D1155058

WITHDRAWN

Kingship and Favoritism in the Spain of Philip III, 1598–1621

The enthronement of Philip III (Philip II's son and heir) in 1598 also meant the rise to power of the Duke of Lerma, the first of a series of European favorites/prime ministers who had a great influence on politics, government, court culture, and the arts during the seventeenth century. This book analyzes the contexts that explain the rise of Lerma, as well as discourses on kingship and favoritism, and governmental and institutional initiatives taken during Philip III's reign (1598–1621) – a key historical period for our understanding of early modern Spain.

Although this book focuses on the reign of Philip III, it also addresses broader historiographical matters. How was power exercised in personal monarchies? What discourses were used to justify royal power? How was kingship publicly represented? How was favoritism conceptualized and legitimized? What was the effect of the rise of the favorite/prime minister upon the constitution of personal monarchies and on political and ideological struggles?

ANTONIO FEROS is Assistant Professor of History, New York University.

CAMBRIDGE STUDIES IN EARLY MODERN HISTORY

Edited by Professor Sir John Elliott, University of Oxford
Professor Olwen Hufton, University of Oxford
Professor H. G. Koenigsberger, University of London
Dr. H. M. Scott, University of St. Andrews

The idea of an "early modern" period of European history from the fifteenth to the late eighteenth century is now widely accepted among historians. The purpose of Cambridge Studies in Early Modern History is to publish monographs and studies which illuminate the character of the period as a whole, and in particular focus attention on a dominant theme within it, the interplay of continuity and change as they are presented by the continuity of medieval ideas, political, and social organization, and by the impact of new ideas, new methods, and new demands on the traditional structure.

For a list of titles published in the series, please see end of the book

Kingship and Favoritism in the Spain of Philip III, 1598–1621

ANTONIO FEROS

CAMBRIDGE
UNIVERSITY PRESS

PUBLISHED BY THE PRESS SYNDICATE OF THE UNIVERSITY OF CAMBRIDGE
The Pitt Building, Trumpington Street, Cambridge, United Kingdom

CAMBRIDGE UNIVERSITY PRESS
The Edinburgh Building, Cambridge CB2 2RU, UK   www.cup.cam.ac.uk
40 West 20th Street, New York, NY 10011–4211, USA   www.cup.org
10 Stamford Road, Oakleigh, Melbourne 3166, Australia
Ruiz de Alarcón 13, 28014 Madrid, Spain

© Antonio Feros 2000

This book is in copyright. Subject to statutory exception
and to the provisions of relevant collective licensing agreements,
no reproduction of any part may take place without
the written permission of Cambridge University Press.

First published 2000

Printed in the United Kingdom at the University Press, Cambridge

Typeset in Ehrhard 10/12pt [VN]

A catalogue record for this book is available from the British Library

Library of Congress Cataloguing in Publication data

Feros, Antonio.
Kingship and favoritism in the Spain of Philip III, 1598–1621 / Antonio Feros.
p.   cm. – (Cambridge studies in early modern history)
Includes bibliographical references and index.
1. Spain – Politics and government – 1598–1621.   2. Philip III, King of Spain, 1578–1621.
3. Lerma, Francisco Sandoval y Rojas, duque de, 1552–1625.   I. Title.   II. Series.

DP183.F47 2000
946'.043 – dc21   99-054217

ISBN 0 521 56113 2 hardback

DP
183
.F47
2000

0 51001 - 6156X6

For Irma

Contents

Contents

Illustrations

Acknowledgments

In writing this book I have acquired many debts of gratitude towards mentors, colleagues, and friends. In particular, I owe perpetual gratitude to Sir John Elliott, whose wise advice and encouragement gave new life to my work. To Richard L. Kagan, J. G. A. Pocock, Orest Ranum, and Harry Sieber, my advisers at the Johns Hopkins University, I owe many thanks for sharing their vast knowledge with me. Juan Gelabert, Ronnie Hsia, Karen Kupperman, and Geoffrey Parker read a preliminary version of this book and made valuable comments and suggestions that helped me to correct mistakes and improve the text. Julio A. Pardos, a friend and colleague for many years, has nurtured me intellectually, helped me to understand the complexity of ideas, and kept me going during difficult times. He and his wonderful family (Paula, Elena, and Pablo) have given me some of the most cherished moments of my life.

Without the advice and suggestions of Fernando J. Bouza Alvarez this book would have been impossible. I am also indebted in many ways to other friends and colleagues for their advice and support: Pablo Fernández Albaladejo, Michael Gilsenan, Javier Varela, María Luisa López-Vidriero, Antonio Manuel Hespanha, Pedro Cardim, Stuart Clark, Araceli Rubio, and Claudia Sieber. Also, without the help and friendship of Sarah Schroth this book would have been much poorer.

While conducting the research for the dissertation that was the basis for this book, I received assistance from the staffs of several archives and libraries. I appreciate the efforts, help, and patience of all who helped me. I would especially like to thank the wonderful staff of the Archivo General de Simancas, and express my gratitude to Don Ignacio Medina Fernández de Córdoba, Duke of Segorbe, for his kind permission to use the Archivo de los Duques de Lerma. Gail Duggan has given new life to the text and saved me from many (too many) errors and embarrassments. My thanks go also to William Davies of Cambridge University Press for his support. I want to acknowledge my gratitude to Virginia Catmur of Cambridge University Press for her careful reading of my typescript and her insightful suggestions for improving it. To complete my research, I received a grant from the Program of collaboration between the United States Universities and the Spanish Ministry of Culture.

Acknowledgments

Finally I wish to thank my spouse Dr. Irma T. Elo. Without her help, advice, encouragement, and patience this book would doubtless never have been completed. Hers is the most important contribution of all.

Abbreviations

I ARCHIVES AND LIBRARIES

ADL	Archivo de los Duques de Lerma, Toledo
AGPR	Archivo General del Palacio Real, Madrid
AGPR Ex. Per.	Expedientes Personales
AGPR Sec. His.	Sección Histórica
AGS	Archivo General de Simancas
AGS CC	Cámara de Castilla
AGS CC CR	Cámara de Castilla, Casa Real
AGS CC DC	Cámara de Castilla, Diversos de Castilla
AGS CC ME	Cámara de Castilla, Memoriales y Expedientes
AGS CC VI	Cámara de Castilla, Visitas
AGS CJH	Consejo y Juntas de Hacienda
AGS DGT	Dirección General del Tesoro
AGS Est.	Estado
AGS GJ	Gracia y Justicia
AGS PT	Patronato Real
AGS SP	Secretarías Provinciales
AHN	Archivo Histórico Nacional, Madrid
AHN CS	Consejos Suprimidos
AHN Est.	Estado
AHN OM	Ordenes Militares
APM	Archivo de Protocolos, Madrid
BFZ	Biblioteca Francisco de Zabálburu, Madrid
BL	British Library
BL, Add.	British Library, Additional
BL, Eg.	British Library, Egerton
BL, Sl.	British Library, Sloane
BNM	Biblioteca Nacional, Madrid
BPR	Biblioteca del Palacio Real, Madrid
IVJ	Instituto Valencia Don Juan
RAH	Real Academia de la Historia, Madrid

RAH CLSC	Colección Luis Salazar y Castro
RAH CP	Colección Pellicer

2 OTHER ABBREVIATIONS

BRAH	*Boletín de la Real Academia de la Historia*
carp.	*carpeta*
Codoin	*Colección de documentos inéditos para la historia de España*
CSPVen	*Calendar of State Papers Venetian*
leg.	*legajo*
exp.	*expediente*
RABM	*Revista de Archivos, Bibliotecas y Museos*

Introduction

"I am writing at the end of an era and the beginning of another about a monarch [Philip III] who never became a real king [*de un monarca que acabó de ser rey antes de empezar a reinar*]."[1] These words, written by one of the most distinguished and influential seventeenth-century Spanish authors, Francisco de Quevedo, represent perhaps the most famous derogatory statement ever made about Philip III of Spain (1598–1621). Quevedo's sharp criticism extended to the royal *privado*,[2] Don Francisco Gómez de Sandoval y Rojas, better known as the Duke of Lerma,[3] and also to his allies and clients, all of whom Quevedo viewed as corrupt and inept. More than personal criticism, Quevedo's words were uttered at a time when the worth of an entire era was assessed in terms of the character and deeds of the individuals in charge of public affairs. By this criterion, Quevedo's appraisal of Philip III, Lerma, and their allies was truly devastating. His denunciation of the king and his closest advisers relegated Philip III's reign to a position of no historical significance, in no way comparable to the reign of Philip III's father, the "extraordinary" Philip II.

But Quevedo's words cannot be read as an impartial assessment of Philip III's reign. Rather, they must be understood within the context of contemporary ideological debates about Philip III's and Lerma's character and the nature of their government. Quevedo was neither the first nor the last to criticize them. Portrayals of Philip as a weak ruler, the puppet of an ambitious and corrupt favorite, appeared already during the very first years of his reign. Accustomed to the style of Philip's father, who ruled without publicly recognizing the assistance of his favorites, some of Philip III's subjects saw in his recognition of Lerma a clear indication that the new king would imitate fifteenth-century Castilian monarchs rather than his

---

[1] *Grandes anales de quince días*, in Francisco de Quevedo y Villegas, *Obras completas*, ed. Felicidad Buendía, 2 vols. (Madrid, 1960), vol. I, pp. 816–55; quotation at p. 817. Quotations from Spanish documents are given in English translation. Difficult, potentially controversial words and concepts are, however, inserted in Spanish following the translation. All translations are mine, unless otherwise noted.

[2] The term "royal favorite" or "favorite" has at least three Spanish synonyms: *favorito*, *privado*, and *valido*. Throughout the book I use all three to refer to Lerma as Philip III's favorite and in discussing early modern theories of favorites.

[3] For clarity I refer hereafter to Don Francisco Gómez de Sandoval y Rojas as "Lerma" or "the Duke of Lerma" even though he did not obtain this title until 1599.

authoritative father. To these uneasy subjects, Lerma's *privanza*[4] evoked memories of one of the darkest moments in Spanish history: the reign of John II of Castile (1406–54). John II too had promoted a single favorite, Don Alvaro de Luna (1385?–1453) and, in doing so, had brought dissension to the court and civil wars to the kingdom. Those who opposed Philip III's decision to grant Lerma an active political role believed that history was repeating itself because the new king did not understand that the presence of a powerful favorite, no matter why he had risen to power, would ultimately jeopardize the king's own authority and the kingdom's political stability.

After the king's death in March 1621 criticism of Philip III and Lerma intensified as a result of the propaganda campaign orchestrated by the Count-Duke of Olivares, Philip IV's favorite from 1621 to 1643. Olivares was a reformist minister who believed that the former rulers, because they lacked political ability, had driven the Spanish crown to a crisis without precedent.[5] Philip III was portrayed as king in name only and Lerma as an opportunist who had risen to power as the result of Philip's many political and personal weaknesses, not in response to institutional needs or because he had superior political abilities. Even worse than their inept efforts to save the monarchy from decline were certain policies that had actively impaired the possibilities for internal and international recovery in the future. Several aspects of the reign were regarded as particularly damaging: Philip III's decision to sign peace agreements with England (1604) and with the Dutch Republic (1609); his readiness to compromise with the rulers of France, Venice, and Savoy; his determination to decree the expulsion of the Moriscos (converted Muslims living in Spain) in 1609–14; his inability to implement measures to resolve the crown's financial crisis; and his acceptance of government officials who used their offices and the state to enrich themselves.

Not all of Philip IV's and Olivares's contemporaries, however, were critical. Some of them saw the attacks on the previous reign as nothing more than a campaign of denigration constructed mainly to justify the new rulers' aggressive international and fiscal policies and to hide the fact that – like Philip III before him – Philip IV had also given enormous power to one favorite, Olivares, whose modes of governing were almost identical to Lerma's. Some of Lerma's and Olivares's contemporaries even believed that the reign of Philip III was an important historical period when attempts had been made to address structural and theoretical problems of the monarchy.

Such divergent views of Philip III, Lerma, and their times should warn historians to avoid simplistic analyses of the period. The past cannot be explained, in

---

[4] When referring to the period when a royal favorite held power sixteenth- and seventeenth-century Spaniards used two terms: *privanza* and *valimiento*. I use both to refer to the period when Lerma was Philip III's favorite and chief minister.

[5] On the campaign against Philip III, Lerma, and their allies during the reign of Philip IV see below, chap. 12 and Epilogue.

Marc Bloch's words, with a few "apothegms of banal psychology which are neither more or less true than their opposites."[6] Unfortunately, modern historians who study the reign of Philip III have typically accepted ideologically motivated views as indisputable historical facts. Their interpretations portray Philip III as an affable and pious ruler who did not possess the strength of character of a great monarch. He usually appears as a *rois fainéant*, or, as John Lynch has written, "the laziest king in Spanish history,"[7] who, according to Roger Merriman, "delegated everything to subordinates and was immersed in the pursuit of pleasure."[8] Modern historians' views of Lerma are roughly similar. As Tomás y Valiente put it, in what to date is the best study of royal favorites in seventeenth-century Spain, if Philip III was lazy, so was Lerma; if the king lacked ideas, so did his *valido*; and if Philip was a pleasure-seeker, so was the Duke.[9] John H. Elliott, in turn, describes Lerma as "an affable, easy-going man, whose prime concern was to enrich his family and to remain in power." Worst of all, according to Elliott, Lerma's lack of political skills prevented him from revitalizing a monarchy in crisis: the "passive and negative regime of the Duke of Lerma," Elliott writes, "was more remarkable for what it left undone than for what it actually did."[10]

Until now, Philip III's reign has received a rather sterile and incomplete assessment, when it has not been altogether neglected. The purpose of this book is to fill this historiographical lacuna by providing an analysis of the social, cultural, political, and intellectual contexts that influenced, and at times were influenced by, Philip's and Lerma's actions. The central argument is that Philip III's reign is critical to understanding the drive to create an absolute monarchy, a process initiated in the second half of the sixteenth century under the leadership of Philip II. The continuation of this process during the reign of Philip III can be seen in the reproduction of similar ideologies, images, and rituals designed to help the monarch and his men justify the sacred foundations of the monarchy. In addition, Philip III and his supporters continued to concentrate power at the center by creating new institutions and by placing favorites at the apex of the monarchical machinery.

While the period clearly shows signs of continuity with the reign of Philip II, it also manifests its own unique character. For example, unlike Philip II, who relied at least formally on multiple favorites and never publicly recognized their political role in the government of the monarchy, Philip III made no secret of the fact that Lerma was his sole *privado*. His preference for a single favorite created the distinct

---

[6] Marc B. Bloch, *The Historian's Craft* (New York, 1954), p. 23.
[7] John Lynch, *The Hispanic World in Crisis and Change, 1598–1700* (Oxford, 1992), p. 18.
[8] Roger Merriman, *The Rise of the Spanish Empire*, vol. IV (New York, 1962), p. 668.
[9] Francisco Tomás y Valiente. *Los validos en la monarquía española del siglo XVII* (Madrid, 1982), pp. 33–6.
[10] John H. Elliott, *Imperial Spain* (London, 1963), pp. 301, 304. See also Antonio Domínguez Ortiz, *Las clases privilegiadas en el antiguo régimen* (Madrid, 1973), p. 111; and Lynch, *Hispanic World*, pp. 22, 35–6.

and influential discourse on the role, characteristics, and nature of the royal favorite, a discourse that was reproduced during Olivares's *privanza*, and which became a focus of the ideological debates of the first half of the seventeenth century. Lerma's political prestige also meant that, at least until the early 1610s, a single faction dominated the court, resulting in a complete reordering of the system of patronage and the nature and characteristics of the political debate at court.

This is not the first study of royal favorites in Spain, but it is the first to analyze the *privado* in terms of the broader implications (political, institutional, cultural, and intellectual) of his function as the king's chief minister. Some historians – Francisco Tomás y Valiente and James Boyden, for example – although aware of the favorites' active role in early modern politics, have considered their rise to power not as a reinforcement and extension of monarchical power, but as "a partial reversal of a trend toward a more impersonal and bureaucratic [by which historians usually mean modern and effective] government."[11] Other historians of the Spanish monarchy have realized that a royal favorite could significantly reinforce royal power, but they only acknowledge the leadership of the "strong and capable" Count-Duke of Olivares, whose policies, methods of government and legitimating discourses are usually accepted as *ex novo* creations, completely distinct from Lerma's practices.[12]

This study does not proceed from either of these assumptions. In contrast to Tomás y Valiente, Boyden, and others, I argue that the presence and power of royal favorites, at least between the 1560s and the 1640s, did not represent a weakening of royal power but its opposite: their active role increased the king's capacity for independent action and inhibited the efforts of monarchical and territorial institutions (both at the center and in the various Spanish kingdoms) to impose limitations on royal power. This thesis was briefly indicated by the Spanish historian Jaume Vicens Vives in a paper presented to the eleventh *Congrès des sciences historiques* (1960). After analyzing the existing institutional and political limitations on the king's power, Vicens Vives described some of the counter-initiatives taken by the rulers: the creation of new and more manageable institutions (*juntas*, committees *ad hoc*, intendants) to circumvent the powerful councils and parliaments; the promotion to high offices of men loyal to the king and his closest advisers (in Spain the so-called counselors of *capa y espada*, experts in "politics," not in law, and committed thus to implementing the king's orders); and the elevation of the royal favorite to the role of chief minister.[13] In Spain, these initiatives began during the reign of Philip II, crystallized under Philip III, and continued without major

---

[11] James Mark Boyden, *The Courtier and the King. Ruy Gómez de Silva, Philip II, and the Court of Spain* (Berkeley and Los Angeles, 1995), pp. 64, 154–6. See also Tomás y Valiente, *Los validos*, chap. 1.2.

[12] See John H. Elliott, *Richelieu and Olivares* (Cambridge, 1984); and John H. Elliott, *The Count-Duke of Olivares. The Statesman in an Age of Decline* (New Haven, 1986).

[13] Jaume Vicens Vives, "Estructura administrativa estatal en los siglos XVI y XVII," in Vicens Vives, *Coyuntura económica y reformismo burgués* (Barcelona, 1969), p. 124.

changes during the reign of Philip IV, at least until the fall of Olivares in 1643.[14] Most historians have identified the influential European favorites/chief ministers as the Count-Duke of Olivares, Cardinal Richelieu, and Cardinal Mazarin, entirely dismissing Lerma, who preceded them. This is an unfortunate historical oversight of the legitimating discourses Lerma promoted, the institutional initiatives he undertook, and the style of government he created, which provided the original blueprint later followed by those better known early modern chief ministers.

This study is not designed as a narrative of each and every event, initiative, idea, and action taken by the Spanish rulers. Rather, the goal is to offer an interpretation of selected themes, problems, processes, and discourses that characterized the period. This new interpretative framework addresses questions of concern not only to students of Spain but also to all students of the early modern period. How was power exercised? What discourses, concepts, and languages were used to justify royal power? What were the limitations of royal power and what were the crown's responses? Also addressed are the conditions and ways in which individuals create their own social, linguistic, and ideological contexts while constrained by these and other contexts. More specifically, this study analyzes the ways in which individuals respond to new political practices and, as a result, to the creation of new concepts and discourses providing a framework for the discussion of politics. Since these issues are examined in the specific context of the Spanish monarchy, this study will present no "general models" necessarily applicable to all early modern European monarchies.

The book is divided into four parts. The first addresses several topics essential to understanding the reign of Philip III and the *privanza* of Lerma: the education of Prince Philip, the family background of Lerma, and sixteenth-century theories on royal favorites as well as changes in these theories during the reign of Philip II. It also examines factional rivalries at the court of Philip II and the attempts by several courtiers to gain the favor of Philip III while he was still prince. Unlike previous works, this analysis of these topics is situated within the linguistic, political, and institutional contexts in which they took place, particularly the theories on royal power promoted by Philip II, the institutional structure of the monarchy, and Philip II's initiatives for limiting the power held by certain royal institutions, a task he accomplished by endorsing new institutions and giving power to selected close advisers.

The second part covers some of the most important issues that attracted the attention of Philip's and Lerma's contemporaries, issues also of interest to modern historians: the nature and ideological foundations of royal power developed during Lerma's *privanza* when political writers began clearly to articulate the principles sustaining the monarch's claims to absolute authority; the way in which political influence was won and conserved in personal monarchies; the increasing complexity

---

[14] See below, chap. 12 and Epilogue.

of the discourse that justified the power of royal favorites; the political and institutional changes provoked by the presence of a royal favorite, now conceived – in theory and in practice – as the king's chief minister; and the forms of government Philip III and Lerma enforced to secure the implementation of their policies.

Parts III and IV explore similar topics but from a different perspective – practical politics. Here chapters are organized chronologically around topics that are central to understanding political developments during Philip III's reign. Part III draws attention to several topics that dominated politics at the beginning of the reign: international affairs, the financial crisis of the monarchy, and the beginning of the criminalization of the political debate. Part IV consists of a study of the political opposition that ultimately led to Lerma's fall in October 1618. The last chapter and the Epilogue analyze the political crisis that developed with Lerma's fall from power. These final sections also examine how the debates about the reign and Lerma's *privanza* influenced the methods and policies of the new monarch, Philip IV, and his favorite/chief minister, the Count-Duke of Olivares, as they tried to halt the decline of Spanish power and solve the political and financial problems that the Spanish crown had faced since the end of the sixteenth century.

Some other topics deserve further mention. In analyzing the reign of Philip III most historians have tended to rely on a few documents, usually the ones produced by Philip's and Lerma's opponents or by foreign observers, mainly the Venetian and other Italian ambassadors to Spain. Many other documents from Philip III's regime have remained largely untouched. Moreover, modern historians have denounced many of the cultural and political propositions promoted by the regime as flattering propaganda, spurious ideological manifestations of corrupt politicians whose only desire was to justify unjustifiable acts. In contrast, this study examines a wider range of documents and critically analyzes texts left behind by Philip III, Lerma, members of their government as well as by their opponents: official documents produced by governmental institutions, the king, the favorite and his closest advisers; letters and reports penned by Spanish and foreign observers; plays, novels, poems, and images; and treatises on royal power, on the constitution of the monarchy, and on the role and characteristics of royal favorites.

This study also reconstructs Lerma's *privanza* from analyses of the policies, discourses, and institutional initiatives he and his allies promoted. There are several justifications for this approach. Firstly, until now the regime's views have been seriously neglected, and they need to be assessed if we want to understand the complexity of the period. Secondly, although it would have been impossible to address all topics – those that captured the attention of Philip III and his men and those that they evaded and left unresolved – some of the latter are implicit in the views of those who opposed the regime's policies and Lerma's role as the king's chief minister (see Parts III and IV and Epilogue). Thirdly, related issues and problems as well as the attitudes of other members of the body politic have been examined by other historians: foreign policies (Geoffrey Parker, I. A. A. Thompson, Bernardo García García, and Paul Allen); financial matters (Juan Gelabert and Ildefonso Pulido Bueno); the policies and alternatives proposed by the Castilian *Cortes* and cities (Pablo Fernández Albaladejo, Charles Jago, I. A. A. Thompson, and José Ignacio Fortea Pérez); the situation and matters that affected non-Castilian kingdoms (John H. Elliott, Fernando Bouza, Xavier Gil Pujol, and Giovanni Muto); and the activities of Queen Margaret and her circle of advisers (Magdalena Sánchez). The reader should consult these studies to complement the analyses and information provided in this volume.[15]

Throughout the book the main character is Lerma, which raises an important issue: the determination of political responsibility during this period. Was Philip III anything more than a cipher, the servant and not the master, of his favorite? The question of whether Philip III was the ruler or the ruled has puzzled modern historians. Most have opted, as seen above, to agree with Philip III's critics in their assumption that, because he did not follow his father's style of government, he must have been a weak monarch, who surrendered the active role in his kingdoms to his *privado*.

This study attempts to reassess a reality that was far more complex than generally recognized. As Orest Ranum has indicated, the modern concept of political responsibility is an important one, but one that, nonetheless, "is severely limited" when applied to the early modern monarchies. The main limitation stems from the political culture of the early modern period, especially from the principle that "the king was the source of political power in the state," which "did not permit ministers to acknowledge, to their credit and detriment, political decisions."[16] In the Spanish monarchy this view was particularly dominant during the reign of Philip II. Despite the fact that Philip II made all his decisions after consulting with his ministers and his favorites, often simply approving their suggestions, he remained throughout his reign a monarch jealous of his prerogatives and his power as the sole sovereign. He never publicly delegated his authority to any of his ministers, he forced everyone to consult him on all matters, and he personally sent orders to all ministers and institutions. And, although Philip II created a privy council (the so-called *Junta de Noche*) to help him rule the monarchy (see Chapter 1), he never permitted its members to take any official responsibility in the decision-making process.

This style of majesty changed during the reign of Philip III, when Lerma's rise to power as the king's sole favorite affected, sometimes in radical ways, the role the monarch played in the government. Many of the ministers and institutions were, for example, ordered to send their suggestions and memoranda to Lerma, who discussed them personally with the king. In addition, debates in the royal institutions could only begin after Lerma had communicated the king's orders to them (see Chapter 6). As we shall see, in theory at least, this style of government was

---

[15] These and other works are cited in the Bibliography.
[16] Orest Ranum, *Richelieu and the Councillors of Louis XIII* (Oxford, 1963), p. 3.

designed to protect the king from criticism by transforming the favorite into the king's protective shield.

But, whatever the intentions, this style also had negative consequences for Philip III's public image, because it conflicted with the model of rulership promoted by Philip II, a model which was never officially challenged or changed during subsequent reigns. The first of these conflicts with Philip II's model of rulership, analyzed in Chapters 5 and 6, resulted from the clash between Lerma's actual role in the decision-making process and traditional political theories that upheld the exclusive sovereignty of the monarch, who could not delegate, in any form, his power to administer the monarchy to his subjects. The second conflict, perhaps the more important, was between official discourses that required the monarch to be the sole protagonist in court life and ceremonies, and the fact that Lerma, during his *privanza*, occupied the king's role in state ceremonies and other activities traditionally linked to the practice of kingship (such as, for example, attending to the claims of the king's subjects and organizing the distribution of royal patronage). As a result, Lerma's *valimiento* was perceived as a period characterized by the weakening of the king's role in the rule of the monarchy, and, therefore, as a radical break with the model of kingship created by Philip II.

In reality, however, Philip III maintained his sole sovereignty by claiming the right of final decision, as demonstrated by his answers to the memoranda from his ministers and royal institutions. On occasion Philip III followed the advice of ministers other than Lerma, and endorsed policies the Duke opposed, especially after 1611. Moreover, Philip III ordered Lerma to leave the court once he decided that his favorite's political views were undermining his own power and reputation.[17] But, as discussed in the Epilogue, both Philip III and Lerma were responsible for failing to grasp the consequences of the theories and practices they promoted, which seriously affected the king's historical image.

---

[17] For a very interesting analysis of Philip III's and Lerma's relationships with the Council of State, the most important royal institution, demonstrating that both played an active role in the everyday ruling of the monarchy, see José Antonio Escudero, "Los poderes de Lerma," in *Homenaje al profesor Alfonso García-Gallo*, 2 vols. (Madrid, 1996), vol. II, pp. 73–86.

PART I

The rising stars

Introduction

In the sixteenth-century Spanish monarchy, as in other early modern personal monarchies, the training and education of the royal heir was no mere academic affair; much was at stake in transforming the prince into the head of the most powerful European monarchy. Instruction in reading and writing was obviously important, as were lessons in geography, mathematics, and languages, music, dance, and art – all aimed at promoting the prince's intellectual growth and maturity. But mastering such matters was hardly sufficient preparation for the future monarch, who would need to acquire an understanding of the constitutional and ideological foundations of the Spanish monarchy as well as to cultivate the virtues and faculties that would enable him to become the genuine lord of his kingdoms.

The prince's education concerned not only Philip II and his advisers but also the king's subjects. In personal monarchies, the king reigned supreme, and his actions greatly influenced the everyday life of the body politic – he controlled the laws of his kingdoms, administered justice, decided matters of war and peace, imposed taxes, and rewarded his subjects. These political practices were complemented by the promotion of theories that required the king's subjects to obey his commands and declared disobedience an unlawful and even sinful act. Accordingly, the personal qualities and virtues of the ruler determined the quality of his government. In monarchies where power was inherited, the only way to ensure the benevolence of a future king was through his education.

Philip's education took place in a far more intricate context than the one customarily presented by modern historians. These scholars have failed to appreciate the complexity of the debate on the foundations of the king's power and have assumed that the Spanish monarchy succeeded in imposing a monolithic ideology. Modern historians claim that disagreements concerned only peripheral matters and never fundamentally challenged a shared political vocabulary or common views on how to conduct politics. But while most political writers of the time shared some basic political principles, there was no consensus on many matters of practical and theoretical importance for the government of the monarchy.

Indeed, contradictory principles were defended not only by political writers but also by the king, by members of his entourage, and especially by those in charge of Prince Philip's education. During Philip II's reign, new conceptions of the king's authority and novel images of royal majesty emerged that ultimately led to the creation of what came to be known as the paradigm of kingship – a king who rules alone and who alone controls his own destiny and that of his kingdoms. According to this paradigm, the king's servants, favorites, and counselors played a secondary role in the government: they merely provided advice to a king who remained the sole possessor of sovereignty. It was this paradigm that Philip II used as a model for the political education of his son.

These new conceptions did not go unchallenged. Those who believed that an ideal king communicated with his subjects and counselors and defended the public good above all else promoted diametrically opposite views of government. They advocated a so-called mixed government in which counselors played an active role as "co-rulers" alongside the king. The views of these sixteenth-century Spanish theorists are reflected in Fray Juan de Pineda's *Los treinta libros de la monarquía eclesiástica* (1594), where he argued that a ruler who abandoned this mixed government would create an entirely new entity where he would inevitably become a tyrant.[1]

The theory of a mixed government was far more than a literary creation – it was an attempt to legitimate the power of the counselors and other members of the body politic. As Foucault has written, even in the so-called absolute regimes power should not be considered a phenomenon of "massive and homogeneous domination of an individual over the rest, one group over another," but should be "analyzed as something which circulates, or rather as something which only functions in the form of a chain. It is never localized here or there, never in anybody's hands." Such a system enabled individuals and institutions other than the king and his supporters to be in "a position of simultaneously undergoing and exercising power."[2] Prior to Foucault, the Spanish historian Jaume Vicens Vives argued that the early modern monarchy was a system in which power was concentrated in the king's hands but was "stratified in three zones." One was controlled by the nobility who forced the monarch to recognize their jurisdiction over their own lands and vassals and their participation in the central organs of monarchical power. A second constituted the representative institutions of the kingdoms – *cortes* and parliaments – while the third was controlled by the central institutions of government which promoted their own political discourses, aimed at legitimating practices which in many cases limited the monarch's ability to exercise his authority.[3] In Spain this third "sphere or zone" was made up of the so-called *consejos*, fourteen in all, that were both central to the configuration of the government and key to the implementation of monarchical policies.

These ideological debates intensified as Philip II grew older and concerns about

[1] Fray Juan de Pineda, *Los treinta libros de la monarquía eclesiástica, o Historia universal del mundo*, 5 vols. (Barcelona, 1594), vol. I, Prologue.
[2] Michel Foucault, *Power/Knowledge: Selected Interviews and Other Writings 1972–1977* (London, 1980), p. 98.   [3] Vicens Vives, "Estructura administrativa," pp. 105–8.

royal succession became increasingly pressing. And here it is important to establish that these ideological debates influenced, and were influenced by, Lerma's quest for power. Chapter 2, "The Making of a Favorite," describes Lerma's family background, education, career, and his attempts to present himself as the consummate courtier and thus worthy of the king's favor. This analysis is followed by a study of the conflicts provoked by Lerma's attempt to become Prince Philip's favorite and an account of Philip II's and his favorites' opposition to Lerma's quest for favor. The core of Chapter 2, however, focuses on the philosophical, political, and cultural underpinnings associated with the surge of royal favorites as major court figures in late sixteenth-century Spain with some commentary on how the Spanish experience can help us assess the phenomenon of favoritism in early modern Europe more generally.

The question of why there were royal favorites in early modern European monarchies has attracted the attention of many modern historians interested in the political and cultural history of this period. The answers to this question have frequently focused on issues of personality and king-craft. In the first case, some historians have maintained that a ruling queen, like Elizabeth I, introduced "male favorites"; some have adduced the alleged homosexuality of James I of England and Henry III of France as a contributing cause. More popular is the explanation citing the existence in the seventeenth century of *rois fainéants*, decadent products of generations of unhealthy marriages (Philip III and Philip IV of Spain) as proof of the decline in the monarchs' intellectual abilities.[4] In more recent years historians have added psychological explanations, claiming, for example, that favorites rose to power because they represented father-figures to young and inexpert kings (Olivares to Philip IV, Richelieu to Louis XIII) – an explanation Elizabeth W. Marvick artfully defends in "Favorites in Early Modern Europe: a Recurring Psychopolitical Role."[5]

Others have emphasized the monarch's personality and style of government. David Starkey, for example, claims that Henry VII of England never had favorites, or never let them flourish, because he was an inaccessible and hard-working king. Unlike his father, Henry VIII was an open king, with a tendency to abandon state affairs to the hands of others (e.g. Cardinal Wolsey), and thus he promoted the public influence of his minions or boon companions.[6] But when applied to the Spanish monarchy, Starkey's interpretation leads to a different conclusion. As Mia

---

[4] For a summary of these views see Keith Cameron, *Henri III. A Maligned or Malignant King? Aspects of the Satirical Iconography of Henri de Valois* (Exeter, 1978); Jenny Wormald, "James VI and I: Two Kings or One?" *History*, 68 (1986); and Simon Adams, "Favourites and Factions at the Elizabethan Court," in Ronald G. Asch and Adolf M. Birke, eds., *Princes, Patronage and the Nobility*, (Oxford, 1991).

[5] Elizabeth W. Marvick, "Favorites in Early Modern Europe: a Recurring Psychopolitical Role," *Journal of Psychohistory*, 10 (1983).

[6] See David Starkey, "From Feud to Faction," *History Today*, 32 (1982); and his *The Reign of Henry VIII. Personalities and Politics* (London, 1985).

Rodríguez-Salgado notes in her study of Philip II, he had favorites because he was an inaccessible and hard-working king – "Philip's desire to withdraw from court for extended periods . . . inevitably prompted individuals to make a bid for power."[7]

The main contribution of this study to the ongoing debate is to place Lerma's rise to power, and, thus, favoritism at court, within the political, administrative, and intellectual contexts of his time. As I have written elsewhere,[8] in different polities political writers and actors developed distinct patterns of epistemological legitimation of and opposition to royal favorites. These distinct theoretical approaches depended on particular political structures, contrasting views of monarchical power, and disparate political traditions. More specifically, the emphasis here is on the way in which late sixteenth-century Spanish political authors characterized royal favorites and how debates about their roles in the government of the monarchy influenced Lerma's quest for Prince Philip's favor. The last chapter in Part I, "Continuity or Reform?," analyzes the beginning of the new reign with specific emphasis on the continuities with the reign of Philip II and also on the perception by Philip III's subjects that a new era in politics, court culture, and international affairs had begun.

[7] M. J. Rodríguez-Salgado, "The Court of Philip II of Spain," in Ronald G. Asch and Adolf M. Birke, eds., *Princes, Patronage, and the Nobility. The Court at the Beginning of the Modern Age, c. 1450–1650,* (Oxford, 1991), p. 219.

[8] On the various early modern European views on royal favorites see Antonio Feros, "Images of Evil, Images of Kings: The Contrasting Faces of the Royal Favourite in Early Modern Political Literature, *c.* 1570–*c.* 1650," in John H. Elliott and Laurence W. Brockliss (eds.), *The World of the Favourite* (New Haven and London, 1999).

The education of a king

Born on 14 April 1578, the son of Philip II and his fourth wife, Anne of Austria (1549–80), Prince Philip became the official heir to the Spanish throne in November 1582. Until then he had been a secondary member of the royal household, one more Infante, but in 1582 he was publicly praised as the one chosen by God to succeed Philip II, because by then all the other male heirs had died: Don Carlos in 1568 (1545–68), Fernando in 1577 (1571–7), Carlos in 1575 (1573–5), and Diego in 1582 (1575–82).[1] In accordance with his new status, he was consecrated as Prince Philip in a swearing-in ceremony, a public rite of passage first celebrated in Portugal in January 1583 and subsequently in Castile in November 1584 and in Aragon in March 1585. Soon thereafter Philip's education as the future king began.

Philip II's first concern was to select the men who would be placed in charge of his son's education and given the task of shielding him from factional struggles. Anxiety over the manipulation of heirs by court factions for their own interests dated at least as far back as the reign of Isabel and Ferdinand, who already at the end of the fifteenth century had endeavored to isolate their heir from the influence of competing interests at court.[2] The intensity of the Spanish monarchs' fears of being used by warring factions was also evident in Charles V's "Secret Instruction" sent to his son, the future Philip II, on 6 May 1543. An able monarch, Charles wrote, must become the head of his entire realm and must do his best to prevent the formation of competing groups because their presence facilitates the development of conditions ripe for rebellion and dynastic conflict. But when factions emerge, an inevitable consequence of royal servants' cultivation of their own interests, the king must not support one above the rest but employ them all to his own advantage.[3]

Philip II was determined to follow his father's advice after his accession to the throne in 1556. Soon thereafter, two competing court factions began to vie for

[1] Esperanza (hope) was Prince Philip's pseudonym in an official cipher in 1585; Carlos Riba García, ed., *Correspondencia privada de Felipe II con su secretario Mateo Vázquez, 1567–1591* (Madrid, 1959), p. 351.
[2] On these topics see José M. March, *Niñez y juventud de Felipe II*, 2 vols. (Madrid 1941–2), vol. I, pp. 247–9, 258, 261–2, 323–4, and vol. II, pp. 73–4; Tarsicio Azcona, *Isabel la Católica* (Madrid, 1964), pp. 8, 27–8, 110–12, 125–6; and Miguel Angel Ladero Quesada, *La hacienda real de Castilla en el siglo XV* (Seville, 1973), pp. 274–6.
[3] Charles V's "Secret Instruction to Prince Philip," 6 May 1543, in Manuel Fernández Alvarez, ed., *Corpus Documental de Carlos V*, 4 vols. (Salamanca, 1973–9), vol. II, pp. 108–9. Charles was I of Spain, from 1516, and V of the Holy Roman Empire; we refer to him throughout as "Charles V."

power – one led by Ruy Gómez de Silva, better known as the Prince of Eboli, and the other by Fernando Alvarez de Toledo, Duke of Alba.[4] Despite the king's efforts to utilize them for his benefit, their presence brought constant bickering to the court as they battled for a control of royal institutions, including the king's household, each trying to overpower the other. So many courtiers were involved in the rival factions – almost all of Philip II's court – that from the late 1560s to the early 1570s many believed that the monarchy was at the edge of a complete paralysis. From the king's viewpoint, however, the most serious damage was done to the education and character of his eldest son, Don Carlos, whose behavior grew increasingly erratic as factional conflicts intensified,[5] a situation that ultimately convinced Philip to exercise firmer control over the political education of his heir.

The king's concerns regarding the men who were to help him educate the crown's heir had already become clear during discussions to select a governor (*ayo y mayordomo mayor*) for the household of Prince Philip's older brother Diego. In a letter dated 20 February 1579 the royal secretary Mateo Vázquez had urged the king to choose a person with exceptional qualities and someone who held his confidence because "if the prince becomes a king while still young, the governor will have too much power." He went on to say that selection of a suitable *ayo y mayordomo mayor* would be difficult because all of the potential candidates had some excellent characteristics but also major weaknesses. The pros and cons of the thirteen candidates were then reviewed, but Vázquez considered only two of them suitable for the task: the Count of Barajas, president of the Council of Castile and Vázquez's first choice, and Juan de Zúñiga, viceroy of Naples, whom Vázquez described as a man of limited political abilities.[6] Although Philip II himself believed none of them was the perfect choice, in the end he chose Juan de Zúñiga, who retained the position of governor and head of the prince's household when Philip officially became the royal heir.[7] The selection of the person responsible for Philip's intellectual development appears to have been less problematic than the choice of the *ayo*, and in 1585 García de Loaysa was appointed to this post.[8]

---

[4] On the conflicts and ideology of the factions see David Lagomarsino, "Court Factions and the Formulation of Spanish Policy towards the Netherlands (1559–1567)," Ph.D. diss., Cambridge University, 1973; William Maltby, *Alba: A Biography of Fernández Alvarez de Toledo* (Berkeley, 1983); Boyden, *The Courtier and the King*; and J. M. Martínez Millán, ed., *Instituciones y élites de poder en la monarquía española durante el siglo XVI* (Madrid, 1992).

[5] On Don Carlos see Geoffrey Parker, *Philip II* (Boston, 1978), chap. 5; and Henry Kamen, *Philip of Spain* (New Haven, 1997), pp. 20, 91–2, 107, 120–2.

[6] Juan de Zúñiga was also Count of Pietrapezia, *comendador mayor* of Castile and the son of Juan de Zúñiga "the elder," who had been Philip II's governor when Philip was a young prince.

[7] "I will think about this, although it is true that I will never find a candidate as good as I would like," Philip II responded to Vázquez's recommendations; see Riba García, *Correspondencia privada*, pp. 196–7.

[8] The appointment of García de Loaysa in AGPR Sec. His. *caja* 113: "Casa del Príncipe Felipe Tercero." García de Loaysa (1534–99) was Governor of the Archbishopric of Toledo and counselor of state and the Inquisition when he was appointed tutor to Prince Philip. He became Cardinal and archbishop of Toledo in 1598; see José M. Martínez Millán, "Un curioso manuscrito: el libro de

The king's ultimate purpose in appointing Zúñiga and Loaysa was to select tutors who proclaimed their total loyalty to his interests and needs and, more important, were "friends" among themselves and unlikely to initiate factional conflict that could damage the prince's character as had happened with Don Carlos.[9] Philip's determination to avoid such an occurrence is evident in the selections he made for his son's household after Zúñiga died in October 1586. As his replacement, Philip II initially intended to appoint Cristóbal de Moura, one of his closest advisers and, as we shall see, truly the king's man, but Moura refused on the grounds of possible opposition from the Castilian nobility because he was by birth Portuguese. Instead, Moura recommended a candidate who was subsequently appointed to the post, Gómez Dávila y Toledo, 2nd Marquis of Velada, Moura's self-declared "creature" (*hechura*) and ally, and who from 1553 to 1568 had served in the household of Don Carlos.[10] Two years later (1589), Philip II decided to appoint Moura to the highest office in his son's household, *sumiller de corps* (grand chamberlain or groom of the stole), believing that Moura's "friendship with Loaysa and Velada" would help to consolidate a climate of unity to secure the proper education of his son and forestall the creation of factional groups that could again bring political instability.[11]

For Philip and his contemporaries the principles and foundations of a proper royal education were as important as the men who had to conduct it. In sixteenth-century Spain, as in other hereditary monarchies, everyone agreed that the prince's education was paramount in transforming him into a worthy ruler. "When a prince is to be chosen by election" the selected one must have demonstrated that he will become a just ruler, wrote Erasmus in *The Education of a Christian Prince* (1516), a book written for the education of Emperor Charles, Philip II's father, but in hereditary monarchies "the main hope of getting a good prince hangs on his proper education, which should be managed all the more attentively, so that what has been

---

gobierno del cardenal Diego de Espinosa (1512?–1572)," *Hispania*, 53 (1993), p. 305, n. 16. On the candidates and the selection of Prince Philip's tutor see Gil González Dávila, *Historia de la vida y hechos del ínclito monarca, amado y santo don Felipe Tercero* [1632] (Madrid, 1771), pp. 13–14. See also Fernando Bouza Alvarez, *Imagen y propaganda. Capítulos de historia cultural del reinado de Felipe II* (Madrid, 1998), pp. 160ff.

9 These views were expressed by Zúñiga in a letter to Philip II; a copy of this letter appears in González Dávila, *Historia de la vida*, pp. 17–18.

10 Velada was appointed governor to Prince Philip on 9 August 1587, AGPR Sec. His., *caja* 113; on the relationships between Moura and Velada see Luis Cabrera de Córdoba, *Historia de Felipe II, rey de España* [c. 1609], 4 vols. (Madrid, 1877), vol. III, p. 229. On Philip II's reasons for appointing Velada see Bouza Alvarez, *Imagen y propaganda*, p. 30. On Velada see Santiago Martínez Hernández, "La nobleza cortesana en el reinado de Felipe II. Don Gómez Dávila y Toledo, segundo marqués de Velada, una carrera política labrada al amparo de la corona," *Torre de los Lujanes*, 33 (1997), pp. 185–220.

11 Cristóbal de Moura, in addition to being Prince Philip's *sumiller de corps*, was gentleman of Philip II's chamber, a member of the Council of State, and Philip II's favorite. He was appointed *sumiller* on 1 Dec. 1589, AGPR Sec. His., *caja* 113. See also González Dávila, *Historia de la vida*, p. 17; and Cabrera de Córdoba, *Historia de Felipe II*, vol. III, pp. 299, 368.

lost with the right to vote is made up for by the care given to his upbringing."[12] The substance of this enterprise, inspired in part by Erasmus's work and Francesco Patrizi's *De regno et regis institutione*,[13] can be found in Fray Juan de Mariana's *De rege et regis institutione* (1599), a book commissioned, or so Mariana claimed, by García de Loaysa,[14] who, like his contemporaries, believed that the prince's education must begin in childhood when the mind was still "like wax," easy to control and manipulate (pp. 154ff). The tutors were told to study the prince's personality and character and to curb – with praise or punishment – those aspects that kept him from engaging in virtuous behavior (pp. 160–1). They were to impose strict norms of behavior, create an environment conducive to elevating virtue, and keep the prince in touch with his subjects so that he would not grow to become an arrogant ruler who could turn into a tyrant or be dominated by undeserving courtiers. He should be made to understand that his principal obligation was to protect the interests of his subjects and ensure the prosperity of his realms (pp. 164–7). Only after the tutors were satisfied that he had internalized these principles were they to teach him specific subjects, such as poetry, music, dance, history, rhetoric, Latin, and so on or let him engage in physical education.

Although only a handful of documents have survived on the exact details of Philip's education, we know that it more or less followed Mariana's model.[15] Philip learned Latin, French, Portuguese, and geometry, and he was introduced to the works of Cicero, Comines, Plutarch, Aristotle, Guicciardini, and other authors, many of whom the prince himself translated into Spanish.[16] Contemporaries also reported that the prince was well versed in religious writings and frequently participated in religious ceremonies, suggesting that he had accepted his destiny to become the champion of the Christian faith. As the result of his education, most contemporaries seemed to have viewed Philip in a fairly positive light. He was

---

[12] Desiderius Erasmus, *The Education of a Christian Prince*, ed. Lester K. Born (New York, 1965), pp. 139–40; for sixteenth-century Spanish views on this topic see Fray Juan de Mariana, *De rege et regis institutione (La dignidad real y la educación del príncipe)* [1599], ed. Luis Sánchez Agesta (Madrid, 1981), pp. 39–51, 155; BPR II-1763: Joan Benito Guardiola, "Retrato de las virtudes y calidades con que debe ser dotado cualquier príncipe para la buena gobernación y acrecentamiento de sus reinos, estados, y señoríos," n.d., fol. 38v; BNM, Mss 11070: "Copia de lo que Bartolomé de Villalva y Estaña escribió al rey don Phelipe Tercero siendo príncipe," fol. 116.

[13] Francesco Patrizi wrote his *De regno* in the late 1470s. It was translated into Spanish in 1591 by Enrique Garcés under the title *Del reino y de la institución del que ha de reinar* (Madrid, 1591). For treatises on the education of the prince in early modern Europe see Quentin Skinner, *The Foundations of Modern Political Thought*, 2 vols. (Cambridge, 1978), vol. I, pp. 113–28, 213ff; and Lester K. Born's introduction to his edition of Erasmus, *The Education of a Christian Prince*. For the Spanish literature on the education of princes see María Angeles Galino Carrillo, *Los tratados sobre educación de príncipes, siglos XVI y XVII* (Madrid, 1948); Michael P. Mezzatesta, "Marcus Aurelius, Fray Antonio de Guevara, and the Ideal of the Perfect Prince in the Sixteenth Century," *Art Bulletin*, 66 (1984), pp. 620–33; and Julia Varela, *Modos de educación en la España de la contrarreforma* (Madrid, 1984), pp. 70–82.

[14] Mariana, *De rege*, pp. 6–7. Further references in the text.

[15] A good summary is in Ciriaco Pérez Bustamante, *La España de Felipe III* (Madrid, 1983), chap. 2.

[16] Jehan Lhermite, *Le Passetemps*, ed. Ch. Ruelens, 2 vols. (Antwerp, 1890–6), vol. I, pp. 219, 240–4, 274–6; vol. II, p. 100. Jehan Lhermite was Philip II's servant and one of Prince Philip's teachers.

depicted as having a lively spirit and a peaceful disposition despite his "weak although graceful body," the result of disease and poor eating habits.[17] Jehan Lhermite, who was perhaps most familiar with the prince, characterized him in his memoirs as "dynamic, good-natured and earnest," as someone willing to undertake even the most difficult tasks.[18] The Venetian ambassadors to the Spanish court also commented on Philip's loyalty and obedience towards his father, a sharp contrast to the behavior of Don Carlos.

There were, however, less flattering observations. Juan de Silva, Count of Portalegre, who was one of the Spanish governors in Portugal and well informed because of his close ties to Cristóbal de Moura, for example, commented that "the prince is immature and less intelligent than Don Carlos,"[19] voicing his contemporaries' belief that the prince lacked political experience. From 1593, Philip II tried to remedy this matter by making the prince a member of his inner council of advisers. The prince's political education, both practical and theoretical, is indeed crucial (certainly more important than his "humanistic" education) to an understanding of Prince Philip's views on royal majesty and power. It is also key to the complex debates on the "ideal" government and the constitution of the Spanish monarchy that took place during the 1580s and 1590s.

At this point it is important to establish certain aspects of the political and linguistic contexts in which Philip's education took place.[20] Two main discourses dominated political debate in late sixteenth-century Spain. One of them advocated a "contractual" view of government which emphasized the duties rather than the powers of the king.[21] Its proponents defended an ascendant theory of political power, claiming that even if God had created power, the authority necessary to exercise it rested in the people who transferred its sovereignty to the king, making him a "public official" obliged to serve the community. This definition of sovereignty as "popular" imagined the monarchy as a system where the king had to rule in collaboration with his counselors who were representatives of the commonwealth and defenders of its rights. Many authors defending this perspective published

---

[17] Reports of the Venetian ambassadors Tommaso Contarini (1593) and Francesco Vendramino (1595) in Eugenio Alberi, *Le Relazioni degli Ambasciatori Veneti al Senato durante il Secolo Decimosesto*, Ser. 1, vol. v (Florence, 1861), pp. 421, 424–5, 446–7. Prince Philip's health remained of great concern to his father Philip II who ordered, for example, Fray Diego de Salazar to visit all the holy places (Santiago de Compostela, Rome, and Jerusalem) to pray for the health of his son; see BL, Eg. 311, "Libro de las peregrinaciones que el Católico rey don Phelipe Segundo, de gloriosa memoria, mandó hacer al padre Diego de Salazar Marañón de la Compañía de Jesús por la salud, vida y feliz sucesión de su querido y amado hijo y rey nro. Sr. don Phelipe III."

[18] Lhermite, *Le Passetemps*, vol. i, pp. 193, 219, 241, and vol. ii, p. 113; see also the report of the Venetian ambassador Agustino Nani (14 July 1596), in *CSPVen*, vol. ix, p. 219; and González Dávila, *Historia de la vida*, pp. 19– 20.

[19] BL, Add. 28377, Portalegre to the Marquis of Poza, 21 June 1592. I thank Dr. Fernando J. Bouza Alvarez for this reference.   [20] See also below, introduction to pt. ii, and chap. 4.

[21] The concept "contractual" does not explain exactly the contents and significance of the theories I discuss in the following pages, but it is more accurate than the term "constitutional" used by some modern historians.

I   Justus Tiel, *Allegory of the Education of Philip III* commissioned by Philip II. In this painting Prince Philip is presented as a knightly prince, while in the background Time (the symbol of eternity) drives away Cupid (the symbol of vain pleasures) and pushes toward the prince the figure of Justice, who offers Philip her sword.

their works in the 1590s, including the Jesuit Pedro de Ribadeneira, whose *El príncipe christiano* (dedicated to Prince Philip) had an enormous influence in early modern Spain after its publication in 1595.[22] Other influential authors include Roa Dávila, whose *De regnorum iustitia* was published in 1591;[23] Fray Juan de Torres, who published in 1596 *Filosofía moral de príncipes*; and Fray Juan de Mariana, better known for his radical theories defending the people's right to kill a tyrant in his *De rege* published in 1599.[24] This "contractual" view of government was also defended by some of Prince Philip's tutors, mainly García de Loaysa, and by many members of the royal councils.

But in the last decades of the sixteenth century, in Spain as elsewhere in Europe, the theory known as *ragione di stato* (reason of state) began to have an increasing influence on political debates and governmental practices. Its promoters, as Bartolomé Clavero has noted,[25] did not entirely dismiss the more traditional views outlined above but tried more explicitly to address the monarch's "specific needs and concrete interests." These authors, also known as Neostoicists and/or Tacitists, were less interested than the "contractual" writers in debating the origins of political power, the best form of government, and the duties of the various members of the body politic, including the monarch. Rather their central concern was to delineate the steps necessary "to preserve the king as a head of the state at all costs."[26] Although none of these authors denied that it was in the best interests of the monarch to respect the rights of his subjects, all believed that "if the preservation of a political order was at stake, then rules of justice or constitutional proprieties had to give way."[27] Three "reason of state" authors had an extraordinary impact in late sixteenth-century Spain. The first was Giovanni Botero, whose seminal work, *Ragion di stato*, was translated into Spanish under the orders of Philip II in 1589, to serve as a guide for Prince Philip's political education.[28] The second author was the Flemish Justus Lipsius, with whom many Spaniards had maintained a regular correspondence since the early 1590s. Especially important was his treatise *Politicorum sive civilis doctrinae libri sex*, whose Latin edition was

[22] The complete title of Ribadeneira's work is *Tratado de la religión y virtudes que debe tener el Príncipe Christiano para gobernar y conservar sus estados, contra lo que Nicolás Maquiavelo y los políticos de este tiempo enseñan*, included in Pedro de Ribadeneira, *Obras escogidas*, ed. Vicente de la Fuente (Madrid, 1952). On Ribadeneira, see Robert Bireley, *The Counter-Reformation Prince* (Chapel Hill, N.C., 1990), chap. 5; and José María Iñurritegui Rodríguez, *La gracia y la república. El lenguaje político de la teología católica y el "Príncipe Cristiano" de Pedro de Rybadeneyra* (Madrid, 1998), esp. chap. 4.
[23] Fray Juan Roa Dávila, *De regnorum iustitia* [1591], ed. Luciano Pereña (Madrid, 1970).
[24] On Mariana see Domenico Ferraro, *Tradizione e ragione in Juan de Mariana* (Milan, 1989).
[25] Bartolomé Clavero, *Razón de estado, razón de individuo, razón de historia* (Madrid, 1991), pp. 16, 28.
[26] Richard Tuck, *Philosophy and Government, 1572–1651* (Cambridge, 1993), p. 56.
[27] *Ibid.*
[28] Giovanni Botero, *Los diez libros de la razón de estado* [1593], trans. Antonio de Herrera y Tordesillas (Madrid, 1613); on Botero's ideas see A. Enzo Baldini, ed., *Botero e la "ragion di stato"* (Florence, 1992); Gianfranco Borrelli, *Ragion di stato e leviatano. Conservazione e scambio alle origini della modernità politica* (Bologna, 1993), chap. 2; a good summary in English of Botero's ideas is in Tuck, *Philosophy*, pp. 65–7.

published in 1589, although the Spanish translation did not appear until 1604.[29] The French writer Jean Bodin was the other member of this influential triad of political authors. His work *Les six livres de la République* was published in French in 1576 and translated into Spanish in 1590; it became one of the most influential books in late sixteenth- and early seventeenth-century Spain, even though it was listed among those banned by the Spanish Inquisition.[30] Reason-of-state principles were endorsed by some of Philip II's closest advisers, including Cristóbal de Moura, Juan de Idiáquez, and Diego Fernández de Cabrera y Bobadilla, Count of Chinchón, to whom Botero dedicated his *"Aggiunte"* – two chapters on neutrality and reputation written in 1598 that Botero incorporated in subsequent editions of his *Ragion di stato*.[31]

These opposing discourses formed the background to the political education of Prince Philip, who received lessons on how to be a monarch delivered in both political languages, as can be ascertained in the instructions Philip II sent to García de Loaysa in 1585[32] and in other documents and institutional practices relating to his education. To become an able monarch, Philip II remarked, the prince would have to master the true meaning of the three principal duties associated with the "office of the king" (*el oficio de Rey*). Most important of all, he must always remember that Spanish monarchs were placed on earth to conserve and promote the true faith within and outside their kingdoms by encouraging and demanding obedience to God's laws. With this goal in mind, the prince's tutors were to teach him to abhor vice and its promoters, deplore the "enemies of our faith," and conserve the true religion even if this meant the loss of his kingdoms or his own demise.[33] These aspects of Philip II's instructions reflected shared beliefs that a would-be ruler had to master the Christian virtues or *virtudes teologales* – piety,

[29] Lipsius's *Politicorum sive civilis doctrinae libri sex* [1589] was translated in 1604 into Spanish by Bernardino de Mendoza, Spanish ambassador in France (1584–91) during the most conflictive period of the Wars of Religion; see Justus Lipsius, *Los seis libros de la política, o doctrina civil, que sirven para el gobierno del reino o principado*, trans. Bernardino de Mendoza [1604], ed. Javier Peña Echevarría and Modesto Santos López (Madrid, 1997). Lipsius dedicated one of his works, *De militia romana* [1595], to Prince Philip. On the correspondence of Lipsius with Spaniards see *Epistolario de Justo Lipsio y los españoles (1577–1606)*, ed. Alejandro Ramírez (Madrid, 1966). On Lipsius's ideas see Gerhard Oestreich, *Neostoicism and the Early Modern State*, trans. David McLintock, ed. Brigitta Oestreich and H. G. Koenigsberger (Cambridge, 1982), pt. I; and Tuck, *Philosophy*, pp. 56–64.

[30] Jean Bodin's *Les six livres de la République* was translated into Spanish by Gaspar Añastro Isunza, who introduced several changes to improve the "Catholic credentials" of a book viewed by some as a work that promoted "atheism" and tyrannical government; see Jean Bodin, *Los seis libros de la república*, trans. Gaspar de Añastro Isunza [1590], ed. José Luis Bermejo Cabrero, 2 vols. (Madrid, 1992). On the censorship of the Spanish translation of Bodin's work – a censorship that centered on "doubtful" religious propositions – see Miguel Avilés Fernández, "La censura inquisitorial de 'Los seis libros de la República,' de Jean Bodin," *Hispania Sacra*, 37 (1985), pp. 655–92. For Bodin's influence in the Iberian peninsula see Martín de Alburquerque, *Jean Bodin na península ibérica* (Paris, 1978). A good summary of Bodin's ideas on royal sovereignty is in Skinner, *The Foundations*, vol. II, pp. 286–301.

[31] On Botero's "Aggiunte" see George Albert Moore's edition and translation into English of Botero, *Practical Politics*, ed. George Albert Moore (Washington, D.C., 1949), pp. 221–46.

[32] Philip II's instructions are reproduced in González Dávila, *Historia de la vida*, pp. 14–17.

[33] *Ibid.*, p. 15.

religion, and faith – which were an indispensable attribute of an ideal monarch because without them, as Ribadeneira alleged in his *El príncipe christiano*, "there is no true and perfect virtue."[34] The second obligation Philip II emphasized had to do with the promotion of a just government. The prince had to understand "the inconveniences and evils suffered by kings who pursued their desires" and that he could become a just and prudent ruler only if he "prevailed upon himself (*vencerse a sí mismo*) by overcoming his passions."[35] Here the king was referring to some of the so-called moral virtues (*virtudes cardinales*), such as temperance and prudence that according to early modern writers led to modesty, abstinence, and chastity.[36] By "prevailing upon himself" the prince would mature into a just king whose main goal would be to protect the right of his subjects to live safely and peacefully throughout his kingdoms and would learn that royal power must be limited by reason and by the constitutional rights of the commonwealth.

But while all authors agreed that the king should be a prudent ruler, not all agreed on the meaning of prudence. Writers who supported more traditional views of the political order agreed with the views of Cicero that truth and honesty were the principal elements of successful human activity,[37] and consequently defined political virtue in general and prudence in particular as the monarch's capacity to distinguish good from evil and follow just and honest policies.[38] The practical corollary of these principles – usually defined as the "real reason of state" or the "Catholic reason of state" – was that a prudent ruler had to defend Christian principles, the Catholic church, and Catholics everywhere at all cost and regardless of the consequences for his kingdoms and himself.[39] Throughout his reign Philip II promoted this image of the ruler as *Defensor Fidei*, and he wished his son to maintain it.[40]

The proponents of reason-of-state theories also believed that prudence was the *sine qua non* of a ruler, but they defined the term differently.[41] To these writers prudence meant the capacity to distinguish what was "useful" from what was

---

[34] Ribadeneira, *Obras*, p. 518. Giovanni Botero and Justus Lipsius also shared these views; see Botero, *Los diez libros*, bk. 5; Lipsius, *Los seis libros*, bk. 1, chap. 3, and bk. 4, chaps. 2–4.

[35] González Dávila, *Historia de la vida*, p. 16.

[36] Mosen Diego de Valera, "Doctrinal de príncipes," in Mario Penna, ed., *Prosistas castellanos del siglo XV* (Madrid, 1959), p. 191.

[37] Cicero, *Libro de Marco Tulio Cicerón en que trata de los oficios, de la amicicia, de la senectud, añadiéndole agora nuevamente las paradoxas y el sueño de Scipión*, trans. Francisco Tamara and Juan Jarava (Salamanca, 1582), bk. 1, chaps. 2–3, fols. 8–13. [38] Patrizi, *Del reino*, bk. 6, chap. 7, fol. 238v.

[39] On this topic see, for example, Pedro de Ribadeneira, "Exortación para los soldados y capitanes que van a esta jornada de Inglaterra, en nombre de su capitán general," 1588; and "Carta para un privado de su Majd. acerca de la desgracia de la armada que fue a Inglaterra, y de lo que acerca de ella se puede considerar para mayor provecho de España," in Fray Pedro de Ribadeneira, *Patris Petri de Ribadeneira confessiones, epistolae aliaque scripta inedita* [*Monumenta Historica Societatis Iesu*, 60] (Madrid, 1923), pp. 347–70 and 109.

[40] See Fernando Bouza, "Monarquía en letras de molde. Tipografía y propaganda en tiempos de Felipe II," in Bouza, *Imagen*, chap. 5. [41] Lipsius, *Los seis libros*, bk. 3, chap. 1, 71.

"harmful" rather than good from evil;[42] accordingly, they emphasized "the importance of *interest* and the power of *necessity*" in deciding what plan to follow and what causes to defend.[43] This interpretation implied continual assessment of the monarchy's strategic interests, of the strength of its enemy, and of the political consequences of the king's actions. Decisive action against rebels and heretics would depend on a given set of circumstances, and at times it might be wise to follow a policy that sixteenth-century Spaniards defined as *política de medios*: compromise with the kingdom's enemies when an aggressive policy could result in defeat or, even worse, the spread of conflict within the realm. The Church had to be defended and so did Catholics within and without the territories controlled by the Spanish crown, but the conservation of royal power had to become the king's highest priority. These views can be found, for example, in a chapter of Botero's *Ragion di stato* where he discusses political prudence with emphasis on the importance of timing and opportunity, but without a single reference to religious or political orthodoxies.[44]

Finally, Philip II addressed the responsibility of administering public affairs. He ordered his son's tutors to ensure that his heir spent time attending to and discussing such matters and that the prince learn to resolve problems, large or small, with the advice of reliable counselors.[45] The supporters of both ideological perspectives indeed acknowledged the king's obligation to seek and listen to the advice of his subjects, but the practical conclusions of the two sides were radically different.

Counsel to the prince was perhaps the most important subject in the works of early modern political writers,[46] all of them inspired by the writings of classical authors, especially those of Aristotle, who in his *The Politics* had written that "a good man has the right to rule because he is better; still two good men are better than one," and proposed that monarchs "make for themselves many eyes and ears and hands and feet" in order to rule extended territories.[47] Even Philip II appears to have accepted this political paradigm, that a capable king ruled with the help and advice of competent counselors, and he himself perpetually encouraged counselors to come to him with their advice. In a letter to his secretary Mateo Vázquez, for example, he wrote that "I would not dare to decide those affairs that I do not understand without receiving advice of those who know them."[48] But his convictions on this topic were most clearly stated in the *Nueva recopilación de las leyes del*

---

[42] *Ibid.*, bk. 1, chap. 7, 26.   [43] Tuck, *Philosophy*, p. 80.
[44] Botero, *Los diez libros*, bk. 2, chap. 6, fols. 40–44v, where Botero outlined twenty-seven recommendations on how to behave in matters of state without including any of the great orthodoxies of which contractual writers were so fond.   [45] González Dávila, *Historia de la vida*, p. 16.
[46] On this topic see J. G. A. Pocock, "The History of British Political Thought: The Creation of a Center," *Journal of British Studies*, 24 (1985), pp. 285–7; and Pablo Fernández Albaladejo, *Fragmentos de Monarquía* (Madrid, 1992), pp. 290–4.
[47] Aristotle, *The Politics*, ed. S. Everson (Cambridge, 1988), 1287b12–36; and Aristotle, *La política*, trans. Pedro Simón Abril [1579] (Madrid, 1919), pp. 145–51.
[48] Philip to Mateo Vázquez, 3 Sept. 1576, in Riba García, *Correspondencia privada*, p. 55.

reino, a compilation of laws published in the 1560s under his orders. The preamble to the chapter on counsel to the king read that "if the kings who must reign and govern their peoples and their universal domains in peace and with justice had no assistance or advice, it is doubtful that they alone would have the strength to withstand and execute such labors."[49]

Upon these principles Spanish political writers in favor of the contractual view of government built a complex theory of the king's councils and counselors, who were depicted not only as the monarch's assistants but as his "understanding, memory, eyes, ears, voice, feet, and hands" and even as "his tongue"[50] and, as a result, they considered the role of the king's counselors to be as consequential as that of the king himself in the government of the monarchy. If the king were the heart of his kingdom, wrote Ribadeneira, then the king's counselors were "the soul, the reason, and the wisdom of the commonwealth"; a political community without counsel was like a body without a soul, a human being without reason, a simple beast.[51] Perhaps even more importantly, these writers perceived the counselors as the only ones who could assure harmony by balancing the king's preeminence with the rights of the other members of the body politic. In the words of Furió Ceriol, the king's counselors were "for the people father, tutor, and curator [and] both the king and the counselors are God's vicars upon earth."[52] These views of the role and qualities of the king's counselors affected their perception of the nature of the Spanish monarchy, imagined now as a mixed monarchy (*monarquía mixta*), one where the authority of the monarch was limited by the power of the counselors and other members of the body politic.[53]

These theories reflected the reality of the complex institutional structure of the Spanish monarchy, in which all matters concerning the "office" of the king were handled by royal councils, a total of fourteen charged, at least in theory, with discussing public affairs and implementing the king's orders.[54] While the Spanish councils lacked full executive authority, they nevertheless played a powerful role in

---

[49] *Nueva recopilación*, bk. 2, tit. 4: "Del Consejo del Rey." See also Felipe II, "Instrucción del señor Don Felipe II a don Diego de Covarrubias, obispo de Segovia, presidente de Castilla" [1588], *Seminario Erudito de Valladares*, 30 (1790), pp. 3–19.

[50] Fadrique Furió Ceriol, *El concejo y consejeros del príncipe* [1559], ed. Diego Sevilla (Valencia, 1952), p. 108; and Marco Antonio Camos, *Microcosmia y gobierno universal del hombre cristiano* (Barcelona, 1592), p. 130.   [51] Ribadeneira, *Obras*, pp. 553–4.

[52] Furió Ceriol, *El concejo*, p. 108. See also Juan López de Hoyos, *Real aparato y suntuoso recibimiento con que Madrid recibió a la serenísima reina doña Ana de Austria* [1572], facsimile edn. (Madrid, 1976), fol. 28v, where the author calls the counselors "fathers of the common-wealth."

[53] On the idea of "mixed monarchy" and the importance of this form of government for the creation of a well-balanced monarchy see Mariana, *De rege*, pp. 37, 102–4; and Roa Dávila, *De regnorum*, pp. 76–9. On these ideas during the reign of Philip III see below chaps. 4 and 6.

[54] These councils were: State, War, Castile, Chamber of Castile, Italy, Flanders, Aragon, Portugal, Navarre, Inquisition, Military Orders, Finance, Crusade, and the Indies. A good summary in English is J. M. Batista i Roca's "Foreword" to H. G. Koenigsberger, *The Practice of Empire* (Ithaca, 1969), pp. 9–35; the best studies are, however, Fernández Albaladejo, *Fragmentos*, pp. 97–140; and Francisco Tomás y Valiente, "El gobierno de la monarquía y la administración de los reinos en la España del siglo XVII," in *Historia de España Ramón Menéndez Pidal*, vol. XXV (Madrid, 1982), pp. 3–214.

the monarchical government. Counselors, although appointed by the king, held their offices in perpetuity and had other important prerogatives as well.[55] They acted as supreme judges, proposed candidates for major and minor offices, distributed patronage, and served as an important link between the crown and the kingdoms, and by the late sixteenth century the councils' increasing independence became the most visible sign of the limitations of the king's authority. The councils came to be viewed, by their defenders and critics alike, as corporate bodies that on many occasions interfered with royal orders and on others simply refused to implement them. Cabrera de Córdoba, for example, described the counselors of Castile as "absolute ministers, who wanted to transform the monarchical government into a republican one . . . and whose custom was to view as a failure everything that they did not conceive or order."[56] To emphasize further the councils' central political role, the supporters of the contractual view of government stressed the councils' right to have free access to the king, and during the 1580s and 1590s, when the education of Prince Philip became a matter of great political concern, they strongly maintained that he should participate in the meetings of the royal councils and "not isolate himself in the royal palace" with favorites and other self-interested courtiers.[57]

By the late sixteenth century these views and institutional structures had come under challenge from practices promoted by Philip II and his closest supporters as well as from writings of authors who subscribed to reason-of-state theories. Counsel to the king was still considered essential in a successful government, but there were new views on how it should be sought and delivered. The prince, Bodin wrote, "should be guided by counsel not only in great matters but also in small," if only because royal resolutions would have greater impact if they were adopted "with the wise and prudent advice of a council, a senate, or a magistrate."[58] Authors such as Bodin did not deny the citizens' right to advise the king, but they proposed to transform the councils from being the king's advisers into the implementers of his will.[59] Few summarized this political view better than Lipsius:

I establish a restrained kind of government, that is, that not only the chief strength and honor be derived from you [the king] but remain with you likewise. Surely it is derived from you when you yourself manage the affairs of greatest importance, or at least ratify and confirm them, lest you dissolve the force of principality in referring all things to the senate and the

[55] See Salustiano de Dios, *El Consejo Real de Castilla (1385–1522)* (Madrid, 1982), pp. 281–4; Luis Cabrera de Córdoba remarks that "one of the most suitable and bold ways to conserve the monarchy is to maintain the royal ministers in their jobs." He also insisted that royal officials' authority "never dies," not even during the transition between reigns; Cabrera de Córdoba, *Historia de Felipe II*, vol. I, p. 39.

[56] *Ibid.*, pp. 42–3; on the existence of the councils as proof not so much of the existence of personal monarchies as of its limitations see Antonio Manuel Hespanha, *História das instituições* (Coimbra, 1982), p. 350.   [57] Mariana, *De rege*, pp. 164–7.

[58] Bodin, *Los seis libros*, bk. 3, chap. 1, vol. I, p. 480.

[59] J. G. A. Pocock, *The Machiavellian Moment* (Princeton, 1975), p. 353.

councils. Kings ... are leaders and not followers of counsel. If you yield anything, then you lose all. That is the condition of *imperium* (power): it cannot be conserved if it is committed to more than one.[60]

From an ideological and practical perspective, these writers forcefully rejected the concept of "mixed monarchy": as Bodin stated, the councils and other institutions were created to give advice but never to be the holders of power because sharing royal sovereignty would destroy the royal majesty, "which is so high and sacred that the subjects cannot have any part of it, great or small."[61]

But these authors also recognized that a king could not solve all matters alone and therefore needed the support of his "friends," a small group of loyal counselors who would help him impose discipline in the body politic. Several authors explicitly proposed that the king create "a private or secret council" composed of two or three of his closest ministers with whom he would discuss all matters submitted for consideration by other institutions,[62] a style of government Philip II followed and asked his son to imitate. Confronted with the increasing independence of the royal councils, Philip II promoted less formal channels of advice and relied on a few chosen counselors who were personally close to him. His conduct helps to explain the career and power of some of the leading advisers in the second half of the sixteenth century: the Duke of Alba, grandee of Castile, counselor of state, and Philip's lord high steward; Ruy Gómez, Philip's *sumiller*, a Portuguese nobleman who eventually became one of the richest and most powerful men in the kingdom; Cardinal Diego de Espinosa, who, after having been named president of the Council of Castile in 1565, became a sort of "senior minister" in whom Philip II "has more confidence and with whom he discusses most business, both concerning Spain and foreign affairs";[63] and the royal secretaries Gonzalo Pérez, Francisco de Eraso, Antonio Pérez, and Mateo Vázquez.[64]

The careers of these men indicate how much power Philip II accorded to

---

[60] Lipsius, *Los seis libros*, bk. 4, chap. 9, pp. 134–5; see also Botero, *Los diez libros*, bk. 2, chap. 10, fol. 52r.

[61] Bodin, *Los seis libros*, bk. 3, chap. 1, vol. I, pp. 503–4; attacks against the idea of a "mixed monarchy" in *ibid.*, bk. 2, chap. 1; and Lipsius, *Los seis libros*, bk. 2, chap. 2.

[62] Bodin, *Los seis libros*, bk. 3, chap. 1, vol. I, pp. 490–1.

[63] Count of Chinchón to Duke of Alburquerque, 12 Dec. 1566; cf. Parker, *Philip II*, p. 30; on the relations between Espinosa and Philip see Lagomarsino, "Court Factions," pp. 230–3. Lagomarsino recalls Cabrera de Córdoba's description of Philip II's treatment of Espinosa: "Philip came to treat Espinosa almost like an equal, going forward to meet him as he arrived for an audience, removing his hat in Espinosa's presence, even sitting on the same level with him" (p. 232), behavior similar to that of Philip III toward Lerma; see below, chap. 5. On Espinosa see also Martínez Millán, "Un curioso manuscrito," pp. 299–344.

[64] The relationship between Philip and his counselors can be followed in the excellent work of Lagomarsino, "Court Factions"; on Alba see Maltby, *Alba*; on Eboli see Boyden, *The Courtier*; on Philip II's secretaries see José Antonio Escudero, *Los secretarios de estado y del despacho*, 4 vols. (Madrid, 1976), especially vol. I, chap. 3; on Gonzalo Pérez see Angel González Palencia, *Gonzalo Pérez, secretario de Felipe II*, 2 vols. (Madrid, 1946); on Antonio Pérez see Gregorio Marañón, *Antonio Pérez (el hombre, el drama, la época)*, 2 vols. (Madrid, 1951); on Mateo Vázquez see A. W. Lovett, *Philip II and Mateo Vázquez de Leça: the Government of Spain (1572–1592)* (Geneva, 1977).

personal advisers whom he placed over all royal institutions, thus making them "the key to the administration and dispatching of public affairs."[65] As seen above, until the 1570s such a model had promoted factional conflicts,[66] but by the late 1570s and early 1580s Philip II had forced his private advisers to cooperate and to coordinate their advice through membership in *ad hoc* committees or *juntas* that replaced individual consultations. He initiated this style of government with the creation of the *Junta de Tres* (Committee of Three) in the late 1570s, culminating in 1585 with the creation of the *Junta de Gobierno* (Government Committee), also known as the *Junta de Noche* (Night Committee).[67] It is important to note that the men who made up this "privy council" also held offices in the Council of State and in Prince Philip's household: Juan de Zúñiga; Cristóbal de Moura; Juan de Idiáquez, a former ambassador to Genoa and Venice; the Count of Chinchón; and Mateo Vázquez, the king's secretary.[68]

Composed of the king's men – loyal to the king and God, as Philip II wrote to Mateo Vázquez[69] – the *junta* offered exceptional possibilities for overcoming barriers erected by the councils to divert the king's will. Philip II's frustration at these obstacles is clearly indicated in a memorandum Alonso Ramírez de Prado, the royal attorney at the Council of Finance, sent to Cristóbal de Moura in 1592. "We navigate," he wrote, "with so many pilots, without authority and order, that all things require too much time and effort to execute, and although we have the possibility of accomplishing great things," we achieve nothing.[70] The councils no longer subscribed to the principle that "absolute obedience to the king is the substance of all communities."[71] The *Junta de Gobierno* was the king's response to his frustration, and it became his intermediary with all royal officials. All the *consultas* and reports from the various councils, ambassadors, viceroys, *chancillerías* (provincial tribunals of justice), and royal servants were first to be discussed in the *junta* and only then sent to Philip II, who simply approved the suggestions of his privy council or further discussed them with its members.[72]

---

[65] Escudero, *Los secretarios*, vol. I, pp. 221–2, 224–5.

[66] H. G. Koenigsberger, "The Statecraft of Philip II," *European Studies Review*, 1 (1971), p. 6; see also Lovett, *Mateo Vázquez de Leça*, p. 201.

[67] References to the *Junta de Tres* in the 1570s in Riba García, *Correspondencia privada*, pp. 17, 25–6, 36; for the creation of the *Junta de Gobierno* see Lovett, *Mateo Vázquez de Leça*, pp. 201–4. On the creation of these *juntas* see Santiago Fernández Conti, "La nobleza cortesana: don Diego de Cabrera y Bobadilla, tercer conde de Chinchón," in José Martínez Millán, ed., *La Corte de Felipe II* (Madrid, 1994), pp. 229–70.

[68] The death of Juan de Zúñiga in October 1586 did not change the structure or the functions of the *Junta de Gobierno* and Philip II continued to consult with Moura, Idiáquez, Chinchón, and Mateo Vázquez, who died in 1591. See Cabrera de Córdoba, *Historia de Felipe II*, vol. III, p. 144.

[69] Riba García, *Correspondencia privada*, p. 178.

[70] AGS CC VI, *leg.* 2793, bk. 6, fols. 944v–45r: Ramírez de Prado to Cristóbal de Moura, Feb. 1592; see Antonio Feros, "El viejo Felipe y los nuevos favoritos: formas de gobierno en la década de 1590," *Studia Histórica*, 17 (1997), pp. 11–36.

[71] AGS CC VI, *leg.* 2793, bk. 6, fol. 938r.

[72] On Philip II's style of government in the 1580s and 1590s see "Estilo que guardó el Rey Nro. Señor Don Phelipe II en el despacho de los negocios" (*c.* 1598), in Escudero, *Los secretarios*, vol. I, pp. 202–6;

It is important to note that, as demonstrated by its membership and functions, the *Junta de Gobierno* had been conceived by Philip II not as a temporary measure to help him to rule the monarchy in his old age, as modern historians tend to argue, but as a political mechanism destined to become a permanent fixture in the government of the monarchy. This intention is clear in the instructions sent to the *junta* by the king in 1593 asking it to serve as his private council and a collective tutor of Prince Philip, the institution through which he would receive his lessons in practical politics. On this occasion he also introduced several changes in the *junta*'s constitution. He installed his nephew, Archduke Albert – Cardinal of Toledo, his *alter ego* in Portugal and future ruler of the Low Countries – as its head, and he added Velada, Prince Philip's *mayordomo mayor*, as a member.[73] The king had two motives for making these changes: to elevate the *junta*'s status by electing one of his relatives as its head and to place the present and future of the Spanish monarchy in the hands of a small group of his closest servants.

His desire for the *junta* to serve as a school for his son's political apprenticeship is also clear from the instructions sent on 26 September 1593 in which he commanded the *junta* to hold daily meetings in the prince's quarters although the prince himself was not expected to attend the *junta*'s meetings in their entirety.[74] The *junta* was to deliberate on all public matters except those that he reserved for himself, such as the distribution of commanderies (*encomiendas*) and knighthoods (*hábitos*) in the military orders, and church and judicial appointments. In addition he expected the *junta* to keep its deliberations secret, and its members to free themselves of their private interests and commit themselves "to serving God, my interests, and the interests of my kingdoms." In conclusion, he emphasized that good advice is perfected only when decisions taken are fully enforced, and, hence, he expected the members of the *junta*, especially his nephew Archduke Albert, to guarantee that his decisions would be implemented without delay by closely monitoring the deliberations and actions of the other royal institutions.

At about the same time, Prince Philip assumed a more prominent role in the government, but it is difficult to know whether the king's decision to involve his son was taken in response to his own deteriorating health or to meet Philip's educational needs. Historians know, for example, that owing to his health Philip II was unable to handle public matters in May–June 1595, March–April 1596, the spring of 1597 and almost the entire year in 1598.[75] In any case, in a memorandum dated 30

a large number of the *consultas* of the *Junta* are conserved in the Instituto Valencia Don Juan (where I have consulted *envíos* 29 and 43–45), and Biblioteca Francisco de Zabálburu (where I have consulted *carps.* 132–4).

[73] In his biography of Cristóbal de Moura, Danvila y Burguero affirms that Philip II's decision to appoint his nephew was suggested by Moura in 1591; Alfonso Danvila y Burguero, *Don Cristóbal de Moura, primer marqués de Castel Rodrigo (1538–1613)* (Madrid, 1900), pp. 709–13; see also, Fernández Conti, "La nobleza cortesana," p. 248.

[74] IVJ, *envío* 29, *exps.* 6–7: "La orden que se ha de guardar en la Junta que ahora se ha ordenado," San Lorenzo, 26 September 1593.

[75] This information is in Geoffrey Parker, *The Grand Strategy of Philip II* (New Haven, 1998), p. 277.

July 1595 the king asked his son to represent him in public audiences and encouraged the prince to take a more active role in the debates of the *junta* by asking questions and then informing the king of the nature of the debate and the *junta*'s resolutions, which they would then discuss together.[76]

Initial accounts of Philip's participation in the government did not paint a favorable picture of the young prince. In a report sent to the Venetian senate in 1595 Francesco Vendramino, for example, wrote that while Philip attended the *junta*'s meetings for one hour, according to rumors "he does not understand state affairs very well although in general it seems that princes improve their ability with time and experience."[77] Philip II's own anxiety was reflected in his request for a report on his son's progress, which García de Loaysa sent to the king in October 1596 outlining the prince's virtues and shortcomings and measures that should be taken to transform the prince into a genuine king.[78] According to Loaysa, who began his report by emphasizing the spirit of friendship and cooperation among members of Philip's household, the prince had all the qualities necessary to a Christian prince: he was religious, devout, and honest, as well as composed, obedient to his father and tutors, affable with his servants, very intelligent, and lacked all vices except for his tendency to sleep too much. Loaysa then went on to emphasize the need to transfer these favorable qualities "from the man Philip to the would-be king," a process that would also require a modification of some unfavorable aspects of Philip's character. Some of the prince's servants worried, for example, about certain of his traits, including his inflexibility, reserved and secretive nature, tendency to withdraw from people around him, and his dignified manners. To inhibit his inclination to be severe with those who sought his company, the prince should be given access to new courtiers, and he should increase his participation in public events. He should also attend the meetings of the councils, not only those of the *junta*, to broaden his political experience and then write reports of their deliberations to be shared with the king.

Philip II's reaction to Loaysa's report remains unknown, but no changes were apparently made in the prince's political education. Instead, a few months later in 1597, Philip II expressed his own views of the royal majesty to his son in a memorandum in which he advised the prince to be pious and obedient to God's law, and remember that all able monarchs administered justice and obeyed the laws of the land.[79] He counseled his son to be kind towards loyal servants and not to forget that his public presentation of himself would determine his authority and reputation. For this reason, the king advised him always to "show his servants a

---

[76] IVJ, *envío* 29, *exp.* 8, "De mano de su Majestad para su Alteza," San Lorenzo, 30 July 1595.
[77] Alberi, *Le Relazioni*, p. 446.
[78] I have used a copy of this document published by González Dávila, *Historia de la vida*, pp. 20–22.
[79] Cf. Manuel Fernández Alvarez, "Las instrucciones políticas de los Austrias Mayores: Problemas e interpretaciones," *Gesammelte Aufsätze zur Kulturgeschichte Spaniens*, 23 (1967), p. 184; see also Cervera de la Torre, "Relación de la enfermedad y muerte del Rey don Felipe II" [1600], in Cabrera de Córdoba, *Historia de Felipe II*, vol. IV, p. 317; and González Dávila, *Historia de la vida*, p. 28.

rough, saturnine, and cryptic face" because "you have to present yourself as a king."[80] Philip II further instructed Prince Philip to "[r]ule by yourself because a king who lets others rule, rules unworthily," but he also told him to select several men "of good manners and virtue" as "friends and favorites" because "to rule properly means taking on many obligations, and to attend to them with success you must embrace counsel and seek the opinions of others. I am content with Cristóbal de Moura, and I am confident that you will be as well."[81]

By 1597, Prince Philip had assumed many key responsibilities in the government of the monarchy,[82] including the signing of all documents and royal orders, which, according to his father, provided him, "already a man, [an opportunity] to help me in the ruling of the monarchy and to prevent a paralysis in the execution of state affairs."[83] Prince Philip's growing influence is also evident in the instructions the king sent to the *Junta de Gobierno* following Archduke Albert's departure to the Low Countries as the governor-general in 1595.[84] Philip II now delegated to his son the responsibility of coordinating the work of the *junta* and the control over the execution of the king's orders, tasks previously performed by Archduke Albert. His new role gave Philip first-hand experience of affairs of state and a chance to create his own circle of political advisers. Nevertheless, those alleged to have intimate knowledge of the king's activities claimed that the king remained firmly in control. "The prince has no authority," concluded, for example, the Venetian ambassador in a report sent in August 1598. Even if the king, he continued, owing to his bad health "can neither understand nor provide for affairs, [he] will not divest himself of his dominion and his empire. So far from resigning while alive, His Majesty does all he can to rule after his death."[85]

---

[80] Fernández Alvarez, "Las instrucciones políticas," pp. 184–5, 187.
[81] González Dávila, *Historia de la vida*, pp. 28, 26.
[82] The contrast between a waning old king and the growing vitality of Prince Philip is apparent in Lhermite, *Le Passetemps*, vol. II, p. 113.
[83] A copy of this royal order in BNM, Mss 18190: "Tres decretos de Felipe II, dirigidos a los consejos sobre que su hijo le empezase a ayudar en los negocios de la monarquía," fols. 38r–39v.
[84] IVJ, *envío* 29, exp. 9: "La orden que se ha de guardar en la Junta," 1597. The *junta* was now composed of Moura, Idiáquez, Chinchón, and Velada.
[85] *CSPVen*, vol. IX, p. 339.

2

The making of a favorite

Modern historians have interpreted Philip II's "desire to rule after his death" as an indication of his conviction that his son's destiny was "not to be the ruler but to be ruled" by one of his favorites. To prevent this, they argue, the king surrounded the prince with his own "favorite ministers" to ensure that the government of the monarchy would remain in competent hands after his death. The Venetian ambassador, Francesco Soranzo, seemed to agree when he wrote that by placing "in the prince's service all his favorite ministers," the king tried "to guarantee that the prince himself" would also embrace them as his own advisers and, more importantly, would let them retain control of the government.[1]

Although Philip II's own assessment of the political abilities of his heir has never been tracked down,[2] it is true that rumors circulated at court (see Chapter 3) alleging that the prince lacked the political aptitude and character of his father. It is, however, difficult to substantiate these rumors, and one should remember that they surfaced during a period when several courtiers were struggling for power and influence. On one side were the king's private counselors – Moura, Velada, Chinchón, and Idiáquez – and on the other was the Duke of Lerma, an aristocrat in title if not in wealth, who from the early 1590s had been a central figure in the life of Prince Philip and who posed the most serious challenge to the power and influence exercised by Moura and his allies. In the competition for the prince's favor, however, Lerma and the king's favorites started on very unequal footing. Obviously intimacy with the old king gave an advantage to those who had his support, whereas Lerma had to depend on the favor of the inexperienced prince and the help of minor royal servants. Moreover, he was keenly aware that royal favor and fortune were difficult to attain and even more difficult to preserve, having been born to a family whose power and wealth had fluctuated during the previous two centuries.

Born in the 1550s, Francisco Gómez de Sandoval, 5th Marquis of Denia, 4th Count of Lerma from 1575, and Duke of Lerma from 1599, was a member of a

---

[1] *CSPVen*, vol. IX, p. 338, report of 31 Aug. 1598.
[2] Philip II's alleged fears concerning his son's character appeared only in books published after 1621; see, for example, González Dávila, *Historia de la vida*, p. 30 (Philip II to Moura), and "Adiciones a la historia de el marqués de Malvezzi" (a supporter and collaborator of the Count-Duke of Olivares during the 1630s), in Juan Yáñez, *Memorias para la historia de don Felipe III, rey de España* (Madrid, 1773), pp. 136, 139.

family that had suffered many reversals in the service of the Spanish monarchs.[3] The Sandovals, like other members of the so-called new nobility, rose to prominence in the aftermath of the Christian territorial advance against the Muslims who controlled the southern part of the Iberian peninsula.[4] They had reached the apex of their power in the early fifteenth century under the leadership of Diego Gómez de Sandoval, Count of Castro from 1426. Titles, lands, and wealth positioned Diego Gómez and his household at the center of power in the kingdom of Castile, and he participated in the fight for power during the turbulent reign of John II (1406–54), when he joined the faction commanded by the Infantes de Aragón (the sons of Ferdinand of Antequera, King of Aragon) against the faction led by the Castilian king, John II, and the king's favorite, Alvaro de Luna, conflicts that after numerous turns of fortune resulted in victory by the faction led by the Castilian king.[5] Having chosen the losing side, Diego Gómez was declared a traitor and lost all his Castilian territories, titles, and offices. Without lands and royal offices he and his household became outsiders in the political affairs of the kingdom of Castile. Only support from his former allies saved him from total ruin. In compensation for land lost in Castile Diego Gómez received new, although much reduced, holdings in the territories belonging to the Aragonese crown, including the towns of Borja, Magallón, Balaguer, and Denia.[6]

Only after the deaths of Alvaro de Luna in 1453 and John II in 1454 was it possible for the Sandovals to contemplate the recovery of their lands and political base in Castile, the family's principal ambition. The first opportunity presented itself during the fight for the crown of Castile led by Isabel of Castile and her husband Ferdinand, the new King of Aragon and grandson of Ferdinand of Antequera, against Henry IV (1454–74), King of Castile and Isabel's brother. Fernando de Sandoval, the head of the family from 1455, took advantage of this

---

[3] Historians do not know exactly when Francisco Gómez de Sandoval was born: the year 1552, given by Salazar de Mendoza, is accepted by most scholars; see BNM, Mss 3277, Salazar de Mendoza, "Crónica de la Casa de Sandoval en 22 elogios" (1600). Doubts about his age surfaced in 1589 when Lerma was made a knight of the Military Order of Santiago; witnesses declared that the candidate was between twenty-eight and thirty-three years of age; see AHN OM, Santiago: *exp.* 7589/1589.

[4] See Salvador de Moxó, *De la nobleza vieja a la nobleza nueva. La transformación nobiliaria castellana en la baja Edad Media* (Madrid, 1969).

[5] On the political feuds during the reign of John II see Luis Suárez Fernández, *Nobleza y monarquía* (Valladolid, 1975), pp. 139ff.

[6] For this summary of the Sandovals' history I relied on the following works: *Memorial de los artículos que están vistos por los señores del consejo en el pleito entre el señor fiscal y el reino, con el señor cardenal duque de Lerma y sus sucesores* (n.p., 1653), hereafter *Memorial de los artículos*; Francisco Gómez de Sandoval Manrique de Padilla, *Memorial dirigido por don Francisco Gómez de Sandoval Manrique de Padilla, duque de Lerma, al rey Felipe IV contra una demanda del fiscal don Juan de Chumacero de Sotomayor, sobre las donaciones y mercedes que le hizo Felipe III al abuelo del litigante* (n.p., n.d.); *Memorial del pleito de tenuta que es entre don Gregorio de Sandoval Silva y Mendoza, conde de Saldaña por la tenuta y posesión de los bienes de los estados y mayorazgo de Lerma, Cea y Ampudia* (n.p., n.d.), hereafter *Memorial del pleito de tenuta*; BNM, Mss 3277, Salazar de Mendoza, "Crónica de la Casa de Sandoval"; and Ismael García Rámila, *El gran burgalés don Diego Gómez de Sandoval, primer conde de Castro (1385–1455)* (Burgos, 1953).

dynastic crisis and promised his support to Isabel and Ferdinand in exchange for the return of the Sandovals' Castilian lands and titles taken from Diego Gómez, a pledge Isabel and Ferdinand signed in 1469.[7]

But to the disappointment of the Sandovals, Isabel and Ferdinand failed to fulfill their part of the bargain. Instead of recovering their former lands, titles, and offices, they received only a small portion, including some relatively unimportant and separated small villages, the most important of which was the little village of Lerma in the heart of the kingdom of Castile. Fernando Sandoval was, however, granted the title of Marquis of Denia and given the promise of a payment of 27,000 ducats in compensation for lost territories, a promise that was never fulfilled, not even when Bernardo de Sandoval, 2nd Marquis of Denia, became Ferdinand's lord high steward and married the king's cousin, Francisca Enríquez.[8]

This short summary of the Sandovals' past glory and misfortunes helps to set the Sandovals', and particularly Lerma's, ambition in a historical context and to establish why, despite their failure to recover Castilian titles, offices, and lands, the Sandovals held a firm conviction that they belonged to the highest echelons of the Castilian aristocracy. Although their possessions, income, power, and influence were never comparable to those of other aristocratic houses in Castile, such as Infantado, Osuna, Alba, Medinaceli, and Medina-Sidonia, their confidence in their membership in this exclusive group never diminished and it was the foundation on which they would build during the reigns of Charles V, Philip II, and Philip III.

After these repeated failures to recover their Castilian lands and titles, the Sandovals adjusted their strategy following the death of Ferdinand and the enthronement of Charles as ruler of the Spanish monarchy in 1517. With Ferdinand's death the Sandovals' Aragonese connection had vanished forever, and under Charles and his successors Castile acquired even greater importance. Only those with an independent power base – aristocrats with large land holdings and vassals in Castile and elsewhere or those fortunate enough to belong to the ruler's inner circle – were able to control their own fortunes. Everyone else had to depend on the support of grandees or become part of a rising court nobility (one almost exclusively dedicated to serving the king), a path the Sandovals now followed.

New avenues for courtly careers available to the less-wealthy nobility had opened up under Ferdinand and Isabel. As the victors of a civil war, they were keenly aware of the dangers posed by a powerful aristocracy and took steps from the beginning of their reign to limit opportunities for independent action by members of the nobility who had often used their wealth and territorial power to challenge and sometimes usurp royal sovereignty. To prevent this, the Catholic Monarchs had to augment their own authority and, at the same time, force the nobility to depend on the

---

[7] A copy of this agreement is in *Memorial de los artículos*, fol. 10v.
[8] See BNM, Mss 3277, Salazar de Mendoza, "Crónica de la Casa de Sandoval," fol. 376r; on how the Sandovals' changing fortune was viewed in the early sixteenth century see Gonzalo Fernández de Oviedo, *Batallas y quinquagenas*, ed. Juan Pérez de Tudela (Madrid, 1983), pp. 377–87.

crown. This they accomplished by restricting the nobility's political influence over the crown's central institutions and by transforming the ruler into the great patron upon whom everyone, including the aristocracy, had to depend.

Historians commonly observe that the most important political reform Isabel and Ferdinand introduced was the promotion of *letrados* (individuals educated in the law) as members of the various royal councils and the simultaneous revocation of the nobility's "natural rights" to be represented in them. Until then, members of the nobility were accepted as "natural counselors of the king" who thus held the right to participate in the decision-making process. But in 1480 a new law stated that only those specifically chosen by the king, regardless of social ranking, could serve on the royal councils. Belonging to a select elite no longer entailed automatic political representation; representation was now viewed as the result of the king's grace.[9]

The Catholic Monarchs also began a process of concentrating all possible sources of patronage and wealth into the king's hands, thus transforming the Spanish monarch into the patron from whom all others received their due. By the early sixteenth century, Spanish kings controlled a long list of rewards at their free disposition: lands, jurisdictions, annuities, monopolies, gratuities (*ayudas de costa*), the right to confirm titles of nobility and create others, the concession of the so-called *mercedes* of honor (such as knighthoods in the four military orders), and, perhaps most importantly, the right to appoint all local, territorial, ecclesiastical, and central officials. The immediate consequence was that everyone else now became dependent on the monarch's favor, transforming the sixteenth-century Spanish monarchy into a sort of welfare state with royal favor representing, in H. G. Koenigsberger's words, "the fuel which kept the wheels of political society turning."[10]

Many sixteenth-century writers recognized that royal control of patronage had transformed relations among the nobility, their clients, and the monarch. Diego de Hermosilla, for example, in *El diálogo de los pajes*, apparently written in 1543, in comparing the situation of the nobility in the fifteenth century to that of his own times, noted that during the former times the nobility held power independent of the monarch and had a capacity to use its own sources of patronage to attract followers, whom they enrolled in territorial and dynastic conflicts. But by the mid-sixteenth century, the nobility had become dependent on the king's favor to such a degree that the only way they could maintain territorial influence was by placing themselves in the service of the king, who had become the sole source of wealth for them and their followers.[11]

Royal favor was even more important for those members of the nobility, like the

---

[9] *Nueva recopilación*, bk. 2, tit. 4, law 4.
[10] H. G. Koenigsberger, "Patronage and Bribery during the Reign of Charles V," in his *States and Revolution. Essays in Early Modern European History* (New York, 1971), p. 166.
[11] Diego de Hermosilla, *Diálogo de los pajes* [*c.* 1543] (Madrid, 1989), pp. 68–9, 75–8.

Sandovals, who despite their impressive titles lacked sufficient income and lands to maintain an independent existence. For these nobles the only avenue to wealth and power was a career in the service of the king. Yet the number of offices in royal institutions open to members of the aristocracy was relatively small. The offices in the councils, with the exception of the Council of State, were reserved for the *letrados*, and although one could aspire to become an ambassador, a viceroy, or a governor, these offices were also limited until the late sixteenth century, when the power of the Spanish king extended to several peninsular, European, and American kingdoms. For this reason, many members of the aristocratic houses aspired to become personal servants of the monarch as palace officials, the number of which began to grow during the reigns of the Catholic Monarchs and Charles V.[12]

With the boom in the number of palace servants the court became identified with "sophistication" and *vivire civile* and a place where nobles could exercise their duties of obedience, respect, and service to the king. Furthermore, as a result of the increasing powers of the ruler, the court rather than the country became the preeminent setting for anyone who aspired to establish his importance. This new preoccupation was analyzed in the new genre of courtesy literature, a genre whose principal exponent was Baldassare Castiglione. His *Il cortegiano*, first published in 1528, was translated into Spanish in 1534 by the Catalan humanist, Juan Boscán, and became an extremely popular book with thirteen editions published during the sixteenth century.[13] As is well known, the first two books of Castiglione's treatise address the many qualities and virtues a capable courtier should possess – excellent lineage; external beauty, good appearance and manners; education, and so on. But while important, these were nevertheless not the most critical characteristics of the "new courtier," now envisioned as an individual whose *raison d'être* was to devote himself entirely to the service of his king. A perfect courtier, Castiglione wrote, should "love and adore the prince he serves over all humans, using all his will, virtues, and arts to please his master."[14] In other words, the perfect courtier's only object of loyalty was the king, but through his commitment to the king's interests the courtier could obtain substantial personal benefits. In the fourth book of *Il cortegiano*, Castiglione presented what he anticipated to be the perfect courtier's ultimate goal: to "gain the love of his prince and by doing so become his *privado*" (vol. II, p. 115). Becoming the king's favorite now was seen as central to achieving access to wealth and influence and was viewed as the only path that guaranteed success in court politics.

[12] On the increasing number of palace servants under the Catholic Monarchs see Azcona, *Isabel*, p. 710; Ladero Quesada, *La hacienda real*, pp. 278–9, and his, *Los Reyes Católicos: La corona y la unidad de España* (Valencia, 1989), p. 105.

[13] On the Spanish edition of *Il cortegiano* see Margherita Morreale, *Castiglione y Boscán: el ideal cortesano en el renacimiento* (Madrid, 1959).

[14] I have used Boscán's Spanish translation of Castiglione's work; Baldassare Castiglione, *El cortesano*, trans. Juan Boscán [1534], facsimile edn., 2 vols. (Madrid, 1985), vol. I, p. 132. Further references in the text.

This was precisely the strategy the Sandovals adopted after the enthronement of Charles in 1517, as they were among the first members of the Castilian nobility to offer support, service, and total loyalty to the king. By choosing this path they temporarily gave up their territorial demands and embarked on an effort to promote court careers for members of the household. Bernardo de Sandoval was the first to succeed when he was appointed governor of the household of Queen Juana "the Mad," the mother of King Charles, in 1519. Although this position was considered marginal at best in the court hierarchy – the queen was living outside the royal court in the Castilian town of Tordesillas because of her alleged mental instability – it nevertheless provided the family with an opportunity to present themselves as Charles's loyal servants. The position was also politically delicate because the queen remained the legal ruler of the Spanish monarchy despite her infirmity. Its importance became evident during the revolt of the *comuneros* (1519–21), a loosely formed urban rebellion against Charles in Castile. In an attempt to legitimate their revolt and reinforce their claims, the *comuneros'* leaders turned their attention towards the neglected queen and took her hostage in 1520 in an attack on Tordesillas. Royalist forces, however, led by, among others, Bernardo de Sandoval, successfully counterattacked, regained the town, freed the queen, and ultimately defeated the *comuneros* in April 1521.[15]

Once again the rewards for the Sandovals turned out to be mixed. As a payment for their defense of Charles's rights, they received the title of a grandee of Castile, a title that confirmed what they already knew – that their house belonged to the Castilian aristocracy and that their lack of wealth was simply the result of historical injustices. To their disappointment, their new title did not alter their position in the court hierarchy. If anything, it deteriorated, as the defeat of the *comuneros* eliminated the last political obstacle to the consolidation of Charles's authority. As the governor to Queen Juana, Bernardo de Sandoval remained a political outsider in his "exile" at Tordesillas for more than thirty years.

The queen's death in 1555 finally made it possible for the Marquises of Denia to attain positions that were in closer proximity to the monarch. Luis de Sandoval, 3rd Marquis of Denia, was the first to obtain an office at court when, in the early 1560s, he was appointed gentleman of the chamber to Don Carlos, Philip II's eldest son. His brother, Fernando Rojas de Sandoval, later joined him in the prince's household as *mayordomo mayor* of the prince. The death of Don Carlos in 1568 momentarily hampered the Sandovals' efforts to become members of the king's inner circle, but in 1570 the appointment of Francisco de Sandoval (the father of the future Duke of Lerma) as a gentleman in Philip II's chamber opened up new opportunities for court careers. At least on paper, the Marquises of Denia now had direct access, if not to the king, at least to those who held the strings of power.

During the sixteenth century, one avenue to the top of the court hierarchy was to

---

[15] On the revolt of the *comuneros* see José Antonio Maravall, *Las Comunidades de Castilla* (Madrid, 1963).

seek the favor of those who were the king's confidants by becoming what Antonio de Guevara – the most influential courtly writer in sixteenth-century Spain – referred to as "the king's favorite's favorite" (*el privado del privado*).[16] In other words, in exchange for protection those lacking direct access to the king offered support and loyalty to his closest servants. But as noted in Chapter 1, the search for favor at the court of Philip II was not a simple matter; it was complicated by the presence of several powerful court patrons and one had to choose with whom to affiliate. When Francisco de Sandoval joined Philip II's court the choice was between the Duke of Alba and the Prince of Eboli, who led competing court factions fighting for power and the king's favor.[17] No direct testimonies have survived to indicate which faction the Sandovals belonged to, but other evidence suggests that the Marquises of Denia tied their fortunes to the Prince of Eboli.[18]

The 3rd Marquis of Denia, Luis de Sandoval (1536–70), for example, married Catalina de Zúñiga, who was a sister of the Count of Miranda and a cousin of Luis de Requesens and Juan de Zúñiga, both important members of Eboli's faction. The choice of Lerma's own bride is in some ways even more revealing. In 1576 Lerma married Catalina de la Cerda, who was the daughter of Juan de la Cerda, 4th Duke of Medinaceli, counselor of state, lord high steward of Queen Anne of Austria – Prince Philip's mother – and one of the most prominent leaders of Eboli's followers at the court.[19] Whatever benefits the Sandovals may have drawn from their alliance with Eboli were, however, short lived inasmuch as in the late 1560s he began to lose ground to the Duke of Alba in the competition for the king's favor. The final blow to the Sandovals' hopes came with Eboli's death in 1573 and that of Medinaceli, Lerma's father-in-law, in 1575.

Indeed, despite the acquisition of palace offices, the Sandovals remained unsuccessful in improving their finances, and when Lerma became the head of the house in 1575, he was faced with an enormous debt. The problem was not that the amount was substantially larger than that accumulated by other Castilian nobles[20] but that the annual income the Sandovals received from their land holdings, ranging from 14,000 to 20,000 ducats, was substantially lower than that received by other grandees, which typically ranged from 60,000 to 120,000 ducats per year.[21] This

---

[16] Antonio de Guevara, *Aviso de privados o despertador de cortesanos* [1539], ed. A. Alvarez de la Villa (Paris, 1914), p. 99. [17] On the court factions in the reign of Philip II see above, chap. 1.

[18] On the Sandovals' relations with Eboli, see Antonio Pérez "A un señor amigo" (n.d.), in Eugenio Ochoa, ed., *Epistolario español*, 2 vols. (Madrid, 1952), p. 561; Leopold von Ranke, *La monarquía española de los siglos XVI y XVII* (Mexico City, 1946), pp. 87–8; and Marañón, *Antonio Pérez*, vol. II, pp. 140–1.

[19] On the palace office of Catalina de la Cerda, see AGPR Ex. Per., 233/21, 588/15, and 661/15.

[20] On this topic see Charles Jago, "The Influence of Debt on the Relations between Crown and Aristocracy in Seventeenth-Century Castile," *Economic History Review*, 26 (1973), pp. 218–36; in Jago's view the financial debts of the nobility became the biggest social problem during the sixteenth century in Castile (p. 226).

[21] For changes in the rental income of the Marquises of Denia see Lucio Marineo Sículo, *Las cosas memorables de España* (n.p., 1530), fols. 23v–25v; BNM, Mss 18731/26, "Relación de las rentas que tienen los duques, marqueses y condes de España"; Pedro Núñez de Salcedo, "Relación verdadera de

prompted Lerma to raise the topic in a memorandum he sent to Philip II in 1585 stating that "my grandparents and parents, with royal consent, have left our house and estate" burdened with debt, and "it has become impossible for us to live or to sustain ourselves."[22] He was not the only one troubled by his family's grave circumstances; they were also of great concern to the king's close advisers, leading the royal secretary Mateo Vázquez to inform the king in 1585 that "the Marquis of Denia finds himself in great need, a situation so seldom seen in men of his quality that he provokes nothing but compassion," and to suggest that the only solution to the family's predicament was royal favor.[23] But the king's aversion to granting economic *mercedes* and the disappearance of many of the Sandovals' protectors from the court during the tumultuous 1570s made it hard to attain royal favor, and Lerma found himself abandoned by the king.[24] Given these conditions, he may well have been sincere in his declaration that he was contemplating a return to his lands in Valencia to spend the remainder of his life attending to his estates.[25] In the end, however, being a courtier by education, he was not prepared for a life as a landed noble.

Not much is know about Lerma's education, which took place under the guidance of his tutor and uncle Don Rodrigo de Castro, the Bishop of Córdoba, but evidence indicates that he took "lessons in prudence, politics, and wisdom" (*prudencia, política y cordura*) and learned skills thought essential for court life – such as riding on horseback, fencing and so on.[26] He was educated for a life at the court, and he knew from the experience of his ancestors that were he to leave it for Valencia, he would forever give up the chance of a courtly career and all possibilities of the king's favor, which, however, remained largely unattainable.

Lerma had failed to obtain Philip II's support chiefly because he lacked strong patrons and supporters, especially after Medinaceli's death and that of his own father in 1575. He was temporarily unable to get any palace office to continue his family tradition until 1580, when the influence of his uncle Rodrigo de Castro, who was by then Archbishop of Seville, got him included in the royal entourage that was

todos los títulos que hay en España" [1597], *BRAH*, 73 (1918), pp. 468–92. The increase in Lerma's income from 14,000 to 20,000 ducats between 1580 and 1597 seems to result from improvements to his lands in Valencia (see AHN CS, *leg.* 4410, *exp.* 180), and from the 3,000 ducats per year he obtained from the lease of his commandery of Mérida (military order of Santiago); see Duke of Lerma, *Descripción e inventario de las rentas, bienes y hacienda del cardenal duque de Lerma* (Valladolid, 1622), fol. 14v. For a comparison of the income of the Marquises of Denia with that of other Castilian nobles see Charles Jago, "Aristocracy, War and Finance in Castile, 1621–1665," Ph.D. diss., Cambridge University, 1969, vol. II, app. 1.

22 AHN CS, *leg.* 4410, *exp.* 180: *consulta* of the Chamber of Castile, 12 Nov. 1585.

23 Mateo Vázquez to Philip II, 12 Jan. 1585, in Riba García, *Correspondencia privada*, p. 351.

24 On Philip II's aversion to granting *mercedes* see below, chap. 3.   25 AHN CS, *leg.* 4410, *exp.* 180.

26 Luis de Góngora's "Panegírico al duque de Lerma," written in 1617; see José Pellicer de Tovar, *Lecciones solemnes a las obras de don Luis de Góngora y Argote* [1630], facsimile edn. (New York, 1971), pp. 622–3. On the education of the nobility see Varela, *Modos de educación*, pp. 83–126; and Isabel Beceiro Pita, "Educación y cultura de la nobleza (siglos XIII–XV)," *Anuario de Estudios Medievales*, 21 (1991), pp. 571–90.

to accompany Philip II on his journey to Portugal. The immediate and most important consequence of this mission for Lerma's career was his appointment as gentleman of the king's chamber. He knew that if he now proved himself an able courtier, doors to new and higher offices would open up, but the king's desire for privacy and the wall his favorites had erected around him denied Lerma access to the king despite his newly acquired position. He remained just another royal official on the royal visits to Portugal in 1580 and to the crown of Aragon in 1585.

Frustrated by the lack of opportunities to attain Philip II's favor, Lerma turned his attention to Prince Philip in the late 1580s to early 1590s. From the works of numerous Renaissance authors as well as his own education and experience, he knew that if he could win the prince's favor he would be well on his way to a successful court career. In this quest he followed practices prescribed by contemporary theories for aspiring courtiers; he knew that, to succeed, he had to "visit, serve, suffer, make himself visible, and persevere."[27] But first he had to gain access to the prince's chambers where he could demonstrate to the young prince his capacity for service, his loyalty, and his courtly accomplishments. His lack of an office in the prince's household was no obstacle because palace etiquette during Philip II's reign gave grandees admission to the king's and the prince's chambers.[28]

But access was not sufficient to guarantee victory, as Guevara and many other sixteenth-century courtly writers had made clear. According to contemporary theories, a courtier needed more than access to his master; he had to please him, ascertain his personal preferences, and fashion himself in his image. "In winning the will and favor of the prince it is extremely important," Antonio de Guevara wrote in his *Aviso de privados*, "to find out the prince's inclinations. A courtier needs to know if the prince likes music, hunting, fishing, and the style of his riding, and once he discovers the prince's preferences he himself must love what the prince loves and follow what the prince follows." The reason why this was so important, Guevara continued, is that princes are humans and thus "they sometimes love more those courtiers who share their own preferences than those who labor hard on their behalf." Guevara's advice left no room for misunderstanding: "Wise Castilians should keep in mind the following principle: everything the king likes should be considered good, while everything he dislikes should be considered bad."[29] The key to success, as the Spanish translator of Giovanni della Casa's *Il galateo* noted, was the courtier's ability to use his actions and language to please those whose favor he was seeking. His virtues and worth were far less important than his capacity "to enchant" the prince with sweet words and good manners.[30]

---

[27] Guevara, *Aviso*, p. 181.

[28] See Matías de Novoa, *Historia de Felipe III, rey de España* [c. 1640s]. *Codoin*, 60–1 (Madrid, 1875), 60, p. 31.   [29] Guevara, *Aviso*, p. 86.

[30] Lucas Gracián Dantisco's *Galateo español* was published in 1585, ed. Ciriaco Pérez Bustamante (Madrid, 1943). *Galateo español* is the Spanish adaptation of Della Casa, *Il Galateo*, published in 1558. The extreme popularity of Gracián Dantisco's adaptation is demonstrated by its fourteen editions between 1585 and 1680.

To gain royal favor, a courtier needed to flatter and please the ruler, and Lerma pursued this strategy with numerous gifts and unending adulation, relying on the assistance of some key insiders in the prince's chamber – mainly Alonso Muriel de Valdivieso, secretary of Prince Philip's privy chamber; Juan de Tassis, the king's postmaster-general; and Juan Pascual, a banker.[31] His efforts were at times, however, thwarted by Moura, Loaysa, and other members of the prince's household who attempted to restrict access only to "those more privileged," a group to which Lerma did not belong.[32] But he demonstrated a remarkable ability to overcome such barriers, arranging secret communication with Philip and finding ways to place himself in the prince's presence. In 1593, for example, Lerma used to his benefit a masque organized by Lhermite for Prince Philip's entertainment. Begging Lhermite for a role in the event "to let me give some pleasure to the prince," a "disguised" Lerma, whose presence was noticed only by Lhermite and Prince Philip, greatly impressed the latter by his ability to linger undetected throughout the entire festivity.[33]

Towards the end of Philip II's reign, political life at the court and Lerma's quest for the prince's favor were also influenced by the proliferation of contradictory opinions about the place of royal favorites at court and in the monarchical structure. The dominant sixteenth-century political paradigm held that the presence and influence of royal favorites were pernicious to the well-being of king and kingdom, a view shared by authors who disagreed about other aspects of monarchical privilege. At the same time, Philip II's style of government – especially his decision to rely on the advice of a small group of favorite counselors – created an atmosphere that permitted the emergence of more positive definitions and theories of the king's *privado*. These evolving theories significantly influenced Lerma's actions, his justifications of them, and the contemporary evaluation of his intentions.

Negative views of royal favorites or, more precisely, of their role in government had a long tradition in Spain. The dominance of John II's favorite Alvaro de Luna in the early fifteenth century helped to create contempt for the *privado* that survived in Spanish political literature for centuries. John's reign came to be viewed as one of the most turbulent periods in history and, thus, as an unfortunate example of a government headed by a *privado*. Fifteenth- and sixteenth-century writers indeed argued that because of his dependence on Alvaro de Luna, John II was despised, his subjects were rebellious, harmony and peace were destroyed, and the entire kingdom was in pandemonium.[34] The story of Alvaro de Luna was frequently utilized to convey moral and political lessons and to remind monarchs that

---

[31] On Alonso Muriel, secretary of Prince Philip's privy chamber, as Lerma's ally see "Papel de don Antonio Hurtado de Mendoza, en el que discurre sobre los principios del oficio de secretario de la Cámara," in Antonio Hurtado de Mendoza, *Discursos de Antonio de Mendoza*, ed. Marqués de Alcedo (Madrid, 1911), p. 62; on Lerma's tactics and helpers see Pérez Bustamante, *La España de Felipe III*, pp. 47–8.   [32] Lhermite, *Le Passetemps*, vol. I, p. 220.   [33] *Ibid.*, vol. I, p. 225.
[34] See Nicholas Round, *The Greatest Man Uncrowned. A Study of the Fall of Don Alvaro de Luna* (London, 1986).

whatever the character of a would-be *privado*, once he obtained royal favor he would reveal his true nature and become an avaricious, selfish, power-hungry, and evil counselor, whose only objective was to expropriate the king's authority. Royal favorites were, insisted an anonymous author in 1493, "palace dogs ... who transformed the king's reason into simple passion."[35]

Towards the end of Philip II's reign, many writers intensified their attacks on royal favorites in conjunction with the ongoing political debate about the duties of the king, the structure of the monarchy, and the nature of royal power (see Chapter 1). The importance of counsel and the role of royal councils in the monarchical government became a central theme in the "mirrors for princes" addressed to Prince Philip urging him to trust his subjects and heed the advice of his councils rather than that of his favorites. In *El príncipe christiano*, for example, Pedro de Ribadeneira argues that to maintain harmony in the realm, the monarch must appoint good counselors and follow their advice and shield himself from the influence of "favorites" and "flatterers," who will only try to insulate him from all criticism and who will support him regardless of the nature of his deeds. The prince should remember that many kingdoms have been destroyed by kings who "had their ears more open to lies and flatteries than to truth and good advice."[36] Juan de Mariana's words were even more explicit. When favorites dominated the court and gained more authority, favor, and wealth than the king's other subjects, they destroyed the foundations of the monarchy by making rulers believe that "royal power is greater than the laws and the community, that the king is the owner of his subjects' property, and that everything, including the law, depends only on the monarch's will." The ultimate goal of favorites was, however, to usurp royal power, and to do so they promoted the king's invisibility by keeping him hidden in the "shadow of the palace." The principal consequences were the transformation of the king into an "effeminate" ruler who "disdained public affairs," neglected his duties as the defender of his subjects' well-being, and left the government and the crown in the hands of his undeserving *privados*.[37]

The defenders of an all-powerful monarch feared the royal favorite for exactly opposite reasons: an influential favorite, according to authors such as Botero, Bodin, and Lipsius, would diminish the possibilities for enhancing the king's power. Machiavelli had already made this point in the early sixteenth century. "It is an infallible rule," he wrote, "that a prince who is not himself wise cannot be soundly advised unless he happens to put himself in the hands of a man who is very able and controls everything. Then he could certainly be well advised, but he would not last long because such a governor would soon deprive him of his state." Instead, Machiavelli argued that while the king should seek advice from his counselors and favorites, he should nevertheless rule alone.[38]

---

[35] R. B. Tate, ed., *Directorio de Príncipes* [1493] (Exeter, 1977), p. 47.
[36] Ribadeneira, *Obras*, pp. 558–9.   [37] Mariana, *De rege*, pp. 37, 97, 105, 110, 165–6.
[38] Niccolò Machiavelli, *The Prince*, ed. Quentin Skinner and Russell Price (Cambridge, 1988), pp. 81–2.

These theories were reproduced in the late sixteenth century by defenders of reason of state. The king's subjects would not accept a monarch's dependence on a single counselor, claimed Giovanni Botero, because it would threaten royal sovereignty and indicate the king's weakness and his incapacity to rule. He further reminded monarchs that if they relied on the advice of a single favorite, their subjects would sooner or later rebel against the *privado* and in doing so "offend the king himself," as the cases of Edward II of England and Queen Joanna of Naples, among others, demonstrated.[39] Order and political stability, these authors believed, required that the monarch be presented as the unique holder of sovereignty, as a vivid image of God. Just as a master should never let a servant become too familiar, neither should a true monarch let a subject share his authority. "Royal rights," wrote Bodin,

cannot be delegated, and are inalienable ... and if for whatever reason a prince communicates his rights to one of his subjects, this subject would become the king's companion, and the king would no longer be a sovereign ... For as the supreme God cannot make another God equal to himself ... so we may also say that the prince, who is for us God's image, cannot make a subject equal to himself.[40]

Political reality during the reign of Philip II, however, suggested that both the king and certain authors considered the *privado* in more favorable terms, a fact that ultimately permitted new theories of his role in government. The king himself seems to have taken a practical view of the matter. Despite being an active ruler and protective of his rights and prerogatives, he never hesitated to call on his counselors to help him control the central institutions of government because he believed that he could not otherwise impose his will on the members of the body politic, a belief that appears to have guided many of his initiatives on the structure of government and a belief he also tried to instill in his son. In 1597, for example, he advised Prince Philip to rule by himself but at the same time not to hesitate to solicit the help of competent and loyal counselors, specifically mentioning Cristóbal de Moura. With this advice, Philip II was telling his son that to have favorites was not necessarily disadvantageous as long as these men were worthy of the king's favor as Moura had been of his.

Moura, who was depicted by his contemporaries as Philip II's most intimate minister,[41] had Philip's complete confidence and enjoyed unlimited access to the king.[42] The king himself implicitly confirmed Moura's political role in 1591, when he gave him the authority to answer all consultations from *juntas* (committees *ad hoc*) and again in 1596 when Moura took charge of transmitting royal orders to all

---

[39] Botero, *Los diez libros*, bk. 2, chap. 11, fol. 52, and bk. 1, chap. 14, fols. 17–19.

[40] Bodin, *Los seis libros*, bk. 1, chap. 10, vol. 1, pp. 349–50.

[41] Report by one Mr. Rolston to Anthony Bacon in Jan. 1594, in Thomas Birch, ed., *Memoirs of the Reign of Queen Elizabeth*, 2 vols. (New York, 1970), vol. II, p. 201.

[42] See also Escudero, *Los secretarios*, vol. I, p. 192.

officials and councils.[43] Philip II's reliance on Moura and other favorites did not, however, challenge the foundations of a personal monarchy, because he never publicly acknowledged their importance in the institutional structure of the monarchy, nor did the favorites themselves publicly boast of their power and influence. According to many of their contemporaries, their political roles simply reflected the monarchy's increasing complexity and responded to the king's practical needs.

For Philip II and many of his servants and contemporaries, the presence of a royal favorite who assisted the king in governing the monarchy did not indicate the ruler's failings but simply reflected new political realities. The novel challenges confronting the Spanish monarch after 1570 were well recognized at the time. The acquisition of new territories and intensifying conflicts with other European powers created more concerns for the king, required the involvement of a growing number of officials, and necessitated the creation of new institutions. The king alone could not possibly resolve all matters, identify all problems, and control all men. By the late sixteenth century Spanish kings had lost faith in the councils and viewed them with suspicion, believing that they circumscribed royal capacity for independent action. Analyzing this situation, E. H. Kossmann has noted that during the sixteenth century monarchs ruled in close collaboration with their councils and parliaments until "these bodies [became] self-willed institutions, ambitious of independent responsibilities, [and then] the absolute king preferred to ignore them and consult only his inner council of ministers."[44] What the king thus needed, many political writers and Philip II himself argued, were men of confidence who, acting as the king's representatives, would help him control state affairs and free his time for the most important public matters. These men would enforce the king's authority but would pose no threat because, in contrast to other royal officials, they could be selected and dismissed at the king's will.[45] This topic is more fully discussed in Chapter 6, but it is important to mention that late sixteenth- and early seventeenth-century rulers and their adherents, unlike most modern historians, believed that the growing influence of royal favorites reflected an expansion of royal power rather than its diminution.[46]

These views, and Moura's governmental position, were particularly influential

[43] Report of the Papal nuncio Borghese, 27 Apr. 1594, in Ricardo Hinojosa y Navajeros, *Despachos de la diplomacia pontificia en España* (Madrid, 1896), vol. I, p. 382; Anthony Standen, an English Catholic refugee in Spain who became a spy for Queen Elizabeth, informed Elizabeth's advisers in Sept. 1592 that Idiáquez and Moura controlled "all matters of secrecy ... much to the discontent of the whole nobility of Spain," Birch, *Memoirs*, vol. I, p. 80; see Lovett, *Mateo Vázquez de Leça*, p. 202, and AGS CJH, *leg.* 376, *carp.* 22, and *leg.* 377, *carp.* 25, which contain many documents signed by Moura transmitting "royal orders" to the Council of Finance; BL, Add. 28379, "Letters and minutes of Christoval de Mora, 1594–1598"; and Add. 28378, "Correspondence of the Marquis de Poza [President of the Council of Finance] with Don Christoval de Mora and others between the 15th of December, 1595, and the 20th of January, 1613," where the letters of Poza to Moura and vice versa occupy fols. 1–201. See also BPR, II-1688, "Vida de Cristóbal de Moura," fols. 93–7.

[44] E. H. Kossmann, "The Singularity of Absolutism," in R. Hatton, ed., *Louis XV and Absolutism*, (London, 1976), pp. 11–12. [45] *Ibid.*; see also Vicens Vives, "Estructura administrativa," p. 124.

[46] See Feros, "El viejo Felipe."

in promoting a less negative and more practical view of the *privado*. In 1594, for example, Fray Marco Antonio Camos wrote about "the *privado*'s office" (*el oficio de privado*) and claimed that his privileged position rested on "having been selected and approved by the king" to help him govern his kingdoms. His role and function were now comparable to those of the president of the Council of Castile, the most prestigious and influential of all high officials, and Camos and others went so far as to suggest that the king should consult him on all matters and undertake no action that had not been approved by him.[47] The description of Moura's relationship with the king written by Luis Cabrera de Córdoba, one of the most important Spanish historians in the late sixteenth and early seventeenth centuries and author of a biography–chronicle of Philip II and his reign, typifies the new discourse on royal favorites at the end of the reign. Moura was said to be a member of the king's "chamber and privy," a "favorite," and also "a minister of higher authority who assists the prince out of love and fidelity ... so that the king might enjoy respite from the responsibility of dealing with persons and affairs."[48]

Lerma no doubt was well aware of Moura's position and the positive recognition given to royal favorites, and in his attempts to legitimate his relationship with Prince Philip, he asked for advice from Antonio Pérez, Philip II's former secretary and someone familiar with Eboli's activities as the king's confidant. Pérez's response came in 1594 in the form of a letter–essay entitled *"A un gran privado"* (To a grand *privado*) in which he outlined both the possibilities and limitations of a royal favorite in the public life of the monarchy.[49] He employed the career of his former patron, the Prince of Eboli, to illustrate that the divisions between the monarch's private and public spheres were not as distinct as some had maintained, and he contended that those who served the king in his private life were inevitably going to assist him in his public activities. Therefore, an aspiring *privado* had to demonstrate abilities that went far beyond those required of a palace servant or a minion – ability to dance, hunt, entertain, and flatter the king. A true favorite, Pérez noted, must realize that the way in which he obtained the king's favor would determine the durability and character of his *privanza*; thus, he should seek the king's support by presenting himself as a wise counselor whose "great understanding and merit" were worthy of the love, respect, and confidence of the king and the obedience of his peers (vol. II, p. 79). But he should also remember one important key to success: to remain the king's humble servant and be modest in his public appearance. The

---

[47] Camos, *Microcosmia*, pp. 120–1.
[48] Cabrera de Córdoba, *Historia de Felipe II*, vol. II, p. 144; vol. III, p. 217, and vol. IV, pp. 65–6.
[49] "A un gran privado," in Antonio Pérez, *Relaciones y cartas*, ed. Alfredo Alvar Ezquerra, 2 vols. (Madrid, 1986), vol. II, pp. 77–80. Further references in the text. In his letter Pérez says that it was Lerma who asked him to put together his thoughts regarding royal favorites. This information is confirmed by Alamos de Barrientos in *Norte de príncipes*, probably written in 1600 and also dedicated to Lerma (see Baltasar Alamos de Barrientos, *Norte de príncipes* [*c.* 1600], ed. Martín de Riquer (Madrid, 1969)); and by Camillo Baldi in *Politiche considerationi sopra una lettera de Anton Perez al Duca di Lerma del modo di acquistar la gratia del suo signore, e acquistata conservare* (Bologna, 1623).

king had to be perceived by his subjects as supreme and if the favorite were to rise above him or people believed that the king's powers were being usurped, the *privado* would face a tragic end and the monarch would lose his reputation (vol. II, pp. 78–80).[50]

In 1594, when Lerma received Pérez's advice, his own future was far from settled. His success in gaining Prince Philip's attention and, apparently, his affection had become a concern to Philip II's favorites, themselves eager to preserve their own influence and secure their positions in the court hierarchy after Philip II's death. They began to look for ways to remove Lerma from the court. The prince's obvious affection towards Lerma made them cautious, and their initial efforts to send him as viceroy to Peru failed; but they succeeded in persuading the king to appoint him viceroy of the kingdom of Valencia in June 1595.[51] His departure did not pass unnoticed by court observers, and neither did the prince's discontent with the "exile" of his favorite.[52]

Lerma's banishment did not last long, however, and he rejoined the court in 1597 "being well received by the prince."[53] His return coincided with Prince Philip's expanding political role, for many court observers a clear signal of things to come. Lerma became the center of attention, and his influence began to parallel that of the old king's favorites, forcing almost everyone to woo him in a fashion customarily reserved for the king's most powerful servants. "I did not wait a second," wrote the Count of Portalegre from Lisbon to Lerma in 1597, "to send you my congratulations on your return to court." Portalegre, a well-informed courtier, was well aware that Lerma could soon become the most powerful man at court, and he expressed his unwavering loyalty and confidence in Lerma's bright future. No doubt, he wrote, "God will restore all your affairs."[54]

But for the time being Lerma's destiny remained in the hands of the old king and his favorites, a fact that posed a constant threat to his future. Apparently unhappy with this situation, Lerma requested an audience with the king in which, following conventional court etiquette which gave him the right to present his services to the king and to ask for a reward in return, Lerma openly discussed his relationship with Prince Philip and the problems it had created. Since 1580, he allegedly told Philip II:

when with the love of a subject and servant I began to serve your Majesty as a gentleman of your chamber, I visited the prince who seems to honor and favor my desires to serve him. Because some of the prince's servants have opposed this, I should make clear that my intentions are noble and that they will adjust to your Majesty's desires. Therefore, kneeling

[50] See also Antonio Pérez, "A un señor grande, y consejero," in Pérez, *Relaciones*, vol. II, pp. 81–5.
[51] Cabrera de Córdoba, *Historia de Felipe II*, vol. IV, pp. 141–2.
[52] Jerónimo de Sepúlveda, *Historia de varios sucesos y de las cosas notables que han acaecido en España y otras naciones desde el año de 1584 hasta el de 1603*, ed. Julián Zarco Cuevas (Madrid, 1924), p. 202; and Lhermite, *Le Passetemps*, vol. I, p. 254.   [53] *Ibid.*, p. 313.
[54] Portalegre to Lerma, Nov. 1597, in BNM, Mss 981, "Cartas del conde de Portalegre," fols. 17r–v.

in front of your Majesty, I want to give you an account of all my actions, presenting the services of my house and its condition, my obligations to avoid its decline, and that I will not do anything that goes against your Majesty's approval.[55]

According to many courtiers, Lerma succeeded in persuading the king to appoint him Prince Philip's *caballerizo mayor* (master of the horse), but it is unlikely that this appointment was all Lerma's doing or that the king had changed his opinion of him so quickly. Rather, his appointment is more likely to have been the result of Prince Philip's influence on his ailing father's will. By August 1598, Philip II was close to death, and when Lerma was sworn in as *caballerizo mayor* (4 August 1598), a new regime was ready to begin.[56]

---

[55] Novoa, *Historia de Felipe III*, 60, pp. 34–5; Matias de Novoa's source was probably a *Relación de méritos y servicios hechos a los reyes de España por varios Duques de Lerma . . . sacados de un privilegio concedido en el año 1603*, BNM, Mss 11260/6. Cf. Sarah Schroth, "The Private Collection of the Duke of Lerma," Ph.D. diss., New York University, 1990, pp. 10–11.

[56] On Lerma's appointment see AGPR Ex. Per., 548/4.

3

Continuity or reform?

In Spain, the transition from one reign to the next was viewed as a natural process and lacked any of the ceremonial and legalistic overtones that characterized the elevation of a new ruler in other polities. There was no coronation oath, no other ceremonies symbolized the transfer of power to the new king, and nothing in the royal etiquette forbade the new monarch being present at the old king's funeral as was the case with French ceremonial which upheld the notion that the old king was "alive in dignity" until his burial.[1] Nor was there an interregnum during which the new king was a "sleeping king" waiting for the time when the royal *dignitas* and human nature were reunited in one body.[2] Rather, upon the death of Philip II, power simply transferred to his son, a process perfectly summarized by a popular saying: "*A rey muerto, rey puesto*" (A king dies, a king rises). Philip III himself stressed the importance of dynastic continuity in a meeting of the Council of State in which he declared himself the veritable successor of his father and, like him, a militant defender of the "true faith."[3]

The appearance of continuity did not, however, restrain Philip III's subjects from anticipating the innovations that were inevitable with the new reign. Of prime concern at the outset was whether Philip III would follow the policies of the old king and how he would confront the declining fortunes of the Spanish monarchy. Contemporaries were also particularly keen to discover whose fortunes would rise and fall, a topic already of considerable attention during the last few months of Philip II's reign. For example, in 1597 the Duke of Feria wrote that as soon as the old king dies "we are on another stage and all characters in this comedy will be altogether new." He returned to this theme more than a year later: "[w]hen the old king leaves this world, another era begins, and we do not know how it will be."[4] Everyone, indeed, knew that while the principles that defined the nature of the

[1] Ralph Giesey, "The President of Parlement at the Royal Funeral," *The Sixteenth Century Journal*, 6 (1976), pp. 25–6.
[2] Richard A. Jackson, "The Sleeping King," *Bibliothèque d'Humanisme et Renaissance*, 31 (1969), pp. 540–51.   [3] González Dávila, *Historia de la vida*, pp. 44–5.
[4] Archive of the Archbishopric of Westminster, Mss E. 2., the Duke of Feria to Thomas Fitzherbert, 28 Feb. 1597 (fol. 15), and 1 June 1598 (fol. 38). I thank Professor Sir John Elliott for letting me use his notes on the Duke of Feria's letters. On the Duke of Feria, Gómez Suárez de Figueroa, see Lagomarsino, "Court Factions," pp. 234–6.

Spanish monarchy remained unaltered, some changes were inevitable.[5] The royal chronicler González Dávila summarized his contemporaries' opinions when he wrote "when a prince dies everything changes. Some will rise and get rich, while others will find their fortunes decline. Some will happily celebrate their good fate, while others will weep for they have lost all. Some will be adored because they are now in charge, while others will be scorned for having lost their power."[6]

It is, therefore, unsurprising that soon after Philip II's death the Duke of Lerma became the center of attention. His appointment as Prince Philip's *caballerizo mayor* shortly before the old king died had already consolidated his position in Prince Philip's household, but a sign of his future role and the new king's high regard for him came on the day of the old king's funeral. On Monday 14 September 1598, the day following Philip II's death, his coffin was removed from the sanctity of El Escorial, and the funeral procession headed towards the church where the new king, his servants, and officials were attending a commemorative mass. After mass, the coffin was transferred to the door leading to the royal sepulcher in the grounds of El Escorial, where Philip III ordered Lerma to deliver his father's body to the priest, Fray García de Santa María, who was in charge of placing the coffin in its final resting place.[7] This was not the only symbolic gesture Philip III made towards Lerma immediately after Philip II's death. On the same day the Venetian ambassador, Francesco Soranzo, further reported that "[Philip II] had hardly expired when the new King confessed and communicated and then withdrew into a secret chamber with the Marquis of Denia [Lerma]. After a while the King came out and the Marquis was declared a member of the Council of State."[8] Lerma's appointment to the most prestigious of all councils, his confirmation as *caballerizo mayor*, and his role in the burial of the old king forcefully announced to all who followed court life in the first moments of Philip III's reign that Lerma was destined to become an active player in the public life of the monarchy.

While Lerma's position became clear, widespread concern over the nature of the regime persisted. The youthfulness of the new king and his perceived political inexperience worried those who took a pessimistic view of the future. "The king died yesterday," wrote Luisa de Carvajal y Mendoza, "and it appears that the new king will make many changes. We hope God will guide him for the good of the church so that he can prevent the ruin of the kingdom; times are dangerous and he

---

[5] Baltasar Alamos Barrientos, *Aforismos al Tácito español* [1614], ed. José A. Fernández-Santamaría, 2 vols. (Madrid, 1987), vol. I, p. 55.   [6] González Dávila, *Historia de la vida*, p. 45.

[7] Cervera de la Torre, "Relación de la enfermedad y muerte del Rey don Felipe II," in Cabrera de Córdoba, *Historia de Felipe II*, vol. IV, pp. 325–6.

[8] *CSPVen*, vol. IX, p. 344. BL Add. 28422, Lerma to his uncle Juan de Borja, 14 Sept. 1598, fol. 6v; see also the report of the papal envoy, Camillo Caetani, 30 Sept. 1598, reporting that Lerma had been sworn in as counselor of state on 18 Sept. 1598; cf. R. Vargas Hidalgo, "Documentos inéditos sobre la muerte de Felipe II y la literatura fúnebre de los siglos XVI y XVII," *BRAH*, 192 (1995), p. 435.

is so young!"[9] Many contemporaries shared the opinion that times were desperate, and writers who advised the new king and his favorite expressed general skepticism about the monarchy's future.

Although the situation of the Spanish monarchy was less critical than that of its European counterparts, the latent discontent of political elites in various peninsular kingdoms that had surfaced towards the end of Philip II's reign concerning what they perceived as his "defective government" threatened to spill over to the new regime. Already several years prior to Philip II's death disapproval concerning his break from traditional forms of government was being voiced by his critics. In the late 1570s one of the royal almoners, Fray Luis Manrique, for example, sent the king a critical memorandum[10] in which he asserted that the king had forgotten that monarchs were God's vicars on earth whose duty was to administer justice and function as "public and prominent prophets" for their subjects (fol. 99v), and to fulfill the obligation to listen to their subjects' supplications and advice and to follow the recommendations of their counselors (fol. 105v). But Philip II no longer behaved in this fashion – he was not seen by the people nor did he consult with his ministers or attend the meetings of the Council of State, one of his most important obligations. Instead he relied only on the advice of one or two favorites and tried to control and execute all state affairs by himself. "Little by little," Manrique claimed, "he had become totally inaccessible, locked in a tower without doors and windows, not seeing anyone or allowing anyone to see him" (fol. 99v).

The tone and content of Manrique's criticism were repeated a few months later by Fray Pedro de Ribadeneira in a letter sent on 16 February 1580 to Cardinal Gaspar de Quiroga, Archbishop of Toledo and Inquisitor-General, concerning Philip II's attempt to annex the kingdom of Portugal following the death of King Sebastian in 1579. For the king's propagandists the annexation was the culmination of a long battle to reunite all peninsular kingdoms, but others, including Ribadeneira, saw it simply as another quest by the king to extend his territories. Philip, Ribadeneira observed, was promoting an unnecessary war "of Christians against Christians, Catholics against Catholics, Spaniards against Spaniards" and exhibited no concern for the common good of his subjects and kingdoms. He went on to note that all estates held a grievance against him: the people because of high taxes; the church and various religious orders because of attempts to usurp their jurisdiction and meddle in their affairs and finances; the counselors because the king never consulted or listened to them; and the grandees because they no longer played a role in the government of the monarchy. The feelings of his subjects had undergone a radical change. At the beginning of the reign, Ribadeneira wrote,

---

[9] Luisa de Carvajal to Isabel de Velasco, 15 Sept. 1598, in Luisa de Carvajal y Mendoza, *Epistolario y poesías*, ed. Camilo María Abad (Madrid, 1965), p. 98.

[10] BNM, Mss 18718/55, Luis Manrique: "Papel a Philipo II", fols. 97r–108r. Further references in the text. I have analyzed Manrique's views in more detail in Feros, "El viejo Felipe."

everyone "loved and had deep affection toward the king, his glory and honor . . . [but] now all are embittered, disgusted and incensed, and even though he is a powerful king who is obeyed and respected, he is not as well regarded and loved as before, and he is no longer master of the wills and hearts of his subjects."[11]

Such critical views became pervasive in the late 1580s and early 1590s. Between 1589 and 1591, for example, Philip II's financial demands and the use of Castilian taxes to subsidize military campaigns in the Low Countries and France led to protests and public demonstrations in several Castilian cities and consequently to the detention of local leaders and the execution of an alderman from Avila. These protests coincided with activities carried out by popular "prophets and visionaries," who augured a dramatic end for a "sinister king," identified as Philip II, and for his kingdoms.[12] In 1591, political tensions also surfaced in Aragon, a kingdom belonging to the crown of Aragon, that developed into riots known as the *alteraciones* (disturbances) of Aragon, a movement against what many Aragonese viewed as Philip II's attempts to abolish the kingdom's *fueros* (constitutions) that he had promised to uphold and defend.[13] In this political environment, several authors (see Chapter 1) published works advocating a return to traditional forms of government, accusing the monarch of trying to impose his absolute power and warning that, if he refused to change, he gave his subjects only one alternative – rebellion.[14]

Criticism of Philip II and his policies intensified at the beginning of Philip III's reign. Several books and pamphlets written in the first few months of the new regime give the impression that most Spaniards agreed that the monarchy was in the middle of a deep-seated and dangerous constitutional crisis affecting the king's relations with his various kingdoms and members of the political elite. Alamos de Barrientos, Antonio Pérez's ally and close comrade, for example, warned the king that Portugal and the kingdoms of the crown of Aragon (Aragon, Valencia, and Catalonia) were heading toward rebellion and disobedience as they grew weary of Castilian domination of their lands. The kingdoms of Aragon had "their laws, customs and government . . . [that] distinguish them from us [Castilians]," and the rebellion of the early 1590s and its subsequent repression had greatly disturbed the

---

[11] Fray Pedro de Ribadeneira to Fray Gaspar de Quiroga, 16 Feb. 1580, in Ribadeneira, *Patris Petri de Ribadeneira confessiones, epistolae aliaque scripta inedita* [*Monumenta Historica Societatis Iesu*, 60] (Madrid, 1923), pp. 24–5.

[12] On the tensions and conflicts in the Castilian cities against Philip II's excessive financial pressure, which culminated in the execution of a noble from Avila, see Cabrera de Córdoba, *Historia de Felipe II*, vol. III, p. 504; José Ignacio Fortea Pérez, *Monarquía y cortes en la corona de Castilla. Las ciudades ante la política fiscal de Felipe II* (Salamanca, 1990), pp. 298–342; on prophets and visionaries during the reign of Philip II see Richard L. Kagan, *Lucrecia's Dreams. Politics and Prophecy in Sixteenth-Century Spain* (Berkeley, 1990).

[13] The best study of this revolt and the politics surrounding it is Xavier Gil Pujol, "De las alteraciones a la estabilidad," Ph.D. diss., University of Barcelona, 1990, chap. 2, "Rebelión y poder real." For a good summary in English see Elliott, *Imperial Spain*, pp. 277–84.

[14] On the people's rights to resist a tyrant see Skinner, *The Foundations*, vol. II, pp. 345–8. See also Ribadeneira, *Obras*, pp. 532–5.

Aragonese and made them increasingly suspicious of Castile and the Spanish kings, who they believed wanted to destroy their kingdoms' liberties.[15]

Even the kingdom of Castile, "the head of the monarchy," Barrientos warned, had become impoverished and full of discontent. Echoing earlier criticism, he declared that the grandees and members of the Castilian nobility had accumulated many debts and continuously complained about their exclusion from the government of the monarchy. Those who occupied key offices believed that they had been mistreated by the old king and that their authority and that of the councils had been annulled by the "universally hated" *Junta de Gobierno*,[16] while the general populace was near collapse from high taxes that had been wasted on "foreign wars."[17] Furthermore, the Iberian peninsula was full of Moriscos, the descendants of the Arab population who had occupied the peninsula for several centuries, who were "as loyal [to foreign kings] today" as they had been when they were able to practice their "perverted faith" in public, even as they appeared to accept the Christian faith and the authority of Spanish kings. One of the many contemporaneous pamphleteers concluded that the "Spanish nation" felt "exhausted, dissatisfied, and disregarded"; that justice was "abolished and ruined"; the royal treasury consumed; the glorious reputation of former years vanished; and the entire kingdom "universally afflicted and discontented."[18]

Some writers and royal officials blamed all problems on Philip II's "defective government" and expressed the hope that the new king would reinstate traditional forms of monarchical administration. Francesco Soranzo, the Venetian ambassador, commented on these views in a report he sent to the Venetian senate on 27 September 1598 in which he summarized his conversation with Luis de Padilla, one of Philip III's ministers in the Council of War, who believed that Philip II's death would change the ways in which state affairs were conducted. With Philip II, Padilla had said, all public affairs were "subject to a single brain [the king himself] who thought he knew all that could be known and treated everyone else as a blockhead." But now that he was gone, Padilla expected the new king actively to seek the advice of his subjects and restore the royal councils to their prominent role thus enabling the king's ministers to participate once again in the arduous task of reversing the decline of the Spanish monarchy.[19]

---

[15] Baltasar Alamos de Barrientos, *Discurso político al rey Felipe III al comienzo de su reinado* [1598], ed. Modesto Santos (Madrid, 1990), pp. 21–2. The author was one of the most conspicuous defenders of the theories of reason of state in Spain.

[16] *Ibid.*, p. 89. On poor appointments of royal officials see BNM, Mss 18275, "Memorial que dieron al duque de Lerma cuando entró en el valimiento del sr. Rey Felipe III," fols. 1v, 2r, 4r (there is another copy of this memorandum, BNM, Mss 13239, Cristóbal de Castro: "Consejos sobre el remedio de males que aquejan a la monarquía," n.d.).

[17] Alamos de Barrientos, *Discurso político*, pp. 21–3, 26–8.

[18] BNM, Mss 2346, "Consideraciones para que Felipe III comenzase a reinar con felicidad" [anon. 1598], fol. 23r. For additional comments on the adverse situation of the monarchy and available alternatives for the restoration of its past glory see below, pt. III, especially chap. 8.

[19] *CSPVen*, vol. IX, p. 346, Francesco Soranzo to the Venetian Senate, 27 Sept. 1598.

Padilla was not the only one who hoped that Philip III would reverse the changes his father had introduced, and from the outset of the reign Philip received many memoranda expressing such wishes. The author of one, entitled "Consideraciones para que Felipe III comenzase a reinar con felicidad," noted that to solve the present crisis, the king must restore a government based on royal councils, eliminate all *juntas*, especially the omnipotent *Junta de Noche*, and realize that to rule with the help of powerful favorites was, as Philip II's experience had shown, counterproductive. Given the grave problems confronting the monarchy, the king should not "rule alone or with the help of one or two individuals"; rather he should rely on advice from dozens, hundreds of counselors who could serve as "the eyes, hands, and feet of their prince" and help him reverse the declining fortunes of the monarchy.[20] Lerma's constant presence at Philip III's side did not deter these pamphleteers, and some even argued that it was possible to conserve the councils' influence in the presence of a royal favorite as long as the king did not permit him to interfere with the councils' authority in the administration of affairs of state. The king, suggested one author, should devise a role for Lerma similar to that played by the Prince of Eboli, who throughout his *privanza* "did not become the king's minister or manage public affairs; neither did he impede the king's ministers in their official duties, nor did he try to take from the councils their right to administer governmental affairs."[21]

Philip III and Lerma seem to have believed that criticism targeted at Philip II allowed them to present Philip III as a ruler with a distinct style of government. In response to his subjects' advice, Philip III initiated what appeared to be a comprehensive program of political reforms soon after taking office. He nominally abolished the "hated *Junta de Gobierno*"[22] and ordered other *juntas* to be dismantled – actions that gave the impression that decision-making was gaining speed and that the councils had recovered their role as guarantors of a just government. This image was further strengthened by Philip III's decision to restore the "glory" of the Council of State by naming almost a dozen new counselors, most of whom had considerable political and administrative experience.[23]

Besides the "reconstitution of proper government" he also dealt with other

---

[20] BNM, Mss 2346: "Consideraciones para que Felipe III comenzase a reinar con felicidad," fols. 23r, 28v–29, 24v.

[21] BNM, Mss 17887, "Advertimientos que se dió a Su Majd.," fol. 39r. Lerma's supporters criticized Philip II and the favorites who succeeded the Prince of Eboli because they did not act in this way.

[22] González Dávila, *Historia de la vida*, p. 45.

[23] RAH, Mss 9/3507, Iñigo Ibáñez de Santa Cruz, "Las causas de que resultó el ignorante y confuso gobierno que hubo en el tiempo del rey nuestro señor, que sea en gloria, y el prudente y acertado modelo de gobernar que ha tomado y procura su majd. con el favor de Dios" ("The causes of the ignorant government of Philip II, and the prudent and faithful government of Philip III", hereafter Ibáñez de Santa Cruz, "Las Causas"). On Ibáñez's views on the *Junta de Noche* and other innovations introduced by Philip II's favorites see fos. 769r–783r. On the reinforcement of the Council of State and, in general, on the measures taken by Philip III at the beginning of his reign see Patrick Williams, "Philip III and the Restoration of Spanish Government, 1598–1603," *English Historical Review*, 88 (1973), pp. 751–69.

complaints of his subjects and declared himself to be a just, merciful, and liberal king, who was concerned, unlike his father, not with extending royal power but with regaining the love, obedience, and respect of his subjects. Such actions, at least in part, responded to prevailing political concerns among Spanish authors. In contrast to Machiavelli's opinion that a monarchy could gain and maintain loyalty only through fear and imposition of royal authority,[24] many sixteenth- and seventeenth-century Spanish writers believed that it was not terror but virtue that gave the monarch his strength. The king's ultimate objective was to acquire the love and respect of his subjects rather than their servile submission. To convey the essence of an ideal relationship between a king and his vassals, Spanish authors employed the image of an extended family. The prince was portrayed as the benevolent father, who guided his children (his subjects) through treacherous waters. The paterfamilias punished them for their faults without hesitation, rewarded them for their good deeds, and supported their views and opinions (counsel) when these served the family's best interests. In the realm, as in the family, the father's authority reigned supreme and rested on a hierarchy that governed relations among family members, a structure essential for an orderly and prosperous future for the household. But to legitimize his authority, the father had to gain the love and respect of his entire family. For these Spanish authors, as for Cicero, there was nothing better "than to be loved, and nothing less suitable than to be feared."[25] This principle can be found in the advice Philip III received shortly after his ascent to the throne: "A king gains the love of his subjects; a tyrant arouses their fear."[26]

The king's actions were also influenced by another key axiom that was central to the counsel given to him concerning proper behavior towards his subjects: a monarch must not regard the love of his subjects as a given fact; rather he must actively seek their devotion. To succeed, the king needed many virtues, most important of all being justice. Without it, Pedro de Ribadeneira wrote in *El príncipe christiano*, "there is no kingdom, province, town, village, household, nor family."[27] But justice was a two-edged sword. It embodied both punishment and reward, and the exercise of one rather than the other would have a disparate impact on the affections of the king's subjects. Punishment, even for those who deserved it, could provoke hatred, as the act of punishment revealed the gruesome face of the king's authority. Here Spanish authors agreed with Thomas Aquinas, who explicitly asserted that if the prince desired popular affection "punishments should be inflicted by other princes and by bodies of judges."[28] The king not only had to

---

[24] Machiavelli, *The Prince*, chaps. 15–17; for Machiavelli's ideas I relied on Pocock, *The Machiavellian Moment*, chaps. 6–7; Quentin Skinner, *Machiavelli* (New York, 1981); and Felix Gilbert, *Machiavelli and Guicciardini* (Princeton, 1965).

[25] Cicero, *Libro de Marco Tulio Cicerón*, bk. 2, chap. 3, fol. 96v.

[26] Alamos de Barrientos, *Discurso político*, p. 102.   [27] Ribadeneira, *Obras*, p. 526.

[28] Cf. Gilbert, *Machiavelli and Guicciardini*, p. 154. See also Baltasar Alamos de Barrientos, *Suma de preceptos justos, necesarios y provechosos en consejo de Estado al rey Felipe III siendo príncipe* [*c.* 1599], ed. Modesto Santos (Madrid, 1991), p. 33.

delegate punishment to others but to present himself as a godlike individual who, while understanding the need to punish offenders, also understood the circumstances that caused them to break the law. A king, like God, had to remember that repentance and reintegration of the criminal (sinner) into the community was the ultimate goal of justice.[29] To prove himself a merciful king, Philip III elected to pardon all who had been punished by his father for their participation in the Aragonese disturbances of 1591–2, a measure that according to the royal chronicler González Dávila led to "millions of acclamations" by the Aragonese, who now considered him a "blessed and pious ruler."[30]

In a further effort to differentiate himself from his father, Philip III presented himself as a liberal king. In the early modern political culture, royal liberality (the king's capacity to reward his subjects) was even more important than mercy and was considered the quintessence of kingship, because it enabled the king to address his subjects' needs and confirmed him as a noble shepherd of his flock. It also served, as Giovanni Botero put it, "to encourage and promote" virtue among the king's subjects.[31] According to early modern writers, royal *mercedes* conferred vitality, strength, and virtue on members of the body politic; acted as magnets by drawing many to the service of the monarchy; and transformed royal servants into perfect citizens of the republic.

The centrality of the discourse on royal liberality during the sixteenth and seventeenth centuries was, no doubt, one of the by-products of the transformation of Spanish kings into great patrons of their subjects,[32] as were the conflicts between them and political elites over the distribution of royal *mercedes*. Indeed, towards the end of Philip II's reign, as in Elizabethan England, the distribution of royal patronage "had the appearance of an inflationary movement: too many suitors pursuing too few privileges."[33] Philip II himself was keenly aware that while acting as a patron brought him benefits, it also posed dangers as the demands for favor escalated. "With many asking and little to give, most people will remain discontented," he wrote to his secretary Mateo Vázquez, "and for this and other reasons I say that the position I hold is a foul one."[34] He attempted to impose limits on the flow of *mercedes* to contain damage to his image and fiscal resources, an action supported by some of his contemporaries, who cautioned against excessive munificence that could transform royal liberality from a noble activity into a destroyer of the king's reputation.[35]

---

[29] See the Spanish version of "On Mercy" (*clemencia*), in Seneca, *Los dos libros de la clemencia*, trans. Alonso de Revenga (Madrid, 1626). Seneca's essay and views on mercy are quoted by Alamos de Barrientos, *Suma*, p. 35.

[30] González Dávila, *Historia de la vida*, p. 76; on the royal visit to Zaragoza see Gil Pujol, "De las alteraciones," pp. 428–36. [31] Botero, *Los diez libros*, bk. 1, chap. 19, fols. 28v–32.

[32] See above, chap. 2. [33] J. E. Neale, *Essays in Elizabethan History* (London, 1958), p. 78.

[34] Philip II to Mateo Vázquez, 3 Mar. 1575; cf. Parker, *Philip II*, p. 126.

[35] See, for example, Machiavelli, *The Prince*, chap. 16; and Lipsius, *Los seis libros*, bk. 2, chap. 17, p. 67; bk. 4, chap. 8, pp. 126–7.

Given the dangers posed by excessive liberality, a discourse on the need for its regulation developed along with writings defending its importance. Most authors who advocated regulatory measures seldom went as far as Lipsius, however, who wrote "let the prince rather give nothing than take from others."[36] Instead most authors outlined measures designed to curb excessive royal beneficence rather than to cancel (or even radically reduce) it because they feared that such changes could severely damage the king's power and position. They told him never to grant offices, rents, or other *mercedes* to those who were idle; liberality "should be the reward of virtue, not the result of a whim."[37] And the prince was not to bankrupt the royal treasury; such an act would not be considered liberality but prodigality and would force the king "to take [from] where he should not, turn to theft, and become a tyrant rather than a king."[38]

Philip II tried to follow such advice. His approach, expressed by the king himself, was simple: to conserve the preeminence of royal power, everyone in the realm "must depend on me, and from me alone receive favor for services they have rendered me."[39] To avoid excessive pressure, he introduced administrative reforms designed to spread responsibility for deciding who should be granted a reward. In January 1588, he reformed the Chamber of Castile, the council in charge of advising him on all matters concerning liberality (including appointments) and justice,[40] and in 1591 he created the office of "Contador de la razón general de mercedes" (general accountant of royal rewards) to record all rewards granted by him, to prevent individuals from seeking and receiving more than one payment for the same service.[41] In the end, however, these measures had a relatively small impact on the number of royal *mercedes* distributed. The king's ministers repeatedly circumvented his orders and brazenly exploited all available opportunities to grant offices and other *mercedes* without first consulting him. They were able to do so by establishing informal agreements among themselves based on reciprocal granting of favors.[42] Faced with this situation and an approaching fiscal crisis, Philip II finally had to opt for more radical measures, and he reduced the number of *mercedes* his ministers were allowed to distribute. In 1595 the well-informed

---

[36] *Ibid.*   [37] Erasmus, *The Education*, p. 263.   [38] Botero, *Los diez libros*, bk. 1, fol. 31v.
[39] Cf. Koenigsberger, "The Statecraft," p. 5.
[40] Lovett, *Mateo Vázquez de Leça*, p. 144. On the reforms and new rules for the Chamber of Castile, introduced on 6 Jan. 1588, see *Nueva recopilación*, bk. 4, tit. 4: "De la Cámara de Castilla"; see also "Advertimientos acerca de la distribución de los memoriales, cartas y otros papeles que se dan a Su Majd., y por su mandado se remiten a los tribunales," rules decreed by Philip II in the 1570s, in Alfred Morel-Fatio, *L'Espagne au XVIe. et au XVIIe. siècle* (Paris, 1878), pp. 204–17.
[41] See AGS Est., *leg.* 2637, n.p., *consulta* of the Council of State, 28 June 1601.
[42] Concerning the Council of Italy and its control over royal patronage see Koenigsberger, *The Practice of Empire*, chap. 3; on censures against the illegal behavior of the councils, see BNM, Mss 8526, "Discurso sobre el gobierno que ha de tener Su Majd. en su Monarquía para conservarla," anon., Madrid, 15 Oct. 1599, fols. 26v–27r.

Venetian ambassador Francesco de Vendramino wrote: "The king gives little and awards only a few *mercedes*,"[43] conduct that had created much discontent. The letters of the Duke of Feria expressed the feelings of many of his contemporaries. In May 1598, he complained that because "I have seen all my services unrewarded my household is in a total ruin." Five months later, shortly after the king's death, he added: "the king has left this world without rewarding my services and honoring me, something that has hurt me a great deal."[44]

Philip III was faced with the legacy of his father's policies, and at the start of his reign he decided to address the threat posed by the increasing number of malcontents. His behavior was not unusual. Across Europe, kings were instructed to be merciful and liberal, almost prodigal, at the outset of their reigns,[45] and Philip III received similar advice: to begin his reign by awarding *mercedes*, especially to those who felt neglected by the former king.[46] He appears to have taken this advice to heart, and in a decree dated 24 November 1598 he ordered the Chamber of Castile to reconsider all petitions which had gone unanswered during the previous reign "because of [Philip II's] continuous ailments and other impediments."[47] The order resulted in the arrival of hundreds of new memoranda requesting *mercedes*. Apparently, his subjects believed that whatever their services to the monarchy, they had a right to a reward simply because "that is what he [the king] has done with others"[48] or because "the king has given away many and great *mercedes*."[49] In the long run Philip III's decision created more problems than it solved – including attacks against Lerma and his allies for having used royal patronage to their own benefit[50] – but in the short term it and other measures enabled him to present himself as a king less rigid than his father and always ready to attend to his subjects' needs.

Had he limited his actions to those designed to appease his vassals, it is quite likely that little opposition to his regime would have materialized at least at the beginning. But this was not the case. From the Duke of Lerma's point of view it was essential to do something about the old favorites of the former king who

[43] For Vendramino's report, sent in 1595, see Alberi, *Relazioni*, p. 446; see also Cabrera de Córdoba, *Historia de Felipe II*, vol. II, pp. 427–31; and Philip II to Mateo Vázquez: "tell me the names of those to whom we are more obliged now, because there is not enough for everyone," in Riba García, *Correspondencia privada*, 2 Dec. 1586, p. 436.
[44] Archive of the Archbishopric of Westminster, Mss E. 2, Duke of Feria to Thomas Fitzherbert, 24 May 1598, and 2 Oct. 1598, fols. 73, 93. For other cases see, Cabrera de Córdoba, *Historia de Felipe II*, vols. III, p. 474, and IV, p. 215; and *CSPVen*, vol. VIII, pp. 443–4, report of Tommaso Contarini, Madrid, 3 June 1589.
[45] Philip II, a king not famous for his liberality, did just this when he became the king of England after his marriage to Mary Tudor; see Penry Williams, *The Tudor Regime* (Oxford, 1979), p. 373.
[46] BNM, Mss 2346, "Consideraciones para que Felipe III comenzase a reinar con felicidad," fol. 23v; and Alamos de Barrientos, *Discurso político*, p. 5.   [47] AHN CS, *leg.* 4415, *exp.* 138.
[48] AGS CJH, *leg.* 376, *carp.* 22, Cristóbal de Moura to Philip III, 24 Nov. 1598.
[49] AGS Est., *leg.* 2636, *exp.* 1, consulta of the Council of State on a memorandum by Alonso de Bazán, 12 Aug. 1601.   [50] On this topic see below, chap. 9.

remained at court and posed a potential threat to his quest for power. But to challenge their continued presence involved discrediting not only their political abilities but also those of the late king.

In Spain as elsewhere, political reform – or its pretense – was seen as "the road to power and influence," something Lerma well understood.[51] He was well aware that the attainment of the king's favor was not sufficient; to monopolize power, he also needed to rid the court of those who could contest his position. The principal threat came from Philip II's favorites who had long controlled power and had placed many friends and followers in important positions of political responsibility.[52] They and "their accomplices" were – Ramírez de Prado informed Lerma – "damned slanderers" who would try to stir up these kingdoms and destroy and vanquish "you and all those who will follow you until their deaths."[53] Thus, the elimination, or at least the neutralization, of the former favorites' political influence became an early priority for Lerma and his devotees. In order to legitimate their actions, they adopted a strategy of identifying the problems of the Spanish monarchy not as structural but as the result of the political incapacity of former rulers. The enthronement of a new king and the rise of a new favorite and ministers were necessary first steps, they claimed, to the restoration of the former glory of the monarchy.

As if in anticipation of the coming campaign the Venetian ambassador Soranzo wrote in August 1598 about the growing displeasure those surrounding Prince Philip had expressed about Moura, Idiáquez, and others: "There are [those] who say that the prince will, perhaps, not carry out all these dispositions made by his Majesty's intimates in their own favor, for they are too greedily seeking their own advantage."[54] Such negative comments about Philip II's intimates increased substantially during the first few months of the new regime. Moura and others were not only portrayed as greedy but were accused of trying to dominate, control, and command Prince Philip and seize royal power into their own hands. Iñigo Ibáñez de Santa Cruz, Lerma's personal secretary, maintained for example that Philip II's favorites "to secure their tyrannical throne, reinforced the power of the *Junta de Gobierno* and proceeded to defame the young prince as someone who was incapable of and deficient in governing this monarchy." Their evil reached such extremes that "they did not stop until they had damaged his reputation with his father, Philip II, and the entire world." Such behavior, Santa Cruz argued, had to be treated as a "crime of *laesa majestatis*" because to raise doubts about the quality of a future king destroyed the harmony between the prince and his subjects and promoted disobedience and rebellion.[55]

---

[51] Kevin Sharpe, *Sir Robert Cotton, 1586–1631. History and Politics in Early Modern England* (Oxford, 1979), p. 119.   [52] BNM, Mss 18275, "Memorial que dieron al duque de Lerma," fol. 2r.

[53] AGS CC VI, *leg.* 2793, bk. 6, fols. 216r, 218r, Ramírez de Prado to Lerma, 13 June and 28 Aug. 1599.

[54] *CSPVen*, vol. x, p. 339.

[55] RAH, CLSC, Mss 9/3507, Ibáñez de Santa Cruz, "Las Causas," pp. 763–4; see also BNM, Mss 18275, "Memorial que dieron al duque de Lerma cuando entró en el valimiento del sr. rey Felipe III,"

The first to be censured were those seen as responsible for spreading rumors about Philip III's lack of character, namely García de Loaysa, Prince Philip's tutor, and Pedro de Portocarrero, Bishop of Cuenca and Inquisitor-General. Lerma and his allies knew that Portocarrero was spreading rumors against the new rulers, and in 1599 the papal envoy Bastoni reported that he had lost his office in the Council of Inquisition because of his critical attitude towards Philip III.[56] Loaysa, in turn, whom Philip II had appointed Archbishop of Toledo in 1598, was ordered to leave the court and serve out his ecclesiastical office in Toledo. His death on 23 February 1599 prior to reaching his destination was attributed by many to the pain of his fall into disgrace and caused little remorse among Lerma's supporters: "This morning the Archbishop of Toledo died bringing peace to everyone; he was an evil creature," wrote Ramírez de Prado to Lerma.[57]

In addition to Portocarrero and Loaysa, Lerma was particularly concerned about the influence enjoyed by Rodrigo Vázquez de Arce, President of the Council of Castile, a person with enormous authority in the kingdom.[58] Lerma and his supporters saw him as their most dangerous enemy and feared that he had the will to resist their attempts to displace him. Ramírez de Prado wrote that "he is a real devil" and that getting rid of him would be more difficult than getting rid of religious authorities who had a deeper understanding of their duty to obey.[59] The definitive attempt to remove Vázquez came in April 1599 when Philip III and Lerma were in Valencia on the occasion of the king's wedding to Margaret of Austria: Vázquez had remained in Madrid, attending to the day-to-day government of the monarchy. To replace him as President of the Council of Castile, the king appointed Juan de Zúñiga, Count of Miranda and Lerma's ally.[60] In anticipation of Vázquez's opposition, Philip III ordered Miranda to take possession of his office "without delay and to make sure that Vázquez obeys my order to leave the presidency,"[61] a command Lerma also transmitted to his uncle Juan de Borja, a counselor of state who had also remained in Madrid serving, among other duties, as Lerma's intermediary and agent.[62] Vázquez's influence among the Castilian elite was such that even the members of the Cortes of Castile, meeting to discuss important fiscal matters, officially challenged

---

fol. 1r. In a book published in 1643 but begun during the reign of Philip III Juan de Vitrián expressed a similar opinion, claiming that the doubts about Prince Philip's ability expressed by Loaysa and the prince's other servants were only the product of their political ambitions and that Philip II never believed them. Juan de Vitrián, *Las memorias de Felipe de Comines con escolios propios*, 2 vols. (Antwerp, 1643), vol. II, pp. 146–7. I thank Julio A. Pardos Martínez for bringing Vitrián's book to my attention.   [56] Cf. Hinojosa y Navajeros, *Despachos*, p. 403.

[57] AGS CC VI, *leg.* 2793, bk. 6, fol. 901v, Ramírez de Prado to Lerma, 23 Feb. 1599. According to Vitrián, Loaysa died of "fever of ambition (*fiebre de ambición*)," Vitrián, *Las memorias*, vol. II, p. 146.

[58] Hinojosa y Navajeros, *Despachos*, p. 402.

[59] AGS CC VI, *leg.* 2793, bk. 6, fol. 216v, Ramírez de Prado to Lerma, 13 June 1599.

[60] AGS Est., *leg.* 184, fol. 167, royal order dated 10 Apr. 1599.   [61] *Ibid.*, fols. 170, 167.

[62] BL, Add. 28422, Lerma to Juan de Borja, 11 May 1599, fols. 63v–64.

the royal order,[63] but in the end these efforts failed and in early May 1599 Miranda took over.[64]

Actions against other former ministers were more subtle than those employed against Loaysa, Portocarrero and Vázquez. Cristóbal de Moura, Philip II's most powerful favorite, was removed from the court but given financial rewards for his past service. In 1599, he received the title of Marquis of Castelrodrigo and the grand commandery of the military order of Calatrava – a very prestigious one that carried with it a high revenue.[65] But he lost his office as Philip's *sumiller de corps*, replaced by Lerma,[66] and the king refused to appoint him President of the Council of Portugal despite his desire for this office, evident in his promise that if he were appointed, he would declare himself a creature of the Duke of Lerma.[67] In January 1600 Philip III ordered him to leave court for his Castilian estate, and in April he was appointed Viceroy of Portugal.[68]

Other members of the *Junta de Gobierno* suffered lesser retribution. Diego Fernández de Córdoba, Count of Chinchón, for example, did not lose his place in the Council of State, although he became increasingly distant from the decision-making process. The Marquis of Velada, in turn, managed to retain his palace office as the king's *mayordomo mayor* until his death in 1615. His good fortune has been a matter of speculation since Philip III's reign. According to Bastoni, the papal nuncio at Madrid, Velada was able to preserve his office because of his opposition to Moura during the last years of Philip II's reign. The most popular explanation, however, depicts Velada as a typical courtier who would do anything, including humiliating himself and worshiping the new favorite, to conserve a place at the royal court.[69]

The fate of Juan de Idiáquez resembles Velada's. Although he lost his palace office as Queen Margaret's *mayordomo mayor* (an office he obtained in the last

---

[63] See Juan Gelabert, *La bolsa del rey. Rey, reino y fisco en Castilla* (Barcelona, 1997), p. 31.

[64] BL, Add. 28422, Lerma to Borja, 31 May 1599, fol. 68: "I received your letter and I am very pleased to know that the Count of Miranda has taken possession of his office as president of the council of Castile." On Lerma's and his supporters' relief when Vázquez died in August 1599, see AGS CC VI, leg. 2793, bk. 6, fol. 218r, Ramírez de Prado to Lerma, 28 Aug. 1599.

[65] AGS GJ, *leg.* 890, royal order of 30 Jan. 1599.

[66] Lerma was sworn in as the groom of the stole on 17 Dec. 1599, AGPR Ex. Per., 548/4. Luis Cabrera de Córdoba, *Relaciones de las cosas sucedidas en la corte de España, desde 1599 hasta 1614 [c. 1614]* (Madrid, 1857), p. 1; Count of Portalegre to Esteban de Ibarra, Dec. 1598, in *Cartas de don Juan de Silva, conde de Portalegre, a los reyes Felipe II y Felipe III, y a diferentes ministros, sobre materias diplomáticas, desde 1579 hasta 1601, Codoin* 43 (Madrid, 1863), p. 555.

[67] BL, Add. 28422, Borja to Lerma transmitting Moura's words, fol. 19v; see also Lerma to Borja, 10 Dec. 1598, and 12 Dec. 1598, in *ibid.*, 10 and 19v. In the latter, Lerma wrote that Moura should be very happy for the rewards he had received and that he did not have any right to complain or ask for more.

[68] BNM, Mss 1739, "Sucesos de el año de 1598 hasta el de 1600," fols. 296ff; Cabrera de Córdoba, *Relaciones*, pp. 50, 56; and Sepúlveda, *Historia de varios sucesos*, pp. 210–11.

[69] Hinojosa y Navajeros, *Despachos*, p. 382; for the most popular explanation of Velada as a typical courtier who was concerned only with himself and without principles see Sepúlveda, *Historia de varios sucesos*, p. 211.

months of Philip II's reign), he was able to preserve his position in the Council of State and continued to play an important political role during Philip III's reign. Some observers attributed his good fortune to his ability to dissemble his feelings and flatter the new favorite.[70] According to others, he survived because, given his humble origins, he did not pose a threat to Lerma, with whom he had maintained a friendly relationship throughout Philip II's reign.[71] It is also possible that Lerma understood the importance of having the assistance of one of the most skillful and experienced ministers in the government of the monarchy.[72] But despite his role, Idiáquez nevertheless remained, as the papal envoy Bastoni predicted, a second-rank man who "would always have an important place in the dispatch of state affairs but who would not have personal influence with the king."[73]

None of the actions described above generated opposition, but Lerma made a major mistake when he let attacks against the former king's favorites spill over to the image of the late king himself. The best example of such a mistake was his consent for the writing and circulation of Iñigo Ibáñez's "Las causas" in 1599.[74] In this pamphlet Ibáñez broadened the attacks against the former favorites to include the king himself, whom he portrayed as an "effeminate and ignorant king, who liked women, gardens, and beautiful buildings." He further argued that Philip II was incapable of comprehending state affairs, forcing his father, Charles V, to appoint strong officials to help him rule the monarchy (fols. 746–9). But, according to Ibáñez, because he disliked strong ministers he surrounded himself instead with "sissies" (*mariniquitos*) and mediocre officials (Mateo Vázquez, Moura, and Idiáquez) who were as inexperienced as their master in governmental affairs (fols. 752–7). "Oh wretched Spain," Ibáñez wrote, "wretched Monarchy, lost, ruined, and wasted" by the obtuse government of this mediocre king and his insubstantial ministers (fol. 760).

Ibáñez's attack, the first critique of the late king "which [was] circulated widely in Spain," as Geoffrey Parker has written,[75] went too far and soon posed a danger to Lerma, who was accused of having masterminded it or, at the least, of being responsible for its dissemination. These accusations eventually forced Philip III to punish Ibáñez, although his retribution was rather insubstantial, to save Lerma.[76]

---

[70] *Ibid.* [71] Cabrera de Córdoba, *Historia de Felipe II*, vol. IV, p. 142.
[72] *CSPVen*, vol. IX, p. 347, report of Francesco Soranzo, 3 Oct. 1598; González Dávila, *Historia de la vida*, pp. 36–7.
[73] Hinojosa y Navajeros, *Despachos*, p. 402; on Idiáquez's important political role see below chap. 6.
[74] See note 23 above. [75] Parker, *Philip II*, pp. 203–4.
[76] Ibáñez was arrested in August 1600; see AGS Est., *leg.* 187: royal order, 24 Aug. 1600. He did not, however, suffer this misfortune for long. In 1602 the king ordered him to accompany Juan de Cardona on a "secret mission," an appointment resulting from "my satisfaction with your zeal, experience, and sufficiency," assuring him at the same time that "I will reward you as you deserve," AGS Est., *leg.* 191: Philip III to Iñigo Ibáñez, 11 June 1602. But Ibáñez never fully recovered from this affair and never regained Lerma's complete favor. His career was further compromised by his alliance with courtiers who criticized Rodrigo Calderón, Lerma's prime favorite, later in the reign. On Ibáñez see Cabrera de Córdoba, *Relaciones*, pp. 55–6, 60, 84, 173, 192, 236, 243, 301, 413.

But most importantly, the pamphlet opened up a public debate on the character of the new regime. In a rebuttal, one Doctor Navarrete, for example, painted an opposing view; he not only defended Philip II's memory but also called attention to threats to the well-being of the monarchy from the new regime.[77] Not surprisingly, Navarrete's portrayal of the former king bore no resemblance to Ibáñez's; Philip II, remarked Navarrete, was "a powerful, Christian, and just king" whose policies were guided by his desire to serve God (fols. 121r–122). He further warned that Philip III should not be exalted at the expense of his father because to question the capacity of any king is "something horrendous, something never heard of or dreamed of" in the Spanish kingdoms (fol. 128). He then went on to discuss the ideal form of government and concluded that the kingdom would no doubt be best served by a monarch who selected "competent and wise counselors" because only the government of a king who received the advice of able ministers could save the monarchy from decline. Employing the same arguments Santa Cruz and others had used in their criticism of Philip II's dependence on favorites, Navarrete warned the new monarch that were he to dismiss the advice of good counselors and rely on favorites, he would find himself and the kingdom in great danger: "these favorites will tyrannize the king and the kingdom. They will only be interested in increasing the power of their own houses, relatives, and families and not the well-being of their king" (fols. 147r–v, 149).

Thus Ibáñez's attacks on Philip II and his favorites opened the door for others to condemn the style of government of the new rulers. Adapting one of the most forceful critiques of Philip II, an anonymous author of a pamphlet entitled "Advertimientos que se dio a Su Majd. sobre los ministros y privados" ("Advice given to the king about his ministers and favorites"), attacked not only Philip II but Philip III and Lerma. "The greatest and most just complaint these kingdoms had against his majesty Philip II," he wrote, "was that the king gave so much of himself to one of his favorites [Moura], that this favorite had at his disposition the control of all governmental affairs and all rewards and individual affairs." His power was so overwhelming that "to obtain their king's liberality Philip II's subjects had first to flatter and submit themselves to the king's favorite on whom depended everything and everyone."[78] It was this dependence that caused "all of the dissatisfaction, bitterness, and displeasure" that characterized the end of Philip II's reign. Although now the old king was dead, his son was acting exactly like his father: "Your Majesty begins his reign in the same way as your father ended his, and this is not a beginning that promises a good end. How is it possible that your Majesty consults all matters of state with just one person and with a person who is not very knowledgeable in all matters?" Philip III's foremost duty as the Spanish king was to conduct himself as a just and caring ruler, resolving all state affairs alone with the

[77] BNM, Mss 11044, Doctor Navarrete, "Respuesta en alabanza del gobierno del rey don Felipe II," fols. 120r–149v. Further references in the text.
[78] BNM, Mss 17887, "Advertimientos que se dio a Su Majd.", fol. 37.

help of virtuous counselors. His reputation would inevitably suffer if his enemies should learn that he had delegated his authority to one of his subjects and that he rewarded only this favorite and his relatives while spending his own time detached from public affairs.[79]

Although both Navarrete and the anonymous author were rather mild in their condemnation and both offered only the most general of advice, the implication of their writings was clear: something had gone terribly wrong at the start of the reign, foreshadowing disastrous times to come. Fray Jerónimo de Sepúlveda was more to the point in his assessment of the nature of the new regime. After Philip II's death, he wrote in his diary, the new king "gave his will to Lerma to such a degree that the king has no other 'yes' or 'no' than that of Lerma. It is thus not a surprise that the populace is saying that Lerma has bewitched Philip III!"[80]

[79] *Ibid.*, fols. 37v–40v.   [80] Sepúlveda, *Historia de varios sucesos*, p. 202.

PART II

The king's *valido*

Introduction

Despite criticism of Philip III and Lerma for promoting, or at least permitting, an attack upon Philip II at the start of Philip III's reign, Lerma's supporters tried to assure the king's subjects that Lerma's role would not affect the structure of court politics and that his position would resemble that of Moura and Philip II's other favorites. A sense of continuity in the transition between the reigns of Philip II and Philip III may be inferred from a curious anecdote that describes events in Briviesca, a town located in the present-day province of Burgos 200 miles north of Madrid, soon after the accession of Philip III. In 1602 an official inspection (*visita*) ordered by the Council of Castile revealed that one local faction headed by the "*caudillo*" Doctor Franco controlled the town's institutions. A witness claimed that soon after Doctor Franco was selected as the head of the faction in 1598, its members

> began to award themselves titles according to their closeness to doctor Franco. Dr. Franco's closest *privado* is called Marquis of Denia [Duke of Lerma]; another is called Cristóbal de Moura; another Don Juan Iriáquez [Idiáquez], and yet another Don Fulano [Gaspar] de Córdoba [Philip III's confessor], and I have heard them refer to each other by these names when they gather at Franco's house.[1]

As this story illustrates, soon after Philip II's death it became common knowledge that the new king had a new favorite and that Lerma's rise to power should not be regarded as a radical break with the past. To facilitate this perception Lerma's supporters took care to portray him in an approving light as a good counselor of his king, someone who could play a positive role in the ruling of the monarchy.

To understand how power was won, conserved, and exercised in early modern Spain, it is important to analyze not only those elements that stressed continuity between the two reigns but also the changes that were taking place. Those searching for power in early seventeenth-century Spain knew well that to gain influence at court it was critical to gain the king's favor. Royal favor, or *gracia real*, to use the language of the period, enabled courtiers to ascend and play a role in court politics. Lerma had been able to obtain Philip III's favor while the new king was a prince, which gave him an enviable advantage over the rest.

---

[1] Francis Brumont, "Le Pouvoir municipal en Vieille-Castile au Siècle D'Or," *Bulletin Hispanique*, 87 (1985), p. 130; the inspection was initiated in 1602.

But it was one thing to gain power and another to conserve it. Lerma knew from personal experience that other courtiers would aspire to win Philip III's favor and try to displace him as the king's favorite. To prevent such a fate, he had to become the sole favorite, the king's *valido*, defined by his supporters as the "most valuable and loved among the king's subjects." Lerma succeeded by becoming the "master of the palace" and controlling the most important palace offices, those that gave access to the monarch. Once there, he surrounded the king with a compact courtly faction made up of relatives, clients, and followers to prevent outsiders from infiltrating the king's inner circle. His ability to maintain control of the king's entourage and household enabled him to stay in power for twenty years, from 1598 to 1618, although after 1611 his position as the king's sole favorite was challenged by other contenders (see Part IV).

What makes Lerma's *privanza* interesting is not only his capacity to conserve his power and influence for so many years but the means by which he accomplished this feat. Lerma did not simply follow the forms and rules of *privanza* employed by former royal favorites; he also created his own. In the attempt to construct and legitimate his power Lerma and his supporters were constrained by institutional, intellectual and symbolic contexts that no doubt influenced their behavior. Principal among these was the official political discourse which affirmed that the ruler in a personal monarchy was the only possessor of sovereignty, an exclusivity which limited the creation of new offices, such as prime minister, which could give the impression that the monarch was sharing the power of administering the government with one of his subjects. No less important was the belief that the king had to be the principal, if not unique, actor in the ceremonials devised to celebrate the power of the monarchy. None of the king's subjects could share the public stage with his master without giving rise to the possible accusation of becoming a second king and, thus, destroying the sacred foundations of the Spanish monarchy. Despite these limitations, Lerma and his supporters exhibited great political imagination that enabled them to institutionalize the position of the *valido* in ways never seen before. Lerma's actions and the theories he and his supporters promoted ultimately helped to transform not only the discourse on royal favorites but also, and more importantly, the discourse on the structure and the constitution of the monarchy.

But the redefinition of the discourse on royal favorites did not come about simply as the result of a linguistic evolution. It mirrored changing political and administrative realities. As J. G. A. Pocock reminds us, "history consists of actions, events, and processes";[2] thus, in the analysis of the past one needs both to reconstruct the different political languages and their evolution and also to examine how political acts "modify the contexts they are performed in, and how some of these modifica-

[2] J. G. A. Pocock, "Texts as Events: Reflections on the History of Political Thought," in Kevin Sharpe and Steven N. Zwicker, eds., *Politics of Discourse. The Literature and History of Seventeenth-Century England* (London, 1987), p. 22.

tions lead to the creation and diffusion of new languages and new contexts."³ The action that helped Lerma transform the discourse on royal favorites was Philip III's decision to permit him to become a *de facto* prime minister, thus making it feasible for the royal favorite to "institutionalize" his power and position. As Maurice Bloch has suggested, those who "acquired power institutionalize it to make it less vulnerable to the attacks of rivals." They accomplish this, he continues, "by creating an office of which they are the legitimate holders."⁴ In Lerma's case, the "institutionalization" of his power and position was *sui generis*, taking the form of a reinforcement of the "personal", rather than institutional, character of the relationship between the king and his favorite.

The study of the institutionalization of the *valido*'s role constitutes the central theme of Francisco Tomás y Valiente's seminal work, *Los validos en la monarquía española del siglo XVII*. He and many who have followed his ideas tend to disregard Lerma's *privanza* and to dismiss the reign of Philip III as a critical moment in this process. They have implicitly adopted a traditional historiographical position which declares that Lerma, as the weak favorite of a weak king, neither influenced the ruling of the monarchy nor helped to transform the dominant political discourses on the king's *privado*. This study, on the contrary, demonstrates how Lerma's decisive voice in the ruling of the monarchy together with new theories, concepts, and images helped to create a more complex image of the royal favorite. Although modern historians have tended to value the word "favorite" as a concept without history, whose "essential meaning" did not change during the sixteenth and seventeenth centuries, my analytical perspective is that historians need to contextualize the use and evolution of political terms while trying to understand why changes in meaning took place.

The dismissal of Philip III and Lerma as weak and incapable politicians has led modern historians to view the reign as a lost opportunity to reinforce royal power and construct an absolutist state. The term that best summarizes these views is "devolution," referring to the alleged delegation of power to the royal councils and the absence of political initiatives from Philip and Lerma. This interpretation of Philip III's reign was first put forward by the English historian Patrick Williams, who has asserted that Philip III's reign can be divided into two clearly differentiated phases. The first, extending from 1598 to 1603, was characterized by Philip III's active participation in the ruling of the monarchy and the "restoration of a government by councils." The second, a radically changed situation, occurs after 1603 when the king, as a result of Lerma's personal influence, supposedly abandoned his responsibilities as a ruler of the monarchy and opted to withdraw to his own palaces in a quest for privacy and personal gratification. According to

³ J. G. A. Pocock, "The Concept of a Language and the *métier d'historien*: Some Considerations in Practice," in Anthony Pagden, ed., *The Languages of Political Theory in Early-Modern Europe* (Cambridge, 1987), p. 30.
⁴ Cf. David I. Kertzer, *Ritual, Politics and Power* (New Haven, 1984), p. 51.

Williams's interpretation, after 1603 a separation between the "court" (Philip III, Lerma, and their closest servants) and the "government" (the royal councils and other institutions) emerged, with the councils acting as virtual rulers of the monarchy.[5] In a new twist of this interpretation, the polemical English historian Henry Kamen has recently asserted that this "devolution" of power to the councils came about as a result of pressure from the political elite to bring back a government based on a "constitutional" ideology, which resulted in the restoration of a more traditional and balanced system of government.[6]

Against these interpretations there is ample evidence to suggest that the new rulers did indeed promote political theories and administrative programs to enhance the king's power and centralize the decision-making process into the hands of Philip III, Lerma, and Lerma's allies and creatures. The theories and political initiatives the new rulers advocated and implemented have never been thoroughly analyzed by modern historians; in fact, many of the actions taken by Lerma and Philip III have never even been mentioned. The political initiatives undertaken during Philip III's reign – the creation of a new *Junta de Gobierno*, the establishment of many other *juntas* to bypass the councils, the appointment of "Castilian" ministers to the institutions of non-Castilian kingdoms and, above all, the placement of Lerma's allies into each and every monarchical institution – were no doubt inspired by similar measures previously adopted by Philip II. But it was under the leadership of Philip III and Lerma that this form of administering the monarchy was extended, and the initiatives they took influenced the ways in which the monarchy was ruled until at least the mid-seventeenth century.

[5] Williams, "Philip III," pp. 751–69.   [6] Kamen, *Philip of Spain*, pp. 319–20.

4

The power of the king

Political historians have tended to underestimate the influence of the many discourses that helped to define the power of the early modern royal majesty. Primarily concerned with institutional forms, they have concentrated on the juridical language which represented the monarch as the lawmaker and the head of a bureaucratic state. The study of the Spanish monarchy is a case in point. Most modern historians indeed argue that the Spanish monarchy was highly bureaucratic, and that Spanish rulers justified their power using theories and images that were less commanding, less sacred, and more secular than those promoted by their European counterparts. A closer look, however, reveals that Spanish monarchs, in their attempt to construct the royal majesty, used a variety of political languages and no less commanding images of the power and nature of kingship. In Spain, as in other early modern European states, constructing a powerful image of the king was indeed viewed as an essential component of a political ideology that permitted monarchs "to rule, to control and order the world, to change or subdue other men."[1] It is true, however, that Spanish rulers operated in a context peculiar to Spain, where by the late sixteenth century monarchs had become inaccessible and almost invisible to all but a select group of their subjects, thus changing not only the place and political significance of the royal palace but also the function of royal rituals and ceremonies in the constitution of monarchical power.

"The eminent power that the king has," claimed Fray Alonso de Cabrera in a sermon preached in honor of the late king Philip II,

derives from God and is communicated by Him. Those who resist and rebel against the king, resist God and break God's established order. The king's subjects have to obey their master who has the place of God upon earth. This is the order that will last in the world until the second coming of Christ when He will recover for himself the whole *potestas* and administration of this His realm.[2]

Fray Alonso's sermon is a striking depiction of monarchical power and of the demand for loyalty and obedience from the king's subjects. Yet in a personal

---

[1] Stephen Orgel, *The Illusion of Power* (Berkeley, 1975), p. 47.
[2] "Sermón predicado en el funeral por Felipe II," in Fray Alonso de Cabrera, *Sermones del maestro Fray Alonso de Cabrera*, ed. Manuel Mir (Madrid, 1906), p. 699.

monarchy, royal power – even in its most absolutist definition – was not the core of the monarchical order. For royal power to be effective, its very nature and characteristics had to become embodied in the person of the monarch, who was the center of the system, the personification of God's will on earth and who as such needed to appear to his subjects "as a divinity, as a hero who has come down from heaven, superior in his nature to the rest."[3]

As in the Balinese court described by Clifford Geertz, in early modern Spain Philip III's contemporaries defined power by defining what kings represented. A monarch – whatever his individual character – exemplified not an individual human but the entire monarchy. Here, too, using Clifford Geertz's words, "the driving aim of higher politics was to construct a state by constructing a king. The more consummate the king, the more actual the realm. . . . If a state was constructed by constructing a king, a king was constructed by constructing a god."[4] In other words, the aim of the king's supporters was to demonstrate that the monarch's power – and thus the monarchical system itself – was not socially created but divinely ordered. The monarch was the possessor of all powers, not because of his office but because of his divine nature.

To construct this mythical monarch, early modern Spanish royalists needed to challenge some aspects of prevailing theories that accepted the human frailty of the king, especially those theories that claimed that the king's power was derived directly from the community. Many political writers agreed that although God was the ultimate origin of power, monarchs obtained their power and authority not directly from Him but through the community. Consequently, they viewed the monarch, not as "a master of the kingdom," but as its administrator and tutor.[5] In accord with these premises, political writers emphasized the monarch's official role and his royal *dignitas* over his human nature, as reflected in the political proposition of the "the king's two persons": one natural, thus weak and perishable; the other public, thus perfect and immortal. These theorists also claimed that the community invested its authority in the king's immortal public person whom they were obliged to obey because he was the possessor of a public office. They also claimed that the monarch's main duty was to prevent his vulnerable natural person, guided by passion and self-interest, from interfering with his responsibilities as tutor of the kingdom.[6]

Monarchs and their supporters began, however, to question some of the central premises of such theories in the last decades of the fifteenth century. Although

[3] Mariana, *De rege*, p. 154.
[4] Clifford Geertz, *Negara. The Theatre State in Nineteenth-Century Bali* (Princeton, 1980), p. 124.
[5] For a survey of these theories see Fernández Albaladejo, *Fragmentos de monarquía*, pp. 72–85. See also above, chap. 1.
[6] The implications of the Spanish theory of the king's two persons has not yet been explored in its entirety; for some aspects of this theory see Bartolomé Clavero, *"Hispanus Fiscus, Persona Ficta*: concepción del sujeto político en la época Barroca," in Clavero, *Tantas personas como estados* (Madrid, 1986), pp. 53–105. The most important general reference remains Ernst H. Kantorowicz, *The King's Two Bodies* (Princeton, 1957).

those serving the Spanish monarch never questioned, at least in theory, the ascendant theory of royal power (that the king's authority comes from the community) or that the king's sacred duty was to serve the common good, they aimed to transform the monarch into a superior human through what Edward Peters has called the "progressive enlargement of the [king's] human character."[7] Indeed, as David Starkey has noted about the English monarchy, Spanish royalists similarly promoted the idea that the king's two persons "fused in the actual person of the king" and, thus, that the king's natural body became endowed with singular qualities justifying, therefore, the transformation of the person of the king (and not the royal insignias representing the public royal *persona*) into "the master-symbol" of monarchical power.[8]

It is possible to find such attempts already during the reign of the Catholic Monarchs (Isabel and Ferdinand) when after their victory in the dynastic civil wars of the late fifteenth century their supporters promoted the idea that although the king's natural person was perishable, the monarch had certain personal qualities that made him unique. The Italian humanist Pietro Martire d'Angheria, who was in Isabel's service at the time, declared in 1488, for example, that Isabel and Ferdinand are like "deities, that came to earth from heaven, inspired by a Holy Spirit and guided by God's hand." They are, he continued, "superhuman ... and everything they think, say and execute excels human nature."[9] Such royal qualities were also seen as inheritable. It was said, for example, that Prince John, the Catholic Monarchs' son, although still young, never behaved as a minor because he was "a king's successor." Similarly, Prince Charles, the future emperor and Isabel's grand-child, was depicted as possessing all the qualities of a king "from the moment he was begotten in his mother's womb," and thus "by nature he was an almost divine man."[10] Castiglione was no less enthusiastic when he declared that Prince Charles, despite his young age (ten years), already

displays such wisdom and such certain signs of goodness, prudence, modesty, magnanimity, and every kind of virtue that if, as everybody expects, the empire of Christendom comes to his hands, it is to be believed that he will eclipse the name of many ancient emperors and equal the fame of many of the most famous men who have ever lived.[11]

Because kings were superior humans who belonged to dynasties selected by God to rule over men, they had an innate good judgment in the ruling of their kingdoms

---

[7] Edward Peters, *The Shadow King. Rex Inutilis in the Medieval Law and Literature, 751–1327* (New Haven, 1970), p. 214.

[8] David Starkey, "Representation through Intimacy," in Ioan Lewis, ed., *Symbols and Sentiments* (London, 1977), p. 188.

[9] Pietro Martire d'Angheria, *Epistolario de Pedro Mártir de Anglería*, ed. J. López Toro, 4 vols. (Madrid, 1953–7), vol. I, pp. 6, 7, Martire de Angheria to Juan Borromeo and Teodoro Papiense, 2 Feb. 1488.

[10] *Ibid.*, vol. III, pp. 101–2, and IV, p. 86, Angheria to Luis Hurtado de Mendoza, 1 Jan. 1513, and to the Duke of Mondéjar and the Duke of Vélez, 13 Nov. 1520. See also the words of the Bishop of Badajoz in *Cortes de los Antiguos Reinos de Castilla y León*, 5 vols. (Madrid, 1857), vol. IV, p. 293.

[11] Castiglione, *El cortesano*, vol. II, p. 149.

and in choosing the course of action most beneficial to the well-being of their communities. By definition, kings could do no wrong. Francisco de Los Cobos, Charles V's powerful secretary, made this point as he described young Philip II:

I assure Your Majesty, I not only do not have to reject anything that he decides, but I am astonished at his prudent, well-considered recommendations, which are more fitting in a man trained all his life in state and other affairs than in a ruler who is so new at it, in years and in authority. He is, sir, devoted to virtue and justice, scorning all that is contrary to them. Wherefore we all accept and respect his advice because in the midst of the gravity and restraint with which he gives it and points out the errors, it is accompanied by a natural majesty and authority that is terrifying.[12]

Royal apologists also tried to demonstrate that those who were born to be kings had both physical and psychological qualities that distinguished them from other humans. Juan Huarte de San Juan believed, for example, that kings, in contrast to common mortals, had their various humors in ideal balance and, thus, their constitution achieved "supreme perfection." Men born to be kings had a full memory (*memoria*) to see the past, full imagination (*imaginativa*) to see the future, and great understanding (*gran entendimiento*) "to distinguish, infer, reason, judge, and adopt" the best for their kingdoms. The exterior appearance and behavior of the king reflected such special interior qualities: perfect beauty of the face (to attract the love of his subjects), blond hair (the middle of two extremes, black and white), medium height, and virtuous behavior. Huarte attributed such qualities to the Spanish monarchs and only to three other historical figures: Adam (the first human created in God's image), King David (God's favorite monarch), and Jesus (God and the son of God).[13]

These ideas greatly influenced the ways in which Spanish monarchs were publicly portrayed. Indeed, Charles V and Philip II understood, as did the rulers described by Clifford Geertz, that "the king's ability to project himself (or, better, his kingship) as the stationary axis of the world rested on his ability to discipline his emotions and his behavior with meticulous rigor."[14] In Spain the process of creating a similar public image of the king reached its height during Philip II's reign. Philip II was now described as a king who always showed an imperturbable face, who controlled his feelings, who made everyone tremble in his presence and

[12] Francisco de los Cobos to Charles V, 1543?; cf. Hayward Keniston, *Francisco de los Cobos, Secretary of the Emperor Charles V* (Pittsburgh, Pa., 1960), pp. 269–70. On Philip II's image see Fernando Bouza Alvarez, "La majestad de Felipe II. Construcción del mito real," in José Martínez Millán, ed., *La corte de Felipe II* (Madrid, 1994).

[13] Juan Huarte de San Juan, *Examen de ingenios para las ciencias* [1575], ed. Esteban Torre (Madrid, 1977), chap. 14, pp. 288, 291–3 and 302–8. Huarte's book was frequently translated into other languages: French (twenty-two editions from 1580 to 1675); Italian (seven editions between 1582 and 1604); English (five editions between 1594 and 1698); Latin (1622), and so on; see Torre's edn., pp. 51–2. See also Castiglione, *El cortesano*, vol. I, p. 149. [14] Geertz, *Negara*, p. 130.

2   Sofonisba Anguisciola, *Philip II*. A portrait of Philip II in his customary
attire stripped of all external symbols of royal power, but represented as a "natural"
monarch in control of his destiny and kingdoms.

even his brightest counselors dumb, and who displayed, in private and in public,
such greatness that his "authority and glory appear divine," comments which were
almost identical to those describing God in Exodus.[15] This personal demeanor was
also reproduced in court portraits, which disclose "an imposing, cold, distant, and

[15] Cabrera de Córdoba, *Historia de Felipe II*, vol. I, pp. 323–4. Exodus 19:22–4, 20:18–21.

majestic image" of the king, stripped of any symbols of royal power but easily recognized, as the Italian humanist Pietro Aretino noted, by the "gesto bel di maestà reale."[16]

The presentation of the king as a commanding and sacred person, the epitome of royal power, consumed the energies of Philip III's close servants from the beginning of his reign. There was, in the first place, an urgency to portray the new king as a deserving inheritor of his ancestors' glories and virtues. This task was accomplished in part by suggesting a mystical continuity between Philip II and his son. Philip II, professed the royal chaplain Fray Aguilar de Terrones in a sermon preached to honor the late king, had many virtues, but one summarized them all – his capacity to recreate himself in the person of Philip III. Referring to the fact that Philip II had died in his palace-monastery of El Escorial, Father Terrones noted that: "He [Philip II] built his monastery as a silk worm builds his cocoon, and he died there. But he emerged from this cocoon as the new king [Philip III], whom I believe to be a superior Philip II."[17] Despite its simplicity, this metaphor gave Father Terrones's listeners the powerful impression of being in the very presence of a miraculous event effected by God in the persons of His chosen monarchs. To make this image even stronger Father Terrones ended his sermon by suggesting that Philip III's subjects could worship the new ruler, not because he received his power from God but because the king was himself a god: "Although the king is a god in human flesh . . . if he is religious and just [as everyone knows Philip III to be], he actually will become God (*El rey es un Dios en carne humana . . . el Rey es hombre, pero si es religioso y justiciero, Dios se torna*)."[18]

This image of the transfer of power from Philip II to his son, characterized not as a "succession" but as a "resurrection" of the former in the person of Philip III, was repeated *ad infinitum* during the first few months of the new reign.[19] For example, Lope de Vega in *A la muerte del Rey Filipo Segundo, el Prudente*, presented his

---

[16] Cf. H. E. Wethey, *The Paintings of Titian. II: The Portraits* (London, 1971), p. 42. On the portraits of the Spanish kings see Fernando Checa Cremades, *Pintura y escultura del Renacimiento en España, 1450–1600* (Madrid, 1983), pp. 349–57, and Jonathan Brown, "Enemies of Flattery: Velázquez' Portraits of Philip IV," *Journal of Interdisplinary History*, 17 (1986), pp. 137–54.

[17] "Sermón que predicó a la Majd. del Rey don Felipe III el doctor Aguilar de Terrones su predicador, en las honras que su Majd. hizo al católico Rey d. Felipe Segundo, que sea en gloria, en San Gerónimo de Madrid, a 19 del mes de octubre de 1598," in Juan Iñiguez de Lequerica, ed., *Sermones funerales en las honras del rey nuestro señor don Felipe II, con el que se predicó en las de la serenísima infanta doña Catalina duquesa de Saboya* (Madrid, 1599), fol. 21r.

[18] *Ibid.*, fol. 23v. On Father Aguilar de Terrones's sermon and in general on preachers and preaching during Philip III's reign see Hilary Dansey Smith, *Preaching in the Spanish Golden Age. A Study of Some Preachers of the Reign of Philip III* (Oxford, 1978); pp. 48–9 on Terrones's sermon.

[19] Iñiguez de Lequerica, the editor of Terrones's sermon and other funeral sermons dedicated to Philip II, reminded his readers that Philip II "has bequeathed us a son so equal to himself in his name and deeds" that the transmittal of power "was not a simple succession but a resurrection of Philip II as Philip III [*que no pareciese sucesión sino resurección*]" in *ibid.*, "Prologue of Lequerica," n.p.; see also "Sermón que predicó el padre Maestro Fray Agustín Dávila de la Orden de los Predicadores, calificador del Santo Oficio, en 8 de noviembre de 1598 a las honras que la ciudad de Valladolid hizo en su iglesia mayor al rey Felipe II nuestro señor," fol. 80v.

3 *Philip III Depicted as a Good Ruler* with allegories and symbols representing royal virtues: prudence, religion, justice, *imperium*.

readers with the image of a dying Philip II surrounded by personifications of the virtues he had mastered during his life – "Religion, Justice, Mercy, Peace, Prudence, Temperance, Truth, and Fortitude" – which accompanied the king to Heaven. Returning to earth, the Virtues were pleasantly surprised to find themselves in front of "a radiant young Philip III, King of Spain and the new Phoenix, / . . . a divine portrait, / and a glorious printed stamp / of the original soul [Philip II]"[20] – a new Phoenix, "expressly chosen" by God, as demonstrated by the deaths of Philip III's older brothers and his own "miraculous" recovery from poor health in his teenage years.[21]

The words, ideas, and concepts embedded in these sermons and poems reappeared as powerful images during the royal entry of Queen Margaret into Madrid in October 1599. As in other monarchies, the royal entries took place when the king officially visited one of the principal cities of his kingdoms for the first time.[22] In its original form the royal entry represented what Malcolm Smuts calls the "communitarian" facet of kingship,[23] as a reenactment of the union between the king and his kingdom, represented in this case by the city. The king was given the keys to the city as a symbol of its obedience, and by accepting them, he swore to protect the city's privileges. By the end of the sixteenth century, and certainly by the seventeenth, the royal entry had become a celebration of the uniqueness of the monarch and of his privileged position in the body politic.[24]

Queen Margaret's entry into Madrid on 24 October 1599 is illustrative. Patterned after the royal entry of Queen Anne of Austria (the fourth wife of Philip II and Philip III's mother), and approved by Philip III after careful study,[25] this entry deployed a liberal use of mythology or what E. H. Gombrich has referred to as the "mythopoetic faculty."[26] Its designers – the Italian sculptor Pompeo Leoni (also involved in the design for the entry of Anne of Austria), the Italian painter

---

[20] "A la muerte del Rey Filipo Segundo, el Prudente," in Lope Félix Vega Carpio, *Obras escogidas de Lope de Vega*, ed. Federico Carlos Sainz de Robles, 3 vols., 2nd edn. (Madrid, 1987), vol. II, p. 98.

[21] BNM Mss 8526, "Discurso sobre el gobierno que ha de tener Su Majd. en su monarquía para conservarla," anon., Madrid, 15 Oct. 1599, fol. 19v.

[22] Gonzalo Fernández de Oviedo, *Libro de la cámara real del príncipe don Juan y oficios de su casa y servicio ordinario* [1530?], ed. J. M. Escudero (Madrid, 1870), p. 102.

[23] R. Malcolm Smuts, "Public Ceremony and Royal Charisma: the English Royal Entry in London, 1485–1642," in A. L. Beier, David Cannadine, and James M. Rosenheim, eds., *The First Modern Society. Essays in English History in Honour of Lawrence Stone* (Cambridge, 1989), p. 76; a good summary of this ceremony is in Roy Strong, *Art and Power* (Berkeley, 1984), pp. 7–11, 44–50.

[24] *Ibid.*, p. 48; on the royal entry in Spain and its evolution, see Checa Cremades, *Pintura y escultura*, pp. 371–83; and Alicia Cámara Muñoz, "El poder de la imagen y la imagen del poder. La fiesta en el Madrid del Renacimiento," in *Madrid en el Renacimiento* (Madrid, 1986), pp. 66–77.

[25] José Martí y Monsó, *Estudios histórico-artísticos relativos principalmente a Valladolid* (Valladolid, 1898), pp. 277–8. The royal approval is dated in Valencia, on 8 Mar. 1599. In this authorization the king also ordered that nothing should be done without his prior permission. On Queen Margaret's entry see also Virginia Tovar Martín, "La entrada triunfal en Madrid de doña Margarita de Austria (24 de octubre de 1599)," *Archivo Español de Arte*, 61 (1988), pp. 385–403.

[26] E. H. Gombrich, "Icones Symbolicae. Philosophies of Symbolism and their Bearing in Art," in his *Symbolic Images. Studies in the Art in the Renaissance* (Chicago, 1985), pp. 128–30.

Bartolomé Carducho, the Spanish painter Luis de Carvajal, the architect Francisco Gómez de Mora, and an anonymous poet – spared no analogies, symbols, or images that could enlarge the already mighty image of the Spanish king.[27] In the first arch, referred to as "the principal arch" in a document approved by Philip III and dedicated to "the Royal Power and Majesty," Philip III was depicted as "a robust man supporting two worlds, the old world and the new." He was also depicted as the possessor of the virtues of Jupiter (the ray as a symbol of punishment), Neptune (the trident as the power over the seas), Mars (the shield as a symbol of defense of the realm), Hercules (the mace as a symbol of the king's inner fortitude), and Mercury (the wand as a symbol of wisdom).[28] Entering through two other triumphal arches, the royal procession reached the church of Saint Mary near the royal palace. "Two magnificent statues more than twenty feet high," designed by Pompeo Leoni, covered the facade of the church. One represented King Philip III and the other Atlas carrying a half-globe on his shoulders with the following inscription engraved on its base: *Divisum Imperium cum Jove* (I shared the *imperium* with Jupiter), as a reference to Philip III's youth when he shared the heavy burden of ruling the monarchy with his ailing father (Jupiter).[29]

Public displays of Philip III as the heir of his ancestors' glories and virtues continued throughout his reign. The king himself actively promoted the presentation of a powerful image of previous Spanish rulers and of himself through the decorations he commissioned for El Pardo, a countryside royal palace close to Madrid, and the Alcázar, the royal palace in Madrid. Although many of the paintings Philip III authorized for the halls in El Pardo have disappeared, the iconographical series painted throughout the palace included the "Judgment of Solomon," the "Triumph of the Eucharist," and the "Story of Achilles," allegories that presented Philip III as a just, religious, and prudent monarch. In addition, he commissioned portraits of his ancestors and of himself, the queen, and their children in apparent homage to the dynasty and as a demonstration that he was a capable successor of monarchs of sublime reputation.[30] These iconographical

---

[27] The different reports on the preparation of this entry mentioned a poet or poets charged with creating the "soul" of the triumphal arches, but they never mentioned who those poets were: Martí y Monsó, *Estudios histórico-artísticos*, pp. 277, 281.   [28] Tovar Martín, "La entrada triunfal," pp. 390–5.

[29] *Ibid.*, p. 402. The texts that described this entry do not explain the meaning of the statue of Atlas; it is important to remember, however, that Pompeo Leoni also designed the last statue of Anne of Austria's royal entry in 1570, representing Philip II as Atlas bearing the world on his shoulders. See López de Hoyos, *Real aparato*, fol. 40.

[30] On decorations in El Pardo see Vicente Carducho, *Diálogos de la pintura* [*c.* 1636], ed. Francisco Calvo Serraller (Madrid, 1979), Dialogue 7, pp. 328–33; José Miguel Morán, "Felipe III y las Artes," *Anales de Historia del Arte*, 1 (1989), pp. 159–75; Rosa López Torrijos, *La mitología en la pintura española del siglo de oro* (Madrid, 1985), pp. 198–203; and Mary Newcome, "Genoese Drawings for the Queen's Gallery in El Pardo," *Antichità Viva*, 29 (1990), pp. 22–30. On the collection of portraits of Philip III's ancestors and relatives see "Memoria de los retratos que sean hecho para la casa Real del Pardo [por Pantoja de la Cruz]," a document published in Maria Kusche, *Juan Pantoja de la Cruz* (Madrid, 1964), pp. 65–7; and J. Moreno Villa and F. J. Sánchez Cantón, "Noventa y siete retratos de la familia de Felipe III por Bartolomé González," *Archivo Español de Arte y Arqueología*, 38 (1937). On the plans

programs were crowned by the placing in the gardens of La Casa de Campo of the magnificent statue of Philip III on horseback, the first of its kind in Spain, and a gift to Philip from Ferdinand I, the Grand Duke of Tuscany.[31]

It could be said that these images and the message they conveyed – that the king's power was sacred and that he alone controlled the lives of his subjects – were very similar to those created and displayed in other European monarchies, thus demonstrating that the Spanish monarchy did not differ from its European counterparts in the images of the royal majesty. What really distinguished the Spanish monarchy was the role that "the master-symbol" of the royal office – the natural person of the king – played in the ritualistic and ceremonial public representation of kingship. Historians of early modern Europe are generally agreed that the French and English monarchies created and perfected the most effective modes of ritualizing kingship to impose the ruler's power over his subjects. As a result, the manipulation of the rulers' public image transformed the French and English monarchies into, in the words of Edward Muir, the "most successful monarchies in late medieval and early modern Europe."[32] In this context, the interest of historians focuses upon the constant public presence of the monarch and the transformation of the court into a public stage where the monarch was the principal actor. According to modern historians, royal power in early modern Europe thus required a splendid *mise-en-scène* where that heavenly creature, the monarch, appeared as the paradigm of absolute power.

The two early modern monarchs who were supreme masters of public ritual were Elizabeth of England and Louis XIV of France. Both understood the need to control, use, and manipulate public ceremonies to transform themselves into the inviolable heads of the court hierarchy and to reinforce the perception that political power was identical to the personal power of the king. Elizabeth's ceaseless travels around her realm, for example, made possible her transformation "into the adored object of her subjects."[33] Monarchs who – like James VI and I, Elizabeth's successor – eschewed public rituals are seen as failures. Muir writes that James VI and I, by avoiding public progresses and ceremonies "for more private ceremonies

to redecorate El Alcázar commissioned by Philip III from Vicente Carducho, which were abandoned when Philip III died in 1621, see Carducho, *Diálogos*, pp. 326–7; and Steven N. Orso, *Philip IV and the Decoration of the Alcázar de Madrid* (Princeton, 1986), pp. 121ff.

[31] The statue was commissioned by Ferdinand I in 1600; Giambologna designed the statue and worked on it from 1606 until his death in 1608 when Pietro Tacca replaced him. See Walter A. Liedtke, *The Royal Horse and Rider. Painting, Sculpture and Horsemanship, 1500–1800* (New York, 1989), pp. 70, 204–5. On the origins of this statue see Edward L. Goldberg, "Artistic Relations between the Medici and the Spanish Courts, 1587–1621: Part I," *The Burlington Magazine*, 138 (1996), p. 114. On contemporary references to this statue see Antonio Liñán y Verdugo, *Guía y avisos de forasteros que vienen a la corte* [1620], ed. Edisons Simons (Madrid, 1980), p. 177. Today the statue is situated in the Plaza Mayor of Madrid, the most important architectural improvement in Madrid during Philip III's reign.   [32] Edward Muir, *Ritual in Early Modern Europe* (Cambridge, 1997), p. 249.

[33] *Ibid.*, p. 246.

that asserted the divine right of kings, undermined in practice the sacrality he so ardently advocated."[34]

Not all European monarchies should, however, be analyzed by comparison with the models of Elizabeth and Louis XIV. Modern historians' attempts to reduce the variety of historical experiences to schematic and general paradigms applicable to all polities can lead to a simplistic understanding of monarchies where the ritualization of power took alternative, but not necessarily less successful, forms. One must situate monarchies within their own historical context to appreciate how rituals and ceremonials were employed and, ultimately, to determine how effectively they enhanced the king's power. For example, at least until the mid-seventeenth century, Spanish kings were particularly successful in defending their power and prerogatives, even though the ritualization and representation of their royal majesty differed substantially and in many ways contrasted sharply with the practices of other European monarchs. One sometimes wonders whether Elizabeth's and Louis XIV's constant recourse to public rituals and ceremonials demonstrates their "masterly" use of public means of propaganda or their complete inability to avoid participating in the public ceremonies viewed by many royal supporters in the late sixteenth century as handicaps to effective imposition of the monarch's absolute power.

Indeed, the guiding principle of early modern Spanish rulers' public behavior, since at least the mid-sixteenth century, was, using John H. Elliott's compelling words, the monarchs' "invisibility, and indeed their sheer inaccessibility."[35] This practice was the culmination of a series of challenges to the established views of royal power, especially those concerning the relationship of the ruler to other members of the body politic. Well into the sixteenth century, Spanish rulers were forced to contend with theories according to which the king's sacred duty was to listen to the advice of the members of the body politic and to be open and familiar. The "face of the king not only pleases," a late fifteenth-century anonymous pamphlet alleged, "it inspires, arouses, pleases, and invigorates the king's subjects."[36] The commonly held view was that an open and public monarch gained the loyalty of his subjects, whereas an aloof and private monarch created mistrust and promoted factions and rebellions. As a result, monarchs were advised to give unlimited access to members of the body politic and to transform the royal palace into a public space, "a place where the king exercises justice personally, where he eats and talks with his subjects," according to *Las siete partidas* of Alfonso X the

---

[34] *Ibid.* On Louis XIV, see Louis Marin, *Portrait of the King*, trans. Martha M. Houle (Minneapolis, Minn., 1988); and Peter Burke, *The Fabrication of Louis XIV* (New Haven, 1992).

[35] "The Court of the Spanish Habsburgs: A Peculiar Institution?", in John H. Elliott, *Spain and its World, 1500–1700* (New Haven, 1989), p. 148. See also Fernando Checa Cremades, "Felipe II en el Escorial: la representación del poder real," in *El Escorial: arte, poder y cultura en la corte de Felipe II* (Madrid, 1989), pp. 17–20.

[36] BNM, Mss 6020, "Advertencias del buen govierno," fol. 77v.

Wise, one of the most influential legal texts in medieval and early modern Spain.[37]

The constant flow of petitioners and others seeking to counsel the king, however, developed into a chronic source of frustration. Already in the late fifteenth century Isabel and Ferdinand had tried to curtail the right of entry into the royal chambers and to restrict it to a select group of servants. But their success appears to have been limited. Queen Isabel, for example, often bitterly complained about the unlimited access her subjects had to her person and private chambers. At the time, available means to limit and regulate access to the queen's private chamber remained primitive and not very effective – "to stay in bed all day, even if I am not sick at all, only because I want to be alone." Even when she was in bed her courtiers failed to leave her alone.[38] The situation began to change with the advent of the Habsburgs. Although Charles, to counteract the mistrust of Spaniards toward a "foreign king," maintained a high level of visibility and accessibility,[39] he challenged old practices by introducing stricter ceremonies of greeting and showing respect to the king. One of his agents in Castile had brought to his attention the political significance of such ceremonies in 1517. "Because authority should descend from the head to the members of the body politic," the king should not allow anyone to become too familiar with him. Instead he should require everyone to observe manners, such as kissing the king's hand and remaining bareheaded in his presence, designed to emphasize the king's superior position.[40]

But even more far-reaching in its impact was the introduction and promotion of a new palace etiquette, one of the first steps in the creation of a new model of Spanish kingship. In 1515 Emperor Maximilian I, Charles's grandfather, had established a new etiquette for Charles's household, which incorporated Maximilian's principle of privacy and certain other elements characteristic of the court of the Austrian and Spanish Habsburgs – a distant king and a strict courtly hierarchy based on one's degree of intimacy with the prince.[41] The primary purpose of the 1515 etiquette was to enforce the prince's privacy by allowing only the *sumiller de corps* to be present when the king went to sleep or got up, and by

---

[37] *Las siete partidas del rey Don Alfonso el Sabio* (Madrid, 1989), pt. II, tit. 9, law 29, "Qué cosa es palacio."

[38] Ochoa, *Epistolario*, vol. II, p. 17, Queen Isabel to her confessor, Hernando de Talavera, 30 Dec. 1494; on Ferdinand and Isabel's contradictory behavior toward access to the royal chambers see Ladero Quesada, *La hacienda real*, pp. 372–3; and *ibid.*, *Los Reyes Católicos*, pp. 82–3.

[39] For a few contemporary references see Antonio Rodríguez Villa, ed., "El emperador Carlos V y su corte (1522–1539): Cartas de D. Martín de Salinas," *Boletín de la Academia de la Historia*, 93 (1903), pp. 55, 93; and Francisco López de Villalobos, *Algunas obras*, 2 vols. (Madrid, 1886), vol. I, pp. 144–5.

[40] Fernández Alvarez, *Corpus documental*, vol. I, p. 69, Cardinal Cisneros? to Adrian of Utrecht, 1517?; on the importance of keeping one's head covered in the presence of the king and the changes introduced by Charles see Elliott, "The Court of the Spanish Habsburgs," p. 152.

[41] For the "Burgundian style" see C. A. F. Armstrong, "The Golden Age of Burgundy," in A. G. Dickens, ed., *The Courts of Europe. Politics, Patronage and Royalty* (New York, 1977), pp. 55–75; and Werner Paravicini, "The Court of the Dukes of Burgundy. A Model for Europe?" in R. G. Asch and A. M. Birke, eds., *Princes, Patronage and the Nobility. The Court at the Beginning of the Modern Age*, c. *1450–1650* (Oxford, 1991), pp. 69–102.

prohibiting everyone from approaching and talking with the king during his lunch and dinner except for officials in charge of serving his food. The etiquette also instituted a hierarchical degree of intimacy with the prince based on spatial criteria. Only the *sumiller de corps* and palace servants with specific missions were permitted entry into the prince's privy chamber. The rooms closest to the prince's chamber, in turn, were reserved, in the following order, for the "huissiers," and the "pensioners, chambellans, maistres d'hostel et gentilzhommes."[42] That Charles V himself regarded this Burgundian model of a distant and private monarch as best suited to his desire to establish a strong monarchy is reflected in the palace etiquette he himself ordered for his son, the future Philip II, in 1548 despite the opposition of many of his Castilian subjects. Again this etiquette emphasized the king's privacy by giving access to the prince's quarters only to a small number of palace officials.[43]

The most important consequence of these principles was the transformation of the royal household and the king's private quarters into a pivotal center of power and influence, into the "primary sphere of the king's rule."[44] The king's chamber, or as the Spaniards called it at the time, the *retrete* ("the most secret part of the house"), was transformed into a "dreadful place where [invisible] Power lurks."[45] The monarch's inaccessibility also gave new meaning to the royal palace by transforming it into the monarch's private space to which he withdrew accompanied only by a small, select group of servants who helped him rule his kingdoms and shared his thoughts, his ambitions, and, ultimately, his power.

Writing on the French court during Louis XIV's reign, Norbert Elias asserts that for the king palace etiquette "was an instrument not only of distancing but of power,"[46] something early modern Spanish monarchs clearly understood. In effect, from tentative beginnings in the reign of Charles V, and much more definitely from the time of Philip II, the strict limitations of *entrée* to the king's privy chambers were accompanied by the monarch's increasing withdrawal from public view.

---

[42] "Ordonnance de Charles, prince d'Espagne, archiduc de Bourgogne . . . pour le governement de sa maison," in M. Gachard, *Collection des voyages des souverains des Pays-Bas*, 3 vols. (Brussels, 1874), vol. II, app. I.

[43] On the new etiquette of the royal palace see Antonio Rodríguez Villa, *Etiquetas de la casa de Austria* (Madrid, 1913); for an excellent analysis of palace etiquette in early modern Spain see Elliott, "The Court of the Spanish Habsburgs," pp. 143–54. On the opposition to this palace etiquette see Helen Nader, "Habsburg Ceremony in Spain: The Reality of the Myth," *Historical Reflections/Réflexions Historiques*, 15 (1988).

[44] Norbert Elias, *The Court Society*, trans. Edmund Jephcott (New York, 1983), p. 119. Elias's words refer to the royal court in general, but given the conditions in the Spanish monarchy the real center of power, the center from which the Spanish monarch imposed his will, was the royal palace, and throughout the early modern period Spanish monarchs concerned themselves more with the royal household and palace than with the royal court in general.

[45] These are the words used by Roland Barthes in his analysis of Racine's plays; see Roland Barthes, *On Racine*, English trans. Richard Howard (Berkeley, 1992), pp. 3–4. On the meaning of the word *retrete* see Sebastián de Covarrubias Orozco, *Tesoro de la lengua castellana o española* [1611], facsimile edn. (Madrid, 1984), s.v. "retrete."

[46] Elias, *The Court Society*, p. 117; see also his *The Civilizing Process: The History of Manners and State Formation and Civilization*, trans. Edmund Jephcott (Oxford, 1994), p. 267.

During Philip II's reign, the inaccessibility and invisibility of the king came to be viewed as key elements in the practice of kingship, and Philip II's supporters began to defend the idea that the king's invisibility was essential for the promotion of obedience and reverence among the king's subjects. Indeed, as soon as he inherited the throne, Philip II stopped attending the meetings of the various councils and the *Cortes*. As a result, his subjects could only speak with him if they were given access to his person and chambers, a right that was reserved to a limited number of palace officials. The king portrayed by Philip II's contemporaries was a king who never spoke in public, who remained aloof and spent much of his time enclosed in his palaces, especially in the palace at El Escorial. Philip II even avoided participation in the public ceremonies (including royal entries), which many modern historians consider the crucial instrument for imposing the king's power.[47] For Philip II public ceremonials became dutiful performances that kept his subjects content, not instruments of political domination.

As with other aspects of kingship, Philip II tried to instill similar behavior in his son, Philip III, and it was during Philip III's reign that the king's inaccessibility was turned into an enduring political axiom, a sort of religion of state and an essential component in the constitution of royal power. Although both English and French rulers also attempted to isolate themselves by retreating into an aristocratic milieu, this practice never replaced the accepted principle that a real king should remain a public king.[48] As the Frenchman Pierre Matthieu observed, the French needed a visible and accessible king because otherwise they would believe that there was no king, whereas Spaniards believed that the power of the royal majesty would increase when the king was invisible and inaccessible.[49] Early seventeenth-century Spanish political authors also noted this distinctive character of the Spanish kingship. Juan Fernández de Medrano, for example, advised the king that "it is a certain kind of religion to retire from your subjects. You should not become familiar with anyone, except with the person who is your oracle [meaning 'favorite'], because *continuus aspectus minus verendos magnos homines ipsa satietate facit.*"[50] Medrano could choose many historical examples to support his views, but he

---

[47] See Parker, *Philip II*, pp. 20–2, 82.

[48] On this topic, see Smuts, "Public Ceremony," p. 85; Orest Ranum, "Courtesy, Absolutism, and the Rise of the French State, 1630–1660," *Journal of Modern History*, 52 (1980), pp. 426–51. For the Russian case, see Valerie A. Kivelson, "The Devil Stole His Mind: The Tsar and the 1648 Moscow Uprising," *American Historical Review*, 98 (1993), pp. 733–56.

[49] BNM, Mss 9078, "Breve compendio i elogio de la vida del rey Don Phelipe segundo de felicissima memoria escrito en francés por Pierre Matiu," fols. 32r–v; cf. Bouza Alvarez, "La majestad de Felipe II," p. 52. See also Conde de Salinas, "Dictamen del conde de Salinas en que se examinan las prerogativas de la corona y de las cortes de Portugal" [1612], ed. Erasmo Buceta, in *Anuario de Historia del Derecho Español*, 9 (1932), p. 378.

[50] This Latin sentence, meaning "if great men are seen often they are less revered," was included by Giovanni Botero (*The Reason of State*, ed. P. J. Waley and D. P. Waley [London, 1956], p. 57) in the Italian version of his *Ragion di Stato*. Antonio de Herrera y Tordesillas did not include this sentence in his Spanish translation of Botero's work.

settled on Emperor Tiberius, who according to Medrano had lived "*Occultum, ac subdolum fingendis virtutibus*" ("Hidden and deceitful, feigning virtue").[51]

Tiberius and others among the ancients were not the only examples evoked by early seventeenth-century Spanish writers to justify their king's inaccessibility and invisibility. As important as these historical models were those taken from Christian doctrine and traditions, including the doctrine of the Holy Sacrament. Diego de Guzmán, Queen Margaret's biographer, for example, criticized those who advocated that the Holy Sacrament be publicly exposed all day, thus visible to everyone at all times. Such exhibition, he feared, would result in a loss of "the respect, reverence, and love due to Him" by transforming the holy representation of Jesus Christ into an ordinary custom. "Those who see me will die, our Lord said. In this way God imposed respect and fear among men," and, according to Guzmán, a monarch, God's representative on earth, should behave similarly by limiting his public exposure and by prohibiting his subjects from attempting to see him outside established (and increasingly exceptional) public ceremonies.[52]

In addition, as these precepts suggest, the king's invisibility meant that the monarch should speak only with a small group of select individuals. If the king were to speak with everyone, he would lose the respect and obedience of his subjects, the author of "Discurso de las privanzas" advised. Taking Tiberius as his example, he further noted that "in [Tiberius's] times the only permitted way to address the prince was by writing, even when the prince was present."[53] Silence was thus considered an ideal way for the Spanish king to establish his preeminence, to protect his power and reputation.[54] In 1598, the year of Philip II's death, Giovanni Botero advocated exactly such behavior when he proposed that a monarch should always keep his thoughts secret and not speak too much. "Men somewhat taciturn and melancholic are more revered than the merry and loquacious; and in sum where the Prince can make himself understood with deeds he ought not to use

---

[51] Juan Fernández de Medrano, *República mixta* (Madrid, 1602), p. 32. The aloofness of Tiberius, a ruler who moved his headquarters far from Rome to distance himself from Senate pressure, is a crucial element in Tacitus's *Annals*, 4.41, 57–8, 67, in Tacitus, *Complete Works*, ed. Moses Hadas (New York, 1942). See also Alamos de Barrientos, *Aforismos*, vol. I, pp. 99–100; Lorenzo Ramírez de Prado, *Consejo y consejeros de príncipes* [1617], ed. Juan Beneyto (Madrid, 1958), p. 24. These three books were dedicated to the Duke of Lerma. See also Antonio de Herrera, "Discurso de cómo se ha de entender que cosa es Majestad, decoro y reputación," in BNM, Mss 3011, Antonio de Herrera, "Primera parte de las varias epístolas, discursos, y tratados dirigidos al rey nro. señor don Felipe IV," fols. 161ff. On the "invisibility" of Philip III as the result of the image of the royal majesty created by Philip II see Javier Varela, *La muerte del rey. El ceremonial funerario de la monarquía española (1500–1850)* (Madrid, 1990), pp. 53ff.

[52] Diego de Guzmán, *Vida y muerte de doña Margarita de Austria, reina de España* (Madrid, 1617), fols. 229v–230. See also Juan Pablo Mártir Rizo, *La Poética de Aristóteles traducida del latín* [1623], ed. Margerete Newels (Cologue, 1965), pp. 44–5, 75.

[53] "Al rey don Felipe III: discurso de las privanzas," in Quevedo y Villegas, *Obras*, vol. II, p. 1393.

[54] Francisco de Gurmendi, *Doctrina física y moral de príncipes* (Madrid, 1615), bk. 1, chap. 6: "De la importancia y excelencia del silencio," fol. 22v; Francisco de Gurmendi, too, dedicated his book to Lerma.

words."[55] To Philip III and his favorite, to use the words of Frank Whigham, "speech and other significations revealed not power but powerlessness, a pleading with the audience for a hearing, for recognition, for ratification."[56]

Philip III's silence in public, his aloofness, and his tendency to be "in solitude with very little court," accompanied always by his favorite, caught the imagination of his contemporaries almost from the start of his reign.[57] Queen Margaret's entry into Madrid late in 1599 was, for example, distinguished by the fact that no one could see the king, who remained hidden from public view accompanied only by Lerma,[58] offering his subjects a still more compelling image of the king, now imagined and depicted as a god and a hero in the triumphal arches and statues displayed in Madrid at the time. Philip III's withdrawal from public view in the company of his favorite continued throughout his reign. This custom met both the king's need to remain aloof from his subjects and Lerma's desire to exercise control over access to the king. After all, Lerma had been told that Philip II "was obeyed and feared even when he had locked himself into his rooms" and that he should promote the king's inaccessibility to establish Philip III's authority and his own influence.[59]

Such principles inspired one of the less understood measures taken early in the reign: the relocation of the royal court from Madrid to Valladolid for what proved to be a period of six years (1601–6). Modern historians have interpreted this event as a manifestation of Lerma's economic self-interest because his Castilian lands were closer to Valladolid than to Madrid. The presence of the royal court – the richest and largest internal market – increased demand for local products of all kinds, and the move clearly benefited Lerma's estates. Only apparently motivated by Lerma's interests, however, the relocation of the court to Valladolid occurred primarily for political reasons. In fact, Philip III had inherited a bankrupt, dysfunctional, and overpopulated court-city, and Madrid's defects "became an emblem for the *mal gobierno* [bad government] of the old regime."[60] Almost immediately after

---

[55] "Aggiunte," in Botero, *Practical Politics*, p. 240. See also "Imagen del silencio y descripción de lo que sus partes representa," in Juan de Jarava, *Problemas o preguntas problemáticas* (Alcalá de Henares, 1546), fols. 156v–168v; and Pliny the Elder, *Historia natural de los animales*, trans. Jerónimo de Huerta (Madrid, 1603), bk. 7, chap. 23, fol. 57.

[56] Frank Whigham, *Ambition and Privilege. The Social Tropes of Elizabethan Courtesy Theory* (Berkeley, 1984), pp. 39, 51.

[57] Simeone Contarini to the Venetian senate 1605; cf. Elliott, "The Court of the Spanish Habsburgs," p. 148. On the treatment of these characteristics by the literature of the period see Antonio Feros, "Vicedioses pero humanos: el drama del rey," *Cuadernos de Historia Moderna*, 14 (1993), pp. 103–31.

[58] Cabrera de Córdoba, *Relaciones*, p. 47.

[59] BNM, Mss 18275, "Memorial que dieron al Duque de Lerma, cuando entró en el valimiento del sr. Rey Felipe III," fol. 2r.

[60] The situation of Madrid, the scandals created by "prostitutes," the increase in the population, the relaxation of customs, and so on, were the subject of considerable debate during the reign of Philip II; see, for example, BFZ, *carp.* 132, fol. 54: report of the *junta* in charge of the "reformation" of customs in Madrid, 4 Sept. 1586. See also Claudia Sieber, "Madrid: A City for a King," paper presented at the meeting of the Society for Spanish and Portuguese Historical Studies, St. Louis, 1987, p. 1.

his accession, Philip III created a special committee to examine the situation in Madrid and the possible relocation of the court to an alternative site and requested the committee to recommend measures that might be taken to create a new court for a new king.[61] Madrid, as depicted in the committee's report, was an over-populated, confrontational, and noisy court full of "vices and sins," where it was impossible to protect the king's privacy because the offices of the councils were located in the royal palace. The committee saw few advantages in keeping the court in Madrid and recommended that it relocate to one of several Castilian cities that in the past had hosted the royal court: Valladolid, Toledo, or Burgos. In the end Philip III chose Valladolid, arguing that he had received reports stating that there was sufficient infrastructure to host the royal family.

The committee also presented Philip III with a set of recommendations to help him avoid a fate for the court in Valladolid similar to the one in Madrid. The king was told to establish rigid controls over who should have the right to live at the court and to remember that it was important to have not "a populous court but a populous kingdom." The committee thus proposed that residence at Valladolid be limited to those who had lived there prior to the relocation of the court and to those who held court or palace offices. Nobles should live on their estates; the councils should be relocated to other cities, with the exception of the Council of State. The dispersal of the councils would mean that those searching for rewards or justice need not go to the court, thereby weakening the power of the councils by separating them from the king's person.

Philip III did not, however, follow all of the committee's recommendations. The councils, for example, were permitted to remain at the court, although their chambers were no longer located in the royal palace as they had been in Madrid. The new rulers did try to restrict the number of residents permitted to live at the court. Immediately before the court's relocation, a royal order was issued prohibiting the entry of all individuals who did not have a letter-patent signed by the committee in charge of relocating the court to Valladolid.[62] According to Luis Cabrera de Córdoba, this measure seems to have succeeded, at least initially, because the new rulers were able to prevent the entry of many "insignificant" individuals – widows, beggars, and idle persons without business or office at the court.[63] Success did not last, however, and soon the problems of Valladolid were similar to those experienced by the court in Madrid. Furthermore, despite assurances of an infrastructure adequate to a royal court, it soon became obvious that it was impossible to maintain the royal family at Valladolid in the decorum to

---

[61] AGS GJ, *leg.* 897, a report without date and author; I thank Dr. Claudia Sieber for drawing my attention to this important document. On the debate over the removal of the court and the constitution of this special committee see Sieber, "Madrid: A City for a King," pp. 4–7.

[62] Luisa de Carvajal to Magdalena de San Jerónimo, letters of 16 Oct. 1600, 29 Jan. and 29 May 1601, in Carvajal y Mendoza, *Epistolario y poesías*, pp. 107, 109, 113.

[63] Cabrera de Córdoba, *Relaciones*, p. 99.

which they were accustomed. This inadequacy was the main reason why Philip III decided to return the court to Madrid in 1606.[64]

Notwithstanding their failure to control unruliness at the court, Philip III's and Lerma's behavior at Valladolid established the style of the new regime regarding the king's public presence. Lerma had taken upon himself to arrange the new royal quarters in Valladolid, which he bought, redecorated, and later sold to the king. The buildings housing the royal family were a complex set of edifices connected through second-floor passages to protect the royal family's privacy, transforming the royal palace into a private space that was opened to the public only on selected ceremonial occasions.[65] Lerma also made available to the king his own palace in Valladolid, La Huerta de la Ribera, an enormous residence located just outside the city on the banks of the Pisuerga River. There the monarch, his family, and entourage could rest and attend the masques, theatrical performances, banquets, naval ballets, and bullfights that Lerma organized to entertain his master.[66] The routine established in Valladolid was followed once the court returned to Madrid. Lerma bought and reconditioned the Quinta del Prior, also known as Huertas del Duque de Lerma, an enormous *hacienda* located in the Paseo del Prado, a suburb of Madrid, where he again organized many spectacles to entertain the king and the royal entourage.[67]

In addition to enjoying the protected spaces at the court, Philip III, accompanied by Lerma, spent as much time as possible in his or Lerma's countryside residences. Lerma, firm in his belief that such retreats were essential to maintain his political independence and to hold the king's favor, was undeterred by criticism accusing

[64] Lerma and his followers justified this move by suggesting that the local government in Valladolid had failed to transform the city into an attractive and well-appointed court. See AGS Est., *leg.* 201/n.p., "Ordenes del duque de Lerma de parte de su Majd. a don Pedro Franqueza sobre diferentes materias," Dec. 1605.

[65] Lerma bought all the buildings from various nobles between 1599 and 1600 and sold them to the king in December 1601. On the royal quarters at Valladolid see the excellent article by Jesús Urrea, "La Plaza de San Pablo como escenario de la corte," in *Actas del I Congreso de Historia de Valladolid* (Valladolid, 1999), pp. 15–29; Luis Cervera Vera, *El conjunto palacial de la villa de Lerma* (Valencia, 1967), chaps. 1–3; José J. Rivera Blanco, *El palacio real de Valladolid* (Valladolid, 1981), chaps. 4–6; Agustín Bustamante García, *La arquitectura clasicista del foco vallisoletano (1561–1640)* (Valladolid, 1983), pp. 395–402.

[66] That La Huerta was useful for Lerma only as far as it could be used to impose his dominion over the king's activities is demonstrated by the fact that Lerma sold it to the king in June 1606 when the court's return to Madrid was a *fait accompli*. On the conditions of this sale, see AGS CC ME, *leg.* 920, *exp.* 8, Memorandum of Lerma, 11 July 1607. See also Cervera Vera, *El conjunto palacial*; and Bustamante García, *La arquitectura clasicista*, pp. 402–3; for a contemporary account of the activities of Lerma and the king at Valladolid see the memoirs of Tomé Pinheiro da Veiga, a Portuguese who lived in Valladolid until the court returned to Madrid: Tomé Pinheiro da Veiga, *Fastiginia o fastos geniales* [1605], ed. Narciso Alonso Cortés (Valladolid, 1916).

[67] On the Quinta del Prior, demolished at the end of the nineteenth century to build the Palace Hotel, see ADL, *leg.* 1/*exp.* 9, and *leg.* 40/*exp.* 8, and AGS CC, Libros de Cédulas, bk. 172, royal decree, 10 Oct. 1605; see also María Isabel Gea Ortigas, *El Madrid desaparecido* (Madrid, 1992), p. 118. In the *relaciones* written by Cabrera de Córdoba are numerous references to the activities organized by Lerma in his residence.

4 *The Carrera of San Jerónimo, or Visit of Philip III to Lerma's Palace.* On the left side of this painting, which portrays one of the most popular venues of seventeenth-century Madrid, the artist reproduces one of Philip III's visits to Lerma's palace, known as "Quinta del Prior" or "Huertas del Duque de Lerma."

him of taking "the king to the countryside to prevent everyone from speaking with him."[68] Thus, Philip – always in Lerma's company but often without members of his own family – spent long periods in El Pardo, which was rebuilt and redecorated under the king's supervision after a fire in 1604, in Aranjuez, and, particularly after 1606, in El Escorial or in Lerma's residences, including the town of Lerma, ostentatiously rebuilt after 1606, and in La Ventosilla, a hunting palace located near Valladolid.[69] These residences were private spaces where indiscreet individuals who did not belong to Lerma's inner circle were forbidden,[70] leaving Philip III, Lerma, and their entourage to hunt, entertain themselves, and attend to the affairs of state free from outside influence.

[68] BNM, Mss 1492, "Papel que escribió el Cardenal Sandoval, arzobispo de Toledo, al duque de Lerma," fol. 32v.

[69] On Philip III's preference for El Pardo, see Fernando Checa Cremades and José Miguel Morán, *El coleccionismo en España* (Madrid, 1985), pp. 228–30; on La Ventosilla and Lerma, see Cervera Vera, *El conjunto palacial.*

[70] See, for example, Cabrera de Córdoba, *Relaciones*, pp. 163–4, 253–4, 286; and AGS Est., *leg.* 200/n.p., report of Pedro de Franqueza, Valladolid, 23 May 1605.

5

In his image and likeness

The monarch's invisibility irrevocably altered the nature of the royal palace from a place where the king communicated with his subjects to a place where he withdrew from public view accompanied only by a select group of servants. For that reason, controlling access to the king became the most important instrument of influence for those who hoped to transform the king's favor into their own advantage. A favorite who managed entrance to the king's quarters could guard his power against all challengers and, at the same time, lay the foundations for legitimizing his own power and exalting his own image. In both tasks the Duke of Lerma proved himself to be particularly adept, transforming himself into the most powerful favorite in Spanish history.

For the king, his palace and his privy chamber became his "primary sphere" of action; for those fighting for power and influence, the monarch's chamber became the only site where dreams of power and influence could be brought to fruition. Consequently, since access to the king required holding one of the few palace offices that carried the right of entry to the king's private chambers, palace offices became far more important and coveted than those of royal secretaries and council presidents. The Count of Portalegre had made this point to his son in the late sixteenth century. "As far as peacetime offices go," he wrote, "be advised that those of a palace nature have an advantage over the rest. They might seem less weighty to you, but they do not hinder, indeed they nourish and facilitate, possibilities of advancement . . . because the prince has more knowledge of those who are in his presence."[1] From the late sixteenth century, accordingly, one finds an increase in references linking major palace offices and royal favorites. Even so, everyone was aware that the holding of a major palace office did not automatically guarantee the king's *privanza* or even his confidence.[2] The Marquis of Velada, for example, was never considered Philip III's

---

[1] Juan de Silva, *Instrucción de don Juan de Silva, conde de Portalegre, cuando envió a don Diego su hijo a la corte* (n.p., n.d.), fol. 17r.

[2] As pointed out by the writer and poet Antonio Hurtado de Mendoza, despite their potential for influence and power, palace offices brought few benefits for their holders without the king's grace (*la gracia del Príncipe es el mejor puesto de Palacio, éste sin ella es moderado y corto*), in "Papel de don Antonio [Hurtado] de Mendoza a pedimento de don Martín de Ibarra, cuando pasó a Flandes a servir al señor Infante Cardenal en el puesto de Secretario de Cámara," en Hurtado de Mendoza, *Discursos*, p. 47.

favorite, even though he served the king as *mayordomo mayor* until his death in 1615.[3]

In early modern Spain three palace offices gave their holders an unquestionable right of *entrée* to the king's chambers. The first was the *sumiller de corps* (grand chamberlain or groom of the stole), who as the head of the privy chamber was considered the king's closest servant.[4] This official had customarily slept in the king's bedroom, but by the late sixteenth century, possibly because of Philip II's desire for privacy, he had begun to maintain separate although permanent lodgings in the royal palace. His most important duty, and certainly the one that gave his office its eminence, was to assist the king in the morning (*lever*) and at night (*coucher*) and while the king ate in his privy chamber. Palace etiquette explicitly established that the king "should never withdraw from the sight of his groom of the stole," who had always to accompany the king in public audiences, visits to the queen's chamber, public ceremonies, and when the king retired to his privy chamber.[5] Early seventeenth- century authors offered an image of the *sumiller* as the king's "brother" with whom the monarch shared everything, including the "selection of royal officials." What in fact gave this position added importance was that the *sumiller de corps* presided over hundreds of other palace officials, including the *gentilhombres de la cámara* (gentlemen of the chamber) who shared with him the privilege of serving the king in his most private retreats. The breadth of the functions assigned to him also explains why Spanish kings were admonished to select this official carefully because "from being a servant he will become your companion and friend, whom you will ask for advice on all matters."[6]

The second principal official of the royal household, the *mayordomo mayor* (the lord high steward), was in charge of feeding and housing the king and held the right to attend all meetings of committees dealing with financial matters, to be informed of royal expenses, and to sign all official payments. In addition, he had the right to enter the queen's chamber in the king's presence, and he oversaw dozens of servants, most important of whom were the *mayordomos* (stewards) and the *gentilhombres de la boca* (gentlemen of the table).

The third key official, the *caballerizo mayor* (the master of the horse), was responsible for the royal stables and all war and peacetime transportation. He also had the right to accompany the king whenever he left the palace – on hunting journeys, visits to his kingdoms, walks, and so on – and he enjoyed the privilege of

---

[3] On the Marquis of Velada and the reasons why he retained his palace office after Philip II's death see above, chap. 3.

[4] Officially, the possessor of the king's privy chamber was the *camarero mayor* (grand chamberlain), but from the last decades of the sixteenth century Spanish kings did not have *camareros mayores*, passing the responsibility of the privy chamber to the *sumiller de corps*.

[5] Rodríguez Villa, *Etiquetas*, p. 48.

[6] Miguel Yelgo de Vázquez, *Estilo de servir a príncipes, con ejemplos morales para servir a Dios* (Madrid, 1614), fol. 15v.

having his quarters in the royal palace and free *entrée* to the privy chamber after the king's *lever*.

The Duke of Lerma, quick to discern the importance of these palace offices, arranged to be confirmed as the *caballerizo mayor* of Philip III immediately after the death of Philip II in 1598, and in December 1598 he was also appointed *sumiller de corps*, replacing Cristóbal de Moura. As a holder of these offices, Lerma had the right to remain in the king's presence at all times and places: in the king's privy chamber, during public audiences, on the king's visits to his kingdoms and countryside palaces, or when the king was hunting, riding, or walking. When, in 1603, Lerma was also appointed the general of the Cavalry of Spain, it became impossible to see or talk with the king inside or outside the royal palace, in peace or in war, without first confronting Lerma, who had become Philip's virtual shadow.[7]

As discussed in Chapter 4, to see the king or to speak with him in public was not consequential. On such occasions the king received his visitors "standing at a console table" where he remained motionless and speechless during the entire audience.[8] It was significant to see and talk with the king only when he had retired to his private chambers, those small, gloomy, dark rooms in the royal palace,[9] where the royal etiquette strictly regulated those who could have access to the king. Only the *sumiller de corps*, plus a few of his aides – including the person in charge of the royal chamberpot – were permitted to enter the king's alcove when the king had retired to bed or had undressed. Spanish royal etiquette did not contain a ceremony such as the French solemn *lever et coucher*, in which a large number of palace officials, members of the royal family, and aristocrats were present.

Palace etiquette further decreed that only after the king had put on his shirt and moved out of his alcove could other individuals see him. But even then, only major palace officials, including the gentlemen of the chamber and the grandees – who were obliged to remain silent and to stand against the wall when the king was washing, working, or eating in private – were allowed in the king's presence in his private chambers.[10] Other servants and royal officials were admitted only in select other quarters, depending on their status and position in the hierarchy of the royal household. The same palace etiquette was followed in other royal palaces, including those where the royal family did not maintain a permanent presence, such as El Escorial, where the royal apartments were even smaller and darker than those in the Alcázar and which were surrounded by an intricate labyrinth of hallways and passages essentially isolating the king's quarters from the rest of the palace.[11] As

---

[7] On Lerma's office as general of the Cavalry of Spain, see Lerma, *Descripción e inventario*, fols. 15r–v.

[8] Elliott, "The Court of the Spanish Habsburgs," p. 150.

[9] *Ibid.*, p. 182. On the uses of the different rooms see Orso, *Philip IV and the Decoration*, esp. pp. 17–24.

[10] On the grandees' right until the end of the sixteenth century to enter the king's private rooms see BNM, Mss 3826, "Lo que el sr. don Duarte en 24 de junio de 1622 entendió del duque del Infantado acerca de la entrada que los grandes tenían en palacio," fols. 95r–v.

[11] On the internal organization of El Escorial see Cornelia von der Osten Sachen, *San Lorenzo el Real de El Escorial* (Bilbao, 1984), pp. 107–18.

Hugh Murray Baillie has observed, the organization of the Spanish royal palaces reinforced the limited access to the king imposed by royal etiquette not only for his many anonymous subjects but also for those who regarded themselves as members of his inner circle.[12]

Following the precedent established by his father, Philip III, from the outset of his new reign, doubtless with the support and the encouragement of the Duke of Lerma, was intent on limiting access to his person. A royal order issued in 1599, for example, stipulated that only those who had the key to the king's chamber, namely major palace functionaries and the gentlemen of the chamber, were allowed to enter the king's private quarters and that they would lose this right if they were caught in the king's private rooms accompanied by unauthorized individuals.[13] Philip III also permanently forbade the grandees from entering his alcove, an exclusion already begun toward the end of Philip II's reign, apparently, at least in part, because of the old king's failing health. Grandees without palace offices could only accompany Philip III to the so-called Sala de las Pinturas (Paintings Hall) or Salón Grande (Great Hall) located outside his most private chambers. Subsequently, the restrictions on the grandees' access to the king went even further when Philip III ordered that a grandee who desired to speak privately with him was required to request an audience, which would then take place not in the king's privy chamber, but in the Pieza Obscura (Dark Room) adjacent to the Sala de las Pinturas in the presence of Lerma as Philip's *sumiller de corps*.[14] From the beginning of the reign, what came to differentiate those who were "in" from those who were "out" was access to the king's person in his private quarters. As the Duke of Medinaceli, Antonio Juan Luis de la Cerda (Lerma's nephew), explained in 1643,[15] the contrast between free access to the king and his private chambers and the necessity of awaiting permission from a valet (*ayuda de cámara*) to cross into the king's chambers was the difference between proof of the king's favor and demotion to the second rank among courtiers. (He himself had enjoyed the coveted favor during the reign of Philip III and suffered its loss when Philip IV came to the throne.)

To control palace life, and ultimately to influence the king, Lerma needed, however, to do more than simply rely on palace etiquette or his own offices. He had to extend his influence over other palace offices. This task he accomplished by relying on members of his extended kin network. Lerma's designs are clearly

---

[12] Hugh Murray Baillie, "Etiquette and the Planning of the State Apartments in Baroque Palaces," *Archaeologia*, 101 (1967), pp. 169–99, especially p. 199, where the author compares the internal organization of the Spanish, German, French, and English royal palaces.

[13] Cabrera de Córdoba, *Relaciones*, p. 3.

[14] See BNM, Mss 3826, "La entrada que los grandes tenían en palacio," fols. 95r–v; and BNM, Mss 8740, "Etiquetas de Palacio, estilo y gobierno de la casa real, ordenadas en el año 1562 y reformadas en el de 1624," fol. 99v. The Dark Room was also used by the king for his private audiences with the presidents of the councils.

[15] "Representación dirigida al Rey por el duque de Medinaceli, acerca de sus servicios personales y pecunarios, y escasa recompensa de ellos," in Antonio Paz y Meliá, ed., *Documentos del archivo y biblioteca del excmo. sr. duque de Medinaceli* (n.p., n.d.), p. 192.

evident in the appointments associated with the king's privy chamber. Almost half of the gentlemen of the chamber, for example, were Lerma's close relatives: two sons, Cristóbal Gómez de Sandoval, the future Duke of Uceda, and Diego Gómez de Sandoval, Count of Saldaña; a brother, Juan de Sandoval, who was also *primer caballerizo* and, thus, Lerma's lieutenant; two nephews, Pedro Fernández de Castro, Count of Lemos since 1600 and also Lerma's son-in-law, and Pedro's brother Fernando de Castro y Sandoval; a brother-in-law, Juan Luis de la Cerda, Duke of Medinaceli and brother of the Duchess of Lerma; and two cousins, Francisco de Borja, Prince of Esquilache, and Juan de Mendoza, nephew of Lerma's uncle Bernardo de Rojas y Sandoval, Archbishop of Toledo.[16] Lerma also appointed other relatives to lesser offices and reserved some for his trusted creatures.[17] The most important of Lerma's clients was undoubtedly Rodrigo Calderón, who became Lerma's favorite and in the end a symbol of the failure of Lerma's government.[18] Calderón, who had served as Lerma's page since 1597, was appointed *ayuda de cámara* to the king in 1598 and secretary of the king's privy chamber in 1601, an office that granted him the right to inspect all memoranda addressed to the king. By placing his relatives and friends in key palace offices, Lerma was able to erect a thick wall around Philip III, who was unable to write or speak to his subjects without being observed or heard or having his papers read by Lerma or one of his relatives and creatures.

But, as in other European monarchies, the king's household was only one part – although admittedly the most important – in the structure of the royal palace.[19] The queen's household, for example, constituted an entirely separate structure, one that Lerma realized he must control in order to remain in power. The queen's free access to the king made her, as Fernández de Navarrete put it, "an important asset for the favorite in his quest for influence but, no doubt, the most dangerous obstacle if she opposed him."[20] Immediately following the establishment of Queen Margaret's household in 1599, Lerma began to pay ceaseless attention to every detail concerning the appointment of servants who would have access to the queen. Ultimately, Lerma would follow a *modus operandi* similar to the one he had adopted with respect to the king's household. Even before the queen's arrival at the court, Juan de Borja, Lerma's uncle, in a letter of 6 May 1599, had recommended to his nephew that he strictly limit the number of the ladies with access to the queen's private chambers and that he carefully consider their qualities. To admit many or to

---

[16] For the various components of the chamber of Philip III see AGPR Sec. His., *leg.* 3, "Gentilhombres de la Cámara de Felipe III."

[17] For example, his cousins Gonzalo Chacón, Bernardo de Rojas y Sandoval, and Antonio de Borja; see AGPR Ex. Per., 214/15, and 913/45.

[18] On Rodrigo Calderón as a symbol of Lerma's failure see below, chaps. 11 and 12.

[19] There was also the royal heir's household, but Prince Philip [IV]'s household was not established until 1611–14: see chap. 12 below.

[20] "Carta de Lelio Pelegrino," written in 1612; in Pedro Fernández de Navarrete, *Conservación de monarquías y discursos políticos* [1626], ed. Michael D. Gordon (Madrid, 1982), pp. 409–10.

admit troublemakers would provide them with opportunities "to meddle too much in affairs" they did not understand, resulting in tensions, troubles, and divisions between the king's and the queen's servants.[21] Initially, though, it appeared that Lerma was unable to impose strict rules regulating access to the queen or was perhaps unconvinced that his power could be challenged from within the queen's household.

In 1602, however, Lerma discovered what he and his supporters believed to be a conspiracy against his *privanza* emanating from Queen Margaret's household. The incident ended in October 1603 with the imprisonment of the Marchioness of Valle, Magdalena de Guzmán, *aya* (governess) to the Infanta Ana (the future Anne of Austria) since November 1601, and her exile from the court.[22] Although the exact role played by Magdalena de Guzmán in what Lerma's creatures defined as a "treason in the royal palace" remains obscure, Lerma and his supporters firmly believed that someone was trying to remove him from power,[23] and indeed her answers to questions posed by the judges conducting the investigation revealed a story of factionalism and conspiracy originating from Queen Margaret's chamber. Magdalena de Guzmán's interrogators paid special attention to one document found in her possession, a letter sent to her by the Countess of Castellar, Beatriz Ramírez de Mendoza. In it, the countess explained what she had told the queen about a conversation she had had with the king:

I entreated the king to rule by himself and to take advice from impartial persons, and the king responded that he was doing just that. I also told him that he should take advice from his wife, because "she loves you very much," and that he should be aware that everything is deteriorating. When I was telling this to the queen, the Duke [of Lerma] entered the room, and she became so extremely disturbed upon seeing the duke that it was pitiful to watch her. The duke approached the queen and asked her what I was saying to which she did not respond. Afterward, the queen, looking at me, responded, "This is how everything goes."[24]

On the surface Castellar's comments concerning Lerma were no different from criticism voiced by those who opposed Lerma's *privanza* at the start of the reign.

---

[21] BL, Add. 28422, Borja to Lerma, 6 May 1599, fols. 64v–65.

[22] Magdalena de Guzmán was detained in October 1603 and exiled from the court without charges in 1605. Although she was dismissed from her palace office, she continued to receive her salary on Lerma's direct orders; see AGPR Ex. Per., 1064/2. On Magdalena de Guzmán see Luis Fernández Martín, "La marquesa del Valle. Una vida dramática en la corte de los Austrias," *Hispania*, 39 (1979), pp. 559–90.

[23] BNM, Mss 18191, "Declaración dada por la Marquesa del Valle en la prisión en que se halla, por cierta traición que acaeció en palacio," fols. 192r–202v. Those in charge of detaining and interrogating Magdalena de Guzmán – Silva de Torres, Diego de Ayala, Juan de Ocón, and Melchor de Teves – were all Lerma's creatures. Given the possible participation of Queen Margaret in what seems a conspiracy against the Duke of Lerma, Magdalena de Guzmán and her nephew Ana de Mendoza were exiled from the royal court without being officially indicted. In Magdalena de Guzmán's file in the royal palace the reason given for her exile is quite euphemistic: "she retired to live in her own house on 4 October 1604," AGPR Ex. Per., 1064/2.

[24] BNM, Mss 18191, "Declaración dada por la Marquesa del Valle," fols. 197v–198r; see also Marí Jesús Pérez Martín, *Margarita de Austria, reina de España* (Madrid, 1961), pp. 119–21.

But memoranda, pamphlets, and diaries could be destroyed and censored before they reached the king's eyes. It was rather more difficult to exert control over someone who could directly speak with the king and who also had the queen's confidence. That Lerma considered the above episode a serious threat to his position is evident in the new etiquette the king enacted for the queen's household on 9 July 1603 immediately after the Marchioness of Valle affair. The new regulations limited access to the queen's private apartments to her *mayordomo mayor*, her *camarera mayor* (grand chamberlain), and her *damas de honor* (ladies-in-waiting). It further stipulated that only the queen's ladies-in-waiting could be present while she ate in her private chamber and that when grandees or others desired an audience with the queen in her private rooms they had to seek the permission of her *mayordomo mayor*.[25] As an additional step to control *entrée* to the queen's chambers, Lerma tried to restrict communication between palace servants and individuals without palace offices. The queen's ladies-in-waiting, for example, were told that they "should not meddle in the affairs of private individuals, must not accept memoranda and petitions from anyone or discuss any affairs with royal ministers and other servants," and must not allow anyone who did not hold an office in the queen's household to visit their rooms.[26]

Lerma also tried to impose his authority through the appointment of the queen's servants as he had done in the household of the king. With the exception of the queen's confessor, the Austrian Richard Haller, and a few ladies-in-waiting, most notably Queen Margaret's favorite, María Sidonia Riderer, Lerma was successful in arranging the appointment of his relatives and creatures to the most important offices in Queen Margaret's household.[27] Lerma's determination to impose his own candidates as the queen's servants was evident with the immediate substitution in 1598 of the queen's first *mayordomo mayor*, Juan de Idiáquez, with Lope Moscoso, Count of Altamira, who was married to Leonor de Sandoval, Lerma's sister, herself a governess to the Infanta Ana from 1603.[28] In March 1604, Altamira was appointed the queen's *caballerizo mayor* and the office of the *mayordomo mayor* passed to the hands of Juan de Borja, Lerma's uncle, who was subsequently replaced by Sancho de la Cerda, Marquis of La Laguna and Lerma's brother-in-law, after Borja's death in 1606.[29]

Another important office in the queen's household, the *camarera mayor*, was also occupied by one of Lerma's relatives. Although Philip II had appointed Juana de Velasco, Duchess of Gandía, to this office in 1598, Lerma expressed his wish to

---

[25] BNM, Mss 1007, "Etiqueta de la casa de la reina," 9 July 1603, fols. 2r, 4r, 24r–27r. See also Dalmiro de la Válgoma y Díaz-Varela, *Norma y ceremonia de las reinas de la Casa de Austria* (Madrid, 1958), p. 105.   [26] BNM, Mss 1007, "Etiqueta de la casa de la reina," fols. 2r, 24v–26v.

[27] On Queen Margaret's confessor and favorite servants see Magdalena Sánchez, "Confession and Complicity: Margarita de Austria, Richard Haller, S.J., and the Court of Philip III," *Cuadernos de Historia Moderna*, 14 (1993).   [28] On Altamira's appointments see AGPR Ex. Per., 521/26.

[29] AGPR Ex. Per., 135/50 (Juan de Borja), and 533/14 (Sancho de la Cerda).

dismiss her only a few months after the enthronement of Philip III.[30] His wish was realized at the end of 1599 when Gandía was replaced by the Duchess of Lerma, Catalina de la Cerda, who became ill in 1603 and was succeeded by Catalina de Sandoval, Countess of Lemos and Lerma's sister.[31] This appointment of Lerma's sister was an important victory for him because, as Orazio della Rena, ambassador of the Great Duke of Tuscany to Spain, wrote, she "was very active, prudent, and so loved by the Duke of Lerma" that he delegated to her many important responsibilities in his attempts to conserve his *privanza*.[32] Lerma also succeeded in promoting other relatives and creatures to assorted offices in the queen's household. At least fifteen of the queen's *damas de honor* were Lerma's relatives. Among them were three of his daughters (Catalina de la Cerda, Juana de Sandoval, and Francisca de Sandoval), two daughters-in-law (Luisa de Mendoza, Countess of Saldaña and heiress of the powerful house of the Infantado, and Mariana de Padilla, who belonged to the house of the Counts of Buendía), several nieces (Catalina de Sandoval, Juana de la Cerda, Isabel de Moscoso), and other relatives who belonged to the houses of the Count of Gandía (Borjas) and the Counts of Casarrubios (Chacón).[33] In addition, Lerma appointed Pedro Franqueza, one of his closest allies, to the important office of the secretary of the queen, whose responsibilities were similar to those exercised by the secretary of the king's chamber.[34]

Lerma also used palace offices both in the king's and the queen's households, especially those of the *gentilhombres de la cámara* and *damas de honor*, to gain the support of the most powerful grandees who, because of changes in the royal etiquette, were now desperately seeking palace offices. A notable example is the Count of Niebla, Juan Pérez de Guzmán, heir of the house of Medina Sidonia, who was appointed Lord High Huntsman and a gentleman of the chamber at the king's household and who had married Lerma's daughter, Juana de Sandoval. Another is the 6th Duke of Infantado, Juan Hurtado de Mendoza, who in turn was appointed a gentleman of the king's chamber and a counselor of state, on 25 August 1603, the day when the Duke of Infantado and Lerma agreed to the marriage of Lerma's son, Diego Gómez de Sandoval, to Luisa de Mendoza, the Infantado's heiress.[35] Moreover, at least five other members of the Mendoza kin network were appointed as ladies-in-waiting in Queen Margaret's household.[36]

[30] See BL, Add. 28422, Lerma to Borja, 26 Nov. 1599, fol. 183.

[31] *Ibid.*, Lerma to Borja, 22 Mar. 1603, fol. 61, where Lerma informed his uncle that Philip III had given his permission to appoint the Countess of Lemos *camarera mayor* of the queen given the poor health of the Duchess of Lerma.

[32] Biblioteca Nazionale Centrale, Florence, Magl. CI. XXV, cod. 796, Orazio della Rena, "Relazione segreta" (1605), fol. 47. I thank Dr. Edward L. Goldberg, director of the Medici Archive Project, who provided me with a transcription of Orazio della Rena's *Relazione*.

[33] AGPR Sec. His., *leg.* 3, "Damas de la Reina Nuestra Señora."

[34] AGPR Ex. Per., 521/26.

[35] AGPR Sec. His., *leg.* 3, "Gentilhombres de la Cámara de Felipe III." It was not a secret that these offices were purely and simply the reward for this marriage; see Cabrera de Córdoba, *Relaciones*, pp. 184–5.

[36] Juana de Mendoza, Beatriz de Mendoza, Ana de Mendoza, Felipa de Mendoza, and another Juana de Mendoza, married to the Marquis of Flores Davila: see AGPR Sec. His., *leg.* 3, "Damas de la Reina."

In addition to exercising control over the appointments to palace offices, Lerma actively promoted Philip III's invisibility (see Chapter 4). In fact, Lerma's habit of retiring with the king to countryside palaces caught the attention of his contemporaries because it made him as invisible and inaccessible as Philip III himself.[37] Such behavior was contrary to all advice and his contemporaries' expectations. The political literature of the period often justifies the existence of royal favorites by reference to the king's invisibility and inaccessibility. If the king's subjects could not speak with or even see the king himself, then it was necessary to have a favorite who could act as the king's intermediary and transmit the subjects' concerns to the ruler. Contemporaries thus claimed that one of the favorite's obligations was to be accessible to the king's subjects and counselors and to listen to their demands and advice.[38] Lerma, however, clearly ignored such advice and gave varied reasons to justify his behavior. In public he attributed his withdrawal from public view to bouts of melancholia and ill-health,[39] yet in correspondence with his relatives and allies Lerma defended his behavior by adopting arguments that Spanish monarchs had used to defend their own tendency to retire from public view: namely, that spending time in public audiences and ceremonies took valuable time away from his duties as the king's chief minister.[40] Regardless of Lerma's justification for withdrawing, he became as invisible as the king to many of his contemporaries, who came to believe that it was even more difficult to see and talk with him than with the king himself.[41]

As in Philip's case, Lerma's increasing privacy promoted a compelling public image of the favorite. The king's use of symbols and effigies to magnify his image as an almighty ruler had followed a practice already evident under Charles V and Philip II and represented a continuity in attempts to create a strong image of the king. But the similar transformation of the image of the royal favorite during the reign of Philip III was a complete novelty. The foundation of such a process was Lerma's perceived intimacy with the king, as if by being in close contact with Philip he automatically was infused with some of the prerogatives and qualities of kings. Indeed, for Lerma, as for the members of the privy chamber in England studied by

---

[37] See, for example, Sir Charles Cornwallis, the English ambassador in Spain, to the Earl of Salisbury, June 1606, in Ralph Winwood, *Memorials of Affairs of State in the Reigns of Queen Elizabeth and James I*, 3 vols. (London, 1725), vol. II, p. 231.

[38] This is an idea constantly repeated by authors on royal favorites during the reign of Philip III, regarding their overall position on the legality and convenience of having favorites.

[39] For Lerma's bouts of melancholia see Cabrera de Córdoba, *Relaciones*, pp. 161, 215–16, 287, 299, 332–3, 475, 478, 489; Lope Félix de Vega Carpio, *Epistolario de Lope de Vega Carpio*, ed. Agustín González de Amezúa, 4 vols. (Madrid, 1941–3), vol. III, pp. 94, 96–7, 120; Francisco de Quevedo y Villegas, *Epistolario completo de don Francisco de Quevedo*, ed. Luis Astrana Marín (Madrid, 1946), p. 36.

[40] See BL, Add. 28422, Lerma to Juan de Borja, 10 Jan. 1599, fol. 27; and BL, Add. 28424, Lerma to Borja, 15 Sept. 1601, fols. 137r–v.

[41] Pinheiro da Veiga, *Fastiginia*, p. 35, and Rubens to Jacques Dupuy, Antwerp, 22 Oct. 1626, in Peter Paul Rubens, *Letters of Peter Paul Rubens*, ed. Ruth Saunders Magurn (Cambridge, Mass., 1971), pp. 148–9.

David Starkey, intimacy with the king "served as a symbol of the high place that [he] held in [the king's] confidence, [and this] confidentiality was in turn what we could call the rational basis of [his] role as royal alter ego."[42]

But if for the monarch the use of grand images, symbols, and allegories to justify power and position seemed a natural practice, the situation was rather more complex for the favorite. As Pérez had advised Lerma in his letter of 1594, early modern authors repeatedly reminded courtiers that they had to honor the monarch's right to be portrayed as the most powerful member of the community. According to widespread belief, favorites who promoted themselves in public would cause not only their own fall from favor but also a political crisis by diminishing the figure and power of the king. "Let him [the courtier or the favorite] be as the Moon and attribute all brightness of his glory to the Sun [the king]," wrote Justus Lipsius.[43] The author of "Discurso de las Privanzas" further asserted:

There is only one sun in the sky, but with the moon it shares its cares and the world. The sun gives the moon its rays and light, and the same happens with the stars. . . . The comparison with the sun and the moon is a very good example, and that is how it should be with the king and the favorite. The moon places itself behind the sun . . . and, therefore, the favorite has to stand behind the king to avoid competing with the king's light.[44]

Favorites during the sixteenth century seem to have followed such advice. Admittedly, certain favorites and royal secretaries were praised as worthy and powerful men who acted as patrons of the arts; nevertheless, they refrained from public display of their special status. Their positions at the court could have been as elevated as Lerma's, but the monarch never explicitly acknowledged their status. All of this changed during the reign of Philip III as a result of Lerma's need to project to the public the image of a powerful and commanding individual.

The king's public recognition immediately transformed Lerma's status at court and opened the door for his public glorification by artists and writers searching for his patronage. It is important, however, to avoid believing that this public celebration of Lerma resulted solely from the artists' need for patronage from the all-powerful favorite. Lerma himself deliberately promoted his public glorification, which he viewed as a *sine qua non* for conserving and increasing his power and influence. According to the royal chronicler Gil González Dávila, Lerma inaugurated "a new style of grandeur" by employing art, pomp, and ceremonies to parade his power in a manner never seen before.[45] In addition, he also inaugurated a historical trend in Europe that resulted in the favorite's transformation into a prime cultural and artistic patron. He became the most important artistic patron of his times, surpassing all others at the Spanish court, including the king himself.

---

[42] Starkey, "Representation," p. 211.   [43] Lipsius, *Los seis libros*, bk. 3, chap. 11, p. 96.
[44] Quevedo y Villegas, *Obras*, vol. II, pp. 1393–4.   [45] González Dávila, *Historia de la vida*, p. 65.

Following the example set by Philip II, Lerma collected numerous paintings, approximately 1,500 between 1599 and 1611, making his collection one of the greatest ever assembled and Lerma the first "non-royal mega-collector" of early modern times.[46] He also undertook an immense program of palace building. Not only did he commission the restoration and rebuilding of what later became the royal palace in Valladolid and his own palace in Madrid (see Chapter 4) but he also authorized the reconstruction of the town of Lerma, the center of his estate, a project considered one of the most important architectural initiatives in seventeenth-century Spain, one which he hoped would provide a splendid architectural facade for his newly acquired political status.[47] Lerma's activities were by no means limited to art and architecture; he also became an important patron of letters, an activity he initiated while serving as Viceroy of Valencia.[48] He commissioned one of the most important history books published during the seventeenth century, the *Historia de la vida y hechos del emperador Carlos V* by his distant relative Fray Prudencio de Sandoval,[49] and he became the most important patron of the theater during the first decades of the seventeenth century.[50]

In early seventeenth-century Spain, a society dominated by concepts of honor and the importance of one's ancestors, Lerma had to aggrandize his position, if not his inner virtues, by embellishing the past deeds of his ancestors and presenting himself as the deserving heir of his glorious relatives. Given the mediocre reputation of the Sandovals during the late sixteenth century, this was not an easy task, and Lerma had to find ways to recreate the past of his family. Here history, poetry, symbols, and images served legend, and legend politics. "Several writers have dedicated to you books of history," the historian Luis Cabrera de Córdoba wrote in dedicating his book, published in 1611, *De historia, para entenderla y escribirla*, to Lerma, and "I [dedicate to you] the source from which all these stories come. [History] is used to write about the antiquity and nobility of your household, the deeds of your ancestors, and the advancements of Your Excellency, in whom today

---

[46] On Lerma as painters' patron and picture collector see Schroth, "The Private Collection."
[47] See Cervera Vera, *El conjunto palacial*; and José Miguel Muñoz Jiménez, "Fray Alberto de la Madre de Dios y la arquitectura cortesana: urbanismo en la villa de Lerma," *Goya*, 211–12 (1989), pp. 52–9.
[48] On Lerma's activities as patron of letters in Valencia see Gaspar de Mercader, *El prado de Valencia* [1600], ed. H. Merimée (Toulouse, 1907); in his work Mercader depicts the kingdom of Valencia as a pastoral paradise ruled by the Shepherd of Denia (Lerma), who governed the kingdom promoting poetry and love and therefore harmony and stability. On Lerma's unimpressive book collection see ADL, *leg.* 52/*exp.* 15, Inventario de los libros del Duque de Lerma, 1611.
[49] Prudencio de Sandoval, *Historia de la vida y hechos del emperador Carlos V* [1604–6], ed. Carlos Seco Serrano, 3 vols. (Madrid, 1955); on Lerma's commission see "Introduction," pp. xvii–xxviii. On Lerma as patron of musicians see Douglas Kirk, "Instrumental music in Lerma, c. 1608," *Early Music*, 23 (1995), pp. 393–408.
[50] See N. D. Shergold, *A History of the Spanish Stage* (Oxford, 1967), chap. 9; Michael D. McGaha's introduction to his edition of Félix Lope de Vega Carpio, *Fábula de Perseo o la Bella Andrómeda* (Kassel, 1985); and Teresa Ferrer Valls, *La práctica escénica cortesana: de la época del emperador a la de Felipe III* (London, 1991), pp. 105–42.

is alive their glory and the rise of their fortune."[51] In addition to history, writers employed genealogy to demonstrate the noble origins of the Sandovals. In 1600, for example, in his *Chrónica del ínclito emperador de España, Don Alonso VII*, Fray Prudencio de Sandoval claimed that the Sandovals descended from royal blood, a claim also made by Salazar de Mendoza in his genealogy of the Duke of Lerma.[52] Neither of the two authors, however, went as far as Diego Matute de Peñafiel, who in his *Prosapia de Christo* (1614), also dedicated to Lerma, contended that Lerma's ancestors included such historical figures as Adam and Eve, Methuselah, Noah, Hercules, and Aeneas, the last also considered an ancestor of the Habsburgs.[53]

Prudencio de Sandoval and others glorified not only the royal origins of the Sandovals but also their heroic deeds. The family was publicly depicted as the rock on which the foundations of the Spanish monarchy could stand, a claim substantiated by their activities during the reconquest of Spain from the Moors and their continued support of the Spanish monarchs against all internal and external enemies. Lerma well understood that a past, especially a glorious past, should be celebrated not only in writing but also in painting. These were the images that would consolidate the brilliant present of the Sandovals under the leadership of Lerma. To this purpose Lerma commissioned the Italian artists Vicente and Bartolomé Carducho to execute numerous tapestries and pictures glorifying his family's deeds and prominently displayed these works in his palaces and many public ceremonies.[54] Lerma's preoccupation with the canonization of the Sandovals' past also explains his commission of Prudencio de Sandoval's history of the reign of Charles V – a period when the Sandovals had been prominent actors at court, vigorous in their defense of Charles's rights as the legal heir of the Catholic Monarchs' legacy and staunch in defense of the king against the *comuneros*.

But for Lerma it was not good enough to idolize the Sandovals if he himself was not included. Although he did not have a bellicose history to offer, he designed depictions of his life and career as a victorious saga of danger and persecution at the

---

[51] Luis Cabrera de Córdoba, *De historia, para entenderla y escribirla* [1611], ed. S. Montero Díaz (Madrid, 1948), p. 4.

[52] Prudencio de Sandoval, *Chrónica del ínclito emperador de España, don Alonso VII* (Madrid, 1600), pp. 187–252; BNM, Mss 3277, Salazar de Mendoza, "Crónica de la casa de Sandoval en 22 elogios, 1600."

[53] Matute Peñafiel, "Discurso y disgresión del capítulo segundo de la segunda edad del mundo," included in Diego Matute Peñafiel, *Prosapia de Cristo* (Baeza, 1614); on this work see Agustín González de Amezúa y Mayo, "Cómo se hacía un libro en nuestro siglo de oro," in his *Opúsculos histórico-literarios*, vol. I (Madrid, 1951), pp. 343–4.

[54] Of all these paintings and tapestries only two survived, *The Siege of Antequera* and *Victory against the Count of Urgel*, both by Vicente Carducho. See Diego Angulo Iñiguez and Alfonso E. Pérez Sánchez, *Historia de la pintura española* (Madrid, 1969), pp. 178–9; and Schroth, "The Private Collection," p. 201. These paintings and tapestries were displayed by Lerma during public ceremonies. See "Relación de lo sucedido en la ciudad de Valladolid" (1605), published as an appendix in Pinheiro da Veiga, *Fastiginia*, pp. 25–6; and José M. Florit, "Inventario de los cuadros y otros objetos de arte de la quinta real llamada 'La Ribera' en Valladolid," *Boletín de la Sociedad Española de Excursiones*, 14 (1906), p. 156.

hands of Philip II's favorites who had been resentful of his increasing closeness to Prince Philip. His constancy under such assaults had demonstrated his will and virtue, making him a deserving candidate for the king's favor. After all, Lerma's contemporaries believed – as the tribulations of Job and Jesus Christ proved – that the ability to master oppression and persecution with constancy and stoicism indicated a person of solid principles. It was then requisite to compare Lerma with the heroes of antiquity, a task undertaken by poets, such as Gaspar Mercader, Luis de Góngora, and Francisco López Zárate, who portrayed Lerma in combat against heinous personifications of Envy trying to frustrate his predestined ascent to power.[55]

Such glorifications of Lerma and the Sandovals served to confirm that Lerma's position at Philip III's court resulted from his inner virtues, not from the action of unpredictable Fortune. Baltasar Alamos de Barrientos, in a work dedicated to Lerma entitled *Aforismos al Tácito español*, succinctly expressed this view:

Your Excellency comes from a house that descends from kings. Your ancestors were illustrious with many public distinctions, their profession being that of [affairs of] state, an art of kings and great persons who belong to a second place after kings. All these qualities are passed to you through their blood. The first and supreme place that the king has given Your Excellency in the ruling of his kingdoms, trusting in you with so much reason, is the result of the fact that you inherited your ancestors' virtues, for they were real and truly certain.[56]

These virtues empowered Lerma to assume his position as Philip's assistant, and numerous writers portrayed him in this role, sometimes with quite extraordinary language. This trend is exemplified by Lope de Vega's *auto sacramental*, a one-act religious play entitled *Bodas entre el alma y el amor divino*, written in celebration of the wedding between King Philip III and Queen Margaret.[57] The play depicts a "sacred" wedding between Divine Love (a portrait of Christ) identified as King Filipo [III] or King Love of Spain and his Queen-Soul named Margaret from Austria, who meets her groom in the city of Divine Love, Jerusalem-Valencia. Another important *dramatis persona* is John the Baptist, who as King Filipo's *aposentador mayor* is placed in charge of announcing the holy wedding and receiving Queen Margaret when she lands in Jerusalem-Valencia. The Queen refers to him as "divine evangelist / marquis, duke, groom of the stole / of the king my husband . . . divine priest."[58] In Spain the use of John the Baptist to symbolize a royal favorite

---

[55] The idealization of Lerma's past started with Mercader's *El prado de Valencia*, pp. 13–14, and reached its apex with one of the greatest poets of the Spanish Golden Age, Luis de Góngora, who in 1617 wrote the "Panegírico al duque de Lerma"; on Lerma's feuds during the reign of Philip II see verses 105–208. See also Francisco López de Zárate, *Varias poesías* (Madrid, 1619), fols. 37r–v.

[56] Alamos de Barrientos, *Aforismos*, vol. I, p. 28.

[57] I used the version of *Bodas entre el alma y el amor divino* included by Lope de Vega in his novel *El peregrino en su patria*, originally published in 1604; see Félix Lope de Vega Carpio, *El peregrino en su patria*, ed. Juan Bautista Avalle-Arce (Madrid, 1973), pp. 193–234.

[58] *Ibid.*, p. 229; in April 1599 Lerma was still Marquis of Denia and *sumiller de corps* of the king. Lerma was in charge of receiving Queen Margaret when she arrived on the coast of Valencia.

carried special meaning. Because he represented virtue and wisdom, a reference to him suggested that the favorite could serve as an elder counselor to a younger king/Jesus, a role Lerma was to occupy with Philip III. Furthermore, Vega's portrayal of John the Baptist symbolized the royal favorite's sacred position. In the play, John the Baptist declares his vital role in a response to Jerusalem's inquiry ("Are you, divine *aposentador*, the king announced by the Holy Scriptures?"):

I am His Angel, as He calls me in the book of your law, the shadow of His Sun. Although the shadow comes after the light, I am the shadow that announces that only He is the light and God. It is more important to name Him who comes after me. The King is God, I am a man, and I come here to lodge Him in you (pp. 226–7).

Lerma took other initiatives to present himself as a mighty courtier. Painted by none other than Peter Paul Rubens, he became the first non-royal person in all Europe outside of Italy portrayed on horseback. By contrast, Philip III was not memorialized in this mode until after his death. In Rubens's painting, *Retrato equestre de Lerma* (*The Duke of Lerma on horseback*) (Plate 5), which Lerma commissioned in 1603, he appears as a victorious warrior adorned with the symbols of his office of the general of the Spanish Cavalry, "a dignity that the [Spanish] kings had reserved for themselves until then,"[59] with battle scenes in the background in reference to the Sandovals' glorious past.[60] As Frances Huemer has noted, Lerma's portrait "inaugurate[d] the great sequence of equestrian portraits of the seventeenth century," but none of the other portraits by Rubens "achieved to the same degree the ceremonial dignity or the statuesque grandeur of the Lerma portrait" in which Rubens represented the royal favorite as a mirror image of the king himself.[61] The representation of Lerma as a royal figure is also evident in other portraits, such as the one by Pantoja de la Cruz painted in 1602 and modeled after one of Titian's portraits of Philip II. In 1606 Pantoja went on to paint a new portrait of Philip III modeled after Titian's Philip II. The portraits of Lerma and Philip III are disconcertingly similar (Plates. 6 and 7).[62]

Lerma's public aggrandizement was crowned by his incorporation into the monarchical ritual. As the king's sole favorite, he was depicted as "the second Sun

---

[59] BNM, Mss 2751, "Historia de Johann Kevenhüller, conde de Franquenburg," 1006. On Lerma's views on this office see BL, Add. 28425, Lerma to Juan de Borja, 22 Mar. 1603, fol. 61v; and Juan de Borja's answer declaring that the office of general of the Spanish Cavalry was the most important office the king could award to Lerma, 26 Mar. 1603, fol. 64.

[60] Sarah Schroth, "The Duke of Lerma and the Art at the Court of Philip III," paper presented at the meeting of the Society for Spanish and Portuguese Historical Studies, St. Louis, 1987, p. 3.

[61] Frances Huemer, *Corpus Rubenianum Ludwig Burchard. Part XIX: Portraits* (London, 1977), vol. I, pp. 21, 25, 134. Huemer asserts (p. 21) that before painting Lerma on horseback, Rubens painted an equestrian portrait of Philip III, now lost. See also John F. Moffitt, "Rubens's *Duke of Lerma, Equestrian* amongst 'Imperial Horsemen,'" *Artibus et Historiae*, 15 (1994), p. 101, who believes that "the idea lying behind the [portrait] ... must have been personally formulated by Lerma."

[62] See Schroth, "The Duke of Lerma," p. 1, who writes that in the two portraits "the figures are interchangeable." Pantoja had already painted Philip III following this model in the last years of Philip II's reign.

5   Peter Paul Rubens, *The Duke of Lerma on Horseback*. In this, the first portrait of a non-royal individual on horseback in Europe, Lerma appears as a victorious warrior adorned with the symbols of his office of General of the Spanish Cavalry with battle scenes in the background in reference to his family's glorious past.

6 and 7   Portraits of Philip III and Lerma by Juan Pantoja de la Cruz. The purpose
of these portraits was to depict the royal favorite as a twin image of the king.

who enlightens Spain."[63] He became the only one who could sit next to the king under the royal canopy, the only one who could represent the king in public ceremonies. Lerma also became the only one whom the king treated in public as his close companion, a role illustrated by one of the *relaciones* describing the kingdom's oath to Prince Philip as its future monarch in 1608: "Toward the Duke of Lerma [Philip III's behavior was different than toward the rest]; in seeing that the duke was approaching, [the king] got up, stepped forward and lovingly (*amorosamente*) embraced Lerma."[64]

"Imitation," according to Erasmus, "aims at similarity ... emulation, at victory."[65] This is exactly what Lerma hoped to achieve through actions that glorified his role as Philip III's favorite. For many years such images helped Lerma to increase his prestige and even to protect him against criticism. But a too-perfect imitation of the monarch could make Lerma vulnerable to the charge that he considered himself equal to his master.[66] After all, as E. H. Gombrich has written, "what people experience as likeness throws light on their perceptual categories."[67] Even if one does not know how Lerma's contemporaries interpreted the similar portraits of Lerma and Philip III by Pantoja de la Cruz or Rubens's portrait of Lerma, one does know that they read many period images in ways unintended by their designers. This was the case, for example, with two gigantic statues designed by Pompeo Leoni, one representing Philip III and the other Philip II, which were presented at the royal entry of Queen Margaret into Madrid in October 1599. As noted in Chapter 4, in Spain dynastic continuity was represented by depicting two monarchs, father and son, supporting a globe on their shoulders.[68] Despite this tradition many of Lerma's contemporaries – Spaniards and foreigners alike – interpreted the two statues in Madrid not as representations of Philip III and Philip II, but as images of Philip III and the Duke of Lerma, the king and his *valido*, who

---

[63] Francisco Márquez Torres, *Discursos consolatorios al excmo. sr. don Cristóbal de Sandoval y Rojas, duque de Uceda, en la temprana muerte del señor don Bernardo de Sandoval y Rojas, primer marqués de Belmonte, su caro hijo* (Madrid, 1616), fol. 83v.

[64] "Relación verdadera en que contiene todas las ceremonias y demás actos que pasaron en la jura que se hizo al Serenísimo Príncipe nuestro señor don Phelipe quarto, en el monasterio de san Gerónimo," celebrated in Toledo in 1608, in José Simón Díaz, *Relaciones de actos públicos celebrados en Madrid (1541–1650)* (Madrid, 1982), p. 55.

[65] Michael C. Schoenfeldt, *Prayer and Power. George Herbert and Renaissance Courtship* (Chicago, 1991), p. 43.   [66] This idea also in *ibid.*, pp. 43–5.

[67] E. H. Gombrich, "The Mask and the Face: The Perception of Physiognomic Likeness in Life and in Art," in his, *The Image and the Eye. Further Studies in the Psychology of Pictorial Representation* (Oxford, 1982), p. 109.

[68] There are many examples of this tradition. For Charles V and Philip II sharing the burden of the globe see Strong, *Art and Power*, pp. 82ff; on the use of this motif by Leone Leoni, brother of Pompeo Leoni, on coins commemorating the passing of the crown from Charles V (Atlas) to his son Philip II (Hercules) see Osten Sachen, *San Lorenzo el Real*, pp. 109–10; and on Queen Margaret's entries into various Italian cities with references to Philip II and Philip III sharing the burden of ruling the monarchy see Banner Mitchell, *The Majesty of the State. Triumphal Progresses of Foreign Sovereigns in Renaissance Italy (1494–1600)* (Florence, 1986), pp. 189–208.

from September 1598 also held administrative and governmental responsibilities that ultimately transformed him into Philip's chief minister.[69]

[69] See, for example, Eloy Benito Ruano, "Recepción madrileña de la reina Margarita de Austria," *Anales del Instituto Madrileño*, 1 (1966), pp. 91–2, and Grimston's English edition of Louis de Mayerne, *The General Histoire of Spaine* (1583), published in 1612. Grimston, who added information from 1583 to 1610, wrote the following words regarding these two statues: "that the Empire was divided between Jupiter and Caesar; and they found in strange characters and an unknown hand at the foot of Jupiter's image, these words: This is the Duke of Lerma," p. 1295.

6

The king's chief minister

The promotion of an expanded monarchy and of an aggrandized image for the king's *valido*, both novel policies, were just two among many initiatives the new rulers undertook. As stated in Chapter 2, even while Philip was still a prince, Lerma had sought his favor in the hope of becoming more than a palace favorite, a minion; he aspired to be the king's *privado* and minister. His transformation into the royal *valido* forced him to confront two important issues: how to expand the *valido*'s role in the management of public affairs and how to provide the theoretical justification for such expansion. In both cases Lerma's *privanza* appeared as an instance of practical and theoretical creativity in the promotion of new forms of government and ingenious theoretical redefinition of the royal favorite and his political capacity.

At the beginning of the reign, the new rulers attempted to convey the impression that the presence of Lerma as the king's favorite would not alter the institutional structure of the monarchy or Philip's wish to restore traditional forms of government (see Chapter 3). However, it soon became clear that Lerma's political role in the monarchy had no precedents in any other period. Indeed, from the outset of the reign, Lerma became Philip III's unique favorite, the only minister who enjoyed Philip's unequivocal confidence. This situation was noted by Camillo Caetani, the papal nuncio in Madrid, in a report written on 30 September 1598: "All public matters and papers are handled by the Duke of Lerma, and no one is able to mention the name of another *privado* in history with so much power."[1] Long after the first weeks of the new regime, Lerma's contemporaries continued to see him as the preeminent player in politics and government, unchallenged at least until the 1610s when a series of crises provoked the rise of other ministers and favorites who shared Philip III's trust with Lerma.

Like other favorites before him, Lerma had recourse to more than one route to participation in the decision-making process. Institutionally, as counselor of state, Lerma held unquestionable rights to advise the king on a regular basis. The records of the Council of State indicate that he regularly attended its meetings, especially when the council discussed matters he and Philip III considered particularly

---

[1] Cf. Vargas Hidalgo, "Documentos inéditos," p. 435.

important, such as Spain's relationship with other monarchies and internal problems that could affect the safety of the monarchy.[2] But Lerma, like later seventeenth-century favorites/prime ministers – Richelieu and Olivares, among them – never considered his participation in the Council of State as his highest priority. Membership in the most prestigious council gave Lerma institutional status, but not much more. He was just one more counselor without special privilege and constrained, like all the others, to marshal support for the royal policies that he favored. As a result, Lerma, like Philip II's favorites, asserted his political influence from outside the institutional structure, by enhancing his role as the king's *valido* and becoming *de facto* prime minister.

The "office of *privado*," according to the author of a pamphlet entitled "Discurso de las privanzas," could help its holder "to control all state matters because the favorite is the master of the king's will," but the *privado*'s position could mean "nothing at all, if he lets the councils, judges, and other ministers have all authority."[3] To become "master of all state matters," Lerma had to transcend the institutional mechanisms and structures that regulated the decision-making process. To succeed, he needed to create a position in the monarchical machinery that could not be challenged by other royal officials. In practical terms, he needed to control the consultation process and become the sole intermediary between Philip III and all governmental institutions.

The institutional and political challenges Lerma had to confront to become Philip's sole intermediary are clearly set forth in a memorandum one Cristóbal de Castro sent to Lerma early in 1599. In it the author analyzed the various styles used by previous royal ministers to confer with the king and described the political implications of each. In one, the councils' presidents met with the king in person (*consulta a boca*), who conferred with each and responded in person. In another, royal secretaries rather than council presidents conferred with the king in the same manner. In yet another alternative, "the presidents of the councils consulted with the king through written *consultas*; they passed their reports to the secretaries, who in turn sent them to the king, who then responded in writing." The danger of these practices was clear to Castro. By conferring with the king in person the councils' presidents "sometimes tyrannized all matters, even the king's will, and were thus able to overpower royal favorites, as had happened with the Prince of Eboli." To avoid this fate, Castro advised Lerma to make sure that Philip III ordered all councils to direct their reports to Lerma so that he alone would discuss them in

---

[2] Historians have traditionally affirmed that Lerma did not participate in the meetings of the Council of State, a manifestation, they argued, of Lerma's complete lack of interest in politics, but more serious studies of the documentation of the council have proved them wrong. On Lerma's alleged lack of interest in politics see Williams, "Philip III"; on Lerma's participation in the meetings of the Council of State see Bernardo José García García, *La pax hispánica. Política exterior del duque de Lerma* (Leuven, 1996).   [3] Quevedo y Villegas, *Obras*, vol. II, pp. 1395–6.

person with the king.[4] Juan de Borja similarly advised Lerma that all consultations with the king must be "written and not spoken." Lerma maintained that it was Philip himself who desired "that all royal ministers consult with him in writing so that he has time to respond and decide what he should do."[5]

Although it is difficult to know whether the king followed his own opinions or Lerma's preferences, Philip III indeed ordered his councils to send "all *consultas*" in writing, a measure he justified by reference to his desire to prevent any discussion of state affairs without his knowledge. Philip's order officially established a practice that had already been in operation since his father's reign; written *consultas* now became the only form of communication between the king, the councils, and other ministers, including Lerma's clients and allies.[6] The only difference between the two reigns, a very important one, was the designation of the royal favorite as the receiver of all documents produced by the royal institutions and the only member of the royal court who was able to consult in person with the king. The councils, special committees, and individual ministers who debated state affairs prepared written reports and sent them immediately to Lerma, who then read them, wrote his own opinions in the margins, and forwarded them to Philip III before he and the king met to discuss the contents of these *consultas*.[7] Lerma's creatures and supporters also knew that the favorite should be immediately informed of all political initiatives before they were sent to the king. In 1617, Alvaro de Quiñones and Lorenzo Ramírez de Prado, for example, both *procuradores* in the *Cortes* of Castile, sent a message to Lerma informing him of a proposal they had prepared for presentation in the plenary meeting of the *Cortes* defending the rights of the king in financial matters and asked Lerma "to revise it and see if it is good for the royal service" with the understanding that Lerma's orders would be followed.[8]

Although the king personally, with Lerma usually at his side, replied to and

[4] BNM, Mss 18725, Cristóbal de Castro, "Memorial que dieron al duque de Lerma," fols. 5v–6r. There are many copies of this memorandum, many of them anonymous; one of these copies, housed in the Instituto Valencia de Don Juan, *caja* 42, *envío* 29, is attributed to Pedro Franqueza, secretary of state and Lerma's favorite.

[5] BL, Add. 28422, Borja to Lerma, 8 Dec. 1598, fols. 19v, 21v; and Lerma to Borja, 12 Dec. 1598, fol. 19v.

[6] AHN CS, *leg.* 4415, *exp.* 137, Nov. 1598; this is the copy of the royal order sent to the Chamber of Castile.

[7] Detailed information about the functioning of the government during Philip III is in BNM, Mss 6713, "Apuntamientos por don Pedro [Rodrigo] Calderón, marqués de Siete Iglesias, sobre los cargos de las visitas," fols. 223r–v; and BNM, Mss 2229, "Interrogatorio por parte de don Rodrigo Calderón," fol. 16r. For an example of this style of government see Lerma's *billete* (note) to the secretary of state, Andrés de Prada, in which the favorite informs him that "the king has read the dispatches [from the Council of State] and he agrees with them and with the comments I have added in the margins," AGS Est., *leg.* 191/n.p., Lerma to Antonio de Prada, 29 July 1608. See also AGS Est., *leg.* 201/n.p., Blasco de Aragón to Pedro Franqueza, 15 May 1605; *ibid., leg.* 204/n.p., Medina Sidonia to Andrés de Prada, 24 Feb. 1606.

[8] AGS PT, *caja* 89, fol. 226, letter of Alvaro de Quiñones and Lorenzo Ramírez de Prado to Lerma, 21 Sep. 1617.

signed all responses to *consultas* from the councils and reviewed matters that required further debate, Lerma was permitted to sign the king's orders – occasionally adding his own opinions – when the reports came from *juntas*, Lerma's allies and clients, and the secretaries of the councils. Philip III's response, for example, to a report prepared by a *junta* charged with drafting proposals to reform the Council of Portugal begins with the following words: "The Duke of Lerma has read this report to me, and I will respond to each recommendation separately," yet Philip III's answers were signed by the favorite.[9] Lerma also maintained a continuous correspondence with several royal ministers, who gave him a deeper, although biased, knowledge of the ways various councils approached state affairs. Such informal correspondence gave Lerma the opportunity to transmit his and the king's thoughts more openly to his friends and allies.[10]

But Lerma's role in the day-to-day administration of the monarchy went well beyond the above activities. Until Philip III's reign royal institutions had received their orders through written orders (*billetes*) signed by the monarch. This practice changed, however, during Lerma's *privanza*. Now all debates in royal institutions began only upon the receipt of *billetes* signed by Lerma transmitting Philip III's orders. The phrasing of these *billetes* indicates Lerma's intention of keeping intact, at least in public, the principle of the king's control; all of them began with the following words: "The king orders." Invariably, the councils replied: "Complying with what the king has ordered through the Duke of Lerma, we have discussed the following matters."[11] Until 1612, this system worked informally. Every council implicitly understood that the king transmitted his orders through the Duke of Lerma as is evident from a *consulta* sent by the Council of State dated 10 October 1611: "With the Council of Portugal the king observes the same system as with the rest: to communicate his orders through *billetes* signed by the Duke of Lerma."[12] In October 1612, however, Philip III made the procedure official in an order sent to the Council of State and most likely to others as well:

Since I have known the Duke of Lerma, I have always seen him serving the king my lord and father [Philip II] and me with much contentment from both. Every day I am more satisfied with how he handles all matters I ask of him, and how well-served I feel. Given this and how much he has helped me sustain the weight of state affairs, I order that you obey the duke in all matters. All members of the council are obliged to tell him all he wants to know, and

[9] AGS Est., *leg.* 435/fol. 22, report of a committee formed by Juan de Borja, Fray Gaspar de Córdoba, the Count of Vilanova, and Pedro Franqueza on the reform of the Council of Portugal, 3 May 1602.

[10] See, for example, BL, Add. 28422, Lerma to Borja, 2 Aug. 1599, fol. 93; and BL, Add. 28423, Lerma to Borja, 28 Aug. 1600, fols. 188v–189.

[11] There are thousands of Lerma's *billetes* among the papers produced by the councils and other royal institutions. The last *billete* with these characteristics I have found was written on 30 Sept. 1618, just a few days before Lerma's dismissal from power on 4 Oct. 1618. For this *billete*, see AGS Est., *leg.* 437/fol. 81.   [12] AGS Est., *leg.* 2641/n.p., *consulta* of the Council of State, 10 Oct. 1611.

although this system began from the moment I inherited these kingdoms, I have decided explicitly to tell and order you now.[13]

As the king's favorite and *de facto* prime minister, Lerma also communicated directly with all Spanish ambassadors, viceroys, and even with the Archdukes Albert and Clara Isabel Eugenia, rulers of the Low Countries.[14] He also met with foreign ambassadors and devoted considerable time to writing and signing papers concerning matters of foreign policy.[15]

It is important to note that the forms of government Philip III and Lerma adopted were not entirely different from those found during the last years of the Philip II's reign. Moura and his colleagues at the *Junta de Gobierno* had also controlled and debated most documents and reports sent to Philip II by his ministers, and Moura himself had signed *billetes* in which he ordered royal institutions to implement the king's orders, and which were very similar to those signed by Lerma. In fact, it may well be that Moura's practice inspired Lerma's.[16] But enormous differences between the two reigns also emerged. Philip II, for example, never publicly recognized the role played by the *Junta de Gobierno* in the political and institutional structure of the monarchy and never publicly acknowledged to his ministers that Moura acted as his intermediary and transmitter of his orders. Moreover, the *junta* itself was composed of several favorites. Even if Moura enjoyed more influence with the king than the rest, no one ever claimed that Philip II considered him his "prime minister" and chief adviser. Even more importantly, the justifications of Moura's role and the creation of the special *juntas* were not political or institutional, but merely circumstantial, the sort of provisional arrangements due, for example, to Philip II's bad health. With one or two exceptions, no one ever accused Philip II of delegating his power and sovereignty to one of his subjects.

The situation altered radically during the reign of Philip III, and so did the consequent political debate. This ideological debate, provoked by Philip III's decision to position Lerma as *de facto* prime minister, did not become public until the 1610s, but Lerma and his allies were aware that the king's decision would be controversial. Explicit criticism, although still kept from public ears, appears in Fray Jerónimo de Sepúlveda's journal which chronicles the changes taking place at court. In one entry, for example, Sepúlveda wrote that Lerma not only "has the support of the king, but he is the king."[17]

---

[13] AGS Est., *leg.* 4126/fol. 59: "Copia de lo que Su Majd. ordenó al Consejo de Estado por Octubre 1612 tocante al duque de Lerma." A copy of this document is in Tomás y Valiente, *Los validos*, p. 157. For the explanation of why the king decided to send this decree at this time see below, chap. 11.

[14] See, for example, Juan de Silva, *Cartas*; *Documentos relativos al archiduque Alberto de Austria, Codoin*, 42–3 (Madrid, 1863); and Antonio Rodríguez Villa, ed., *Correspondencia de la infanta archiduquesa, doña Isabel Clara Eugenia de Austria, con el duque de Lerma y otros personajes* (Madrid, 1906).

[15] See AGS Est., *leg.* 634/fol. 34: Lerma to Pedro Franqueza, 13 Oct. 1604, where Lerma explains that he had spent the whole day writing to the archdukes and to various ambassadors and viceroys.

[16] See above, chap. 2.   [17] Sepúlveda, *Historia de varios sucesos*, p. 262.

The portrayals Philip III and Lerma had to counteract were even more negative in a report Simeone Contarini, the Venetian ambassador in Madrid, sent to the Venetian senate in 1605, a report later circulated among Philip III's own courtiers.[18] Contarini praised Philip III for his piety, his belief in justice, and his understanding of state affairs; but he also noted the monarch's lack of interest in playing an active role in ruling the monarchy: the king, Contarini asserted, preferred solitude and dedicated only "three or four hours each day" to state affairs. It was Philip III's disengagement from public matters, Contarini remarked, that enabled Lerma to become "the real king," who controlled not only the king but also the councils and made key decisions without consulting either. Contarini's portrait of Lerma was even less complimentary. Although he depicted Lerma as a "good courtier," he also described him as greedy, melancholic, and capricious, a poor statesman who was unable to fulfill the responsibilities that came with his position.[19]

Sepúlveda's and Contarini's observations were more than negative personal descriptions. They disclosed the existence in Philip III's court of contrasting views regarding the government of a monarchy, the qualities of a good monarch, and the role the king's favorites could play in the government of the realm. Both Sepúlveda and Contarini, like many of their contemporaries, believed there was but one perfect form of monarchical government, one in which the monarch ruled supreme aided by his councils and counselors. In early seventeenth-century Spain any other way of ruling could only be perceived as a disease in the body politic produced by the treacherous and selfish behavior of royal favorites, or worse by the stupidity and weakness of the king himself. This political view posed a serious problem for Philip III and Lerma. If they were unable to justify Lerma's role in government, many of Philip's subjects would believe that they were living in a moment of political crisis produced – as Contarini and Sepúlveda indicated – by the king's incapacity to rule alone and Lerma's desire to usurp royal power.

To challenge such an interpretation, Lerma promoted an entirely different view of the nature and foundations of his *privanza*. Citing reason of state, Lerma's supporters avoided discussion of the king's obligation to hear, if not to obey, his councils and counselors, and emphasized the king's complete freedom to decide

---

[18] I used the Spanish version attached to Cabrera de Córdoba, *Relaciones*, pp. 563–83. References are to pages 562, 563, 579, and 569. The Italian version is in Niccolò Barozzi, and Guglielmo Berchet, eds., *Relazioni degli Stati Europei. Lette al Senato dagli Ambasciatori Veneti nel secolo Decimosettimo*, Serie 1: *Spagna*, vol. 1, (Venice, 1856), pp. 277–337. There are dozens of manuscript copies of Contarini's report in the Spanish archives, which demonstrates its popularity. For an example of the circulation of this report in the 1610s see Vega Carpio, *Epistolario*, vol. IV, p. 37.

[19] In 1611, Lord Digby, the English ambassador to Madrid, expressed similar views in a letter to his friend Sir John Holles: "as you well know, [the Spanish court] is absolutely governed by the Duke of Lerma, not with restriction and measure as great ministers and favourites do in other kingdoms but with that fullness and absoluteness that the king is not spoken of, the Duke's name is only used"; "Lord Digby to Sir John Holles, Madrid, 29 October 1611," John Holles, *Letter book of John Holles*, in *Historical Manuscripts Commission: Manuscripts of the Duke of Portland*, vol. IX, (London, 1923), p. 103.

what was best for the commonwealth, even the administrative structure of the monarchy and the power of the favorite. These ideas were advanced in a bold response, written probably by Juan de Idiáquez, to Contarini's report. Idiáquez forcefully dismissed Contarini's allegations that Philip III lacked political proficiency and was a puppet of the Duke of Lerma.[20] Idiáquez's line of defense was to claim that Philip III was so skillful in matters of state that "he does not need advice to make decisions" and that when the king chose to listen to his counselors' advice, it was not because he depended on them but because he wanted to please his subjects. Furthermore, Philip did not always consult his councils because many matters of state were *arcana imperii* (secrets of empire), not to be disclosed to others. Most importantly, the power of the king, Idiáquez claimed, must be viewed as absolute, and himself as extraordinary, with "a judgment so exceptional that no one can question him." Recalling the ideas put forward by Lipsius, Bodin and others, Idiáquez further confirmed that "the councils were created to be consulted only when the king has doubts." Their constitutional role, he argued, restricts them to be occasional helpers of the king, not co-rulers.

Idiáquez also provided a laudatory portrait of Lerma and, at the same time, presented a thorough justification of Lerma's political activities. To counteract Contarini's assertion that Lerma decided state affairs and patronage without consulting the king, Idiáquez cited the difficulty of assessing such a charge, because no one "knows what happens between them," and maintained that all who publicly or privately asserted that "the Duke of Lerma proceeds in an absolute fashion and that the king is Lerma's servant, behave irresponsibly." In reality, Idiáquez continued, the king's love is the "real foundation of Lerma's power. [Lerma] sometimes resolves common or unimportant matters without consulting the king, but he does not decide any important matters of state, which are decided when the king and the Duke meet in private."

Consistent with Idiáquez's defense of his *privanza* and in an attempt to avoid accusations of usurping Philip III's authority, Lerma was very careful to present himself as a mere minister/servant of the king, as his humble spokesman. In his *billetes* Lerma always stated that he was simply transmitting the king's orders and always included this heading: "The king has ordered me to present this matter to you."[21] He insisted that he merely advised the king in state matters; it was the king

---

[20] There are at least two versions of this document: one is in RAH CP, vol. 23, fols. 73v–91v, and is anonymous. This copy contains references to the death of Queen Margaret, which means it was written after 1611. The other copy, the one I used, is in BNM, Mss 8741, "Respuesta que hizo don Juan de Idiáquez, de el Consejo de Estado de su Maj. a la embajada que Simon Canturini [*sic*] hizo a la República de Venecia" (n.p.). This copy does not contain references to the death of Queen Margaret, but the rest of the text is identical.

[21] Lerma adopted this position not only when he had to write to the various royal institutions, but also when he wrote to the *Junta de Gobierno* or to his creatures. See, for example, AGS Est., *leg.* 202/n.p., Lerma to Pedro Franqueza, 12 Nov. 1605; a similar document in *ibid.*, Lerma to Pedro Franqueza, 9 July 1605, on the same topic, Lerma insisting that "the king wants to know everything about this matter."

who decided what to do. His attitude, hopefully the position of all good ministers, was to accept the king's decision without complaint and to obey without delay his monarch's orders.[22] Lerma's sensitivity to any language that could compromise Philip III's public image, and at the same time endanger his privileged position, is illustrated by an alteration to a royal decree announcing the king's intention to give Lerma an office in the kingdom of Valencia. A draft of this decree, prepared by Pedro Franqueza as secretary of state, attributes the king's decision to his gratitude for Lerma's many services to the crown and also acknowledges that "the weight of the government of my kingdoms rests on his shoulders with my entire satisfaction (*que el peso del gobierno de mis reinos carga sobre sus hombros con entera satisfacción*)," a phrase that was erased some time before Philip's decree was made public.[23] As Lerma wrote in several letters, he simply wished to be perceived not as a king-like royal favorite but as "the humblest slave of Your Majesty (*humildísimo esclavo de su Majestad*),"[24] who works "harder than anyone else" for the well-being of the king and the kingdom.[25] On many occasions Lerma also stated his only goal, chosen long ago: "to serve a king who deserves everything I can do for him, a king to whom I owe everything."[26] Always, he said, he wanted to make sure that everyone knew "the love and will with which I serve our lord (*amo*), which is the only thing that really matters to me."[27]

Although Lerma carefully considered the arguments he used to justify his role in his communications with royal ministers, creatures, and allies, he nevertheless needed to legitimize his position, and, consequently, to promote a new vision of the royal favorite's role in government. The dominant paradigm of the time presented the royal favorite as the king's man, not as a representative of the kingdom or the community. By the terms of this paradigm, the favorite who played a role in the resolution of state affairs could only do so by usurping – with or without his master's consent – the king's sovereignty. In fact, the monarch's consent was difficult to defend since late sixteenth- and early seventeenth-century political writers believed that royal power "had to be exercised personally" by the king; thus, the notion of a king delegating his sovereignty to one of his subjects was a contradiction in terms.[28] If the prince were to share or delegate his sovereignty, he would make a companion of his servant, whose power would be equal to that of the king. In *De legibus* the Spanish Jesuit Francisco Suárez explicitly stated that a monarch could not delegate sovereignty to another individual; otherwise, he would create two monarchs, resulting in a radical transformation of the commonwealth which then would become "a body with two heads, a monstrous outcome that could only harm the government of the realm." In case some of his contemporaries had

---

[22] BL, Add. 28425, Lerma to Borja, 11 Sept. 1603, fol. 109v.   [23] AGS Est., *leg.* 196/n.p., 1603.
[24] BL, Add. 28425, Lerma to Philip III, 27 Aug. 1617, fol. 481.
[25] *Ibid.*, Add. 28423, Lerma to Borja, 4 July 1600, fol. 85v.
[26] *Ibid.*, Add. 28424, Lerma to Borja, 2 Sept. 1602, fol. 391v.
[27] *Ibid.*, Add. 28425, Lerma to Borja, 26 June 1605, fol. 294.
[28] Richard Bonney, "Absolutism: What's in a name," *French History*, 1 (1987), p. 99.

any doubts regarding the extension of these principles, he also claimed that the monarch could not delegate even the daily administration of the kingdom to others because "[t]he crown is the responsibility of the monarch ... and [he] cannot neglect that responsibility or delegate it to someone else. The ruler cannot separate the power of sovereignty from his everyday duty to rule the kingdom."[29] Some of Lerma's contemporaries regarded a royal favorite who shared the king's power as a public recognition of the king's inability to assume his responsibilities, transforming him into a *"rex inutilis,"* a king in name only. From a practical perspective, to admit that a royal favorite acted as a *de facto* prime minister ultimately subverted what Orest Ranum has defined as one of the most pervasive political "fictions" in early modern Europe, which defined the monarch as the ultimate or the only person responsible for all political decisions in the realm.[30]

The search for alternative theories to justify Lerma's active role in the monarchy began early in the reign. A number of authors interested in new forms of government claimed that, by the early seventeenth century, the existence of "political favorites" was no longer a governmental novelty. They cited the precedent of Philip II, one of the most powerful Spanish monarchs, and asked why his son should not also have favorites. There was, however, a complication confronting those who supported Philip's decision to place Lerma as his intermediary: the functions Philip III delegated to Lerma were far more complex than those assumed by Philip II's favorites. The way Lerma's supporters responded to this theoretical challenge permitted the development of a new literary genre that forever changed the way in which Spanish political writers addressed the topic of *privanza*. The new genre, a mirror-for-favorites, created in imitation of the mirror-for-princes, attempted to define the virtues, characteristics, and the institutional status of a "perfect" favorite. The novelty present in these mirrors-for-favorites was not only their exclusive dedication to the topic of the *privanza* but their tacit acceptance of the royal favorite as an essential component in the structure of personal monarchies.

The first problem to be elucidated by authors interested in royal *privanza* was whether a king should have only one or several favorites. Until the reign of Philip II everyone seemed to believe that the ideal situation included multiple favorites in order to avoid a concentration of power that would endanger the king's supreme position as the head of the monarchy. Lerma's supporters, however, attempted to demonstrate that the opposite was true; multiple favorites produced factional conflicts that could imperil the stability of the monarchy and, ultimately, the power of the king. Baltasar Alamos de Barrientos addressed this topic in *Norte de príncipes,*[31] a book intended as a practical guide to help Lerma become a perfect

---

[29] *De legibus* was published in 1612; see Fray Francisco Suárez, *De legibus* [1612], ed. Luciano Pereña, 6 vols. (Madrid, 1971–7), vol. v, p. 11.   [30] Ranum, *Richelieu,* p. 3.

[31] Alamos de Barrientos wrote this memorandum between 1599 and 1600; see Alamos de Barrientos, *Norte de príncipes.* Further references in the text.

"principal minister" (*ministro principal*) of the king, a book considered the first of a long series of mirrors-for-favorites. Following, among others, Lipsius's theories, Alamos agreed that a good monarch should have "many counselors," but he also maintained that the king needed a sole *privado* whose role and functions essentially differed from those of the king's counselors. To defend his position, Barrientos borrowed a principle often used to justify personal monarchies: "unity of power at the top" (a sole ruler), the element that gave stability to personal monarchies and made them the ideal form of government. The same should prevail just below the king, who should invest his confidence and favor in just one *privado*, as exemplified in sacred history by the case of Joseph of Egypt among others (pp. 53–4).

The argument for a single favorite was most forcefully made by Juan Fernández de Medrano, one of Lerma's clients. Medrano expressed his opinion in the dedication to Lerma of his *República mixta* (1602) again by underscoring the importance of conserving unity of power at the top: one king and only one favorite. "The boat that has two captains," he wrote,

will be in constant danger of sinking. The empire that depends on more than one cannot conserve itself. If in the fourth heaven inhabited by the sun that illuminates the earth we put another sun, the earth will burn. Although this kingdom and monarchy appear as the image of many bodies, there is only one body that has only one soul that rules the rest.[32]

None of these authors, however, addressed the issue of how to legitimize the powers Lerma had acquired. They addressed practical governmental matters or simply flattered Lerma. What he really needed was an explicit theory that simultaneously defended his role without questioning the ideological foundations of the monarchy. The theoretical support Lerma needed came in 1609 when his confessor, Fray Pedro de Maldonado, completed a manuscript entitled "Discurso del perfecto privado," which, based entirely on Lerma's experience, revolutionized the way royal favorites were depicted in seventeenth-century Spain.[33] Maldonado intended to refute the arguments that had been made against royal favorites; in particular, he wanted to challenge the claim made by sixteenth-century authors that the existence of favorites posed a threat to the political stability of the crown. He recognized that opposition to royal favorites resulted from the existing political paradigm of a monarch who could lose freedom and eminence by depending on one of his subjects. Against this view Maldonado described the favorite as the "noblest and most virtuous part of the monarchy" (just below the ruler) and claimed that the existence of favorites responded to the natural order of things ordained by God. His was, indeed, an elitist view of nature and of political systems, in which favoritism appeared not as a mechanism to corrupt the essences of the body politic, but as the

[32] Fernández de Medrano, *República mixta*, "Dedication to Lerma," n.p.
[33] Dozens of copies of Maldonado's manuscript are preserved in the Spanish archives. My comments on Maldonado are based on one of these copies, BNM, Mss 18721/48, n.p.

main instrument used by God and his most selected creatures to create stable and well-defined natural and human orders. According to Maldonado, for example, the sun which shines on the entire earth gives more light to some parts than to others; the soul gives life to the body but favors especially the head and the heart; God, who gives life to all humans and creates them in His image, favors some over others. Even Jesus Christ gave singular favor to two apostles, John and Peter. So it was with the king, who cared about all his subjects but especially favored one.

Although Maldonado's views on the royal favorite already represented a radical departure from prevalent theories, it was his definition of the favorite and of the favorite's relationship with the monarch that extended his influence beyond his times. Until then the prevailing definition of a *privado* was simple: a courtier who, for whatever reason, enjoyed the king's favor. But in his pamphlet Maldonado introduced a more complex definition. "The *privado*," he wrote, "is a man whom [the king] has chosen among the rest for a particular kind of equality based on love and perfect friendship (*escogido entre los demás para una cierta manera de igualdad, fundada en amor y perfecta amistad*)." Maldonado's reference to "a particular kind of equality," "love," and especially to "perfect friendship," gave Lerma and his supporters the theoretical justification for Lerma's political role without questioning the political foundations of a personal monarchy.

The language of friendship has been neglected by modern historians in their analyses of early modern political relationships. Today, friendship usually describes private associations between individuals and does not typically allude to the political connections individuals have with the state and society. Moreover, when contemporary friendship and politics combine, the result is usually perceived as corruption, the infringing of private interests on the public good. Those interested in the structure and functioning of the early modern state also find friendship a concept too vague for convincing historical explanation of influential figures or complex subjects like the changing nature of monarchical power in early modern Europe. Francisco Tomás y Valiente – undoubtedly one of the best scholars of the royal favorite in early modern Spain – contends, for example, that early modern authors who explained royal favorites in terms of their friendship with the monarch were prisoners of a medieval concept of the monarchy in which political relationships were personal (feudal) in nature. The Renaissance, he claims, brought changes that led to the "modernization of the state" and, consequently, to the institutionalization and politicization of the relationships between the king and his ministers, and among the ministers themselves.[34] But when seventeenth-century writers depicted the favorite as the king's friend, they were not simply borrowing concepts from previous eras but were employing a concept which had significant meaning in the linguistic framework of their own time. Moreover, in the context of

---

[34] Tomás y Valiente, *Los validos*, pp. 130–5.

Lerma's *privanza*, to describe the favorite as the king's friend had important implications for the development of a discourse aimed at legitimizing the favorite's role without devaluing the power, majesty, and position of the king in the body politic.

The revolutionary effect of Maldonado's definition of the *privado* as the king's friend resulted from the existence of a familiar and influential discourse on friendship in early modern Spain. Friendship in early modern Europe referred to public alliances among individuals as well as to a private relationship between two men – what the sociologist Niklas Luhmann calls "everyday and special friendship."[35] In the former, friendship referred to patron–client relationships, what early modern writers called "common friendship," in which friends were understood as allies, protectors, and advisors who were necessary for one's advancement at court.[36] In cultivating "common friendships" courtiers were advised to acquire a multitude of supporters and/or clients to exercise influence or to gain royal favor. In contrast, an ideal or perfect friendship was understood as an exclusive and highly intense relationship between two men, the perfect state to which all men should aspire.[37]

Throughout sixteenth- and seventeenth-century Europe, Cicero's words on friendship profoundly influenced the ways individuals viewed themselves as members of a complex and extended society: "Nothing else in the whole world is so completely in harmony with nature and nothing so utterly right in prosperity and adversity alike."[38] Friendship was not, however, a mystical relationship and to be maintained it needed to be nurtured by following a well-defined set of rules. Friendship, it was said, required friends to share experiences and, more important, intimacy. Thomas Aquinas, for example, assured his readers that "living together is required for friendship as its proper act"; friends desire to live together owing "to a likeness of friendship to sensual love in which we observe that lovers desire most of all to see the persons they love. They prefer this sense, sight, to the other external senses because the passion of love begins especially by seeing . . . and is preserved

---

[35] Niklas Luhmann, *Love as Passion*, trans. Jeremy Gaines and Doris L. Jones (Cambridge, Mass., 1986), p. 81. For a general analysis of early modern theories on friendship see Maurice Aymard, "Friends and Neighbors," in *A History of Private Life. III: Passions of the Renaissance*, ed. Roger Chartier; trans. Arthur Goldhammer (Cambridge, Mass., 1989), pp. 447–91.

[36] Castiglione, *El cortesano*, vol. I, pp. 148–9.

[37] Martire de Angheria to the Count of Tendilla, 30 Sept. 1488, in his *Epistolario*, vol. I, p. 87. In the following pages I draw my argument from Spanish authors or from authors who influenced Spanish writers during the sixteenth and seventeenth centuries. Many others also addressed this topic, but I have kept the number of quotations to a minimum. For an analysis of the evolution of theories on friendship from ancient times to the sixteenth century see Luigi Pizzolato, *La idea de la amistad*, trans. José Ramón Monreal (Barcelona, 1996); Antonio Manuel Hespanha, "La economía de la gracia," in his *La gracia del derecho. Economía de la cultura en la edad moderna* (Madrid, 1993), pp. 156–9; and Mark Morford, *Stoics and Neostoics. Rubens and the Circle of Lipsius* (Princeton, 1991), chap. 2.

[38] Cicero, "De Amicitia", in his *Libro de Marco Tulio Cicerón*, fol. 162v. On Cicero's ideas on friendship, see Pizzolato, *La idea de la amistad*, pp. 165–95.

by this sense."[39] In addition, friends had important duties toward each other. Unlike a flatterer (false friend), whose sole reason "to court" the other is to obtain an immediate benefit, a true friend offers trust, advice, and support in times of trouble.[40] In sum, a real friend had to share his feelings and ideas as well as his wealth, honor, titles, and offices, thus creating a communion of wills, a fusion of the souls that transformed friends into "one soul in two bodies." This fusion of souls, the human element that determined personality and outer image, allowed classical and early modern authors alike to assert that friends were identical, clone images of each other.[41]

Such characteristics and consequences of a true friendship made friends ideal companions especially for those who decided to follow a court career.[42] But what about monarchs? According to sixteenth-century authors, rulers also had to confront problems, criticism, tension, and frustration and needed the support of those who loved them, their friends. In sixteenth-century Spain, however, there were few references to friendship between monarchs and their subjects; there were, in fact, negative views about the possibility of friendship between a king and one of his subjects. A few authors referred to the king's counselors as his friends, but most political writers viewed their relationship not as a "true friendship" but as the result of the *ministerium* both had to fulfill.[43] The relationship between the monarch and his counselors was not voluntary but a duty, which distinguished it from perfect friendship.

Even royal favorites were seldom depicted as the king's friends in sixteenth-century Spain. The concepts of friendship and kingship seemed mutually incompatible. Classical and early modern writers alike believed that only individuals of similar status and qualities could establish friendships,[44] an impossibility for a monarch and one of his subjects. Under the logic of friendship, a king would be obliged to share with his subject not only his feelings and ideas but also his power and royal sovereignty.[45]

It was this theoretical aspect of friendship that Lerma's supporters attempted to

---

[39] Thomas Aquinas, *Commentary on the Nicomachean Ethics of Aristotle*, ed. C. I. Litzinger, 2 vols. (Chicago, 1964), vol. II, pp. 726, 854. See also Seneca, *Epistolae Morales*, ed. Richard M. Gummere, 3 vols. (London, 1925), letter 9, vol. I, p. 49; Juan Luis Vives, *Obras completas*, ed. Lorenzo Riber, 2 vols. (Madrid, 1948), vol. II, p. 1261. In Spanish the words *amigo* and *amiga* also mean "lover"; see Covarrubias Orozco, *Tesoro*, *s.v.* "Amores," pp. 109–10. For Justus Lipsius's ideas on this topic see Morford, *Stoics and Neostoics*, chap. 2.   [40] Guevara, *Aviso*, pp. 23–6.

[41] See, for example, Leone Ebreo, *Dialoghi di Amore*, trans. Garcilaso de la Vega, el Inca, 1590, facsimile edn. (Seville, 1989), fol. 20v; Aristotle, *La ética de Aristóteles*, trans. Pedro Simón Abril [1580] (Madrid, 1918), bk. 9, chap. 4. On Aristotle's ideas on friendship see Pizzolato, *La idea de la amistad*, pp. 80–107.

[42] Pedro de Ribadeneira, *Tratado de la Tribulación* [1589], in Ribadeneira, *Obras*, p. 384.

[43] Pizzolato, *La idea de la amistad*, p. 242.

[44] Aristotle, *La ética*, bk. 8, chap. 1, 335; and bk. 8, chap. 3, 343, and chap. 6, 352.

[45] *Ibid.*, bk. 8, chap. 7, 355; see also Aquinas, *Commentary*, vol. II, p. 738: "kings whose friendship people in humbler walks of life are not likely to have." See also Patrizi, *Del reino*, bk. 8, chap. 11, fols. 342v–44.

redefine in order to legitimize his governmental responsibilities. At the start of the reign, Juan Fernández de Medrano presented an image of the favorite as the king's good friend by asserting that since antiquity all prudent monarchs had had "a servant who became a loyal friend . . . to whom the king gave authority over the rest" and whose functions were to moderate the king's lust for power, tell him the truth, and help him rule the monarchy.[46] But it was not until Maldonado defined the *privado* as the king's friend that the meaning and uses of the word "favorite" expanded and a more complex theory to justify the favorite's role was developed. The reason why Maldonado's definition of the *privado* had such an impact was twofold. First, as noted above, the concept of perfect friendship was widely used and understood in the society of his time. To use Niklas Luhmann's words, the concept of perfect friendship was already "systematized" and could be used to explain the relationship between a monarch and his favorite.[47] Although the presentation of the favorite as the king's friend could be perceived as a political novelty, it certainly was not a linguistic one. Second, the concept of the favorite as the king's friend gave Lerma and his supporters an almost perfect theory with which to challenge all those who believed that a favorite with powers like Lerma's challenged the exclusive right of the king as the unique holder of sovereignty. If the favorite was the king's friend, then the king was in no danger of diffusing royal power and prerogatives because the *valido* was his other self, the clone of the king himself.

Maldonado's influence among his contemporaries can be seen in the many plays and treatises published after 1610 which include dialogues between monarchs and their favorites who refer to each other with phrases like "great friend of mine," "particular friend," "confidant of the secrets of my soul," and "I will make you my equal."[48] The implications of this language can be seen in a play entitled *Comedia famosa de Ruy López de Avalos, o Primera parte de don Alvaro de Luna* written by Antonio Mira de Amescua, a client of the Count of Lemos, toward the end of Philip III's reign. Although the principal characters in the play are John II and his favorite don Alvaro de Luna, who appears as a virtuous favorite, Mira de Amescua used Lerma's career to create his portrait of a *valido* who had responsibilities in the rule of a monarchy but did not usurp the king's sovereignty. In the play, after promising each other "their most loyal and pure friendship," King John asked Alvaro de Luna, "If you were the king what would you give me as a proof of your love?" Alvaro de Luna replied:

My *potestas* would be yours, / you would be king; / I would be a mute statue / following your will, / my being would unite with yours, / and both together our two natures would look like one/ and thus, I would not give you anything / because already you would be the absolute master of the kingdom and me.[49]

[46] Fernández de Medrano, *República mixta*, p. 83.   [47] Luhmann, *Love as Passion*, p. 82.
[48] On this topic, see Miguel Herrero García, "La monarquía teorética de Lope de Vega," *Fenix*, 3 (1935), 3: 306–29.
[49] Antonio Mira de Amescua, *Comedia famosa de Ruy López de Avalos (Primera parte de don Alvaro de Luna)*, ed. N. E. Sánchez-Arce (Mexico City, 1965), p. 61.

So influential was this language of friendship that Philip III himself adopted it when he addressed the Duke of Lerma. In explaining Lerma's rise to power, for example, Gil González Dávila, Lerma's contemporary and Philip III's biographer, wrote that:

the king declared his grace to Lerma and asked him to help the king handle affairs of state given that Lerma was his Friend, which is the greatest honor that a king can give to one of his subjects. In all the papers from the king answering Lerma's reports, and I have seen many, the king always signs Your Friend, and the Duke always responds with these words, Humble Slave of Your Majesty.[50]

"Your friend" (*vuestro amigo*) is precisely the term Philip III used in several letters he sent to Lerma in August 1617.[51]

The language of friendship can also be found, at least implicitly, in one of the most important documents produced during the reign of Philip III: the so-called decree of signed delegation sent by Philip III to all councils in 1612 in which Philip III ordered all his ministers to obey Lerma's orders as if they were his own. Although Tomás y Valiente and other modern historians have interpreted this document as a delegation of sovereignty and proof patent of Philip III's inability to rule, a consideration of the language of friendship reveals another possible interpretation. Instead of delegating his power and preeminence, the king was simply presenting Lerma as his public voice, his other self, his living image. A similar interpretation can be found in a document written in 1622 in defense of the Duke of Uceda, Lerma's son and his successor as Philip III's favorite. The author of this defense reworked the theory of the king's two bodies (natural and public) by implying that "for the time being" both persons are united in the king. Additionally, he states that all humans have the right to have a friend, and the monarch as a private individual also possessed this right. But because the monarch was also a public person his private friend became his public favorite, spokesman, and representative. In all public matters, he wrote, "the favorite is a mere executor of the king's will, and as such no one can limit the favorite's actions in public life (*en lo exterior y público*) because every time the favorite leaves the king's chamber he transforms himself into the prince (*viene su príncipe transformado en él*)."[52]

Lerma's supporters did not hesitate to use such theories and language to explain, justify, and legitimize Lerma's role in the decision-making process. He was, for example, depicted as "his master's voice in all matters concerning the community, not because of his office but because he is the incumbent of his master's favor," and no one had the right to interfere with his activities just as no one had the right to interfere with the actions of the king.[53] Hence, when Lerma recommended a course of action or gave orders, it was not because he had usurped the king's power but because he was the king's representative. The monarch and his favorite, as Fernández de Caso noted in a reference to Philip III and Lerma, had similar wills and

---

[50] González Dávila, *Historia de la vida*, p. 40.   [51] BL, Add. 28425, fols. 478–81.
[52] BNM, Mss 11569, "Memorial del pleito contra el Duque de Uceda," fol. 220r.   [53] *Ibid.*

natures because "they are joined together as if they were only one."[54] Such arguments served Lerma's supporters in their presentation of their patron as the coarchitect of all policies during Philip III's reign and raised no awkward questions about the king's sovereignty.

Positioning Lerma at the apex of the government as *de facto* prime minister was the most innovative, certainly the most controversial, political initiative taken by Philip III during his twenty-three years as ruler of the Spanish monarchy. It led, in turn, to a revolution in government intended to reinforce the monarch's power. With very few exceptions modern historians argue that Lerma's rise represents the beginning of an aristocratic assault on state power aimed at transforming the monarchy into a defender of aristocratic social and political privileges.[55] It is indeed a fact that Lerma used his position as Philip's favorite to enrich himself and promote his relatives, clients, and supporters, but it is equally important to remember that he acted as the head of the Sandovals, not as the leader of a unified aristocratic class. More important is that Lerma's activities as the head of his family and as a royal favorite demonstrate the complex symbiosis between the monarch's need to expand state power and the nobility's need to consolidate their privileged social and political position. Indeed, as the Italian historian Giorgio Chittolini has recently stated, the early modern state must be understood as a "system of institutions, of powers and practices, that had as one of its defining features a sort of programmatic permeability to extraneous (or, if one prefers, 'private') powers and purposes while retaining an overall unity of political organization."[56] No one has better articulated the compatibility between the royal favorite's "private" interests and the benefit of his master than Louis XIV of France, who wrote in his *Mémoires*: "If he [the prime minister] despoils you of part of your glory he unburdens you at the same time of your thorniest cares. The interest of his own greatness engages him to sustain yours. He wishes to preserve your rights as a possession that he enjoys in your name, and if he shares your diadem with you, he at least works to leave it intact to your descendants."[57]

Louis XIV's words are corroborated by the experiences and characteristics of Spanish royal favorites. Since the reign of Philip II, all *privados* came from the echelons of the court nobility and owed their careers and riches to the king's favor rather than to their territorial holdings. Once selected as the king's favorites, their power and influence stemmed not from their independent capacity for action but from their position as intimate servants of the king, who always had the option to replace them if he felt that they threatened his own preeminence – as Philip II did

---

[54] Fernández de Caso, *Oración gratulatoria al capelo del ilustrísimo y excelentísimo señor cardenal duque* (n.p., 1618), n.p.

[55] See Perry Anderson, *Lineages of the Absolutist State* (London, 1974); and especially Tomás y Valiente, *Los validos*, "Introduction."

[56] Giorgio Chittolini, "The 'Private,' the 'Public,' the State," in Julius Kirshner, ed., *The Origins of the State in Italy, 1300–1600* (Chicago, 1996), p. 46.

[57] Louis XIV, *Mémoires for the Instruction of the Dauphin*, ed. Paul Sonnino (New York, 1970), p. 130.

with Eboli, Philip III with Lerma, and Philip IV with Olivares. If the ruler decided to discard one of his favorites, nothing could stop his fall – neither his offices nor riches, creatures, or allies. Moreover, while in the king's favor, the favorite reinforced rather than diminished royal power even while accumulating private riches and enlarging his own territorial holdings. Dependence on the king's favor was such that the favorite's fall from power inevitably led to a loss of prestige for his whole house besides a loss of riches and territorial influence, as the experiences of Lerma and Olivares demonstrate.[58] An imposing and quasi-absolute royal power therefore permitted the rise of powerful favorites, at least between 1550 and 1650, whereas the weakening of the monarch's authority caused their disappearance from the political scene.[59]

As the king's favorite, Lerma took upon himself the task of bolstering, in theory and practice, the king's authority. It was during Lerma's *privanza* that theories of reason of state received increasing official support, resulting in the reprinting of Botero's *Ragion di stato*; the publication of the Spanish translation of Lipsius's *Politicorum sive civilis doctrinae libri sex*; and, for the first time, the circulation of works defending reason of state penned by Spanish writers, such as, for example, Fernández de Medrano, Baltasar Alamos de Barrientos, and Sancho de Moncada.[60] By promoting these theories, Philip III and Lerma wanted to challenge traditional theories which presented the Spanish monarchy as a "mixed monarchy," claiming – as Lerma's grandson wrote in 1623 – that the government of the Spanish monarchy was *regale* (*gobierno real*), a government by one, not *politicum* (*gobierno político*), a government by many, and that the Spanish king was not a "prince," a *primus-inter-pares*, but a "monarch" and thus "the lord and master of the crown, not its tutor or administrator."[61] The contemporary preoccupation with theories of reason of state appears succinctly in a scene that Miguel de Cervantes included in the second part of his hugely popular *Don Quijote de la Mancha* (1615), in which Don Quijote recalls that he and his friends have been discussing "what people know as reason of state and methods of government (*modos de gobierno*), correcting this abuse and condemning

---

[58] On Lerma's case see below, Epilogue.

[59] On these themes see Vicens Vives, "Estructura administrativa," p. 124.

[60] On their works see references in the Bibliography; for an excellent guide to which books were popular in the first years of Philip III's reign among those who supported the new rulers, see the diary of Girolamo Sommaia, an Italian student who lived in Salamanca from 1603 to 1607: *Diario de un estudiante de Salamanca. La crónica inédita de Girolamo da Sommaia (1603–1607)*, ed. George Haley (Salamanca, 1971). In his diary the most frequently named books, which he and his friends and colleagues read, discussed, bought, borrowed or copied, are Machiavelli, *The Prince* and *The Discourses*; Castiglione, *The Courtier*; Gracián Dantisco, *El galateo español*; Lipsius, *The Six Books of Politics, On Constancy*, and *Epistles*; Mariana, *De rege* and *Historia de España*; Jean Bodin, *The Six Books of the Commonwealth*; Botero, *Relationi* and *Ragion di stato*; and the works of Tacitus and Seneca.

[61] Gómez de Sandoval Manrique de Padilla, *Memorial dirigido* pt. II, fols. 18v–19r. See also the report sent to Lerma by the Count of Salinas in 1612 stating that the Spanish monarch had more powers in his kingdoms than all other monarchs in theirs: Conde de Salinas, "Dictamen."

that, reforming one custom and abolishing another.... To such a degree did they fashion the commonwealth that it was as if they had taken it to the forge and brought away a different one."[62]

Theories claiming absolute power for the ruler proliferated and a thorough program of institutional reforms was implemented in order to reduce opposition to the king's orders and to give precedence to "execution" over "counsel." The king's right to implement his orders took precedence over his duty to receive advice from the royal counselors. From the beginning of the reign, Lerma was well aware that as the king's prime minister he had to confront a complex and formalized political structure. In theory the monarch was to make policy with the guidance of his ministers and counselors and choose a course of action which the royal institutions were obliged to obey and dutifully implement.[63] In reality, the cooperation of the royal institutions was far from automatic and by the first decades of the seventeenth century references to the councils' obstructionism became rather common. A *consulta* the Council of State sent to Philip III in 1611, for example, complained that the Council of Portugal, instead of executing Philip's orders, "discussed them again and again as if matters had not yet been decided and resolved by the king."[64] By the turn of the century, the royal councils were also depicted as inept bodies controlled by incompetent ministers whose only goal was to defend their own privileges and interests, giving no consideration to the common interests of the realm or the needs of the king. In 1601 Lerma himself criticized several counselors of the Indies for opposing administrative reforms designed to expedite the implementation of the king's orders and proposed their removal as the only way to introduce "law and order in the council, because the passions of these counselors are damaging general and specific affairs alike."[65] But, as Spanish rulers and their close servants often found, these counselors, once appointed, were nearly impossible to remove from office.[66]

The only available means of imposing royal authority was by exploiting to the maximum the monarch's capacity for independent action, which, in turn, created, in John H. Elliott's words, a "government of creatures." Convinced, as Sharon Kettering has noted in her analysis of political practices during the reign of Louis XIII of France, that "institutional procedures alone were insufficient . . . the crown had to supplement its authority with patron–broker–client ties . . . used to

---

[62] In Cervantes Saavedra, *Obras completas*, ed. Angel Valbuena y Prat (Madrid, 1943), chap. 1, p. 1250. The book was dedicated to the Count of Lemos, Lerma's son-in-law.

[63] On this topic see I. A. A. Thompson, "The Rule of the Law in Early Modern Castile," in his *Crown and Cortes. Government, Institutions and Representation in Early-Modern Castile* (Aldershot, 1993).

[64] AGS Est., *leg.* 2641/n.p., *consulta* of the Council of State, 10 Sept. 1611.

[65] AGS Est., *leg.* 186/n.p., Lerma to the Count of Miranda, 21 May and 5 Apr. 1601. In pts III and IV I tackle more specific examples of the councils' resistance to the implementation of the king's orders and theories, defending the role of these institutions in the government of the monarchy.

[66] See above, chap. 1.

manipulate political institutions from within, to operate across institutions, and to act in place of institutions."[67] In addition to the use of patron–client networks to manipulate or circumvent royal institutions, Philip III also decreed the establishment of parallel institutions, the so-called *juntas* (committees *ad hoc*), and created (following his father's advice) a privy council to help him and Lerma control the monarchical machinery.

As noted in Chapter 1, Philip II had earlier instituted a special council, the *Junta de Gobierno*, to help him rule the monarchy in the last years of his reign and had advised his son also to create a "secret council" with "a few of your closest advisors."[68] Both Philip III and Lerma were familiar with the operations of this *junta*, as both had participated in its deliberations,[69] and it appears that they intended to create a similar privy council.[70] However, its unpopularity and the new king's own efforts to demonstrate his desire to restore traditional forms of government precluded Philip III from carrying out his plans (see Chapter 3). But once the *Junta de Gobierno* and its activities were no longer a matter of public debate, in the early months of 1601, Philip III ordered the institution of a new privy council known as the *Junta de Dos*, the *Junta de Tres*, or the *Junta de Cuatro* (Committee of the Two, of the Three, or of the Four).[71] The members of this new *junta* were Juan de Idiáquez, Fray Gaspar de Córdoba (the royal confessor), the Marquis of Velada (Philip III's *mayordomo mayor*), and Pedro Franqueza, who acted as its secretary and held a right to vote following a custom set by Mateo Vázquez during Philip II's reign. Shortly after its establishment, the *junta*'s membership changed when the Count of Miranda replaced Velada in July 1601. The places left vacant by the death of Fray Gaspar de Córdoba in June 1604 and the imprisonment of Pedro Franqueza in January 1607 were never filled.[72] Toward the end of its existence the *junta* had only two members, Idiáquez and Miranda, and it formally disappeared after the Count of Miranda retired from public life in

---

[67] Sharon Kettering, *Patrons, Brokers, and Clients in Seventeenth- Century France* (New York, 1986), p. 5. See also William Beik, *Absolutism and Society in Seventeenth-Century France. State Power and Provincial Aristocracy in Languedoc* (Cambridge, 1985).

[68] Cf. Albert Mousset, *Felipe II* (Madrid, 1917), pp. 26–7.

[69] For an example of a meeting of the *Junta de Gobierno* attended by Lerma see AGS Est., *leg.* 2636/fol. 40, 10 Sept. 1598; on the dissolution of the *junta*, see above, chap. 3.

[70] The interest of the new rulers in the workings of the *Junta de Gobierno* became manifest when Philip commissioned a detailed report of the *junta*'s operations entitled "Estilo que guardó el rey nuestro señor don Phelipe Segundo en el despacho de los negocios, desde que comenzó a valerse del secretario Matheo Vázquez hasta que murió"; see Escudero, *Los secretarios*, vol. I, pp. 202–6. Some authors, for example Baltasar Alamos de Barrientos, advised Lerma to appoint several private counselors to help him in his role as the king's chief minister. See Alamos de Barrientos, *Norte de príncipes*, p. 79.

[71] These names do not refer to different committees but simply to the number of ministers who attended the meetings of this *junta*; to avoid confusion I hereafter refer to this as the *Junta de Gobierno*. The first *consulta* of this *junta* I found is dated 3 February 1601; see AGS Est., *leg.* 186/n.p.. The junta met at least six other times in February 1601 (5, 6, 9, 17 (twice), 21, and 23 Feb.).

[72] The last meeting of the *junta* in which Franqueza participated was 16 January 1607; see AGS Est., *leg.* 2025/fol. 5, *consulta* of the *Junta de Tres* (Miranda, Idiáquez, Franqueza), 16 Jan. 1607.

April 1608.[73] Thereafter, Lerma held individual consultations with Idiáquez and the new royal confessor Fray Luis de Aliaga.

The *junta*'s mission was clear from the start: to review the *consultas*, letters, and reports the councils, ambassadors, individual ministers, and special committees sent to the king and to offer Lerma and Philip III guidance in governmental matters, both domestic and international. In a meeting held on 3 February 1601, for example, the *junta* discussed letters sent by the Count of Miranda to Lerma concerning the need to dissolve the *Cortes* and move the court to Valladolid, revised *consultas* from the Council of Finance, discussed several appointments to "the secret Council of Milan," and considered the charter for the importation of pepper from the colonies.[74] Despite their important role, Lerma did not allow them to meet in person with the king; like other royal officials, they had to convey their opinions to Lerma in written reports.

Among the *junta*'s members, only Pedro Franqueza can strictly speaking be considered a client of the Duke of Lerma.[75] Born in Igualada, a small town in Catalonia, Franqueza moved to the court in the 1580s when he was appointed to several minor offices in the Council of Aragon. Later, as royal secretary for the kingdom of Valencia, he had the opportunity to work with Lerma, who was viceroy of Valencia from 1595 to 1597. In 1599 Franqueza became Lerma's protégé when the royal favorite – traveling at the time with the king in Valencia, Catalonia, and Aragon – needed someone with an extensive knowledge of the affairs of these kingdoms.[76] Franqueza's activities extended far beyond the responsibilities of the office he assumed in 1600, secretary of state in charge of Italian affairs.[77] He was an active political force in the Council of State and in the new *Junta de Gobierno*, and the mastermind, together with Alonso Ramírez de Prado, of the many fiscal initiatives taken during the first few years of Philip III's reign, and although Franqueza never obtained any of the key offices in the councils, Lerma's favor moved him to the apex of power and influence at the Spanish court (see Plate 8).[78]

The rest of the initial members of the *junta* must be viewed as Lerma's allies rather than his clients. Born in the 1530s, the Count of Miranda had served under Philip II as viceroy to Catalonia and Naples, president of the Council of Italy – an office he retained until 1601 – and a counselor of state. Many of his contemporaries

---

[73] The last *consultas* of this *Junta*, now called the *Junta de Dos*, are dated February 1608; see AGS Est., *leg.* 2025/fol. 72.

[74] AGS Est., *leg.* 186/n.p., *consulta* of the *Junta de Cuatro*, 3 Feb. 1601. In the other *consultas* of the *Junta de Gobierno* I have located, the members of the *junta* discussed as wide a range of *consultas* as they did on 3 February 1601.

[75] For Franqueza, his career, relationship with Lerma, and fall in 1607 accused of corruption see now Josep M. Torras Ribé, *Poders i relacions clientelars a la Catalunya dels Àustria* (Barcelona, 1998).

[76] On how Franqueza gained Lerma's confidence, see Escudero, *Los secretarios*, vol. I, p. 228.

[77] Pedro Franqueza was also secretary to the queen and secretary of the Inquisition. On his appointment as secretary of state in 1600, see Torras Ribé, *Poders i relacions clientelars*, pp. 160–1.

[78] Cabrera de Córdoba, *Relaciones*, p. 92.

Este rretrato, es de quien porsu Ingenio, y virtud merecio ser Secretario, de los Señores Reyes Philipe 2. y del 3. de eftado, siruioles 4 5. años continuos, con Real, y General aprouacion en los mayores negocios, que se les ofrecieron a ambos Monarcas en dicho tiempo, y quando mas merecio el premio de sus seruicios fue preso, y defpojado de los oficios, mercedes, y detoda su hacienda por la Imbidia. Senteciole yndefenso el Miedo. hizole morir en la carcel y nocente, la Ingratitud. y con auer hecho mucho vien amuchos sòlo semostro agradecido, quien le dió Sepultura en la Santa Insigne, y Singular, Yglesia de San Iusto y Paftor, de la Villa de Alcala de Henares, y lostres, que eftabã mas beneficiados fueron causa de todos eftos Males referidos. Murió el Año 1 614. de Hedad de 6 8. años.

P.º de Villafranca, fculptor Regis, ft. 1 655.

8   Pedro de Villafranca, *Pedro Franqueza*. As Lerma's man of confidence, Pedro Franqueza was one of the most powerful ministers during the reign of Philip III. Detained in 1607 on charges of corruption, the fall of Franqueza also signified the first major crisis of Lerma's *privanza*.

considered him "one of the best ministers of his times,"[79] and it is, thus, not surprising that Lerma placed him in many privileged positions, including the presidency of the Council of Castile.[80] The special relationship between Miranda and Lerma was confirmed in December 1601 when Francisca de Sandoval, Lerma's daughter, married Diego de Zúñiga y Avellaneda, Duke of Peñaranda and heir of the Count of Miranda.

The third, and permanent, member of the *Junta de Gobierno*, Juan de Idiáquez, was also an individual with ample political experience and talent. During the reign of Philip II, Idiáquez had been an ambassador in Genoa and Venice, a counselor of state and a member of the *Junta de Noche*. In a sense, Philip II's death diminished Idiáquez's political influence, for he never became intimate with the new king (see Chapter 3); nevertheless, he remained important as a counselor to Philip III and Lerma. Both seemed to trust his advice, and he became the most influential counselor of state, a permanent member of the *Junta de Gobierno*, and president of the Council of the Military Orders. Idiáquez also provided personal counsel to the king and his favorite in the form of hundreds of reports on various matters of state written from 1598 until his death in 1614.[81]

The creation of the *Junta de Gobierno* was one of several institutional and political initiatives aimed at extending the king's influence to each and every one of his kingdoms. Prime among these initiatives was the creation of temporary *juntas* staffed by Lerma and some of his closer allies which functioned mainly to attend to specific tasks that required urgent responses. Although similar *juntas* had already existed during Philip II's reign,[82] it was not until the reign of Philip III that these committees took a more systematic form.[83] One of their advantages was that Philip could create and dismiss them at will, and appoint their members without the interference of any royal minister or institution.[84]

---

[79] Contarini, "Relación," in Cabrera de Córdoba, *Relaciones*, pp. 569–70; Sepúlveda, *Historia de varios sucesos*, p. 43; and Gil González Dávila, *Teatro de las grandezas de la villa de Madrid, corte de los reyes católicos de España* (Madrid, 1623), p. 379.

[80] On Miranda's appointment as president of Castile see above, chap. 3; a summary of Miranda's career can be found in Antonio de Herrera y Tordesillas, *Elogio a don Juan de Zúñiga Bazán y Abellaneda, primer duque de Peñaranda* (Madrid, 1608).

[81] Idiáquez received written petitions from Lerma to study the *consultas* of the councils. After analyzing the different documents, Idiáquez wrote his opinions and sent them to Lerma; see AGS Est., *leg.* 195/n.p., 19 Oct. 1603, Idiáquez's *billetes* to Franqueza, and Idiáquez to Lerma, informing him that he had received Lerma's petition to study several documents related to Italian matters and that he had sent his advice. The first of these reports can be seen in AGS Est., *legs.* 185, 186 (1600–1).

[82] See Lovett, *Mateo Vázquez de Leça*, pp. 144–6, 202–3; and A. W. Lovett, *Early Habsburg Spain, 1517–1598* (Oxford, 1986), pp. 122–3.

[83] See the Count-Duke of Olivares's "Nicandro o Antídoto contra las calumnias que la ignorancia y envidia ha esparcido para deslucir y manchar las heróicas e inmortales acciones del Conde-Duque de Olivares después de su retiro," in John H. Elliott and J. F. de la Peña, eds., *Memoriales y cartas del conde duque de Olivares*, 2 vols. (Madrid, 1978–81), vol. II, p. 257.

[84] Many of these *juntas* focused their attention on matters of defense and the monarchy's overseas territories, as was the case, for example, with the *Junta de Guerra de Indias* and the *Junta de Fábricas*, both charged with matters that had formerly been under the jurisdiction of the Council of Indies and

Although Philip III and Lerma created new institutions of government with relative ease, they found it far more difficult to control the existing councils. As noted above, the king could not dismiss appointed counselors. Furthermore, some of the established councils, specially the Chamber of Castile, had acquired regulative powers regarding the appointment of royal officials to all but the Council of State, the Council of War, and some diplomatic offices. Officially, the king held the right to designate office holders; in reality, he was forced to choose from a list of candidates put together by the chamber.[85] Confronted with legal procedures and aware of the need to place their own loyal ministers on the royal councils, Philip III and Lerma opted to introduce legal reforms to increase their control over the selection process.

The Count of Miranda in particular played a crucial role as president of the Council of Castile and of the Chamber of Castile. In 1602 Cabrera de Córdoba, echoing rumors circulating at court, reported that Philip III was planning to give the Count of Miranda the exclusive right to propose candidates for vacant posts.[86] Although this measure was never implemented, in October 1602 Philip III ordered the Chamber of Castile to limit its shortlist of candidates to three individuals and made it clear that Miranda's vote would carry more weight than the votes of the other four counselors.[87] That same year Philip III sent a new ordinance to the Council of Finance stating that candidates for vacant posts on this council would no longer be selected by the entire council but by a committee made up of the president of the Council of Finance (Juan de Acuña), the president of the Chamber of Castile (Miranda), and two counselors, one from the Council of Finance and the other from the Council of Castile.[88] Additional steps to place the control of appointments in the hands of Lerma's men included the creation of the *Junta de Cámara de Indias* (Chamber of the Indies) in 1600, a small committee composed of the president and three members of the Council of the Indies, all of whom were appointed by the king.[89]

But the thread that unified all these attempts to create a compact team of government was Lerma's network system. Philip III's appointments between 1598 and 1618 were not confined to allies, relatives, and clients of Lerma, but, at least until 1611, a majority of the most important monarchical offices were filled by those who considered themselves members of Lerma's faction. The use of patron– client

the Council of War. Most important of these special *juntas* were, however, those that dealt with matters of finance, which became more permanent than the others and were asked by the king to exercise control over all aspects of royal finances, thus becoming a key element in the revolution in government that took place during Lerma's *privanza*. On these *juntas* see below, chaps. 8–9.
[85] On the Chamber of Castile see Salustiano de Dios, *Gracia, merced y patronazgo real. La Cámara de Castilla entre 1474–1530* (Madrid, 1993); on the role of the Cámara in the appointment of royal officials see pp. 313–26. [86] Cabrera de Córdoba, *Relaciones*, p. 140.
[87] AHN Est., *leg.* 6408, *consulta* of the Chamber of Castile and Philip III's answer, October 1602.
[88] *Ordenanzas del Consejo de Hacienda de 1554, 1579, 1593, 1602 y 1621* (n.p., n.d.), fol. 38v.
[89] On the creation of the Chamber of Indies see J. J. Real Díaz, "El Consejo de la Cámara de Indias: génesis de su fundación," *Anuario de Estudios Americanos*, 19 (1962).

networks to control the decision-making process was certainly not new. Earlier, Philip II and his favorites had also placed loyal individuals carefully in the belief that their appointees would defend the king's interests and authority. Cardinal Espinosa, Philip II's chief minister, kept detailed records of all members of the councils, their characteristics and their loyalty to the king's policies; he also recorded possible candidates for consideration to new appointments.[90] Moura himself had emphasized the importance of loyal men placed advantageously in a letter to the Marquis of Poza, who, after his appointment to the presidency of the Council of Finance, was told that "we put you in this office not to serve the council but to promote what is best for us [the king and his favorites]."[91] It was not until Lerma's *privanza*, however, that this practice became more generalized. In the very first months of the reign, it was evident that to be a client, an ally, or a relative of the Duke of Lerma had become the key to offices and influence.

Those selected for the echelons of the governmental machinery came basically from three groups: Lerma's relatives, Lerma's private servants, and previous council members who were willing to offer their services to the new favorite. Although not the only relatives Lerma promoted during his *privanza*, Juan de Borja, the Count of Lemos, and Juan de Acuña occupied some of the most important institutional offices during the reign of Philip III. Juan de Borja, Count of Mayalde, was Lerma's uncle, and from September 1598 until his death in September 1606 became Lerma's confidant and one of the most active ministers. Borja, like many of the ministers appointed to high offices during Lerma's *privanza*, had gained ample political experience during Philip II's reign. Born in Valencia in the early 1530s,[92] Juan de Borja was appointed ambassador to Lisbon in 1569 and to the Emperor Rudolf II in 1576. He returned to Spain in 1581 as a lord high steward of Empress Maria, an office he held until Empress Maria's death in 1603. The start of Lerma's *privanza* in September 1598 brought new and important offices to Juan de Borja. Appointed counselor of state toward the end of 1598, in 1599 he became senior counselor of the Council of Portugal, a sort of acting president in a council whose official president was the king. He also participated in many *juntas* Philip created to address the intricate situation of the royal finances.[93]

Born in 1576, Pedro Fernández de Castro, Count of Lemos since 1600, was Lerma's nephew and son-in-law. Lemos's political career began in 1603 when he was appointed president of the important Council of the Indies, an office he occupied until 1609. The post was critical because at the time of Lemos's appointment Philip III and Lerma needed to improve the council's effectiveness in order to obtain greater benefits to the crown from the Indies. In 1609, when Lemos

---

[90] See Martínez Millán, "Un curioso manuscrito."

[91] BL, Add. 28378, Moura to Poza, 8 June 1596, fol. 92v.

[92] On Borja's place of birth see his memorandum to Philip II in AHN CS, *leg.* 4411/fol. 169, 9 Oct. 1588.

[93] The correspondence between Juan de Borja and Lerma, September 1598 to the summer of 1606, is collected in BL, Mss Add. 28422 to 28425.

left the council, he was again appointed to an important position, this time as viceroy of Naples with the goal of reinforcing the royal prerogatives and increasing Naples's share in the financing of the monarchy.[94] Other important family connections influenced appointments and promotions during Lerma's *privanza*. Such was the case, for example, with Juan de Acuña, who was a relative of the wife of the Duke of Uceda, Lerma's son and heir. Until the reign of Philip III, Juan de Acuña's career had followed an ordinary path along the *cursus honorum*. After Philip's accession, however, Acuña was appointed president of the Council of Finance (1602) and president of the Council of the Indies (1609); and in 1610 he moved to the presidency of the Council of Castile, an office obtained as a result of the increasing influence of the Duke of Uceda and against the wishes of the Duke of Lerma.[95]

Others were Lerma's *hechuras* in every sense of the word: they owed everything to him and, thus, could be expected to show unquestioned loyalty to him. Among those who rose to political eminence via Lerma's private service, two stand out: Rodrigo Calderón and Juan Bautista de Acevedo. Rodrigo Calderón, Lerma's page during the 1590s, after September 1598 became Lerma's private counselor.[96] As was the case with Franqueza, Calderón's high position in the court hierarchy – some of his contemporaries considered Calderón the most powerful individual after Lerma – stemmed from his personal connections with the royal favorite, his only official duty being that of secretary of the king's chamber. Juan Bautista de Acevedo was born in the 1550s and served as Lerma's eldest son's tutor and his agent at court while Lerma acted as viceroy of Valencia from 1595 to 1597. Once Lerma became Philip III's favorite, Acevedo was appointed Bishop of Valladolid (1601), Inquisitor-General (1603), and President of Castile (1608). His career was later remembered as one of the most fantastic cases of good fortune because from being "a nobody Acevedo reached the most important offices and dignities in Spain."[97] These and many others – Alonso Ramírez de Prado, Diego Sarmiento de Acuña, Pedro Manso, Jerónimo de Villanueva, to name a few – considered themselves the loyal friends and collaborators of the Duke of Lerma and supporters of the king's interests. Their advice became central to Philip's and Lerma's determined efforts to halt the declining influence and strength of the Spanish monarchy.

[94] On Lemos's activities in Naples and his political role in the factional struggles during the last years of Lerma's *privanza* see below, chaps. 11–12.

[95] On this topic see below, chap. 11; on Juan de Acuña's career see Angel González Palencia, ed., *La Junta de reformación* (Valladolid, 1932), doc. 65.

[96] AGS CC DC, *leg.* 35(1)/*exp.* 7, "Consultas hechas por los jueces del Marqués de Siete Iglesias, Rodrigo Calderón." On contemporaries' perceptions of Calderón see the report of the Florentine ambassador, Orazio della Rena, in Biblioteca Nazionale Centrale, Magl. CI. XXV, cod. 796, fol. 47v.

[97] Francisco Bermúdez de Pedraza, *Hospital real de corte* (Granada, 1644), fol. 21.

PART III

Monarchy in action

Introduction

In 1607, three years after a devastating fire destroyed portions of El Pardo, its restoration began with the ceiling of the Queen's Gallery where new paintings depicted the story of Joseph from Genesis.[1] At the heart of this story are Pharaoh's dreams in which God warns of a looming crisis that will follow seven years of prosperity and tells him that to avoid such a fate he should find "a man of vision and wisdom and place him in charge of the country." Following God's advice, Pharaoh places Joseph in charge of his household and commands his people to follow Joseph's orders. Only with respect to the throne, Pharaoh tells him, "Shall I rank higher than you." Pharaoh then gives Joseph "his signet ring, mounts him in his viceroy's chariot ... [and] makes him ruler over all of Egypt," at the same time stating that "I am the Pharaoh, yet without your consent no one will lift hand or foot throughout Egypt."[2]

Seventeenth-century Spaniards, like other early modern Europeans, were accustomed to reading the present as a fulfillment of the past and as a sign of God's will. In this context Joseph's story helped them interpret events taking place during Philip III's reign: just as Pharaoh was warned of a looming crisis, Philip III received numerous memoranda alerting him to the possibility of deep financial troubles and other threats to the well-being of the Spanish kingdoms. The parallels between the story of Joseph and Philip III's reign concerned more than the matter of prediction. Although no one knows who chose this story for the decoration of the Queen's Gallery, its subject matter appeared to justify the presence of a royal favorite, Lerma, who acted as the king's *alter ego* in the ruling of the monarchy. The story of Joseph conveyed a well-defined message: to have a *valido* did not indicate a weak and worthless ruler but a prudent monarch who confronted a crisis by selecting, just as Pharaoh had done, "a man of vision and wisdom" to help him rule his kingdoms.

Modern historians appear unaware of the intended message of these historical analogies and unconvinced by the images, theories, and discourses promoted by Lerma and discussed in Part II of this volume. Although they acknowledge that Lerma and his allies were rather clever in promoting images and theories as a *post facto* justification of Lerma's influence, these historians seem to believe that his

---

[1] Newcome, "Genoese Drawings," pp. 23–5.   [2] Genesis 41.

quest for power and influence had only one objective: to enrich himself, his household, and his allies. In turn, they see Philip III as a weak monarch whose lack of interest in finding solutions to the problems faced by the Spanish monarchy left Lerma free to pursue his personal, and undeserved, greatness.

The few historians who have paid attention to Philip III's reign maintain that Philip III and Lerma were actors without the necessary political skills and ability to confront the serious crises facing the Spanish monarchy at the turn of the sixteenth century. For those who argue that Philip III and Lerma showed no interest in ruling the monarchy or in imposing royal authority, the word that best describes the reign of Philip III is "abandonment."

Robert Stradling, for example, summarizes widely held opinions by asserting that "the *valimiento* of the Duke of Lerma was not so much a case of government as – quite literally – the absence of it." Philip III's desire was "to live the private domestic life of one of his grandees," whereas Lerma wished "to capture power for no positive or dynamic purposes, but merely in order to neutralize it." During Lerma's *privanza*, Stradling continues, "nobody ruled in Madrid; a world empire was run on an automatic pilot."[3] According to modern historians, the consequences of this political "abandonment" were disastrous for the Spanish monarchy and led to the inexorable decline of the Spanish empire. Philip III's reign is thus commonly viewed as "a lost opportunity" in the history of Spain. John H. Elliott best articulates the conclusions of modern historians that the ineptitude of rulers such as Philip III and Lerma meant that "old problems were left unresolved, new problems began to accumulate, and a new generation of court favorites, lacking the sense of responsibility of their immediate predecessors in government, squandered the opportunities for retrenchment and reform provided by the return of peace."[4]

Yet a careful analysis of the forms of government created by Philip III and Lerma demonstrates that the active rule of the monarchy was by no means abandoned. Moreover, recent investigations of international policy during Philip III's reign by Bernardo García García and Paul Allen demonstrate, for example, that both Philip III and Lerma were actively involved in finding solutions to conflicts that had carried over from the reign of Philip II and in reappraising the Spanish monarchy's position on the world stage.[5] Similarly, both of them participated actively in the debates about solutions to the financial crisis which faced the Spanish monarchy from the start of the reign. Studies by Ildefonso Pulido Bueno and Juan E. Gelabert, among others, demonstrate that Philip III and Lerma proposed several fiscal initiatives and that their lack of success resulted as much from the complex

[3] Robert A. Stradling, *Philip IV and the Government of Spain, 1621–1665* (Cambridge, 1988), p. 8.
[4] John H. Elliott, "Yet another crisis?" in Peter Clark, ed., *The European Crisis of the 1590s* (London, 1985), p. 309.
[5] García García, *La pax hispánica*, insists that the Duke of Lerma played an active role, and Paul Allen, "The Strategy of Peace: Spanish Foreign Policy and the 'Pax Hispanica', 1598–1609," Ph.D. diss., Yale University, 1995, makes the same case for Philip III.

structures of the Spanish monarchy and the problems caused by Philip II's policies as they did from the alleged ineptitude of Philip III and Lerma.[6]

Part III draws attention to several issues that dominated politics during the first ten years of the reign: the confrontational relationship with France despite the Peace of Vervins in May 1598; the war with Elizabeth of England that did not end until 1604; the long and costly conflict in the Low Countries, which was not solved until 1609 and then only provisionally; the disastrous financial situation; and the problem of the Moriscos, who were ultimately expelled from Spain between 1609 and 1614. An analysis of the documents from this period clearly shows that the Spanish crown under Philip III and Lerma debated and tried to address all of these problems. Their policies differed radically, however, from those promoted by Philip II. Departing from the expansionist policy of his father, Philip III upheld the priority of conservation, which meant abandoning territories, such as the United Provinces, considered until then an inalienable part of the Spanish monarchy. The "pacifist" policies of the new regime, which Lerma was crucial in defining, also meant that the new rulers followed less aggressive policies toward other European powers, especially France and England, than had been the case under Philip II. For the new rulers the changing international circumstances in Europe and the critical financial situation of the Spanish monarchy meant that Spain could no longer afford to act as Europe's policeman and instead had to choose its interventions carefully and to focus on those that seemed most likely to advance the monarch's desires for territorial and political conservation. The failure of these policies should not be viewed as proof of their inadequacy but as the result of serious mistakes in their implementation and of an international situation over which the Spanish monarchy had little control, especially the political, economic, and military recuperation of France under the leadership of Henry IV and the continuous resistance of the United Provinces. To the extent that success is measured by the preservation of the territorial integrity of the Spanish monarchy, Philip III and Lerma did rather well in the end.

The implementation of Philip III's and Lerma's political vision was obstructed by opponents of the new policies and, perhaps even more detrimentally, by members of Lerma's inner circle. At first glance it may be difficult to assess political dissension during Philip III's reign given the control Lerma and his allies established over governmental institutions. It is important to remember, however, that administrative control in and of itself did not eliminate all political and ideological conflicts. Theories defending the need for councils' control over the king's power persisted, thus making the councils important political actors during Lerma's *privanza*. In addition, some individuals appointed to head the councils viewed many of the institutional and political measures implemented by the king and his

---

[6] Ildefonso Pulido Bueno, *La real hacienda de Felipe III* (Huelva, 1996); and Gelabert, *La bolsa del rey*, esp. chaps. 1.1 and 3.1.

favorite as a direct attack on their power and privileges. These personal and ideological conflicts were reinforced by royal ministers who opposed the regime's policies, especially those with respect to the Low Countries and the peace with England.

Philip III's and Lerma's policies were perhaps most seriously undermined by the behavior of some prominent members of Lerma's own governmental team. According to contemporary opinion, the imposition of a government based on a monopolistic faction provoked an exponential increase in political corruption. Scandals caused by the immoderate behavior of royal ministers were not new to the Spanish monarchy, but during the reign of Philip III political corruption became a topic of central importance in the ideological debate, especially after 1607. The detentions in that year of two of the most prominent members of Lerma's inner circle, Pedro Franqueza and Alonso Ramírez de Prado, and the trials of Rodrigo Calderón, Lerma's principal favorite, created the impression that political corruption permeated Philip III's and Lerma's government. Much of Chapter 8 focuses on the charges against Lerma's allies and related themes, including theories of corruption in early modern Spain and examination of how the detention of Lerma's clients weakened his grip on power. The chapter ends with a discussion of the increasing "criminalization" of politics in the second half of the reign. Until around 1609 political controversies had centered on the nature of Lerma's *privanza* – the legitimacy of his role in the government and the consequences of the regime's policies. Thereafter, the debate shifted to a focus on the ethics of his actions, with his enemies arguing that monopolistic favorites brought about widespread corruption.

Part III ends in 1609 after the corruption scandals concerning the detentions of Franqueza and Ramírez de Prado, which coincided with two of the most important political measures of Philip III's reign: the signing of the Twelve Years Truce with the United Provinces (1609–21) and the expulsion of the Moriscos (1609–14). The Twelve Years Truce marked – at least symbolically – the end of Philip II's policies towards the Low Countries and signaled the abandonment of the principle that military pressure would continue until Catholicism was imposed throughout the territory and the United Provinces were once again under Spain's authority. Although the Truce was justified on tactical grounds – the monarchy's critical financial predicament – in reality the agreement symbolized Philip III's and especially Lerma's belief that the monarchy had to abandon its claims over selected territories to protect its nucleus in the Iberian peninsula and its Italian possessions.

The need to defend the signing of a truce with the Dutch rebels, a measure opposed by many key members of the military and aristocratic elites, led Philip III to decree the expulsion of the Spanish Moriscos. Modern historians have commonly depicted the expulsion – one of the most controversial decisions taken during the reign of Philip III – as a timely development of a "racist" perception of the "other" among the Spanish elites, resulting from a deepening conviction that the Moriscos could not be transformed into "true" Christians and from the presumption that they constituted internal enemies of the Spanish monarchy. Although these justifications for the expulsion were put forward, I argue that the decision was taken principally to deflect criticism of Philip III's decision to sign the Twelve Years Truce with the Dutch and to establish him as a true Catholic monarch.

.

7

"We need miracles"

On 5 July 1599, Lerma informed his uncle Juan de Borja of the latest developments in the *Cortes* of the crown of Aragon and expressed his hope that "His Majesty will become the most beloved and respected monarch ever and that we will be able to accomplish deeds worthy of his holy fervor."[1] At the time, however, many of Lerma's contemporaries believed that the Spanish monarchy was surrounded by enemies and misled by untrustworthy friends, utterly ruined and internally divided, and that only a miracle could help the king improve the state of the monarchy.

The monarchy's critical predicament became a central topic of debate, but if all agreed on the severity of the disease, not all agreed on its causes. There were, for example, those who believed that the ultimate cause was the envy of other monarchies, which wished to limit and, if possible, destroy Spain's power. The Duke of Sessa, Philip III's ambassador to Rome, expressed this view in a letter to Baltasar de Zúñiga, Spain's ambassador to France: "Truly, sir, I believe we are gradually becoming the target at which the whole world wants to shoot its arrows."[2] Other Spaniards placed the blame on Philip II's policies, especially on his attempts to extend the influence of the Spanish monarchy throughout Europe and the world, and pointed to the fact that the period from 1570 to 1598 was characterized by continuous conflicts, enormous expenses, and military efforts that had driven the Spanish monarchy to financial bankruptcy and political crisis.[3]

At least until 1596–7, the state of the royal finances did not affect Philip II's policies. As modern historians have explained, Philip II's strategic vision beheld Europe "as a society broken by civil war between nations, whose reconstruction called for a new imperialism" to be led by the Spanish monarchy. Three elements were key to his imperial scheme: the need to secure the safety and integrity of Christendom against the Ottoman empire and its allies; the reestablishment of

---

[1] BL, Add. 28422, Lerma to Borja, fol. 78.
[2] Duke of Sessa to Baltasar de Zúñiga, 28 Sept. 1600; cf. Parker, *The Grand Strategy*, p. 111.
[3] The increasing financial burden is, perhaps, best understood by examining the growing expenditures of the Spanish monarchy in its war effort in the Low Countries: by 1577 the Spanish monarchy had spent 1 million ducats per year in its efforts to recapture the provinces that rebelled in the 1560s. This amount increased to 3 million by 1588 and to more than 4 million by 1594. See I. A. A. Thompson, *War and Government in Habsburg Spain, 1560–1620* (London, 1976), p. 288; and Geoffrey Parker, *The Army of Flanders and the Spanish Road, 1567–1659* (Cambridge, 1972), pp. 241–7.

unity in the church throughout a Europe divided after the reformation; and the spread of Christianity throughout the world.[4] This strategic view of Spain's role in world affairs, defined by Geoffrey Parker as "messianic imperialism," required, according to Philip II and his favorites, valor rather than prudence, expansionism rather than conservation.[5]

By 1596, however, Philip II and his favorites became aware that their policies were not bringing positive results and that internal opposition was mounting. The crown had proved unable to defeat the rebels in the Low Countries despite the financial resources and military forces they invested. France was beginning to show signs of recovery and a resolve to stop Spain's intervention in its internal affairs. Elizabethan England also seemed stronger than before: it had created a powerful fleet, maintained its support of the rebels in the Low Countries as champions of European Protestantism, and increased its control over Catholic Ireland. The letters exchanged between Cristóbal de Moura, Philip II's chief favorite, and the Marquis of Poza, president of the Council of Finance, during 1596 point to the political tensions created by a strategy that required enormous financial resources and the indefinite expansion of these resources. In all his messages Poza insisted on three main points: that all sources of royal income had been consumed; that increasing financial needs were forcing the king to give important political roles to other members of the body politic, especially the Castilian *Cortes*; and that it was the king's duty to plan for the future by ending the conflicts and restoring the integrity of public finances. To do so, the monarch had to change his priorities by favoring conservation over expansion.[6] In the same year, Martín de Padilla, *Adelantado* of Castile, further insisted that "no power exists that can maintain continuous wars, and even for the greatest monarch it is important to conclude wars rapidly." If, Padilla continued, the monarch cannot find rapid solutions to the conflicts in the Low Countries and other European territories, "the patient [meaning the Spanish monarchy] will soon die."[7]

Confronted with failure and political opposition, in the last two years of his reign Philip II adopted measures that appeared at least on the surface as a provisional dismantling of his "grand strategy." On 29 November 1596, the king ordered a suspension of all payments to bankers in an effort to alleviate the weight of the public debt and liberate some cash to attend urgent military expenses.[8] Two years later, after having spent 1 million ducats in an effort to keep Henry IV from becoming king of France, Philip II acknowledged his defeat and signed the Peace of Vervins agreeing to return all territories taken by Spain during the civil conflicts in

---

[4] Tuck, *Philosophy*, pp. 65–7.

[5] Geoffrey Parker, "David or Goliath? Philip II and his World in the 1580s," in Richard Kagan and Geoffrey Parker, eds., *Spain, Europe and the Atlantic world. Essays in Honour of John H. Elliott* (Cambridge, 1995), pp. 245–66.   [6] BI., Add. 28378, Moura to Poza, 18 May 1596, fol. 41v.

[7] Cf. Kamen, *Philip of Spain*, p. 308.

[8] Modesto Ulloa, *La hacienda real de Castilla en el reinado de Felipe II* (Rome, 1963), pp. 532–7.

France.[9] Four days after endorsing the peace with France, on 6 May 1598, with the consent of his son and heir Prince Philip, the monarch signed a royal decree naming his daughter Isabel Clara Eugenia and her husband-to-be, Philip II's nephew Archduke Albert, as sovereigns of the Low Countries,[10] explicitly acknowledging his defeat and asserting that pacification of the Low Countries could not succeed through repressive policies but required a certain degree of respect toward the customs and political traditions of his subjects in Flanders.[11]

Despite these measures, Philip II left many problems unresolved. It was generally agreed that the new rulers needed to confront the crises of the monarchy without delay. Some unresolved problems required an immediate answer (what to do, for example, with the Marquisate of Saluzzo, a northern Italian territory occupied by the Duke of Savoy, Charles Emmanuel, a Spanish ally), whereas others involved long-run strategic considerations (relationships with France, England, and, above all, the rebels of the United Provinces) and called for a redefinition of Spain's role in world politics.

Modern historians have viewed the steps taken by Philip II near the end of his reign as temporary and circumstantial; they certainly did not connote the end of the Spanish monarchy's "messianic imperialism," but a tactical retrenchment to permit its recovery.[12] Philip II, historians argue, was simply following the advice of his father, Emperor Charles, who asserted that when obliged to negotiate with other powers, a monarch may agree to the unavoidable, but he should never agree to anything that affects religion, sovereignty, or property rights over territories because to relinquish something, even a little, would inevitably lead to the loss of all.[13]

If one considers only Philip III's public declarations at the beginning of his reign, it seems that he was prepared to follow his father's strategic vision concerning the role of the Spanish monarchy in European affairs. In his first address to the Council of State, for example, Philip III presented himself as the faithful heir of his ancestors and a champion of the Catholic faith, which he promised to defend even if it meant the loss of all of his kingdoms. Voicing traditional political views, Philip advised his ministers that "all matters of state you discuss have to be adjusted to the precepts of divine law"; in other words, the defense of the Catholic faith was to take priority over all other considerations. Do not forget, he told his counselors, that "if the cause of the war is good and just, God will support us."[14] These were the views of a militant king with an activist policy, and they were propagated in poems and

---

[9] The Peace of Vervins was signed on 2 May 1598. José Luis Cano de Gardoquí, *La cuestión de Saluzzo en las comunicaciones del imperio español (1588–1601)* (Valladolid, 1962), pp. 18ff.
[10] Parker, *The Grand Strategy*, p. 279.
[11] Parker, *The Army of Flanders*, pp. 247–51; Fernández Albaladejo, *Fragmentos*, p. 193; and Jonathan I. Israel, *The Dutch Republic. Its Rise, Greatness and Fall, 1477–1806* (Oxford, 1995), p. 254.
[12] Elliott, "Yet another crisis?" p. 307.   [13] See Parker, *The Grand Strategy*, p. 89.
[14] In González Dávila, *Historia de la vida*, pp. 44–5.

royal entries proclaiming the new king to be a champion of the Christian faith and a conqueror of men and lands in all corners of the world.[15]

But such public declarations of continuity hid complex ideological shifts that were simultaneously taking place with respect to how the Spanish monarchy should confront other European powers and set its long-run goals and priorities. Although its approach to dealing with European powers did not crystallize definitively until 1609, the new regime pursued policies aimed at conservation rather than expansion and favored negotiation over conflict. Francesco Contarini, the Venetian ambassador in Madrid, expressed this new political vision succinctly when he wrote that a key characteristic of the new regime was its "lively desire for peace."[16] In practical terms this strategy meant the adoption of policies aimed at ending ongoing conflicts and protecting those territories considered the nucleus of the monarchy – the kingdoms in Spain and Italy[17] – while attempting to gain the collaboration of other kingdoms for the resolution of the monarchy's financial predicament.

How Philip III's subjects perceived the situation facing the Spanish monarchy is reflected in the words of González de Cellorigo, one of the most perceptive analysts of Spain's situation in the early seventeenth century, when he wrote that these "times are the worst ever."[18] Cellorigo found it easy to identify the causes of the ills of the Spanish monarchy: an alarming decline in population, the monarchy's financial bankruptcy, and, most importantly, the loss of the unique virtues that had enabled Spain to become the most powerful monarchy that ever existed. The first two ailments meant the weakening of some of the key foundations upon which the greatness of a monarchy was built: "a sound financial and economic base" and "a large population engaged in productive activity."[19] The third suggested that Spain had become a place where virtue was despised and vice praised, a country inhabited by "bewitched beings, living outside the natural order of things."[20]

Despite such pessimistic views, not everyone anticipated the future with apprehension; after all, they believed that God had given humans the capacity to analyze problems and that rulers had at their disposal the science of politics "to conserve the monarchy and prevent its downfall."[21] According to such views, the first thing a new prince had do was to learn from his ancestors because precedents "can give life

---

[15] See, for example, Vega Carpio, *Obras escogidas*, vol. II, pp. 98–9; Francisco de Medrano, *Poesía*, ed. Dámaso Alonso (Madrid, 1988), pp. 193, 327. On Philip III's public intentions at the beginning of his reign see also Allen, "The Strategy of Peace," p. 57.

[16] Report of 6 Nov. 1599; *CSPVen*, vol. X, p. 385.

[17] For a more interesting view of the complexity of the political debate regarding the Spanish monarchy's European policies during the first years of the new reign see Charles Howard Carter, *The Secret Diplomacy of the Habsburgs, 1598–1625* (New York, 1964), chap. 5: "The Ultimate Question: War or Peace?"

[18] Martín González de Cellorigo, *Memorial de la política necesaria y útil restauración a la república de España* [1600], ed. José L. Pérez de Ayala (Valladolid, 1991), pp. 7, 94.

[19] Tuck, *Philosophy*, pp. 80, 81.

[20] González de Cellorigo, *Memorial*, p. 79; cf. Elliott, *Spain and its World*, p. 240.

[21] González de Cellorigo, *Memorial*, p. 54.

9 Pedro Antonio Vidal, *Philip III*. The king is portrayed as a militant king, a
champion of the Christian faith and a conqueror of men and lands in all
corners of the world.

to future enterprises and let us imitate the good things of the past,"[22] which implied the existence of a golden age worth imitating and a need to discern the causes of decline in order to cleanse the kingdom of all evil.[23]

There were many reasons why seventeenth-century Spaniards viewed the reign of the Catholic Monarchs, Isabel and Ferdinand, as the golden age of the Spanish monarchy. Under their leadership, for the first time in centuries, the peninsular kingdoms – at least those belonging to the crowns of Aragon and Castile – had been united in pursuit of a common destiny designed to impose Christianity as the sole faith in the Iberian peninsula. They were also perceived as the monarchs who restored peace to the kingdom, promulgated new laws to promote the well-being of the commonwealth, created new governmental institutions, and controlled corruption in their lands. Peace and prosperity spared their subjects from waging internal and foreign wars and enabled them to cultivate the peninsular kingdoms and to create, in the words of González de Cellorigo, the conditions necessary to transform the Spanish monarchy into the most powerful political entity in Europe.[24]

This view of Isabel and Ferdinand's reign as the golden age of Spanish history in contrast to the conflict-ridden and, ultimately, unsuccessful reign of Philip II raised many questions for Philip III and Lerma. Could Spain possibly maintain an active role in European politics with a strategy like Philip II's? Should the defense of Catholicism take priority over other strategic interests? Should they try to preserve and defend all territories claimed by Spain or should they opt to conserve only those that made up the core of the monarchy? According to many of Philip's subjects there was only one answer to all these questions: the Spanish crown should not try to obtain glory through conquest or the defeat of its enemies but should secure the conditions that would conserve the Spanish monarchy intact. A prudent monarch, according to Alamos de Barrientos, was obliged to evaluate not the causes of a conflict or the religious and ideological characteristics of Spain's enemies, but the advantages and disadvantages that old and new conflicts brought to the monarchy. Alamos himself believed that Lerma should recommend that Philip III end all conflicts in which Spain was involved, especially in the Low Countries, and preserve, by any means available, the peace with France. But, above all, Philip III should be told not to begin new wars or other conflicts. Instead, the king should promote a policy of temporary retrenchment so that his monarchy could "concentrate upon itself with renewed vigor to recover its natural ardor," the only way, according to Alamos, that Spain could regain the power, territories, and influence it had lost during the last years of Philip II's reign.[25]

The course of action Philip III, Lerma, and their supporters could pursue in Spain's conflicts depended not only on their personal preferences but, especially in the beginning of the reign, on the views of other members of the body politic and on

---

[22] Cabrera de Córdoba, *De historia*, p. 11.
[23] For this mythical golden age, see Elliott, *Spain and its World*, pp. 248–52.
[24] González de Cellorigo, *Memorial*, p. 93; see also pp. 94–5.
[25] Alamos de Barrientos, *Norte*, p. 96.

the fact that a policy of peace was far easier to recommend than to implement. Many royal officials continued to support the policies pursued by Charles V and Philip II and believed that the destiny of the Spanish monarchy was to govern the Christian world with the consequent right and duty to intervene in European conflicts, especially those provoked by Protestant forces. These officials also defended the so-called unity of the Spanish monarchy and the duty of the Spanish monarch to defend the integrity of all territories belonging to the Spanish crown, from the kingdoms in the Iberian peninsula to those in Italy, from the Netherlands to the Indies.

Among the problems confronted by the new rulers perhaps the easiest was Spain's relationship with France. The Peace of Vervins, signed in May 1598, allowed both monarchies to address disagreements without resorting to armed conflict. There were occasional conflicts (the war between France and Savoy for the Marquisate of Saluzzo; Henry's support of the Dutch rebels; or the conspiracies between Spanish ministers and some French nobles to instigate internal conflicts to weaken Henry's power) but all of them were solved in a timely fashion. Both monarchs and their closer ministers concluded that this was a time of peace and, in fact, agreed to open talks in the hope of establishing a matrimonial alliance between Henry IV's heir and one of the Spanish Infantas.[26]

Although France was Spain's historical enemy, Elizabeth's promotion of piracy against Spanish ships, her open support of the rebels in the Low Countries, her attempts to weaken Spanish control over the Indies, and her plans to colonize and "reform" Ireland made England a priority in Philip III's foreign policy, although the conflict with Elizabeth appeared from the beginning less urgent than those with the French and the Dutch. Lerma and his supporters believed that if the crown were to win the war in the Low Countries they had to neutralize Elizabeth; therefore, in the words of Paul Allen, the "keystone of Spanish foreign policy in 1599 was precisely the peace with England."[27] But Philip III also felt pressure from within and without the Spanish kingdoms to protect the English and Irish Catholics by not settling the conflict with Elizabeth. Although Philip III never yielded to the pressure from some of his ministers and from the English refugees to reinvigorate the plans for the conquest of England, in 1601 he approved a less ambitious enterprise: the creation of a fleet whose aim was to help the Irish rebels "free the Irish Catholics by reestablishing the true religion."[28] Its complete failure persuaded

---

[26] On the relationships between France and Spain in the first years of Philip III's reign see Antonio Eiras Roel, "Política francesa de Felipe III: las tensiones con Enrique IV," *Hispania*, 118 (1971); David Buisseret, *Henry IV* (London, 1984), pp. 83–5, 111–14; Cano de Gardoquí, *La cuestión de Saluzzo*, pp. 20–1; and Bernard Barbiche, "L'Exploitation politique d'un complot: Henri IV, le Saint-Siège et la conspiration de Biron (1602)," in Yves-Marie Bercé and Elena Fasano Guarini, eds., *Complots et conjurations dans l'Europe moderne* (Rome, 1996), pp. 271–88.

[27] Allen, "The Strategy of Peace," pp. 69–74; see also the report of the Count of Miranda and the royal confessor to Philip III on 25 January 1602; cf. Federico Eguiluz, *Robert Persons, "el architraidor"* (Madrid, 1990), pp. 409–11.

[28] See AGS Est., *leg.* 249, n.p., a report dated Mar. 1612 on the Irish campaign.

Philip III and Lerma to abandon all attempts to attack territories under English control and to pursue other tactics, including looking to the future and to Elizabeth's successor,[29] even contacting the Scottish candidate, James VI, in anticipation of a future agreement between the two monarchies. Once James became king of England in 1603, the Spanish authorities committed all their efforts toward reaching a peace agreement with the new king, which was ultimately signed in 1604–5.[30]

The question of the Low Countries posed the new rulers even more demanding and complex problems than Spain's relationship with either France or England. One of the complicating factors had to do with the legal status of the United Provinces. During the 1560s and 1570s Spaniards viewed the rebels as Spanish subjects and the troubles they provoked as an internal crisis. Philip II's failure to defeat the rebels, however, radically transformed this situation. By the 1580s and 1590s the United Provinces had gained a new status, equivalent in the eyes of its inhabitants to an independent polity. They saw nothing that connected them to the Spanish king, while few if any considered the possibility of returning the provinces to Spanish rule. Equally important, in resisting "Spanish aggression," the United Provinces had become "one of the great powers [military, naval, and political] of Europe."[31]

During the first years of the reign the Spanish government continued to identify the inhabitants of the United Provinces as "rebels" who should be pacified and reintegrated into the Spanish monarchy. This was, however, more a legal fiction than a reality. Like many other Spaniards, for example, Alamos de Barrientos viewed Flanders as one of the Spanish kingdoms, although he chose to include the conflict with the rebels of the United Provinces in the chapter on "foreign wars" where he also discussed Spain's struggles with England and France. More importantly, in his advice to Philip III and Lerma, Barrientos acknowledged that the rebels had offended the Spanish crown, but he thought it now impossible to reinstate Spanish authority. To forgive them and restore their privileges was far better than to continue a military campaign that had brought no benefits to Spain.[32]

Philip III and Lerma seemed convinced, like Barrientos and others, that peace was the only available solution, although it would not be easy to implement.[33] The regime's views on the conflict are evident in a letter from Juan de Borja to Lerma on 25 March 1601 and in Lerma's reply to his uncle.[34] Borja began with blunt reflections about the Spanish failure to defeat the Dutch rebels and stated that to invest more money and men in the pacification of the Low Countries, as some royal ministers had petitioned, seemed therefore ludicrous. The Spanish crown did not have enough funds to make its currently required payments to Flanders, much less

---

[29] See Albert J. Loomie, *Spain and the Early Stuarts, 1585–1655* (Aldershot, 1996), chap. 7.
[30] On the peace agreement with England see below, chap. 8.
[31] Israel, *The Dutch Republic. Its Rise*, p. 253; on this topic see also chaps. 11–17.
[32] Alamos de Barrientos, *Discurso político*, pp. 32–7, 75–7.
[33] Israel, *The Dutch Republic. Its Rise*, pp. 254–5.
[34] BL, Add. 28423, fols. 454r–455r, Borja to Lerma, and Lerma's answer, 25 Mar. 1601.

to finance a grand military campaign. In opposition to calls for renewed military effort and warnings that a peace agreement with the United Provinces was likely to lead to rebellion by loyal provinces as well, Borja asked the king to "suspend" the conflict "at least temporarily." If such an agreement was impossible, it was not because it would hurt the interests of the monarchy, Borja went on, but because too many people benefited from the war. The timing for such a peaceful solution was now perfect, because the agreement was to be signed by the Archdukes. Any criticism would be directed against them; their reputations would suffer, not the king's.

Lerma's answer to his uncle demonstrated, however, that the situation was far more complex. The conflict in Flanders, he wrote, "is the major problem we have … and none other has me more awake (*desvelado*) and worked up." The best solution was, as Borja had indicated, a truce with the rebels, a measure the king had ordered his envoy Fernando Carrillo to pursue, but of which nothing had yet come. Failure to achieve a truce involved more than opposition from royal ministers: the king's reputation was at stake. Before Philip could publicly declare his desire for a truce, it was required that the rebels "petition it first," and so far there was no indication that they were ready to do so. Increased Spanish military efforts were necessary to isolate the rebels from their allies, which, according to Lerma, explained the regime's policies toward France and its overture towards England, both measures taken by the new regime in the first years of the reign.[35]

In addition to international conflicts, the new regime had inherited from Philip II a disastrous financial situation, which not only limited the possible solutions to external conflicts but also posed a potential threat to Lerma, whose enemies could use it to weaken Lerma's influence over Philip III.[36] The topic of royal finances was indeed one of the central concerns of those who supported and advised Philip III and Lerma. Without money, wrote Ramírez de Prado, "there will be no peace, and justice and religion will disappear, and, therefore, we must do everything humanly possible" to obtain the financial resources needed by the crown.[37] He reiterated this topic in a later report to Lerma on 11 January 1600, noting Philip II's enormous expenditures during the last five years of his reign and explaining that the new king, given his many obligations, could hardly be expected to manage with less.

The Count of Montesclaros, the king's representative in Seville, described the state of the royal finances in dramatic tones in his address to the city aldermen as he attempted to persuade them to approve the financial aid (*servicio*) voted by the Castilian *Cortes*. According to Montesclaros, a monarchy rested on two principal

---

[35] See also BL., Add. 28424, Borja (1 Apr. 1601) to Lerma, and Lerma's answer (5 Apr. 1601), fols. 5–6; Parker, *The Army of Flanders*, pp. 250ff; on the regime's policies towards the conflicts in Flanders, see also below, chap. 9.

[36] AGS CC, *leg.* 2793, bk. 6/fols. 216–217v: Ramírez de Prado to Lerma, 13 June 1599, fol. 216. On Lerma's awareness of the potential political consequences of the crown's financial crisis, see BL., Add. 28422, fol. 8r, Lerma to Borja, 30 Oct. 1598.

[37] AGS CC, *leg.* 2793, bk. 6, Ramírez de Prado to Lerma, 7 July 1599, fol. 905.

foundations: reputation and power. Now, he claimed, the Spanish monarchy was losing its reputation; only two decades ago the Spanish armada had defeated the powerful Turkish fleet at Lepanto, but now a handful of pirates were able to attack the Spanish coastline without opposition. Spain's loss of reputation was due to its loss of power, more specifically to the absence of financial resources to support its power. The situation was grave indeed because the king had no money to maintain his person and household, to pay his ministers and officials, and even more importantly, to defend his kingdoms and defeat his enemies.[38] Although there was much rhetoric in Montesclaros's words, they fairly represented the state of the royal finances. Only one month after Philip III had inherited the throne, the Council of Finance sent a *consulta* indicating that the king had nothing but debts and that only quick measures would enable the monarchy to pay the salaries of royal ministers and soldiers as well as the debts and interest to the bankers and the expenses of protecting his territories in Italy and the Low Countries.[39]

The rulers were faced with a limited set of remedies. They could try to increase revenues, reduce expenses, and/or improve the administration of the royal treasury. No measure was without difficulty, and some had the potential to endanger the regime's stability. Few believed it possible to increase existing fiscal demands on the kingdom of Castile. For forty years Castile had shouldered most of the support of the monarchy, and since 1596 a murderous plague had killed many Castilians, disrupting the economy and reducing the number of taxpayers. Philip III and Lerma were warned that if they tried to impose additional taxes on Castile they could expect strong opposition, perhaps even rebellion. Instead, they were told to reduce expenses radically and to implement new fiscal policies designed to make possible the redemption of all debts (*desempeño*) and the balancing of the royal finances.[40]

Most of the ministers who advised Philip III and Lerma on these matters agreed that the bulk of the crown's expenses resulted from the maintenance of a powerful military machine. To reduce these expenses, Spain needed to reach permanent peace agreements with England and, especially, with the United Provinces, but the Spanish crown could not obtain immediate relief from the costs of "foreign wars" because it could not achieve peace until 1605 and 1609. Military campaigns were not the only causes of fiscal problems, and some ministers deplored the steady increase in expenses which had been kept under control during the reign of Philip II. In November 1599, for example, a *junta* headed by the royal confessor Fray Gaspar de Córdoba released a proposal for a radical reduction in the expenditures

---

[38] BL, Sloane 3610: "Lo que el marqués de Montesclaros refirió a boca en el cabildo de Sevilla en 3 de octubre de 1600 sobre la concesión de millones," fols. 22–4.

[39] *Consulta* of the Council of Finances, 21 Oct. 1598; cf. Gelabert, *La bolsa del rey*, pp. 29–30.

[40] See, for example, Alamos de Barrientos, *Discurso político*, pp. 118–19; BNM, Mss 8526, "Discurso sobre el gobierno que ha de tener su Majestad en su monarquía para gobernarla," 15 Oct. 1599, fols. 29–30v; and BPR, Mss II/2227, "Cosas que han resuelto en la Junta con el padre confesor," 9 Nov. 1599.

of the royal households and a substantial cut in the number of *mercedes* with financial benefits attached, which the new regime was distributing. The *junta* asked that the expenses of the royal households be cut by at least 50 percent, a reduction to the level of spending during the reign of Philip II.[41] The new rulers, however, seemed to lack the will to follow these recommendations. Rather than reducing royal *mercedes*, for example, Philip III increased them substantially to compensate Lerma for his services and to enable Lerma to reward his allies and supporters.[42] Expenses of the royal household also continued to grow and eventually doubled from the half-million ducats per year during the reign of Philip II to more than 1 million, an amount that was not significantly reduced at any time during Philip III's reign.[43]

Given the difficulties of reducing military expenses and the regime's refusal to cut others, the only alternatives left were to look for new sources of revenue and to create new financial institutions that would give the rulers greater control over the royal treasury. Regarding the former, the regime tried to implement some rather extreme measures, demonstrating not a well-designed fiscal plan but a state of desperation. In addition to asking his affluent subjects for "voluntary donations," in October 1600, Philip III issued a royal order known as the "decree of the silver" which instructed all private individuals and the church as well to compile inventories of their silver holdings. All silver was to be handed over to royal officials to be melted down and used for the issuing of new silver coins.[44] The most controversial measure adopted by Philip III and Lerma at the beginning of the reign, however, was the decision to issue devalued copper coins (*vellón*),[45] a measure adopted only after intensive debate about its legality and possible future consequences, to help the crown pay part of its debts.[46]

Lerma's supporters in the Council of Finance soon realized that such measures were only partial cures for a very sick body. But alternatives were limited. The only one that could, perhaps, offer a long-term solution was to negotiate with the *Cortes* of Castile, which provided a large portion of the monarchy's budget. To open negotiations with the Castilian *Cortes*, however, meant an assessment of political as well as fiscal matters. Which fiscal petitions could be taken to the *Cortes*? Under

---

[41] *Ibid.*   [42] See above, chap. 3, and below, chap. 10.

[43] On this topic see Antonio Domínguez Ortiz, *Crisis y decadencia de la España de los Austrias* (Madrid, 1969), pp. 77–80.

[44] This measure was, however, never fully implemented because of the strong opposition it provoked. See González Dávila, *Historia de la vida*, pp. 77–80.

[45] Gelabert, *La bolsa del rey*, p. 30; see also pp. 21–22.

[46] On the difficulties seen by Philip III, Lerma, and their closest advisers as arising from the manipulation of the coinage see, for example, AGS Est., *leg.* 186/n.p., *consulta* of the *Junta de Gobierno*, 17 Febr. 1601; AGS CC, *leg.* 2793 bk. 6/fols. 55–56v, *consulta* of the *Junta de Hacienda* and royal answer, 31 Aug. 1602. In 1617 Lerma himself publicly opposed the minting of new *vellón* because earlier experiences had demonstrated that this was "an inconvenient measure"; see BNM, Mss 5570, "Copias de los pareceres que el Sr. Duque de Lerma ha dado en las consultas que se han hecho a Su Majd. desde el 22 de junio de 1613," vote of the Duke of Lerma in the meeting of the Council of State held on 22 Mar. 1617, fols. 154r–v.

what conditions could the monarch accept the *servicio* of his Castilian subjects? These issues were discussed in July 1600 in a session of the Council of State, whose members advised the king to ask Castile once again for a sacrifice in the defense of the monarchy, reminding them of their obligations to provide the king with sufficient funds for the conservation of the monarchy.[47]

The debate over the fiscal obligations of Castile formed part of a wider discussion of monarchical government. As the counselors of state indicated, the kingdom had a duty to respond to the king's call, especially in cases of extreme necessity, but the monarch also had the obligation to establish the justice of his claims in discussions with the kingdom's representatives. Even among the defenders of the king's absolute authority, thinkers like Bodin and others influenced by his writings on royal sovereignty believed that the king could not impose new taxes or increase those already implemented without consulting his subjects.[48]

This controversy had intensified by the 1590s when the Castilian *Cortes* began to play a more active political role as a result of Philip II's growing financial needs.[49] In his negotiations with the Castilian *Cortes*, Philip II had obtained approval of a new *servicio*, "the millions" (*millones*), signed by the kingdom in April 1590, which amounted to 8 million ducats to be paid over six years. One of the conditions the *Cortes* imposed at the time was that the *servicio* be considered "exceptional" and not subject to renewal without the approval of the cities.[50] The weight of these provisions became clear in 1596 when Philip II tried to extend this *servicio* and to eliminate its original conditions. Although the *Cortes* eventually renewed it, it also wanted to use its newly acquired power to impose stricter clauses – demanding, for example, the right to control the allocation of the funds by proposing that 60 percent (1,400,000 ducats per year) be spent entirely on the *desempeño* (debt repayment) of the royal treasury, a proposal that Philip II rejected.[51]

When Philip III became king in September 1598, the Castilian *Cortes* summoned by Philip II in 1596 was still in session. The new rulers had many reasons to hope that the *Cortes* would again sign a new agreement regarding the *millones*, but they also believed that reaching such an agreement would be too onerous politically. The alternative, as viewed by Ramírez de Prado, was "to avoid the tiresome business of negotiating with the *Cortes* because it was never going to provide additional benefits and would just make us waste time when we cannot afford to do

---

[47] AGS Est., *leg.* 2023/fol. 31, *consulta* of the Council of State, 4 July 1600; reproduced in Mariano Alcocer y Martínez, ed., *Consultas del Consejo de Estado*, 2 vols. (Valladolid, 1930–2), vol. I, pp. 25–7.

[48] On this debate in seventeenth-century Spain see Charles Jago, "Taxation and Political Culture in Castile, 1590–1640," in Kagan and Parker, eds., *Spain, Europe and the Atlantic world*, pp. 48–72.

[49] See Fernández Albaladejo, *Fragmentos*, p. 263; and I. A. A. Thompson, "Castile: Polity, Fiscality, and Fiscal Crisis," and "Castile: Absolutism, Constitutionalism, and Liberty," in Philip T. Hoffman and Kathryn Norberg, eds., *Fiscal Crises, Liberty, and Representative Government, 1450–1789* (Stanford, 1994), p. 185.

[50] On the conditions imposed by the *Cortes* on the first *servicio of millones* see Fernández Albaladejo, *Fragmentos*, pp. 264–6.

[51] *Ibid.*, pp. 268–9; see also Miguel Artola, *La hacienda del antiguo régimen* (Madrid, 1982), pp. 109–11.

so."[52] Philip III shared these apprehensions, and one of his first acts was to adjourn the *Cortes* without reaching any type of agreement.

The new rulers soon found, however, that it was impossible to improve the monarchy's fiscal situation without the support of Castile, an awareness that moved the king to summon a new *Cortes* almost immediately after the old had adjourned in the hope that the new representatives would be more willing to put the "universal" interests of the monarchy above those of their own cities.[53] The negotiations with the new *Cortes* did not prove to be any easier than they had been during Philip II's reign, but in September 1600 the *Cortes* acceded to paying 18 million ducats over six years. All Castilian cities, except Madrid and a few others, consented to this new *servicio*; the agreement was signed by the king and the Castilian representatives on 1 January 1601.[54] The *Cortes* succeeded in imposing new conditions, however, including its right to control the "destiny of the funds collected to pay such *servicio*," a clause that transformed Castile and its institutions into an administrator of their *servicios* to the crown. Furthermore, the *servicio* was to be considered a loan, not a gift, making renewal dependent on the crown's respect for Castile's conditions. The king also agreed not to increase other taxes and *servicios* during the period in which the current agreement was in effect.[55]

According to modern historians, the *Cortes*'s approval of the *servicio* and the king's acceptance of its conditions demonstrated not only the increasing power of the cities but also the weakening of monarchical authority during Lerma's *privanza*.[56] The *Cortes*'s approval of a *servicio* of this magnitude suggests, however, that the crown could rely on enough political instruments to impose obedience on other members of the body politic. In fact, an analysis of the relations between the crown and the *Cortes* confirms the concerted efforts made by the former to convince the representatives and the aldermen of Castilian cities to approve a *servicio* that was extremely unpopular. To accomplish this, the government conducted an intense ideological campaign led by a group of well-chosen spokesmen who constantly emphasized the kingdom's sacred duty to help the king in case of extreme necessity. At the same time, the regime orchestrated well-planned political initiatives designed to enhance monarchical control over Castilian cities and their

[52] AGS CC, *leg.* 2793, bk. 6, Ramírez de Prado to Lerma, 7 July 1599, fol. 906.
[53] Gelabert, *La bolsa del rey*, pp. 31–2.
[54] On the difficulties concerning the negotiations between the king and the *Cortes* see reports by the Venetian ambassador Francesco Soranzo, in *CSPVen*, vol. IX, pp. 404, 406–8, 424.
[55] Fernández Albaladejo, *Fragmentos*, pp. 271–3.
[56] Three historians have suggested the need to pay more attention to the role played by the *Cortes* of Castile in the political process during the seventeenth century: Charles Jago, "Habsburg Absolutism and the Cortes of Castile," *American Historical Review*, 86 (1981), pp. 307–26; I. A. A. Thompson, "Crown and *Cortes* in Castile, 1590– 1665," originally published in 1982, now in his *Crown and Cortes*, chap. 6; and Pablo Fernández Albaladejo, "Monarquía y reino en Castilla: 1538–1623," originally written in 1982, now in Fernández Albaladejo, *Fragmentos*, pp. 241–83; see also Jago, "Fiscalidad y cambio constitucional en Castilla, 1601–1621," in José Ignacio Fortea Pérez and Carmen María Cremades Griñan, eds., *Política y hacienda en el Antiguo Régimen* (Murcia, 1993); and Fernández Albaladejo, *Fragmentos*, pp. 284–99.

representatives. The first mechanism the crown used was its capacity for patronage – the promise of rewards to those representatives and aldermen who supported the crown's interests – a practice frequently employed during Philip III's reign.[57] The use of royal patronage to gain the support of the *Cortes* and the cities was complemented by the activation of patron–client networks, which integrated not only members of the court but also local officials. Some of these networks were headed by Lerma and his allies, who used their influence and connections to promote the king's interests.[58] In addition, Lerma, his allies, and his relatives also acquired local offices in Castilian cities with a vote in the *Cortes*. (Lerma himself held offices in eight of these cities.) They participated in the meetings of the *Cortes* and supported proposals favoring the king's policies. Lerma acted as *procurador* (city representative) in the *Cortes* of 1607 and 1615; other active members included the Duke of Infantado (1615 and 1617); Juan de Acuña (1607); and Lorenzo Ramírez de Prado, the son of Alonso Ramírez de Prado (1611, 1615, and 1617).[59]

Perhaps the weakest aspect of modern studies of the relations between the Castilian *Cortes* and the regime, which makes their conclusions rather tentative, is modern historians' tendency to analyze these relationships in isolation from other monarchical financial initiatives. Most historians disregard the appointment of members of Lerma's team as counselors of finance, the reform of the council itself, and, more importantly, the creation of a parallel organization dedicated to the control of royal finances in Castile and in other kingdoms of the monarchy. From the start of the reign Philip III, Lerma, and their close counselors had sent a clear message about the need to impose tighter control over the Council of Finance, which they tried to accomplish by appointing new members and radically changing the Council's structure and functions. The Council of Finance and other councils shared a political culture that embraced the idea that the primary purpose of the monarchical government was to promote and protect the law, even if this meant that the king's rights were limited and royal orders were not implemented. The

---

[57] There is no analysis of these practices although there are dozens of documents with information on what the *procuradores* (city representatives) asked for and what they received. In 90 percent of the cases the *procuradores* received public bonds with a capital of 50,000 *maravedíes*, a very small amount, which in many cases the *procuradores* were unable to cash. The documents with the petitions of the *procuradores* and the royal replies can be consulted in AHN CS, *legs*. 4410–22; some of these documents have been transcribed in Manuel Danvila y Collado, "Nuevos datos para escribir la historia de las Cortes de Castilla en el reinado de Felipe III," *BRAH*, 8 (1886); and *El poder civil en España*, 6 vols. (Madrid, 1885–6), vol. VI. On the monarchy's practice of not paying the dividends resulting from these bonds see AGS CJH, *leg*. 528/fol. 152, *consulta* of the Council of Finance, 2 Oct. 1614.

[58] Again, there are no studies of these patron–client networks that helped to establish political connections between the center and the periphery. For a few examples of this practice see BPR Mss II/2422, "Correspondencia del conde de Gondomar relacionada con el servicio de millones durante su corregimiento en Toro"; and Fernando de Acevedo, *Copia de una carta de Fernando de Acevedo a la ciudad de Córdoba en razón de la concesión del servicio de millones* (Madrid, 1619).

[59] On Lerma's local offices see Lerma, *Descripción e inventario*; on Lerma's direct participation in the cities' debates see Cabrera de Córdoba, *Relaciones*, pp. 332–3, 341, 343; and Pinheiro da Veiga, *Fastiginia*, pp. 13–14.

Marquis of Poza, President of the Council of Finance from 1596 to 1602, made this point in a letter to Cristóbal de Moura in which he accused the *letrado* members of his and other councils of obstructing the execution of royal orders and paying more attention to the rights of individuals than to those of the crown. The solution, Poza advised, was to introduce additional "robe and sword" (*capa y espada*) members into all councils. Although these individuals were less knowledgeable about the law, Poza claimed, they would certainly be more inclined to execute royal orders.[60]

With this idea in mind, the new rulers implemented a series of reforms and changes in the Council of Finance in 1602. The first was the substitution of Poza, a president appointed by Philip II with close political ties to Moura, by Juan de Acuña, an expert counselor linked to Lerma's faction.[61] Acuña's appointment was accompanied by the addition of several new counselors, almost all of whom were non-*letrados* politically connected to Lerma and his allies: Juan Pascual, a banker and Lerma's ally since Philip II's reign; Cristóbal de Ipeñarrieta, Juan de Borja's client; and Diego Sarmiento de Acuña, Lerma's client.

The addition of loyal ministers to the Council of Finance was accompanied by revisions in the ordinances that regulated its structure and functions. The new ordinances, signed by the king in 1602, combined the council's two branches, one dedicated to the collection of taxes and the other to their administration, into one body that was to be in charge of all financial matters.[62] In addition, Article 24 of the new ordinances prohibited the Council of Finance from involvement in suits brought by individuals against the crown and ordered the council to dedicate all of its time to attending to the needs of the crown.[63]

As a complement to these institutional reforms, the regime created parallel institutions, or *juntas*, made up of Lerma and his men, dedicated to enhancing the king's control of the public budget and finding ways to obtain new resources. Already in November 1599 an informal committee headed by the royal confessor, Gaspar de Córdoba, had recommended that the king create a permanent special committee which would function to control the resources that belonged to the monarchy, to develop new means for reducing the public deficit, and to search for new sources of revenue.[64] The king followed up on this recommendation

---

[60] BL, Add. 28378, Poza to Moura, 31 Mar. 1596, fols. 1–2v. "*Capa y espada*" denoted members of the nobility as opposed to university-educated "*letrados*."

[61] On Poza, his connections with Moura, and Lerma's mistrust of him see Carlos Javier de Carlos Morales, *El Consejo de Hacienda de Castilla, 1523–1602* (Avila, 1996), pp. 173–8. On Juan de Acuña see above, chap. 6.

[62] "Ordenanzas del Consejo de Hacienda, Contaduría Mayor de ella, Oidores y Contadores de la Contaduría Mayor de Cuentas," 26 Oct. 1602, in *Ordenanzas del Consejo de Hacienda*, fol. 36v. On the various reforms of the Council of Finance see Tomás García-Cuenca Ariati, "El Consejo de Hacienda (1476–1803)," in Miguel Artola, ed., *La economía española al final del Antiguo Régimen* (Madrid, 1982), pp. 405–502; Juan E. Gelabert, "Sobre la fundación del Consejo de Hacienda," in Fortea Pérez and Cremades Griñán, eds., *Política y hacienda en el Antiguo Régimen*, pp. 83–95; and Carlos Morales, *El Consejo de Hacienda*, pp. 19–54. [63] "Ordenanzas del Consejo de Hacienda," fols. 39v–40.

[64] BPR, Mss II/2227: "Cosas que se han resuelto en la Junta con el padre Confesor," 9 Nov. 1599.

immediately and in August 1600 ordered the creation of the first *junta* of Finance, whose members consisted of Gaspar de Córdoba, the royal confessor; Juan de Borja; Pedro Franqueza; and Alonso Ramírez de Prado.[65] More important was the creation in 1603 of a permanent *junta* of Finance (*Junta de Hacienda*) to oversee all institutions in charge of royal finances. They were to review all fiscal proposals made by monarchical institutions, conduct the search for new sources of revenue, and control the debt-reduction process. Ramírez de Prado explained the main reason for the formation of this *junta* in a letter to Lerma in which he expressed the need for an expeditious and active (*expeditiva y breve*) implementation of royal orders because the Council of Finance delayed the execution of such orders and was unable to find new sources of revenue.[66] The *Junta del Desempeño General*, as it was to be called, was created by royal decree on 5 May 1603; its members were Lerma, the Count of Miranda, Fray Gaspar de Córdoba, Alonso Ramírez de Prado, and Pedro Franqueza, who had "total and complete power over the administration of royal finances and over finding new sources of revenue without limitation."[67]

At the same time, the new rulers toyed with the idea of bringing all the kingdoms, and not only Castile, to the defense and conservation of the Spanish monarchy. As John H. Elliott has pointed out, the Spanish monarchy was perhaps the most representative case of what he calls "composite monarchies," polities with diverse territories, which although legally under the sovereignty of a single ruler, had, in reality, their own constitutional regulations. In each territory the king possessed a different set of powers and capacities for independent action.[68] In all, except in the Indies and Navarre, the king had to deal with a political culture which prohibited the monarch from taking any action without first consulting his subjects; he also had to manipulate institutions charged with protecting the rights of the kingdoms and their inhabitants. Furthermore, in several kingdoms, such as Portugal, Catalonia, and some Italian territories, the Spanish monarch and his representatives had limited control over the appointment of public officials and tax collection. Spanish monarchs had to comply with constitutional regulations and be prepared to engage in lengthy, time-consuming negotiations with kingdoms trying to impose limitations upon the king's powers in exchange for financial support. In theory, Spanish monarchs accepted this state of affairs without questioning its basis; in practice, they avoided visits to non-Castilian kingdoms in order to evade political and constitutional limitations to their powers. As a result, Spanish monarchs had to depend increasingly on the fiscal and political collaboration of Castile

---

[65] See AGS Est., *leg.* 184/n.p., royal order dated 4 Aug. 1600.

[66] AGS CC, *leg.* 2793, bk. 6, Ramírez de Prado to Lerma, 31 Oct. 1602, fol. 193v. See also *ibid.* Philip III to the Council of Finance, 27 Sept. 1603, fols. 27–8.

[67] A copy of the royal decree creating this *junta* in RAH CP, vol. 15, fols. 164r–165v; on the activities of this *junta* see below, chap. 8.

[68] John H. Elliott, "A Europe of Composite Monarchies," *Past and Present*, 137 (1992).

while the participation of other kingdoms in the defense of the monarchy was further reduced.

By the late sixteenth century the king and his closest ministers began to view the constitution of the monarchy in profoundly negative terms. The Spanish monarchy had become an unstructured polity in which the various kingdoms were only nominally under the king's authority. Most kingdoms did not contribute financial resources to the treasury and refused to alter the situation, claiming constitutional privileges which the king could not afford to challenge because of the threat of rebellion. The non-Castilian kingdoms saw the Spanish monarch as a Castilian king who neither spent time in their territories nor attended to their problems, an indifferent and absentee king who wanted to transform his non-Castilian kingdoms into dependent provinces.[69]

Modern historians have correctly claimed that the regime failed to attract substantial numbers of non-Castilian elites to serve in the government of the monarchy. No doubt, Philip III's invisibility increased the symbolic magnitude of a central royal majesty even while it diminished his influence in kingdoms where political constitutions upheld the idea of a public king who consulted with the other members of the body politic. Although it is true that Philip II had also been an invisible king, Philip III took this behavior to extremes. Philip II, who initiated the process of identifying the Spanish monarchy with Castile, still visited Flanders and Portugal and attended the *Cortes* in the kingdoms of the crown of Aragon on several occasions. In contrast, Philip III never visited any of his kingdoms outside the Iberian peninsula, and even there he stayed mainly in his Castilian possessions with the exception of two visits to Valencia, one symbolic visit to Aragon and Catalonia in 1599, and one to Portugal in 1619. The results of Philip III's inaccessibility were devastating in the long run. The Spanish monarchy was now controlled by the Castilian elite, and a strong sense of political loyalty among its nobility and urban elite emerged, which helped the king to consolidate his power throughout the kingdom. But nothing of the sort happened among the elites of non-Castilian kingdoms, which led to a growing sense of alienation and the development of a powerful discourse on cultural and political diversity among the Spanish kingdoms.[70]

[69] On this topic see the writings of a Catalan, Fray Juan de Pineda, who in his analysis of the Roman empire underlines the idea that Rome became a monarchy when the various provinces started to be ruled by the ruler's *alter egos* and not by their own rulers, as was the case in the Spanish monarchy: Pineda, *Los treinta libros de la monarquía eclesiástica*, vol. III, p. 15. On the increasing perception of the Spanish monarch as a Castilian and "absentee monarch" by his non-Castilian subjects and the political implications of these views see John H. Elliott, *The Revolt of the Catalans* (Cambridge, 1963); and Fernando Bouza Alvarez, "La nobleza portuguesa y la corte madrileña hacia 1630–1640. Nobles y lucha política en el Portugal de Olivares," *Mélanges de la Casa de Velázquez*, 35 (1999).

[70] For the situation in Catalonia see Elliott, *The Revolt of the Catalans*; in Aragon see Gil Pujol, "De las alteraciones a la estabilidad"; in Valencia see James Casey, *The Kingdom of Valencia in the Seventeenth Century* (Cambridge, 1979); and in Portugal see Fernando Bouza Alvarez, "Portugal en la monarquía hispana (1580–1640): Felipe II, las cortes de Tomar y la génesis del Portugal católico," Ph.D. diss., Universidad Complutense de Madrid, 1987.

This failure, however, should not be attributed, as it has been by some historians,[71] to Philip III's and Lerma's abandonment of their responsibilities to rule the entire territory claimed by the Spanish monarchy. Like his father before him, Philip III tried to avoid involvement in the intricate politics of the non-Castilian kingdoms, but he and his favorite did not abandon all attempts to extract from them as many fiscal resources as possible.[72]

The problem posed by the non-Castilian kingdoms became the focus of debate among Philip III's ministers regarding the crown's policy toward the kingdom of Portugal. Many of Philip's ministers viewed Portugal as a rich kingdom because of its extensive imperial possessions and its monopoly over the spice and slave trades. Portugal, however, contributed nothing toward the maintenance of the Spanish monarchy as a result of the conditions Philip II had accepted at the time of Portugal's forced integration into the Spanish monarchy.[73] Lerma's rise to power opened up possibilities for greater control over Portugal's economy and finances, if only because some of Lerma's allies, especially his uncle Juan de Borja, had strong political connections in Portugal. It was Borja, in fact, who in July 1600, when the needs of the monarchy were widely known, told Lerma that the king should and could get what he needed from Portugal,[74] even though every time the king asked for help the kingdom responded with the same words, "there is nothing (*no hay nada*)."[75] This response made Lerma furious. Although he agreed that the king had the duty to respect and to defend the privileges enjoyed by Portugal, he also felt that Philip III had the right "to make use of the kingdom's finances," which were in a better condition than those of any other kingdom because in "twenty years nobody has touched them, whereas the monarchy has had to rely on resources from Castile for Portugal's defense." Lerma's words express an opinion that was gaining ground among the monarchy's supporters: that despite their laws, privileges, and constitutions, the various Spanish kingdoms ought to form a unified body under the authority of their king. Lerma went on to say that no one should promote divisions and differences among them because "all lawfully belonged to the king (*todos son justamente del rey*)."[76]

To benefit from Portugal's assumed riches, some of Philip III's ministers simply proposed a reform of the Agreements of Tomar, especially those that curtailed the king's capacity for independent action in the kingdom. In the end, however, the

---

[71] This is, for example, the position of Elliott and Gil Pujol.
[72] AGS CC, *leg.* 2793, bk. 6, fol. 218v, Ramírez de Prado to Lerma, 28 Aug. 1599.
[73] On the process that resulted in the inclusion of Portugal into the structure of the Spanish monarchy and the contents of the agreements between Philip II and the kingdom (the Agreements of Tomar), see Bouza Alvarez, "Portugal en la monarquía hispana," *passim.*
[74] BL, Add. 28423, Borja to Lerma, 3 July 1600, fol. 143.
[75] *Ibid.*, Borja to Lerma, 24 Aug. 1600, fol. 188v.
[76] *Ibid.*, Lerma to Borja, 28 Aug. 1600, fols. 188v–189.

king favored Idiáquez's position of avoiding such changes because they might increase discontent among Portuguese subjects;[77] he approved the proposal expressed in Lerma's correspondence with Borja: the creation of a new administrative structure which would coexist with other more formal institutional channels both at the court and in Lisbon and which would be controlled by his clients who could help the king gain access to Portugal's financial resources.

The regime's first step was the creation of the so-called *Junta da Façenda* made up of "Castilian ministers" (Molina de Medrano, Diego de Herrera, and Francisco Duarte) and located in Lisbon. The *junta*'s ordinances, conceived by Alonso Ramírez de Prado and approved by the king on 29 March 1601, stated that it was to inform the court on the state of Portugal's finances; to control how Portuguese ministers spent resources sent by the monarchy for the kingdom's defense and the expenses of its viceroy; to prevent the development of illegal trade between Portugal and the East Indies; and to establish and secure tight control over Portugal's commerce with its colonies.[78] To complement this *junta* in Lisbon, the king approved the creation of a *Junta de Hacienda* of Portugal at the court, which was made up of three Portuguese ministers who also served in the Council of Portugal (the Count of Vilanova, Enrique de Sousa, and Pedro Alvarez Pereira) and five Castilian ministers (Juan de Acuña, Fray Gaspar de Córdoba, Pedro Franqueza, Juan Pascual, and Alonso Ramírez de Prado). The duties of this *junta* consisted of studying reports sent from Lisbon, finding ways to increase Portugal's contribution to the finances of the monarchy, and opening negotiations with Portuguese bankers to diversify the monarchy's sources of loans.[79] The existence of these committees and the monarchy's fiscal policies for the kingdom apparently led to discontent among Portuguese subjects who, according to Borja, "have become suspicious that the king refused to visit the kingdom because it seems to them that Portugal has been reduced to a province, as if it had been conquered (*les parece que aquel reino se ha reducido a provincia como si hubiera sido conquistado*)."[80] Despite the growing discontent among the Portuguese, both *juntas* continued to function until 1608, which seems to indicate that Philip III and Lerma found them useful. Data

[77] See the debate on these matters in the meeting of the Council of State held on 2 Nov. 1603: AGS Est., *leg.* 2636/fol. 125.
[78] AGS CJH, *leg.* 409/n.p., "Billete que hizo el duque de Lerma con una instrucción que hizo el licenciado Alonso Ramírez de Prado para los que van a Portugal," 29 Mar. 1601. On the creation of this *junta* see also Santiago de Luxán Meléndez, "El control de la hacienda portuguesa: la Junta de Hacienda de Portugal, 1602–1608," in Fortea Pérez and Cremades Griñán, eds., *Política y hacienda en el Antiguo Régimen*, pp. 377–88.
[79] AGS CJH, *leg.* 409/n.p., royal decree, Apr. 1601, and *leg.* 435/fol. 27, report of the *Junta de Hacienda* de Portugal, indicating members, rules, and responsibilities. On this *junta* see also Francisco Paulo Mendes da Luz, *O Conselho da India* (Lisbon, 1952), pp. 84–5, and Luxán Meléndez, "El control de la hacienda portuguesa."
[80] AGS Est., *leg.* 2636/fol. 125, *consulta* of the Council of State, 2 Nov. 1603.

collected by Peter Thomas Rooney indeed shows a steadily increasing flow of revenues from Portugal during the early years of Philip III's reign.[81]

The "miracles" Lerma had hoped to achieve in order to transform Philip III into the greatest of all kings did not happen during the first four years of the regime. Too many mishaps, both international and internal, prevented the desired achievement. Nevertheless, the beginning of the reign was clearly marked by the efforts of the king and his minister to confront the troubled political inheritance left by Philip II. During this period they appeared to be in control of political discourse and direction. This was, however, a time when a few of Lerma's clients and supporters acquired too much power, too much control over some of the most important affairs of state, too much influence over the favorite and the decision-making process.

[81] Peter Thomas Rooney, "Habsburg Fiscal Policies in Portugal, 1580–1640," *Journal of European Economic History*, 23/3 (1994), pp. 547, 550, 552–3. Portugal was not the only kingdom the crown pressed for more money. Following the example set in Portugal additional *juntas* were created between 1600 and 1608 in Flanders and the Spanish territories in Italy. On the *Junta de Hacienda* of Flanders see AGS Est., *leg.* 2023/fol. 56, royal decree, 10 May 1603; on the *Junta de Hacienda* of Italy see Giovanni Muto, *Le finanze pubbliche napolitane tra riforme e ristorazione* (Naples, 1980), pp. 56–7. On fiscal matters during the Habsburg period in the kingdoms of Catalonia, Aragon, and Valencia see Artola, *La hacienda*, pp. 159– 208; Gil Pujol, "De las alteraciones a la estabilidad," pp. 15–31; and Casey, *The Kingdom of Valencia*.

8

A corrupt regime?

From many points of view 1604 and 1605 can be considered the golden years for Philip III and Lerma. During these two years the strategy adopted in the first few months of the reign began to bear fruit. To the north, the peace with France was holding without major setbacks despite latent tension between the two monarchies.[1] On the Italian peninsula the Duke of Savoy maintained his desire to become an important player in European politics as an ally of Spain. Everybody agreed that peace between France and Spain had helped to relax political tensions in Italy where Spanish power seemed to remain supreme.[2]

During these years major progress was also made in Spain's relations with England. The death of Elizabeth in March 1603 and the enthronement of the Scottish king, James VI, as James I of England, immediately opened a possibility for peace, which both monarchies clearly desired. After almost thirty years of continuous confrontation, in August 1604 the Spanish and English representatives signed the Treaty of London in which both monarchies pledged a peace that lasted until the 1620s.[3] While it is true that some of the English viewed this peace as confirmation of the Spanish monarchy's critical state,[4] Lerma and his allies saw in it a chance for internal recovery. Although the Spanish negotiators had been unable to impose religious tolerance for the English Catholics, they nevertheless obtained several other provisions important to conserving the political and economic strength of the monarchy: a complete halt to the actions of pirates and buccaneers against Spanish ships and Spain's dominions in the Old World and the New, an end to England's support of the rebels in the Low Countries, a reestablishment of

---

[1] On these tensions see Alexandre Cioranescu, *Le Masque et le visage. Du baroque espagnol au classicisme français* (Geneva, 1983), pp. 15–16; and Davis Bitton and Ward A. Mortensen, "War or Peace: A French Pamphlet Polemic, 1604–1606," in Malcolm R. Thorp and Arthur J. Slavin, eds., *Politics, Religion and Diplomacy in Early Modern Europe. Essays in Honor of De Lamar Jensen* (Kirksville, Mo., 1994), pp. 127–41.
[2] Cano de Gardoquí, *La cuestión de Saluzzo*.
[3] The best analysis of the Anglo-Spanish negotiations and the Treaty of London is Allen, "The Strategy of Peace," chaps. 5–6.
[4] See, for example, Sir Charles Cornwallis to "the Lords of the Councell," Valladolid, 31 May 1605, and to "Lord Viscount Cranborne, Principall Secretary to his Majestie," Valladolid, 2 June 1605, in Winwood, *Memorials*, vol. II, pp. 74, 76.

commercial relationships, and the acceptance of Spain's monopoly over the Americas.[5]

As a consequence of the peace with England and a series of financial successes (some of them unanticipated, such as the increase in the amount of American silver sent to Spain), there was a growing feeling of self-confidence toward the conflict in the Low Countries. Only one month after the signing of the peace with England, the Spanish army, led by the new commander Ambrosio Spinola, conquered Ostend after a three-year siege. This victory was important because it signaled a resurgence in Spain's offensive capacity in Flanders, which manifested itself in 1605 through several victorious campaigns, which, even if they did not result in the total defeat of the United Provinces' army, did help to reestablish a Spanish presence in the region.[6]

Other events at the time also contributed to the feeling of well-being among Philip III's subjects and made Philip III and Lerma believe that God continued to protect the Spanish crown. On April 1605 a male heir, the future Philip IV, was born, his birth coinciding with Philip III's ratification of the Treaty of London. As Pinheiro da Veiga, a Portuguese living in Valladolid, noted, the concurrence of the peace with England, Spanish victories over the Dutch rebels, and the birth of Prince Philip created a feeling of hope among many of Philip III's subjects and a belief that the future was going to be stable, prosperous, and peaceful.[7]

To Lerma, the political situation during these years seemed to be completely under control; his power and influence were flowing smoothly. Indeed, until 1605 Lerma had been able to accumulate power and riches without generating much opposition. Those who complained, criticized him, or stirred up the tranquil political waters at court were promptly punished. In December 1605, for example, Lerma ordered the punishment of Father Castroverde, described as a "friar much noted to be inclined after the manner of Prophets of the Old Testament to speak liberally in the pulpit" and who "is lately banished from the court and this city, by reason of a sermon lately preached before the king." Sir Charles Cornwallis, James I's ambassador to the Spanish court, summarized the reasons for Castroverde's banishment by repeating the friar's words: "Princes being the heads and the substances of common wealthes were in these days the shadows of one private man, who according to his own humour governed all things."[8]

[5] Allen, "The Strategy of Peace," pp. 286–8. On the religious issue see Loomie, *Spain and the Early Stuarts.*

[6] That Spinola's military campaigns against the United Provinces was intended "to force" the rebels to ask for a truce or peace was defended by contemporary writers; see, for example, Antonio Carnero, *Historia de las guerras civiles que ha habido en los estados de Flandes desde el año 1559 hasta el de 1609 y las causas de la rebelión en los dichos estados* (Brussels, 1625), p. 557. On these campaigns see Parker, *The Army of Flanders*, pp. 249–50; Israel, *The Dutch Republic. Its Rise*, pp. 256ff; and Allen, "The Strategy of Peace," chap. 7.   [7] Pinheiro da Veiga, *Fastiginia*, pp. 44–9.

[8] Sir Charles Cornwallis to the Earl of Salisbury, Dec.? 1605, in Winwood, *Memorials*, vol. II, p. 174. See also Cabrera de Córdoba, *Relaciones*, pp. 266–7. Cabrera de Córdoba is not as explicit as Cornwallis in indicating the reasons for Castroverde's banishment from the court on 3 Dec. 1605, but he added that

Father Castroverde's criticism of Philip III and Lerma was neither original or new, nor was his fate uncommon. His comments on Lerma's influence over the king echoed the condemnations voiced by participants in the so-called "treason in the royal palace" that resulted in the banishment of the Marchioness of Valle from the court in 1603.[9] Nor were Castroverde's words different from the words included in several placards distributed in Madrid and Valladolid in January 1603 proclaiming that Philip III's only virtue was "Ignorance" and Lerma's was "Greed", and that the combined influence of a king who "is not a king" and of a greedy and worthless favorite would drive the kingdom to its total destruction.[10] The fate of those who either publicly or privately condemned Lerma's role and actions demonstrates his determination to repress all opposition and shows how difficult it was to organize resistance to the king, his ministers, and the royal favorite in early modern Spain.

A political system like the early modern monarchy provided few possibilities for organizing systematic opposition to the ruler or his government, and such opportunities were further reduced during periods when a single court faction controlled power and the royal favor. One obstacle to opposition was a political culture that upheld the idea of absolute political obedience to a ruler who was depicted as a superior being whom none of his subjects could judge or resist. To criticize the king publicly or privately was viewed as an act of treason and, consequently, as an attempt to destroy the peace of the kingdom. During the reign of Philip III this vision prompted Fray Juan Márquez to remind other preachers of their duty to denounce all ills affecting the community, but, he reminded them, they must show unquestionable respect toward the monarch. Otherwise, he noted, "the people cannot be expected to obey royal orders. This is why God so carefully forbade everyone to speak ill of monarchs or to slander their actions."[11] The correct attitude of the king's subjects at all times was to obey without question; one of the characters in Cervantes's play *La elección de los alcaldes de Daganzo* asserted:

> Leave alone those who rule because they know
> Better than us what has to be done.
> If they are bad rulers, pray for their improvement;
> If they are good rulers, ask God not to take them away.[12]

These principles also justified official censorship and legal regulations forbidding the publication of books and pamphlets containing "offensive language affecting

"many persons were not very happy with Father Castroverde's punishment because they liked to hear him for the good doctrine he preached."

[9] See above, chap. 5.
[10] These placards are reproduced in Sepúlveda, *Historia de varios sucesos*, p. 317.
[11] Fray Juan Márquez, "Opúsculo del maestro Fray Juan Márquez: si los predicadores evangélicos pueden reprehender públicamente a los Reyes y Prelados Eclesiásticos," *La Ciudad de Dios*, 46 (1898), p. 181.
[12] Miguel de Cervantes Saavedra, *Teatro completo*, ed. Florencio Sevilla Arroyo and Antonio Rey Hazas (Barcelona, 1987), p. 764.

the fame of princes, kings, and those close to them."[13] Since no one was closer to the king than his favorite, as the royal chronicler Antonio de Herrera y Tordesillas noted, all offenses against the royal favorite were treated as "offenses against the king," which in turn justified Lerma's persecution of those who opposed him or his creatures.[14]

Establishing complete control over private and public opinion was, however, impossible even for favorites as powerful as Lerma. Once he and his allies had monopolized the right to advise the king and had made it plain that they would punish all opposition, the regime's opponents resorted to the only way left to express criticism: the politics of compliment. That praise of the powerful could embody criticism was well understood by early modern Spaniards. They could express views on how rulers should and should not behave in guides, or mirrors, laying out the steps to be followed by rulers who sought to attain the virtues necessary to good kings rather than the vices of tyrants. These same "mirrors" could apply to favorites and other ministers. What on the surface appeared to be flattery could on occasion be interpreted as a radical attack on their activities and programs. Few have expressed better than Erasmus the possibilities available in the use of panegyrics and other complimentary writings. In a letter to his friend Jean Desmarez, Erasmus justified his *Panegyric for Archduke Philip of Austria*, Philip III's great-grandfather:

> Those who believe panegyrics are nothing but flattery seem to be unaware of the purpose and aim of the extremely far-sighted men who invented this kind of composition, which consists in presenting princes with a pattern of goodness in such a way as to reform bad rulers, improve the good, educate the boorish, reprove the erring, arouse the indolent, and cause even the hopelessly vicious to feel some inward stirring of shame.

Erasmus compared himself to Paul, the apostle, who in his attempts to extend the influence of Christianity did not hesitate to avail himself of the rhetorical force of this "sort of holy adulation."[15]

To praise and compliment rather than to criticize openly was the path taken by several writers during Philip III's reign, which explains the increase in the number of panegyrics dedicated to Lerma after 1605 and the increase in the number of

[13] BNM, Mss 12179, report of Pedro Manso, President of the Council of Castile, censoring Juan de Mariana's works, Oct. 1609, fol. 141r; on censorship and ideological control in Spain see Virgilio Pinto Crespo, *Inquisición y control ideológico en la España del siglo XVI* (Madrid, 1983). The regulations controlling what could be published were complemented by a penal system that treated attacks against monarchs and their ministers as treason; see Kagan, *Lucrecia's Dreams*.

[14] "Discurso cómo se ha de entender qué cosa es majestad, decoro y reputación," in BNM, Mss 3011, Antonio de Herrera, *Primera parte de las varias epístolas, discursos, tratados de Antonio de Herrera dirigidos al rey nro. sr. don Felipe IV*, fols. 164v–165r.

[15] Erasmus to Jean Desmarez, Feb. 1504, in Desiderius Erasmus, *The Correspondence of Erasmus*, ed. A. H. T. Levi (Toronto, 1974), letter 180, p. 81; the English version of the *Panegyric for Archduke Philip of Austria*, in Desiderius Erasmus, *Collected Works*, vol. XXVII. On this topic in seventeenth-century Spain see Feros, "Vicedioses pero humanos."

books, pamphlets, and dramas in which a royal favorite occupied a central role.[16] Plays written by Damián Salucio del Poyo, *La próspera fortuna de Ruy López de Avalos* and *La adversa fortuna de Ruy López de Avalos*, and Tirso de Molina's *El vergonzoso en palacio* are cases in point.[17] In these plays, especially in those by Del Poyo, the royal favorite is viewed in a positive light. He is depicted as a minister who, acting as a loyal adviser and a good servant, helps the king to follow a road of virtue and good government.

But even as straightforward panegyrics of the royal favorite, these plays focussed the attention of their audiences on important events and ideas. In his study of early modern literature Stephen Greenblatt has asserted that "even those literary texts that sought most ardently to speak for a monolithic power could be shown to be sites of institutional and ideological contestation."[18] This is precisely what happened with Del Poyo's and Molina's plays on favorites. In them the *valido* is certainly imagined as a virtuous character, as perfect as an earthly angel, but audiences could interpret them in many ways. They could, for example, believe that the favorite portrayed by Del Poyo and Molina was a model, an idealized figure, not an expression of the authors' views of the actual favorite, Lerma. The Portuguese Pinheiro da Veiga, for example, interpreted these plays and other panegyrics exactly this way: he believed that the authors' intention was to depict how a favorite "should be," not how Lerma was.[19] Del Poyo and Tirso de Molina did indeed present their favorites as models, as ideal courtiers, who were always concerned with the interests of the community and not their own, who forgave their enemies, and who did not fear contradicting the king even at the risk of losing power and influence – as, in fact, happens in Del Poyo's plays. These idealized models contrasted radically with the "real" images of Lerma spread by the participants in the "palace conspiracy of 1603" and by writers such as Fray Jerónimo de Sepúlveda and preachers such as Castroverde.

Other central characters in the plays attracted the attention of audiences and readers: at the service of the favorites were corrupt clients who used their patron's confidence and favor to enrich themselves, to persecute their enemies, and ultimately to threaten their patron's power and position. None of the plays makes clear who is responsible for permitting these opportunists to penetrate the inner sanctum of the court, but all the dramas imply that their presence is made possible by a system based on favoritism rather than on merit and virtue. Perhaps the most

16 On this topic see Mary Austin Cauvin, "The *Comedia de Privanza* in the Seventeenth Century," Ph.D. diss., University of Pennsylvania, 1957; and Raymond MacCurdy, *The Tragic Fall: Don Alvaro de Luna and Other Favorites in Spanish Golden Age Drama* (Chapel Hill, N.C., 1978).
17 Damián Salucio del Poyo's plays about Ruy López de Avalos were not published until 1612 and 1614, but Salucio wrote them between 1600 and 1604; see Luis Caparrós Esperante, *Entre validos y letrados. La obra dramática de Damián Salucio del Poyo* (Valladolid, 1987), pp. 65–6; Tirso de Molina's play was not published until 1624, but it was written in 1606; see Tirso de Molina, *El vergonzoso en palacio*, ed. Everett Hesse (Madrid, 1983), p. 14.
18 Stephen Greenblatt, *Shakespearean Negotiations* (Berkeley, 1988), p. 3.
19 Pinheiro da Veiga, *Fastiginia*, p. 61.

important moral impact of these plays was their authors' belief that a favorite had to worry not so much about those who criticized him – his "real friends" who felt obliged to tell him the truth – but about those who flattered him, the "false friends" who were only interested in their own power and advantage.

It is difficult to know whether Salucio del Poyo and Tirso de Molina referred to real events and individuals or just reproduced conventional ideas about the dangers of political ambition at court. What is known, however, is that after 1605 criticism increased substantially, not so much against Lerma himself as against his favorites and close collaborators. Certainly, criticism against Pedro Franqueza, Alonso Ramírez de Prado, and Rodrigo Calderón (against whom there was an assassination attempt in 1604)[20] had existed before 1605, but until then Lerma had always protected his clients by trying to silence all those who went public with their censures. After 1605, however, he could not prevent the spread of rumors about the corrupt behavior of some of his closest aides.

Everyone who had business at Philip III's court knew, for example, that Pedro Franqueza was the most influential minister and that "he [was] extremely expensive (*costosissimo et carissimo*)"; as Orazio della Rena observed in his report to the ruler of Florence, those who came to see him with modest gifts got absolutely nothing in return. Orazio della Rena's views on Calderón were similar: "No one can talk with him if he comes empty-handed." Indeed, because he had become Lerma's main adviser (*es padrone dell'orecchio del duca*) Calderón was portrayed as a minister who "has tyrannized everything and imposed his own ways to negotiate," which involved gifts and bribes.[21] Khevenhüller, the emperor's ambassador to Spain, went even further by claiming that some of Lerma's creatures had transformed the court into a marketplace where everything – justice, offices, and *mercedes* – was sold to the highest bidder. Khevenhüller further believed – and he was perhaps the first to state this point of view explicitly – that Lerma was ultimately responsible for the behavior of his clients.[22]

Khevenhüller was a very well-connected courtier with close ties to the queen, to the queen's favorite, María Sidonia, and to the queen's confessor, Richard Haller.[23] His comments indicate a change in attitude; he and other critics were now describing not only corrupt individuals but a corrupted regime. Lerma's *privanza*, some began to say, had elevated corruption to levels never seen before, as a result, they argued, of the monopoly Lerma and his faction enjoyed over the king. A

[20] Cabrera de Córdoba, *Relaciones*, p. 227.
[21] Biblioteca Nazionale Centrale, Florence, Magl. CI. XXV, cod. 79, Orazio della Rena, "Relazione segreta" (1605), fols. 46v and 48. Simeone Contarini, the Venetian ambassador who also wrote a report on the situation of the Spanish court in 1605, shared Rena's views; see in Cabrera de Córdoba, *Relaciones*, p. 571.
[22] "Relación que hace el conde de Franquenburg al emperador," 1 Jan. 1606, in BNM, Mss 2751, "Historia del conde de Franquenburg," 1138–9.
[23] On the "Austrian circle" in Philip III's court see Magdalena Sánchez, *The Empress, the Queen, and the Nun: Women and Power at the Court of Philip III of Spain* (Baltimore, 1998), *passim*.

monopolistic faction serving an all-powerful favorite gave its members the sensation of invulnerability and its enemies the confirmation that if power and ambition corrupt, absolute power and ambition corrupt absolutely.

Many observers of Philip III's court believed that Lerma knew how his clients behaved but simply refused to prosecute them and instead protected them. Lerma was aware of what was going on, at least partially. In a letter dated 9 July 1605, for example, he informed Franqueza that the royal confessor Fray Diego de Mardones had told him of complaints against Ramírez de Prado who "is destroying everything."[24] Lerma also received a warning that if he was unable to stop Ramírez de Prado and Franqueza, he himself would eventually become the subject of condemnation. Such was the message conveyed in a report from a certain Juan González de Guzmán to the royal confessor Mardones asserting that it was good for Lerma to count on friends who could inform him "about the misdeeds committed by some royal officials. Otherwise, [Lerma's] reputation will be endangered because it is quite common among the people to criticize not the person who committed the misdeed but the person who gave him power and influence."[25] Guzmán's purpose was not only to denounce the power and influence gained by Pedro Franqueza but also to warn Lerma that given "his powerful hand, Franqueza could destroy the royal treasury and even the whole commonwealth in a way that would make it impossible for the king and Lerma to reverse the damage."[26]

Until early in 1606, at least officially, Lerma was still willing to defend Ramírez de Prado and Pedro Franqueza against those who accused them of defrauding the royal treasury. Lerma went so far as to send a *billete*, drafted by Franqueza and Ramírez de Prado, to the Council of Finance, blaming its members for the exhaustion of the royal treasury and ordering that all the money in the hands of the council's officials be immediately transferred to the coffers of the *Junta del Desempeño*. To make his wishes perfectly clear, Lerma ordered the council to end all "replies and complaints" against these orders or the *junta*'s actions and threatened the counselors with an investigation to determine whether some of them were responsible for fiscal malfeasance.[27]

Believing that Lerma's support was unwavering, Franqueza and Ramírez de Prado even had the audacity to send a report (known as the *consulta del desempeño*) to Philip III on 13 February 1606 in which they claimed that they had laid the foundation for the fiscal recovery of the monarchy and had brought the public deficit under control. "We have resolved the problem of the public deficit in a way no one has expected," they wrote, assuring the king that they had been able to pay all debts and had obtained sufficient resources to cover both ordinary and extraordinary

---

[24] AGS Est., *leg.* 202/n.p., Lerma to Franqueza, 9 July 1605.
[25] AGS CC VI, *leg.* 2792, bk. 1, fol. 186r.   [26] *Ibid.*
[27] *Ibid., leg.* 2793, bk. 6, fols. 467r–v, Lerma to the Council of Finance, 11 Jan. 1606; see also fols. 26r–v, a report sent by Ramírez de Prado and Franqueza to Philip III justifying the need to criticize publicly the Council of Finance and indicating that they had prepared the *billete* to be sent to the Council of Finance which only needed Lerma's signature.

expenses for the coming years.[28] In a similar report, this time addressed to Lerma, Franqueza and Ramírez de Prado reiterated their claim of success and expressed their belief that they deserved the largest *mercedes* ever granted to any of the king's servants as well as their expectation that Lerma would champion their request as "our true patron and lord."[29]

The report of Ramírez de Prado and Franqueza was truly extraordinary, and, had it been true, the central aim of Lerma's government would have been achieved: the financial recovery of the monarchy. But few, if any, believed their pronouncements. Instead their report gave some of Lerma's opponents, such as Queen Margaret and her allies, an opportunity to regain the political initiative they had lost after the affair of the Marchioness of Valle in 1603 by concentrating their criticism on what they believed to be the weak link in the chain of command created by Lerma.[30]

Even Lerma himself did not have much faith in the veracity of Ramírez de Prado's and Franqueza's claims. Despite their assertions, Lerma knew that the fiscal crisis threatening the future of the Spanish monarchy had worsened rather than improved, and he doubted that anything had been done in the last three years to improve the situation. In a long response, Lerma suggested that the two had misinformed the king by presenting a rosy picture of a bleak situation. He reminded his creatures that they had failed to include in their reports all the information necessary for a full assessment of the state of the royal finances. They had not, for example, included the amount of unpaid debts for the years 1603–5, omitting those relating to the "army of Castile, the prisons, borders, galleys, salaries of palace servants and ministers and officials of the councils, plus all the quantities that had to be paid to the bankers to reduce the public deficit."[31] Lerma further noted that other parts of their reports also contained misstatements or inaccurate information. Now the king knew from their report how much money had entered the royal treasury, but nowhere in it could he find the sum total of expenses. Lerma also reminded them that if the agreements with the Genoese Ottavio Centurione and other bankers had brought momentary relief, they had also brought a serious increase in the amount of interest the monarchy would have to pay in the future. The Duke of Lerma ended his reply by adding that it was already clear that the monarchy would find it difficult to pay its ordinary expenses in 1606 and that the extraordinary ones, unpredictable but sure to come, would make the

---

[28] *Ibid.*, fols. 29–32v, Pedro Franqueza and Alonso Ramírez de Prado to the king, 13 Feb. 1606.

[29] *Ibid.*, fols. 33–34r, Franqueza and Prado to the Duke of Lerma, 13 Feb. 1606.

[30] On Queen Margaret's criticism of the *Junta de Desempeño* in general and the activities of Prado and Franqueza in particular see Pérez Bustamante, *La España de Felipe III*, pp. 124–5; see also María Jesús Pérez Martín, *Margarita de Austria, reina de España* (Madrid, 1961), pp. 148–9; and Sánchez, *The Empress*, pp. 135–6.

[31] AGS CC VI, *leg.* 2793, bk. 6: "El Sr. Duque de Lerma para lo del desempeño; pondré aquí lo que a mi se me ofrece sobre estos papeles del desempeño," fol. 913.

10　Juan Pantoja de la Cruz, *Queen Margaret*. The Queen, perceived by many as
an opponent of Lerma and his policies, played an important role in bringing
public charges against some of Lerma's favorites.

financial situation as critical as before despite Ramírez's and Franqueza's rhetorical claims to the contrary.[32]

By the summer of 1606 hope was replaced by despair. In a *billete* to Franqueza dated 29 July Lerma noted that debts were growing uncontrollably while "we are witnessing the complete desolation of Castile," a situation that "worries me a great deal." This *billete* also demonstrated that Lerma's attitude toward his two ministers was beginning to change and that he was willing to tolerate criticism of his former protégés. The reason for Lerma's new attitude is unknown, but it could be related to the fact that much of the criticism directed against Franqueza and Ramírez de Prado began to be voiced by Lerma's relatives and close allies, who charged the two with political corruption and inability to revive the dying royal treasury.[33] Ramírez de Prado was also aware of this changing mood. "All those who write to his excellency [Lerma] criticizing us," he wrote to Franqueza, "not long ago praised us, saying that never before existed men who were able to do as much.... Now all is forgotten, deserved rewards become complaints and promises are not fulfilled."[34]

But the Duke of Lerma continued to rely on his two clients because he believed they could still assist him in solving the problems of the royal treasury or at least help him maintain financial administrative structures, such as the *Junta del Desempeño*.[35] The regime's intention to maintain an independent body under the king's and Lerma's direct control became clear on 16 December 1606 when the king signed a decree establishing the *Junta de Hacienda* modeled after the *Junta de Desempeño*.[36] Although the main task of this new *junta* was to reduce the public deficit, the scope of its jurisdiction was broader than that of its predecessor. It received from the king, for example, "absolute jurisdiction (*plena potestad*) to administer, benefit, and collect all my rents without any restraint," and all councils (including the Council of Finance) and other royal institutions were ordered "to obey and execute the *junta*'s orders as if they were mine (*como si yo por mi Real persona lo ordenara y mandara*)." That the *junta* represented a more ambitious step in the attempts to solve the financial problems of the monarchy becomes clear when one considers its much larger membership, a total of ten high royal officials, a membership that also demonstrated that Franqueza and Prado were no longer the only crucial players in fiscal matters.[37]

---

[32] *Ibid.*, fol. 917.

[33] For the Countess of Lemos's attacks on Lerma's favorites see Biblioteca Nazionale Centrale, Florence, Magl. CI. XXV, cod. 79, Orazio della Rena, "Relazione segreta" (1605), fol. 47.

[34] AGS Est., *leg.* 266/n.p., Lerma to Franqueza, 29 July 1606; this file also contains reports sent to Lerma by the royal secretary Juan de Ciriza and Juan de Mendoza, Marquis of Hinojosa and Lerma's cousin, on these matters, Franqueza's letter to Ramírez de Prado, and Ramírez de Prado's bitter response.   [35] AGS CC VI, *leg.* 2793, bk. 6, fol. 917v.   [36] *Ibid.*, fols. 116r–117v, 16 Dec. 1606.

[37] In addition to the Duke of Lerma, the Count of Miranda (President of the Council of Castile and Lerma's ally), and Gerónimo Xavierre (Philip III's confessor), other members of the *junta* included Juan de Acuña (President of the Council of Finance), Alonso Ramírez de Prado, Pedro Franqueza, Pedro de Avila (Marquis of Navas, and *mayordomo* of the king), Cristóbal de Ipeñarrieta (counselor of

The new *junta* began work only four days after its establishment, although in its first meeting, held in Lerma's lodgings, it addressed only practical and organizational matters.[38] But the situation was changing rapidly. Despite the appearance of normality the end of the political careers of Ramírez de Prado and Franqueza was quickly approaching. Until now modern historians have attributed the fall of Ramírez de Prado and Franqueza to a conspiracy organized by Lerma's enemies, Queen Margaret and her allies, and a few courtiers who wanted to weaken his hold on power by attacking his creatures. The reality, however, was more complicated, for Lerma himself played a central role in the fall of his clients, in an apparent attempt to keep the criticism of his clients from discrediting him as well. By 1606 Lerma had already concluded that to save his fiscal plans and, perhaps, even his own position as the king's favorite, he had to free himself from dependence on Ramírez de Prado and Franqueza. Fernando Carrillo, in 1606 still one of Lerma's confidants, sent a report to Philip III in 1616 informing the king that since March 1606 he had been secretly investigating "the actions of Pedro Franqueza, Ramírez de Prado, and others" and that all the evidence he had unearthed had been sent directly to Lerma.[39]

The results of Carrillo's investigation led directly to the detention of Ramírez de Prado on 26 December 1606, only ten days after the creation of the *Junta de Hacienda*. At first rumor denied that his arrest was linked to his official position as a minister of finance,[40] but a few days later his detention was clearly tied to his governmental duties.[41] Only seven days after Ramírez's arrest, Fernando Carrillo was instructed to prepare a thorough report on Franqueza's crimes, a report that was subsequently discussed in a meeting attended by Lerma, the Count of Miranda, Fernando Carrillo, and Gerónimo Xavierre (the king's confessor) on 18 January 1607. The report sent to the king starts with the following recommendation:

By Lerma's order and in his presence we have discussed the report on the activities of Pedro Franqueza, a report that the Duke [of Lerma] has already presented to Your Majesty. After

the Council of Finance), Melchor de Molina (royal attorney in the Council of Finance), and Pedro de Contreras (Secretary of the Council of Finance), as the *junta*'s secretary.

[38] AGS CJH, *leg.* 466/fol. 236, *consulta* of the *Junta de Hacienda*, 20 Dec. 1606. The same day another *junta*, in this case the *Junta da Façenda de Portugal* whose members were Lerma, Ramírez de Prado, Pedro Franqueza, and Pedro Alvarez Pereira (counselor of the Council of Portugal), also met to discuss the fact that this *junta* was now under the jurisdiction of the *Junta de Hacienda*. *Ibid.*, fol. 237, *consulta* of the *Junta de Hacienda*, 20 Dec. 1606.

[39] AGS CJH, *leg.* 542/n.p., Fernando Carrillo to Philip III, 4 Aug. 1616.

[40] Contemporary sources indicate that Ramírez de Prado was detained after he was accused by the Count of Benavente, viceroy of Naples, of trying to marry his son Lorenzo Ramírez de Prado to a daughter of Juan Bautista de Zapata, a bride that the Count of Benavente wanted for his own son; on this affair and Prado's detention see Joaquín de Entrambasaguas, *Una familia de ingenios: Los Ramírez de Prado* (Madrid, 1943), pp. 24–5. It is important to remember that Juan Bautista de Zapata belonged to the house of the Count of Barajas, Diego Zapata, husband of María Sidonia Riderer, Queen Margaret's favorite. On the relationship between Queen Margaret and the Zapatas see Cabrera de Córdoba, *Relaciones*, pp. 165, 425, 451–2, 461; and Pinheiro da Veiga, *Fastiginia*, p. 46.

[41] Cabrera de Córdoba, *Relaciones*, p. 297: report dated on Dec. 30, 1606.

studying the charges against Franqueza, we conclude that he is guilty as charged, and given that Your Majesty is obliged to punish such crimes, we believe Your Majesty must order his detention.

Philip III's answer was immediate and unequivocal: "I order the Duke of Lerma to arrange for the detention of Pedro Franqueza," an order that was executed on the following day, 20 January 1607.[42]

A few months after the detention of Ramírez de Prado and Franqueza, Fernando Carrillo presented the official charges against both ministers, more than 500 in each case, while he tried to insulate Philip III and Lerma from blame for their association with the ministers. Carrillo presented the two as evil men who, blinded by their greed, had betrayed the trust of their benefactors.[43] His reports tell a story of two prominent royal officials who received large sums of money and gifts from Genoese and Portuguese bankers interested in controlling the finances of the Spanish monarchy; from Italian princes who wanted to influence Philip III's foreign policy; and from aristocrats, nobles, and royal ministers in search of royal *mercedes* and offices.[44] In these charges Carrillo constructed what appeared to be a "simple" story of corruption of two royal officials who despite their recognized abilities and experience could not contain an insatiable desire for mundane riches.

It was easy for Carrillo to construct the charges of corruption against Franqueza and Prado. He simply had to make the case that both had violated the laws that prohibited the use of public office for private profit. Judges and all members of the councils, from porters to counselors, were prohibited from receiving "gifts" from any person who had business with the councils or lawsuits or trials pending in the tribunals because it was thought that behind their "liberal" behavior the givers' intention was to bend laws and justice to their own benefit. The members of the Council of Finance were particularly subject to such regulations. All were forbidden to receive anything from anyone concerned with royal finances, especially bankers; they were also prohibited from investing in royal bonds.[45] Franqueza and Ramírez had clearly broken such laws, as both had received numerous "gifts" and

---

[42] AGS CC VI, *leg.* 2796, bk. 11, fol. 3: *consulta* of the *junta* in charge of judging Pedro Franqueza's crimes, 18 Jan. 1607, and Philip III's answer. For a description of Pedro Franqueza's detention see Julián Juderías, "Los favoritos de Felipe III: don Pedro de Franqueza, conde de Villalonga y secretario de estado," *RABM*, 13 (1909), pp. 223–5; Pedro Alvarez Pereira, member of the Council of Portugal, and of the *Junta da Façenda de Portugal* with Franqueza and Ramírez de Prado, was also detained the same day.

[43] For the charges against Ramírez de Prado see AGS CC VI, *leg.* 2796, bk. 10, fols. 184–200v; for the charges against Pedro Franqueza see BNM, Mss 960: "Cargos que resultan de la visita hecha a don Pedro Franqueza, conde de Villalonga." Franqueza did not defend himself against these charges and died in prison in 1614. Ramírez de Prado, on the contrary, defended himself – helped by his son Lorenzo Ramírez de Prado – against the accusations, but he also died in prison in 1608; for Ramírez de Prado's defense see AGS CC VI, *leg.* 2794, bk. 6, fols. 4–94v.

[44] It is important to note that the public charges do not mention the names of those who bribed Franqueza and Prado, except for the Genoese and Portuguese bankers.

[45] See Margarita Cuartas Rivero, "El control de los funcionarios públicos a finales del siglo XVI," *Hacienda Pública Española*, 87 (1984).

bribes from bankers, courtiers and many other individuals. As Fernando Carrillo put it in his charges against Ramírez de Prado, the accused "taking advantage of the authority provided by his offices, abused and transformed them into a source for private ends and interests."[46]

But something altogether more alarming appeared in Carrillo's charges against Franqueza and Prado. In early modern Spain, as in other European polities, corruption could convey a more serious meaning than a violation of individual responsibility; it was also perceived, in the words of J. P. Euben, as "a disease of the body politic." From this perspective, corruption "has less to do with individual malfeasance than with systematic and systemic degeneration of those practices and commitments that provide the terms of collective self-understanding and shared purpose."[47] Carrillo used precisely this meaning of corruption in some of his charges against Prado and Franqueza, charges that presented the most critical view of their activities and, at the same time, questioned some aspects of the governmental system headed by Lerma.

One can examine, for example, the allegations against Pedro Franqueza who was accused of "vainly and ambitiously" recording in his private journal all offices, *mercedes*, titles, and lands he had accumulated during his career and the flattering opinions he held of himself.[48] "Thanks to my great valor and prudence in all matters," Franqueza wrote, "and because I am zealous, careful, loyal, and maintain secrecy in royal affairs . . . I became such a favorite of the king that deservedly I was placed in control of [*pasaron por mis manos*] all important affairs of government, war, finance, and patronage" (fols. 3v–4r). Franqueza went on to write that his political abilities and virtues were such that "the government of the monarchy would suffer badly in my absence" (fol. 4r). In referring to Franqueza's remarks, Carrillo attempted to portray him as a man who wished to reach a position of status, honor, and power inappropriate to his social origins. In early modern Spain ambition was understood not only as the desire for personal enrichment but also for power or, as Saint Augustine stated, "a perverse desire for exaltation."[49] An ambitious individual, and this is how many sixteenth-century writers depicted the royal favorite, wanted to become equal to his master if not to become the master himself.

Carrillo's accusations against Franqueza and Ramírez de Prado also touched upon other important themes. The principal charge against Franqueza, a charge brought also against Ramírez, was that the two had attempted to change the way the

---

[46] AGS CC VI, *leg.* 2796, bk. 10, "Cargos contra don Alonso Ramírez de Prado," fol. 184.

[47] J. P. Euben, "Corruption," in Terence Ball, James Farr, and Russell L. Hanson, eds., *Political Innovation and Conceptual Change* (Cambridge, 1989), pp. 222–3; on early modern Spanish meanings of corruption see *Diccionario de Autoridades*, [1726], 3 vols., facsimile edn. (Madrid, 1969), *s.v.* "corrupción."

[48] Given that the charges against Ramírez de Prado and Franqueza were similar, I focus my analysis on the charges against Franqueza based on the copy in BNM, Mss 960, "Cargos que resultan de la visita hecha a don Pedro Franqueza, conde de Villalonga," fol. 3v. Further references in the text.

[49] Cf. Arthur Kirsch, "Shakespeare's Tragedies," in John F. Andrews, ed. *William Shakespeare. His World, His Work, His Influence*, vol. II (New York, 1985), p. 518.

monarchy was ruled, not because they wanted to benefit or extend royal authority but because they wanted to usurp all power and influence to advance their own personal interests. Carrillo accused Franqueza, for example, of masterminding the creation of the *Junta del Desempeño* in collaboration with Ramírez de Prado to appropriate the lawful jurisdiction of the Council of Finance (fols. 7r–v) and of trying to seize the king's prerogatives "by appropriating for himself the resolution of *consultas* and the distribution of *mercedes*, both belonging to the royal majesty" (fol. 5r).

Carrillo did not make any direct or indirect references to Lerma or to his role in the ruling of the monarchy. Instead, what he tried to convey was a clear distinction between individuals, like Franqueza and Ramírez, who did not have the right to occupy the positions they held or to exercise the functions they claimed for themselves, and individuals, like Lerma, whom the king had selected to serve as his helpers and representatives. But anyone who read Carrillo's charges against Ramírez de Prado and Franqueza, whose trials were public events closely followed by courtiers and royal officials, could easily conclude that their activities simply reproduced what Lerma had done with respect to the power of the king. Lerma had also promoted the creation of new royal institutions, had responded to the *consultas* sent by the councils, and had distributed royal patronage. No doubt some believed that to find the source of the monarchy's ills one should not search the system's lower echelons but rather at the top. It is easy to see how Lerma, the king's favorite, and a close ally of the two ministers only weeks before their detention, could become the next target of those who aimed to depose him from his position as Philip III's favorite.

Aware that criticism of his creatures could also pose a danger to himself, Lerma took steps to control the potential damage before and after their detention by managing the investigation into their affairs. He appointed Fernando Carrillo to investigate their wrongdoings in 1606 because, as noted above, he was a former client of Juan de Borja, Lerma's uncle, a member of the Chamber of Castile and of the Bureau of Queen Margaret's household. Although this is not known for certain, it is also possible that Lerma had persuaded his eldest son, the Duke of Uceda, to appoint Carrillo as his agent and as tutor to Luisa de Sandoval, Uceda's daughter.[50] Lerma thus believed that Carrillo would shield him from potential damage resulting from the deeds of his most prominent clients. Carrillo in fact insisted that both Franqueza and Ramírez de Prado were solely responsible for their sins and crimes, which they had committed without the knowledge of those who supported and favored them. By permitting and ordering the detention of his creatures, Lerma

---

[50] For further details on Carrillo's career see AGPR Ex. Per., 35/23; BNM, Mss 7377, "Memorial del Duque de Lerma a Felipe IV," fols. 350r–v; AGS CC ME, *leg.* 920/fol. 51: Memorandum of Fernando Carrillo to Philip III, 10 October 1607; and "Doña Francisca Fajardo, viuda de Don Fernando Carrillo, presidente de Indias, a Felipe IV," 8 June 1622, in González Palencia, *La Junta de Reformación*, doc. 54, pp. 344–56.

further demonstrated that he did not hesitate to protect his own interests at the expense of others, including his closest creatures, especially if they had attracted attention by their scandalous behavior. This is how Lerma's contemporaries interpreted the fate of Franqueza, who, it was said, fell from power despite the fact "that before his detention Franqueza and Lerma had been very intimate."[51] In public, however, Lerma presented himself as the protector of the common good, a person who was willing to destroy his own men when they dared to corrupt the body politic.[52]

Despite these precautions, Lerma was unable to prevent the charges of political corruption against his creatures from becoming a powerful weapon for those who opposed him and his policies. Corruption indeed became a central theme of political debate during the rest of Philip III's reign. Why this happened had less to do with the extent of corruption than with the political context in which these charges were made. Modern historians have often argued that at the turn of the seventeenth century and during the following decades administrative and political corruption rose to levels previously unknown and that simple and sporadic faults became "the system" (*la fraude érigée en système*).[53] An English historian, Joel Hurstfield, has explained the apparent increase in political corruption in the English monarchy by emphasizing changes that took place in the nature of the government between the late Tudors and the Stuarts. During the sixteenth century, Hurstfield notes, monarchs personally controlled the everyday tasks of government and chose their assistants based on their political–administrative experience, as did Elizabeth. The Stuarts, James and Charles, however, placed their personal desires above the needs of the state and promoted men without political experience or aptitude. Patronage was used by both the Tudors and the Stuarts, but the aims and the results were radically different. Although Elizabeth employed patronage to promote her own men, her actions were viewed as legitimate because she promoted men of "outstanding ability" who, in turn, chose men of quality for the lower echelons of government. Under the Stuarts, however, "ability gave place to physical charm, and political and administrative talents were rated as inferior to superficial personal attributes." In other words, "patronage had been corrupted into favouritism. Patronage is not entirely corrupt. Favouritism is, because it sacrifices the long-term needs of the state to the ephemeral tastes of the monarch."[54]

[51] BNM, Mss 722, "Advertencias que se dieron a Don Rodrigo Calderón, marqués de Siete Iglesias, nombrado para la embajada de Venecia: ¿Cuál le es mejor a vuesa señoría, quedarse en su oficio o irse a su embajada?" [1612], fol. 165r.   [52] BNM, Mss 8741, "Respuesta que hizo don Juan de Idiáquez."
[53] See Hugh Trevor-Roper, "The General Crisis of the Seventeenth Century," in Trevor Aston, ed., *Crisis in Europe, 1560–1660* (London, 1965), pp. 73–5; Vicens Vives, "Estructura administrativa." On the debates over the role and extension of political and administrative corruption in early modern Europe see Jean-Claude Waquet, *Corruption. Ethics and Power in Florence, 1600–1770*, trans. Linda McCall (University Park, Pa., 1992), pp. 1–18.
[54] Joel Hurstfield, *Freedom, Corruption and Government in Elizabethan England* (Cambridge, 1973), p. 153.

Hurstfield's view of England essentially corresponds to what modern historians have written about Spain during the reigns of Philip II and Philip III. One can simply substitute Elizabeth for Philip II and the Stuarts for Philip III. The former, historians argue, concerned himself with the well-being of the commonwealth and always considered the interests of the state above all else, whereas the latter placed his personal needs and pleasures ahead of the well-being of the monarchy. Philip II selected ministers who possessed the same qualities as their king, whereas Philip III chose ministers, such as Lerma, who were preoccupied with enriching themselves, their relatives, and clients. Lerma's desire for riches contaminated the entire system and explained the alleged spread of corruption during his *privanza*.

It is, however, difficult to find evidence to support the view that political corruption became more widespread during the reign of Philip III than in former times. The crimes of Franqueza and Ramírez de Prado were not exceptional either in theory or practice. The notion that money was the key that opened the doors of success at court was already an accepted idea during Philip II's reign. Alonso de Barros's *Filosofía cortesana moralizada*, a book published in 1587 and dedicated to Mateo Vázquez, Philip II's powerful secretary, provides a clear example.[55] In his book Alonso de Barros outlined the difficulties confronted by everyone who tried to start or maintain a career at court. Barros, following popular courtesy books published during the sixteenth century, explained that a courtier had to possess many outstanding qualities and must work hard to perfect himself. But the would-be courtier also needed to know that the most important weapons for success at court were "flattery" and "prodigality." With flattery, he wrote, the would-be courtier would be able to deceive other players and to hide his own lack of merit. With prodigality (meaning in this case bribes and gifts) the would-be courtier, in turn, would obtain favor, offices, attention, and, most importantly, power and influence. There was, Barros insisted, a maxim at court that perfectly summarized how a courtier should behave when confronting those who held the strings of power and influence: "Do not ask for a helping hand if your hand is not full [of money] (*No pidas la mano ajena si la tuya no va llena*)."[56]

Barros's ideas reflected reality. The pervasive existence of bribes and gifts is demonstrated by a *visita* to the Council of Finance in 1596 toward the end of Philip II's reign. Of the seventy-seven royal officials who were investigated, seventy-four were found guilty of enriching themselves and of accepting bribes and "gifts" from

---

[55] Alonso de Barros, *Filosofía cortesana moralizada* [1587], ed. Trevor J. Dadson (Madrid, 1987), *passim*. Barros's *Filosofía cortesana* became one of the most popular books ever published in Spain.

[56] During the sixteenth century numerous treatises were published in which the social importance of gifts was discussed, and in which attempts were made to distinguish between a gift, a symbol of sociability, and a bribe, a sign of corruption. The classical work on the gift and its social functions is still Marcel Mauss, *The Gift. The Form and Reason for Exchange in Archaic Societies*, trans. W. D. Halls (New York, 1990). For early modern Iberian theories on this topic see Bartolomé Clavero, *Antidora. Antropología católica de la economía moderna* (Milan, 1991); and Hespanha, "La economía de la gracia," in Hespanha, *La gracia del derecho*. See also Waquet, *Corruption*, pp. 119–43.

private individuals, of appointing relatives to offices, of buying and selling offices, and of delaying payments of salaries to royal servants. Perhaps it should be noted that Alonso Ramírez de Prado, at the time serving as royal attorney in the council, was one of the three ministers found innocent.[57]

It could be argued that the crimes of these low-ranking officials were trifling peccadilloes compared to those committed by Franqueza and Ramírez de Prado during Lerma's *privanza*. But Philip II's reign offers its own examples of high-ranking officials who were accused of crimes as significant as those of Franqueza and Ramírez de Prado. Such was the case with the king's two personal secretaries, Francisco de Eraso and Antonio Pérez, two of the most powerful men during Philip II's reign. As David Lagomarsino has written, Francisco de Eraso's "peculations and abuses were so notorious that there was no doubt that evidence of them would abound; Eraso had survived for so long not because his crimes were discreet, but simply because his favour with the King had discouraged attempts to bring him to task." When Philip II's favor toward his personal secretary weakened, Eraso became the target of his many enemies and when confronted with a long list of charges opted to resign from his office.[58]

Antonio Pérez's case was somewhat different. That the royal secretary had been able to enrich himself as a result of the king's favor was notorious at the time, but until the 1570s Pérez had been able to prevent all attempts to strip him of power on charges of corruption. Pérez's fate changed when he got involved in a political conspiracy which allowed his enemies to accuse him of ordering the death of Juan Escobedo, Don Juan de Austria's secretary, and when he, in turn, implicated Philip II as the mastermind behind the plot. To stop Pérez from endangering the king's reputation, a *visita* was immediately conducted to establish legal motives for his detention. Pérez was found guilty of selling his favor and influence to bankers, courtiers, and other royal ministers, and, worst of all, of having usurped powers and jurisdictions that did not belong to the sphere of his office.[59] In the end Pérez's fall from grace was the result of losing Philip II's favor, not of the crimes he was accused of committing. Pérez himself noted that behind the accusations of corruption lay a conspiracy orchestrated by his enemies who persecuted him by "taking advantage of the disfavor that His Majesty shows now unto me."[60] Corruption, or the intermingling of power and finance, he pointed out, was widespread at Philip

---

[57] On this *visita* see Cuartas Rivero, "El control de los funcionarios públicos," pp. 145–73; on Philip II's fears of permitting *visitas* against members of the Council of Finance see Riba García, *Correspondencia privada*, pp. 24–5. For the author of a memorandum sent to Philip III in 1599 [BNM, Mss 8526, "Discurso sobre el gobierno que ha de tener su Majd. en su monarquía para conservarla"] the reason for the rampant rise in corruption among royal officials was the lack of political will among Spanish rulers, including Philip II (fol. 18v).

[58] For the charges against Francisco de Eraso see Lagomarsino, "Court Factions," pp. 141–47.

[59] On the accusations against Antonio Pérez see Parker, *Philip II*, chap. 8, and Kamen, *Philip of Spain*, pp. 162–7; on the *visita* against Pérez, and his defense, see Gustav Ungerer, *La defensa de Antonio Pérez contra los cargos que se le imputaron en el proceso de visita (1584)* (Zaragoza, 1984).

[60] *Ibid.*, p. 20.

II's court, and one's fate was determined not so much by one's own actions as by the extent to which one enjoyed the king's favor.

The cases of Eraso and Pérez demonstrate that corruption was indeed a powerful political weapon in the struggle for influence during the reigns of both Philip II and Philip III. Charges of corruption were politically effective, as Joel Hurstfield has indicated; "because the very word corruption is vague and extraordinarily difficult to define, it has, quite understandably, become the stock-in-trade of political controversy." Corruption, he concluded, "is the easiest charge to make and the most difficult to refute."[61] It is not so important to ascertain when corruption was most prevalent, but rather how accusations of corruption varied in different periods. Under Philip II accusations of corruption against political enemies were not often used, perhaps because political struggle was rather fluid with no faction being able to exercise absolute control over power at the court. In contrast, during the reign of Philip III, Lerma and his allies monopolized the king's attention and favor, and the only way others could challenge their dominance – given that the doors of dissent were closed – was to break the king's confidence in his favorite and creatures. To accomplish this goal nothing was more effective than "to criminalize" the struggle for power: to transform the public debate into a debate on ethics and the morals of those who belonged to the king's inner circle.

There are clear signs that this "criminalization" of the political debate was already taking place before 1607, but this transformation became evident after the detention of Franqueza and Ramírez de Prado. By orchestrating the detention of his clients, Lerma had hoped to end the scandal, but the fall of his two creatures created a new political dynamic. Their detention made it possible not only to question their morality but also to question the man who had promoted and protected them for so many years. More importantly, Lerma's active participation in the critique of Franqueza and Ramírez de Prado gave other courtiers the right to express openly their concerns about the condition of the realm. Lerma's adversaries now saw their opportunity to take advantage of charges of corruption at the very center of the royal government.

The detention of the two ministers led to a political crisis that toppled Lerma's closest favorite, Rodrigo Calderón, who was himself made aware of the threat by an anonymous poem that circulated at court: "See how other *privanzas* died / Be afraid of the Third Philip / Because, although he takes time to punish / He is preparing to do so."[62] The author's predictions did not take long to materialize, and immediately after Franqueza's detention, Philip III, pressured by a wave of public anger against Calderón, ordered an official *visita* into his activities.[63] Calderón's fate differed, however, from those of Franqueza and Prado because of his close ties to

---

[61] Hurstfield, *Freedom*, p. 139.   [62] BPR, Mss II/2423, fol. 42.
[63] The judges who investigated Calderón were the Count of Miranda, Fernando Carrillo, Gerónimo Xavierre, and Juan de Idiáquez, all Lerma's close collaborators. On this visita see BNM, Mss 6713, "Descargos de don Rodrigo Calderón," fols. 212r–v.

Lerma. In June 1607 he lost his office as the secretary of the king's chamber, his only punishment. At the same time, he received a royal decree pardoning him for all past deeds and forbidding anyone from publicly persecuting and criticizing him.[64] Despite this lenient treatment, Calderón anticipated further trouble and in a letter to Sor Luisa de la Ascensión, one of his spiritual advisers, dated 4 October 1607,[65] he requested guidance "because we live in a world full of dangers for the body and the soul." Calderón also informed Sor Luisa that he had asked for the king's and Lerma's permission to retire from public life because "I do not want to endure any longer this precarious and dangerous life at court." But if God's will is that "I should continue with this life, bad as it is, and condemn myself and go to Hell, then let us obey His sacred will."

The fate of his clients also threatened Lerma despite his continuous attempts to avoid criticism. That he also had received what he called "gifts" from foreigners and Spaniards alike was, as Simeone de Contarini informed the Venetian senate in 1605, "common knowledge."[66] To prevent these "gifts" from being interpreted as "bribes" by his adversaries, Lerma and his supporters resurrected the distinction between the virtue of "giving" (*dar*), understood as everyone's social obligation, and the vice of "giving with intention" (*dar con intención*). Lerma made this point explicit in his last will, which he drafted during his *privanza* and in which he specified that, although his only intention as Philip III's *privado* was to promote the common good, he recognized that he had accepted gifts (*recibí dádivas*):

I always understood that they were given to me as proofs of good will and not with the intention of forcing me to commit unjust acts. If I realized this was the real intention, I always returned the gifts to their owner, and thus if any other gifts were given to me with bad intentions without my knowledge, I order my successors to return them to whom they belong.[67]

Idiáquez employed the same reasoning in his response to Contarini's report, asserting that Lerma "does receive gifts" but commits no crime because he does so "with the king's consent and pleasure." Lerma, Idiáquez continued, is a virtuous man and "he will never favor anyone who tries to damage the king's or the kingdom's well-being."[68]

Lerma's and Idiáquez's words appear, however, to be an attempt to silence those who insisted that everyone who was a part of Lerma's government was corrupt. Between 1606 and 1608 Lerma was also becoming the target of accusations that charged him with using the king's favor to enrich himself, his family, and his allies. The problem was not that Lerma had accumulated riches, titles and lands because

---

[64] The royal decree pardoning Calderón is dated 7 June 1607; for a few copies of this royal pardon see BNM, Mss 1492, fols. 296–297v; AGS CJH, *leg.* 480, *carp.* 22/n.p., and BPR, Mss II/2423, fols. 5–6.
[65] Rodrigo Calderón to Sor Luisa de la Ascensión, in Manuel Serrano i Sanz, *Apuntes para una historia de escritoras españolas*, 3 vols. (Madrid, 1975), vol. I, pp. 61–2.
[66] Cabrera de Córdoba, *Relaciones*, p. 569.
[67] ADL, *leg.* 11, *carp.* 42: "Cláusulas del codicilio del duque de Lerma," n.d., n.p.
[68] BNM, Mss 8741, "Respuesta que hizo don Juan de Idiáquez."

of Philip III's favor but that the amount was too large and that he had monopolized the best fruits of royal patronage. Royal favorites were not the only ones who transformed royal favor and political service into affluence for themselves and their relatives. During the sixteenth century secretaries and ministers were quick to take advantage of their positions to gain control over lands, income, and offices in Spain as in other European monarchies. Such extensive use of one's position for personal gain suggests that the accumulation of wealth was not of necessity a corrupting influence of power and self-interest, nor was it simply the result of weak kings incapable of resisting the demands of rapacious ministers. In early modern societies power and wealth formed two sides of the same coin. Power required wealth as an exterior manifestation of prestige and as a prerequisite for securing a large retinue; wealth required power, or better, royal favor. To understand Lerma's activities and to place them in a broader context, one should consider the interconnections of politics and wealth, what Joseph Bergin has called the "unmediated cohabitation" of power and profit.[69]

Philip III's open public support of Lerma as his sole favorite did indeed bring tangible benefits to Lerma and the Sandovals. Until 1598 they could only have dreamt of becoming one of the most powerful families in the kingdom, but the death of Philip II and Lerma's instantaneous rise to power as the new king's sole favorite opened the door first to power and influence and then to wealth and fortune.[70] Although on occasion Lerma refused to accept monetary *mercedes* which came from the royal treasury,[71] his desire to accumulate wealth clearly paralleled that of Cardinal Richelieu for whom "nothing seemed too much or too insignificant."[72]

But before money and lands, Lerma and his family had another urgent need: the acquisition of a new title of nobility commensurate with the Sandovals' new eminence. Their desire was fulfilled when the king awarded Lerma the title of Duke of Lerma in November 1599, a Castilian title, which made him twice grandee of Castile and elevated him to a status equal to that held by the most important nobles in the kingdom – the Dukes of Infantado, Alba, Medina Sidonia, Medina de Rioseco, and Osuna.[73] Once the title was granted, Lerma quickly set out to increase the income and lands of his family's estate. Although unable to recover the lands possessed by his ancestors,[74] he received many other royal *mercedes* that rapidly

---

[69] Joseph Bergin, *Cardinal Richelieu. Power and the Pursuit of Wealth* (New Haven and London, 1985), p. 5.

[70] What follows is not a detailed description of Lerma's fortunes. I refer those interested in this matter to Antonio Domínguez Ortiz, *La sociedad española en el siglo xvi*, 2 vols. (Madrid, 1963), vol. I, pp. 363–6.

[71] See, for example, BL, Add. 28424, Lerma to Borja, 31 May 1601, fol. 54, and Lerma to Borja, 25 Aug. 1601, fol. 124v, in which Lerma explains to his uncle his rejection of several substantial economic rewards because of the "poor situation" of the royal treasury.

[72] Bergin, *Cardinal Richelieu*, p. 78.

[73] On the title of Duke of Lerma see *Memorial del pleito de tenuta*, fols. 7r–v.

[74] For the circumstances of Lerma's failure to regain the lands of his ancestors or a monetary compensation see below, chap. 9.

increased the wealth of his house. These included funds associated with his palace offices (20,000 ducats per year in salary); the grand commandery of the Military Order of Santiago (1599), whose annual revenues amounted to more than 20,000 ducats; more than 200,000 ducats in gratuities and gifts;[75] commercial monopolies, such as the right to import wheat from Sicily, a right Lerma sold after numerous complaints for 72,000 ducats, which he then invested in royal income-generating ventures in Italy and Aragon;[76] a share in the slave trade;[77] and a gift of 50,000 ducats after he announced to the king the arrival of the fleet with American silver.[78] Lerma also accepted jewels, paintings, and other gifts of enormous value from Philip III, from foreign princes, and from private individuals. The parliaments of the crown of Aragon (Valencia, Catalonia, and Aragon) also adopted a practice of compensating the favorite for his "good services" to strengthen the harmony between the king and his subjects.[79] In addition to royal favors and other official gifts, Lerma accepted grants from his relatives to help him reduce the debts of his estate: 24,000 ducats annually from his uncle Bernardo de Rojas y Sandoval, Archbishop of Toledo, and 56,000 ducats paid on one occasion by another uncle, Cardinal Tomás Borja.[80] The best proof of Lerma's new circumstances is that in less than ten years (from 1598 to 1608), his annual income rose from about 20,000 ducats to 150,000 ducats – an amount superior to the income generated by the estates of the Dukes of Osuna, Infantado, Escalonia and Alba, equal to the income of the Duke of Medina de Rioseco, and surpassed only by that of the Duke of Medina Sidonia.[81]

Although some of Lerma's contemporaries viewed his enrichment as the natural result of his position as the king's favorite, by 1607 many started to believe that he had gone too far. In the political culture of the times a too biased use of royal patronage could endanger the king and his favorite. "The king is in his kingdom as

---

[75] Lerma, *Descripción e inventario*, fol. 14v. There are differences of opinion concerning the amount received by Lerma in *ayudas de costa*; Lerma maintained that he received "only" 108,000 ducats (fols. 15v–16r). The royal attorney, Juan de Chumacero, in the trial of Lerma immediately after the death of Philip III in 1621, maintained that the amount was 568,000 ducats: see Ciriaco Pérez Bustamante, "Los cardenalatos del duque de Lerma y del cardenal infante don Fernando," *Boletín de la Biblioteca Menéndez y Pelayo*, 7 (1934), p. 525; according to Lerma's grandchild, the second Duke of Lerma, the amount was 182,409 ducats (Gómez de Sandoval Manrique de Padilla, *memorial*, pt. I, fol. 6).
[76] *Memorial del pleito de tenuta*, fols. 16ff.
[77] APM, Protocolo 1848, "Relación de las cuentas del Duque de Lerma," Valencia, 16 Nov. 1604, fol. 1212v. [78] Cabrera de Córdoba, *Relaciones*, p. 16.
[79] *Ibid.*, p. 161: gifts (valued at 3,500 ducats) from the king because Lerma was sick, and gifts (valued at 40,000 ducats) from courtiers and allies for the same reason (p. 336). Lerma received a great number of gifts from foreign princes; see, for example, Schroth, "The Private Collection," pp. 24ff. For the case of the kingdom of Aragon see Gil Pujol, "De las alteraciones a la estabilidad," p. 435.
[80] APM, Protocolo 1848, "Relación de las cuentas del Duque de Lerma," fol. 1212.
[81] See BNM, Mss 7423, "Todos los Grandes, Marqueses, y Condes desde 1598 hasta 1616," fols. 104ff; in Lerma, *Descripción e inventario* he declared that his income was 119,915 ducats annually, 80,891 ducats from his entail, and 39,024 ducats from his salaries and the *encomienda* (land concession); he also declared houses and furniture valued at 55,672 ducats.

a father with many children," Botero wrote in his *Los diez libros de la razón de estado*, indicating the king's obligation to avoid a partial distribution of *mercedes* that favored only his favorite or those selected by the favorite, leaving the rest of the royal servants empty-handed. Partiality would lead to envy and animosity, and those without rewards would "oppose the king to bring the downfall of his favorite as they did Edward II in England over his inordinate preference for Hugh Despenser."[82] The king was also told that he alone should control the distribution of all *mercedes*. No monarch should let others, neither ministers nor especially favorites, manage royal liberality because loyalty and love are directed to the person who controls and distributes royal favors. The king who fails to control royal patronage will jeopardize his authority "while the court seethes with faction and the kingdom with strife."[83]

At the time of the scandals involving Ramírez de Prado and Franqueza, Lerma's contemporaries began to claim that although the favorite deserved *mercedes*, he had received too many, a practice seriously detrimental to the well-being of the kingdom. Even the *Cortes* of Castile approved an official memorandum accusing Lerma of trying to appropriate income voted by the kingdom to support the crown in compensation for territories taken from his ancestors.[84] In the midst of the criticism of Lerma and his allies, Maldonado wrote his influential "Discurso del perfecto privado," and among his many points he included a thorough defense of the favorite's right to accumulate riches in compensation for his extraordinary services to the king. "Royal patronage," he wrote, "is like a mine, and the favorite has all the rights to mine it."[85]

Lerma's contemporaries were just as bothered by the enrichment of his relatives and creatures as by his own personal enrichment. Both Lerma and his contemporaries knew that the prestige of a household was not based solely on the status and power of its most distinguished member. In addition, Lerma perfectly understood that a patron who did not reward his supporters, delayed payment of *mercedes*, or in other ways ignored his clients' needs could not maintain his base of support. The realities of failed obligations made the topic of unhappy clients conspiring against their masters an extremely popular topic in the Spanish drama of the seventeenth century.[86] The Duke of Lerma was no stranger to such complaints. Ramírez de Prado sent numerous letters warning Lerma that he was still waiting for well-deserved rewards. In 1603, for example, he complained that he had not received all the *mercedes* he had earned, whereas others had received more than they deserved:

---

[82] Botero, *Los diez libros*, bk. 1, fol. 18v.   [83] *Ibid.*, bk. 1, fol. 19.

[84] *Memorial de los artículos*, fol. 26v. Lerma sent the king an answer to the *Cortes*'s memorandum later in 1606. Lerma was able, however, to gain the support of the king and several ministers in his attempts to recover part of the territories taken from his ancestors by accepting the ownership of eleven villages that belonged to the crown. On this topic see AGS DGT, *leg.* 335, *exp.* 1.

[85] BNM, Mss 18721/48, n.p.

[86] See, for example, Mira de Amescua, *Comedia famosa de Ruy López de Avalos*, pp. 67–9.

"I know that Your Excellency is powerful and can do whatever you desire; now I need your support in my affairs, and I am confident that there are rewards for me, especially because others have been rewarded even when they do not deserve or appreciate their awards."[87] When confronted with complaints from his creatures, Lerma addressed them in the language of respect and friendship. "I do not want to be viewed," he wrote in response to one of Ramírez de Prado's numerous complaints, "as useless by my friends, and I have already said many times that they deserve all the help I can provide."[88]

Numerous contemporary anecdotes confirm that Lerma's favor and support were viewed as crucial for obtaining royal patronage. In 1605 the Portuguese Tome Pinheiro da Veiga reproduced one of the most popular, the story of a soldier who grew tired of being unable to obtain an audience with Lerma and decided to petition Philip III instead. The king responded, "Go and talk with the duke." "If I were able to talk with the duke," answered the soldier, "I would not have come to see Your Majesty."[89] Even if the story were untrue and merely satirical in tone, it accurately summarized political reality. Lerma's influence over the distribution of patronage was so evident that his contemporaries believed him to be the only one who could transform a desire into a reality, a situation that converted Lerma into the "most solicited, begged, obeyed, and served" person at court.[90]

As a result, Lerma received hundreds of memoranda requesting his support, although he was known to reserve the most lucrative rewards for his relatives, supporters, and allies. Matías de Novoa's complimentary portrait of Lerma presents him in this capacity as a good lord who "intercedes on behalf of those who have served the duke and awards them vice-royalties, judicial offices, generalships, titles of nobility, knighthoods, and commanderies of Military Orders, bishoprics, and ecclesiastical revenues."[91] Lerma helped and promoted, as Suárez de Figueroa pointed out, "an infinite number of men, but particularly those who honored themselves with the title of 'servant of the duke.'"[92]

Already in 1599 the emperor's ambassador to the Spanish court, Johann Khevenhüller, had informed his master that "in this year His Majesty has made big and numerous *mercedes*; the bigger ones went to the Marquis of Denia [Lerma], [and] his relatives,"[93] and the same pattern continued throughout the reign. Indeed, Philip III granted almost half of the seventy new titles of nobility to the Sandovals or to related members of other noble families.[94] Lerma's relatives also received some of the most important commanderies of the Military Orders and

---

[87] AGS CC VI, *leg.* 2793, bk. 6, fol. 948r, Ramírez de Prado to Lerma, 30 Nov. 1603; for other similar cases, see *ibid.*, fols. 903r, 907r, 911r–v.

[88] *Ibid.*, fol. 912r, Lerma to Ramírez de Prado, 28 Mar. 1600.

[89] Pinheiro da Veiga, *Fastiginia*, p. 35.   [90] González Dávila, *Historia de la vida*, p. 42.

[91] Novoa, *Historia de Felipe III*, 60, p. 59.

[92] Cristóbal Suárez de Figueroa, *Hechos de don García Hurtado de Figueroa* (Madrid, 1613), vol. II, p. 547.   [93] BNM, Mss 2751, "Historia de Johann Khevenhüller, conde de Franquenburg," 898.

[94] On the titles of nobility granted by Philip III, see González Dávila, *Historia de la vida*, pp. 252–4.

some other offices viewed as important sources of benefits. Vice-royalties were also given to his family. The 6th Count of Lemos, Francisco Ruiz de Castro, Lerma's brother-in-law, became Viceroy of Naples in 1599, an office he held until his death in 1600, and the 7th Count of Lemos, Pedro Fernández de Castro, Lerma's nephew and son-in-law, occupied the same office from 1609 to 1616; Juan de Sandoval, Lerma's brother, was appointed viceroy of Valencia in 1604; and Francisco de Borja, Lerma's cousin, was appointed to the vice-royalty of Peru in 1614.

Church offices were another convenient source of reward at Lerma's disposal. Bernardo de Rojas y Sandoval, Lerma's uncle, received the most important of these offices when he became Archbishop of Toledo in 1599; and Tomás de Borja, another of Lerma's uncles, occupied the Bishoprics of Málaga (1599) and Córdoba (1602) and in 1616 became Archbishop of Zaragoza. Lerma also rewarded those who entered into matrimonial alliances with his family, such as the Enríquez, Admirals of Castile. As soon as the marriage contract was signed between Lerma and the Enríquez, Philip III ordered the Council of Finance, despite the crisis in the royal treasury, to pay the new couple 100,000 ducats as the bride's dowry. For the groom there was to be another royal gift: the right to export wheat from Seville, a *merced* whose estimated value was 100,000 ducats.[95]

Lerma's liberality toward his clients was no less impressive. Although definitive proof is lacking, there seems to be no doubt that Lerma's creatures together with his relatives received the best fruits of royal patronage. Many received titles of nobility, including Pedro Franqueza, who received the title of Count of Vilallonga; Diego de Sarmiento y Acuña, a member of the Galician gentry, who became Spanish ambassador to the English court and received the title of Count of Gondomar; and Rodrigo Calderón, who from being the son of a modest soldier, Francisco de Calderón, became Count of Oliva and later Marquis of Siete Iglesias, and who even dreamt of becoming a grandee of Castile with Lerma's support. Juan Bautista de Acevedo was another case in point. From being a modest priest who tutored Lerma's son, Acevedo became Bishop of Valladolid, Inquisitor-General, and President of the Council of Castile. Lerma's support also enabled his creatures greatly to increase their fortunes. In 1607, at the time of his imprisonment, Pedro Franqueza, for example, had a personal patrimony valued at more than 1 million ducats, and the same was true of Calderón, whose wealth exceeded that of many members of the old nobility.

But in the end this monopolistic control of royal patronage attracted criticism, and by 1609 many were decrying Lerma's distribution of royal patronage, as reported on 9 May 1609 by Cabrera de Córdoba, who echoed rumors that Lerma was upset because everyone blamed him for not giving them what they wanted and accused him instead of favoring only his own men.[96] The growing criticism

---

[95] For the matrimonial agreement see AGS CC ME, *leg.* 920, *exp.* 51, memorandum of Fernando Carrillo, tutor of Luisa de Sandoval to Philip III, 10 Oct. 1607.
[96] Cabrera de Córdoba, *Relaciones*, p. 368.

convinced many of Lerma's contemporaries that the royal favorite was in the last moments of his *privanza*, and his likely downfall was described in dramatic tones. On 5 September 1607, for example, the self-declared prophet Gabriel Escobar was detained and accused of predicting that in 1608 "Jews and Muslims will be converted ... King Philip III will die, and so will several ministers, in particular the Duke of Lerma, and many other ministers will also lose their heads."[97]

In this atmosphere of criticism, to hold on to his power Lerma needed to do more than simply defend himself against charges of corruption. He had to demonstrate that he remained Philip III's sole favorite. In October 1607 he startled everyone when he expressed his desire to retire from public life. "A piece of news," wrote Cabrera de Córdoba, "that has surprised everyone at the court. No one believes him, however, and suspects that he wants something; only time will tell what it is."[98] Lerma's design soon became clear: "His retirement has come to nothing because the king has not accepted his request."[99] Thus, Lerma's ploy to gain a public demonstration of the king's favor was, at least temporarily, successful.

But in the end Lerma failed to isolate himself and his *privanza* from the charges brought against Franqueza, Ramírez de Prado, and Calderón. To put it simply, in the view of Philip III's contemporaries Lerma's *privanza* had become wholly entwined with corruption, and the crimes perpetrated by Franqueza and Ramírez were viewed as only the tip of the iceberg, just a tiny example of widespread corruption brought about by an over-powerful favorite. Commenting on the detention of the two ministers, a contemporary witness wrote:

the year 1607 started with the fall of several *privados* and their deserved detention because of their corrupt behavior in usurping the royal finances and oppressing the community. Such were their crimes that they weakened the greatest empire ever seen to such a degree that everyone, from the king to the lowest peasant, became poor and needy. Only these false counselors and unjust favorites were prosperous, full of riches and favors for their protectors and underlings.[100]

Even more serious for Lerma and his supporters was the discovery that those who criticized them – and indirectly the king – were becoming bolder. On the morning of 17 July 1608 officials in charge of keeping order at the court (*alcaldes de casa y corte*) sent in a note to Lerma informing him that the night before someone had hung several placards in strategic places (on the doors of the royal palace and of the court jail). The strong words on the placards had "scandalized" the royal officials who read them:

---

[97] Cf. Ronald Cueto, *Quimeras y sueños: los profetas y la monarquía católica de Felipe IV* (Valladolid, 1994), p. 171. [98] Cabrera de Córdoba, *Relaciones*, p. 317, Oct. 1607.
[99] *Ibid.*, p. 322.
[100] BNM, Mss 4072, Gabriel de Peralta: "Memorial de cosas sucedidas en España y a sus gentes," fol. 138v.

O miserable Spanish people,
Who are not able to remedy the insolence
Of this tyrannical *privado*,
Whose absolute and ignorant government
Is destroying and endangering you and your king.

Those who found the placards expressed their complete support for the favorite and promised not to rest until they had detained and punished those who dared to write such monstrosities.[101] The authors of these placards, however, were never identified. Clearly they marked an important new stage in the rising tide of criticism.[102]

---

[101] BNM, Mss 12179, report of the *alcaldes de corte* to Lerma, 17 July 1608, fol. 109.
[102] For a few examples, see Cabrera de Córdoba, *Relaciones*, pp. 344–5; and BNM, Mss 19344, "Vida del ldo. Gregorio de Tovar por sí mismo," fol. 179v.

9

The regime's answer: peace and Catholicism

As stated above, the detention of Franqueza and Ramírez de Prado revealed that those Lerma had placed in charge of fiscal matters had done absolutely nothing to solve the monarchy's financial difficulties. Philip III and Lerma received messages to this effect throughout 1607 and beyond, not only from the Council of Finance but also from the *Junta de Hacienda*, now controlled by Juan de Acuña and Cristóbal de Ipeñarrieta, who transformed it into a mere appendage of the Council of Finance.[1] The new spirit of those who controlled royal finances from 1607 onward was made clear toward the end of February 1607 when the *junta* presented an extended report to the king, written by Ipeñarrieta. His basic point was that the monarchy's debts now totaled almost 20 million ducats, and that financial resources sufficient to meet them had not grown. Philip III's answer revealed the pessimism that permeated the ruling circles and also the realization that the king now depended on the political will of the members of the Council of Finance, which Lerma had accused only a few months earlier of trying to curtail the crown's efforts to solve its financial problems and of mishandling royal finances.[2]

The situation, already desperate, seemed to have worsened when the *junta* sent another *consulta* to the king a few days later. A meeting had been called to discuss a petition Lerma had made in the king's name to sign a contract with the Genoese banker Carlo Stratta, who had agreed to sign a new *asiento* with the crown, providing 300,000 ducats per month to sustain the army in Flanders in order "to reduce the rebels to the obedience of the king." The *junta*'s response left no room for misinterpretation of its position on the matter: there were no revenues with which to sustain a new *asiento*, and instead the king should reduce the amount of money he sent to Flanders (100,000 ducats per month) and begin to think about

---

[1] The new *Junta de Hacienda* held its first meeting on 24 January 1607, just four days after Franqueza's detention; see AGS CJH, *leg.* 474/n.p., *consulta* of the *Junta de Hacienda*, 24 Jan. 1607. This *Junta of Hacienda* existed from January 1607 until at least October 1613 (AGS CJH, *leg.* 520/fol. 207). In all of the *junta's consultas* I have studied the report to the king is always the same: the *junta*, agreeing with the Council of Finance, claims that "there is no money, and there are no ways to change this situation"; see, for example, AGS CJH, *leg.* 474/fol. 314, *consulta* of the *Junta de Hacienda* asserting that it was impossible to send – as requested by the king – 80,000 ducats to the Count of Fuentes, Governor of Milan, given the "critical situation of the royal finances as we have told your Majesty so many times," and Philip III's answer begging the *junta* "to try as best as you can" (*así lo procurará en todo caso*).

[2] AGS CJH, *leg.* 474/n.p., *consulta* of the *Junta de Hacienda*, 24 Jan. 1607, informing the king that the debts to the bankers, counselors, and other royal officials amounted to 19,717,296 ducats.

ways to end the conflict. Philip III's answer demonstrated his growing anger toward the council, but also his impotence: "What I really need is to know that you are doing everything possible to get me the money I have asked for, because if we were able to make this supreme effort now we would avoid new and significant expenses later. Do what you can and inform me about all your steps and initiatives."[3] Philip III received no encouraging news from the ministers in 1607 or afterwards. The dynamic was always the same: the king desperately requested funds; and his counselors refused his requests.[4] Given this situation, no one seemed particularly surprised when Philip III decided to sign a royal decree on 7 November 1607 declaring the monarchy bankrupt and ordering the consolidation of all public debts by renegotiating the conditions of all loans with those who had lent money to the crown.[5]

At the same time, Philip III and Lerma tried to preserve some elements of their earlier fiscal initiatives, especially those designed to reduce the burdens on the royal treasury by involving all Spanish kingdoms in the maintenance of the monarchy. The new element in this strategy was to give more responsibility to the representatives of the kingdom of Castile rather than to place a few select individuals in charge of royal finances. It was Lerma himself who, as a member of the *Cortes* summoned in April 1607, proposed that the kingdom of Castile be placed in charge of the *desempeño*.[6] This step was only the first in a new strategy to deal with fiscal matters, and it was followed by the signing of a contract between the crown and its bankers to establish a more convenient method and a time frame for the repayment of its debts.[7]

In addition, after 1607 the crown also attempted to reduce the number of *mercedes* in the form of financial grants, ordering all councils "not to award so many annuities and *ayudas de costa* because the royal treasury can endure no more expenses."[8] To complement this order, the regime now tried to instill a new

---

[3] *Ibid.*, fol. 421, *consulta* of the *Junta de Hacienda*, and the royal answer, 31 Jan. 1607 and 9 Feb. 1607.

[4] See, for example, *ibid.*, fol. 315, *consulta* of the *Junta de Hacienda*, 3 Oct. 1607 on Lerma's petitions.

[5] "Yesterday an edict was issued," reported the Venetian ambassador Francesco Priuli on 8 Nov. 1607, "suspending payment and assigning a million of gold a year, that is 600,000 crowns for the interest on 12 millions, 400 to be applied to the extinction of the debt," *CSPVen*, vol. XI, p. 56. On the link between Ramírez de Prado's and Pedro Franqueza's downfalls and this decree see Fernández Albaladejo, *Fragmentos*, pp. 274–6.

[6] *Ibid.*, pp. 274ff.; José Ignacio Fortea Pérez, "El servicio de millones y la reestructuración del espacio fiscal en la Corona de Castilla (1601–1621)," in Fortea Pérez and Cremades Griñán, eds., *Política y hacienda en el Antiguo Régimen*, p. 56; Gelabert, *La bolsa del rey*, pp. 44–8. The Council of Finance's view of this agreement is in AGS CJH, *leg.* 474/n.p., *consulta* of the Council of Finance, 19 Oct. 1607.

[7] On this topic see Pulido Bueno, *La real hacienda de Felipe III*, pp. 253–70.

[8] This order, signed by Lerma, was included in a *consulta* of the Council of State, 27 Sept. 1607, AGS Est., *leg.* 208/n.p.; this order was part of a "general reformation" as documented in an order sent by the Duke of Lerma to the Count of Miranda, President of the Council of Castile, in Oct. 1607: see González Palencia, *La Junta de reformación*, doc. 2, p. 4. Orders to curtail the number of *mercedes* with financial grants were issued in later years; see AGS Est., *leg.* 254/n.p., that included similar orders signed by Lerma and dated in 1613 and 1614.

mentality in the royal servants. Previously, those who held royal offices had expected such offices to be the avenue for additional compensation. Countering such expectations, some of Philip III's advisers recommended that the king deny additional *mercedes* to ministers who had already received several. Instead, he should convince his ministers that it was not appropriate to serve the monarch with a "mercantile" mentality (*tan interesada y mercantilmente*). Individuals who had received the honor of becoming royal servants should serve the king and be satisfied with the salaries awarded for their services.[9]

None of these measures, however, made much of an impact, as the councils – and not only Lerma and his supporters – vehemently resisted any proposal that would mean the loss of an important source of political influence. The councils' views on the matter are reflected in the response to Lerma's order written by the Council of State:

Although it is just and necessary to look after the royal treasury and to avoid excessive expenses, to eliminate royal liberality – the virtue that makes the king more magnificent – is unworthy of the greatness of your majesty... To stop distributing *mercedes* will produce great affliction and disaffection (*desamor*) among the soldiers, will give strength to our enemies, and will discourage our friends.[10]

The Council of State did agree, however, to moderate the number and to support only those petitioners who truly deserved a reward. But even this promise was quickly broken. In 1611, for example, the council announced that it was no longer possible to obey the king's order to limit the number of *mercedes* because of the large number of deserving petitioners.[11]

Counselors and royal servants, like royal favorites, were well aware that any reduction in royal patronage would have an immediate impact on their own position and status. Joel Hurstfield explains the logic of this situation when he remarks that in early modern Europe "office having been gained by patronage ... was itself the instrument of patronage.... Through patronage, if successfully operated, lay the path to wealth and the extension of power."[12] By the early seventeenth century royal patronage had become an important royal instrument for the promotion of loyalty throughout the kingdoms; it was also a store of riches, power, and influence used by other members of the body politic. Counselors knew

---

[9] Aliaga to the king, 18 Aug. 1610, in BNM, Mss 1923, "Papeles del Padre Confesor Fray Luis de Aliaga, tocantes a los diversos negocios de que se le ha pedido parecer," fol. 208. Attempts to reduce the number of *mercedes* with financial grants attached were central to the government of Philip IV and his favorite Olivares, but as in the case of Philip III and Lerma their efforts were a complete failure. On Philip IV's and Olivares's policy see "Memorial sobre las mercedes," a document sent by Olivares to Philip IV on November 1621, and the introduction to this document by Elliott and de la Peña, *Memoriales*, vol. I, pp. 1–11.

[10] AGS Est., *leg.* 208/n.p., *consulta* of the Council of State, 27 Sept. 1607.

[11] AGS Est., *leg.* 4126/fol. 8, *consulta* of the Council of State, Mar. 1611.

[12] Hurstfield, *Freedom*, p. 304.

this well. For them, as for others active in the politics of the early modern court, loss of influence over the distribution of patronage endangered their personal economic advancement and, in addition, angered their friends and adherents. The counselors' views on royal liberality clearly show that during the reign of Philip III they continued to view themselves not only as defenders of the king's rights and powers but, more importantly, as defenders of the realm and of individual subjects. Their duty, they constantly argued, was to dispense justice, in this case liberal justice, to the king's subjects without regard for the monarchy's financial capacity to reward all deserving petitioners. In 1620 the Council of Castile made precisely this point regarding Philip III's renewed attempts to halt the growing number of *mercedes*:

> It is well known that from the moment that this Council was created its duty was to protect and help all His Majesty's servants and to reward those who had served him well. This duty is even more appropriate in this present time because royal servants are so numerous and many of them poor and destitute.[13]

The only other area in which Philip III and Lerma could realistically reduce expenses without interference from others was in the military, and here the king and his favorite were persistent, particularly in their attempts to end the conflict in Flanders. Some foreign observers of the Spanish court foresaw in the fall of Franqueza an imminent and radical change in Spanish policy toward the conflict in the Low Countries. "The fall of Franqueza," wrote Francesco Priuli, the Venetian ambassador, "is thought likely to bring about peace with the Dutch; for the war was kept alive chiefly by him on account of the money he made by it. In this opinion the English ambassador concurs."[14] A few years later Fernando Carrillo also noted the connection between the fall of Franqueza and the signing of the truce with the Dutch, although his explanation differed from Priuli's. Carrillo believed that Franqueza's corrupt actions provoked the most serious financial crisis in decades, which in turn "led to the destruction of the kingdom and forced the king to sign the peace with Holland and to sign the decree suspending payments in 1607."[15] It is well known that Franqueza opposed the signing of a truce with the Dutch on several occasions, accusing Archduke Albert and his servants of promoting peace out of regard for their own interests without consideration for the reputation of the monarchy.[16]

---

[13] AHN CS, *leg.* 4421/fol. 158, *consulta* of the Chamber of Castile, 12 Sept. 1620.
[14] *CSPVen*, vol. x, p. 457: Francesco Priuli to the Venetian senate, 20 Jan. 1607.
[15] AGS CJH, *leg.* 542/n.p., Fernando Carrillo to Philip III, 4 Aug. 1616. Jonathan Israel believes that the real cause behind the cease-fire agreement of April 1607 "was the news of the major breakthrough achieved by the Dutch in the Far East in 1605." See Jonathan I. Israel, *The Dutch Republic and the Hispanic World, 1606–1661* (Oxford, 1982), pp. 4–5, 8, 14.
[16] See, for example, AGS Est., *leg.* 2025/fol. 5: *consulta* of the *Junta de Tres* (Juan de Idiáquez, Count of Miranda, and Pedro Franqueza) on the truce with Holland.

The regime's answer: peace and Catholicism

Whether or not Franqueza's detention played a part, the negotiations with Holland for a peace agreement accelerated after 1607, although the "spirit of peace" had grown steadily since 1605 among some of Philip III's subjects. During Ambrosio Spinola's military campaign against the Dutch in 1605, for example, Justus Lipsius published a letter he had written in 1595 asking the Spanish king to sign a peace with the rebels, maintaining that only peace could lead to political stability.[17] Lipsius was not alone in believing that peace was the only alternative; some of the king's ministers, and even the king himself, believed as much. In an instruction he sent to Spinola on 16 April 1606, for example, Philip III ordered his commander to seize all chances to reach a truce with the rebels, which at the time was seen as a key step toward a more durable peace.[18] A few months later, in December 1606, the Council of State openly discussed whether to end the conflict with the United Provinces, a conflict that had brought few results despite the large sums of money and numbers of men deployed.[19]

Two of Lerma's closest collaborators, Juan de Idiáquez and the Count of Miranda, expressed similar views. At a meeting of the *Junta de Gobierno* on 16 January 1607 attended by Miranda, Idiáquez, and Franqueza, Idiáquez openly stated that a "truce with the rebels is what would suit us best in this war, and what we have most desired in recent years." The only prerequisite Idiáquez expressed was that the king must impose strict conditions on the rulers of the United Provinces, including the prohibition of trade with the colonies in the New World, a provision that was also included in the peace treaty with England. Miranda was even more adamant about the need for peace in the Low Countries. Knowing that the rebels had already contacted Spinola concerning peace negotiations, Miranda declared that the "truce is so convenient that it deserves all of us going out to receive it with the cross and holy water." Philip III's answer to their advice was no less forthright, and he ordered them to do everything possible to reach a truce with the rebels, which was, he affirmed, "so convenient."[20]

That these statements were more than simply words is demonstrated by the signing of an agreement for the suspension of arms by the Archdukes on 13 March 1607,[21] a temporary cessation of hostilities made possible only because the rebels also desired "to negotiate."[22] This temporary agreement became the first step in a long process leading to a more permanent settlement, a process that took more time than anticipated because of the opposition of some Spanish ministers and

[17] Tuck, *Philosophy*, pp. 60–1.
[18] Antonio Rodríguez Villa, *Ambrosio Spinola, primer marqués de los Balbases* (Madrid, 1904), p. 131.
[19] Parker, *The Army of Flanders*, pp. 250–1.
[20] AGS Est., *leg.* 2025/fol. 5, *consulta* of the Junta de Gobierno, 16 Jan. 1607.
[21] Rodríguez Villa, *Ambrosio Spinola*, pp. 158–9.
[22] Israel, *The Dutch Republic. Its Rise*, pp. 399ff and his *The Dutch Republic and the Hispanic World*, pp. 18–23.

disagreements among the Dutch and the Spanish regarding the final treaty, whether it should be a truce or a peace, and the nature of its final provisions.[23]

Opposition to a peace agreement with the Dutch came from ministers who believed in Philip II's policies towards the Dutch rebels and saw in the politics of negotiation the seeds of the destruction of the Spanish monarchy's power and influence in Europe. These ministers included Diego de Ibarra, who in 1607 served in the Low Countries; the counselor of state Juan Fernández de Velasco (Duke of Frías); the Duke of Osuna (a grandee who had served in the army of Flanders); and the Count of Fuentes, who was the Duke of Alba's nephew and Governor of Milan. To them and their supporters a truce with the rebels meant the legitimation of the Dutch Republic as an independent polity despite the fact that it had been established by rebellious subjects in defiance of their legitimate sovereign, the King of Spain. The signing of the truce also meant the recognition of political rights for a community of "heretics," thereby violating the essence of the Spanish monarchy, which existed to defend the Catholic faith. The situation was further complicated by the fact that many Catholics, whom the Spanish king had the sacred duty to protect, lived among the heretics. Last but not least, for these ministers the end of hostilities in the Low Countries meant the dismantling of the last barriers for the protection of other Spanish territories. A peace with the United Provinces, they claimed, would have a domino effect, and soon other territories – the Italian ones for sure and probably even the peninsular territories – would escape from Spanish control.[24]

Modern historians have customarily seen the views above as a "respectable" and "compelling" ideological position, whereas they have interpreted arguments in favor of peace as reflective of Philip III's and Lerma's weak and cowardly personalities and of Lerma's personal interests. In the words of Jonathan Israel, for example, Lerma desired peace with the Dutch because this was a conflict "of which he had no first-hand knowledge." To continue the conflict "would have been to encourage the king to rely on advice and experience other than his own," opening the door to other men who could have threatened Lerma's control over Philip III's favor.[25]

The reality was, as always, more complex and, although Lerma and his allies

---

[23] It is not my intention to describe all the steps of the peace negotiations between the Dutch Republic and the Spanish monarchy but to describe the most important moments and analyze their significance in the context of Lerma's *privanza*. Two classic analyses of these negotiations are Rodríguez Villa, *Ambrosio Spinola*; and José María Rubio, *Los ideales hispanos en la tregua de 1609 y en el momento actual* (Valladolid, 1937). Two more recent analyses are García García, *La pax hispánica*, pp. 48–74, and Allen, "Strategy of Peace," chaps. 9–10.

[24] See Rodríguez Villa, *Ambrosio Spinola*, pp. 169–70, 184, 194–5; and Rubio, *Los ideales hispanos*, pp. 63–4. Israel, *The Dutch Republic and the Hispanic World*, pp. 29–33 also reproduces critical comments against the impending truce with the Dutch Republic among the Spanish elite but considers their arguments a mask to hide their personal interests in the continuation of the war: "While the opponents of the truce in both Spain and the Republic thus consisted of coalitions of small minority groups with special interests in the war, on both sides these factions needed to present their arguments comprehensively in terms of national, strategic, and religious interest. They could not afford to appear to be narrowly based or narrowly motivated" (p. 31). [25] *Ibid.*, p. 10.

mainly justified their views on the conflict in the Low Countries with reference to its disadvantage for the royal finances, they also were defending a distinct strategic vision of the Spanish monarchy's role in Europe. In Spain debates about peace and war reflected ideological views on the best ways to conserve the Spanish empire and the virtues its rulers should possess to avoid a decline in Spanish power and influence. These debates did not originate during Philip III's reign, and the need for peace in the Low Countries was forcefully defended by Eboli and his faction during the reign of Philip II. Indeed, from the start of the conflict in the Low Countries in the 1560s, Eboli believed that the only way to conserve the empire intact was not through force but through "collaboration" among the kingdoms and by acceptance of each kingdom's unique characteristics.[26] In practical terms this view implied that in cases of rebellion the immediate response from the rulers should not be military intervention but a negotiated settlement to reestablish political harmony. In a memorandum addressed to Philip II, Furió Ceriol, a writer ideologically linked to Eboli's faction, proposed such a solution and tried to demonstrate that the politics of repression adopted by the crown had brought catastrophic results: the spread of rebellion, the destruction of the land, and the loss of numerous lives. An alternative, and more effective, way to recover the rebellious provinces was by promoting a government based on understanding and respect of the unique conditions in each of his kingdoms,[27] a position also defended by some of Philip III's advisers at the beginning of his reign.[28]

But it is important to remember that Philip's and Lerma's views regarding the conflict in the Low Countries diverged from those defended by the Ebolists. The problems posed by the conflict in Flanders had become radically different. By 1607, the main concern was no longer the most effective measures for reintegrating the rebellious provinces into the Spanish monarchy, a goal (as seen in Chapter 7) no longer believed possible. The current aim was to halt a disastrous conflict without damaging the political reputation of Philip III. In orders to his representatives in the Low Countries, for example, besides expressing his desire for peace, Philip III made clear that he would sign a peace agreement only on the following conditions: refusal to recognize the United Provinces as an independent polity; explicit refusal for the Dutch to participate in trade with the colonies in the New World; and the promise that Catholics living in the Dutch Republic could maintain and practice their religion.[29] Lerma also defended these conditions, but he showed a more practical perspective inspired by the notion of prudence promoted by the theorists of reason of state, who emphasized the monarchy's obligation to value the possible rather than the ideologically ideal. In a meeting of the Council of State held on 17 January 1609, for example, Lerma discussed each of the issues raised by the

---

[26] See Lagomarsino, "Court Factions," pp. 251–6.
[27] "Remedios dados por Fadrique Furió Ceriol a su Majd. para el sosiego de las alteraciones de los Países Bajos de los Estados de Flandes," in Furió Ceriol, *El concejo*, pp. 175–85.
[28] See above, chap. 7.   [29] See Rubio, *Los ideales hispanos*, pp. 74–5.

opponents of a peace agreement with the Dutch. He recognized that the problem of American trade had no easy solution: the monarchy, he said, could insist upon a provision in the agreement forbidding Dutch commerce with America, but the concession alone would not restrict Dutch trade, simply because the Dutch had a more powerful fleet than Spain. This reality, Lerma continued, had to be considered now and in the future, but it should not interfere with the negotiations. Regarding the king's obligation to defend the Catholics in the United Provinces, Lerma reminded his colleagues that during forty years of war the number of Catholics living in the Low Countries had decreased dramatically. To achieve religious tolerance for the Catholics in the United Provinces, it was important to establish civil concord, and he hoped that peace would bring an improved environment for the practice of the Catholic religion as was the case, or so he believed, in England.[30] When Lerma noted the financial impossibility of conducting war his remarks, by implication, went far beyond the immediate discussion and touched upon the dominant ideology of the reign of Philip II, the defense of all territories at any cost. The implicit proposition was that the phase of expansion begun with the reign of Charles had come to an end.[31]

The Italian writer Giovanni da Costa, a defender of the theories of reason of state, set forth the arguments that reinforced the position of Lerma and his allies on the conflict in the Low Countries in a book published in 1610 and entitled *Ragionamiento sopra la triegua de Paesi Bassi.*[32] Although Costa first defended Philip III's decision to sign the truce with the Dutch by claiming that all Christian princes were obliged to promote peace, he also saw the truce as resulting from the king's belief that his monarchy was in serious crisis and that it was necessary to reassess its strategic goals. If a body, Costa wrote, has a cancerous part, the only way to save it from fatal contamination was to cut off the sick member, as allegedly did Augustus Caesar and other Roman emperors, who decided to abandon quarrelsome conquered provinces to save the core of the empire.[33] True reason of state, he concluded, bound the king to avoid endangering the whole polity through a pursuit of impossible dreams, and in the specific case of the Dutch Republic, a truce was the only way to save both the reputation of the Spanish king and his realms.[34]

---

[30] There are no data confirming, or denying, Lerma's belief that the situation of the Catholics living in the Dutch Republic improved after the signing of the Twelve Years' Truce in 1609, although it seems clear that, at least in certain territories of the United Provinces, the truce (as well as religious conflicts within the Dutch Reformed Church) made possible some level of tacit tolerance (by not enforcing the ordinances forbidding Catholic worship) and a more active missionary campaign organized by the *Missio Hollandica*. On this topic see Israel, *The Dutch Republic. Its Rise*, pp. 377–95; and Christine Kooi, "Popish Impudence: The Perseverance of the Roman Catholic Faithful in Calvinist Holland, 1572–1620," *Sixteenth Century Journal*, 26 (1995). I thank Dr. Christine Kooi for sharing with me her views on this topic.

[31] Lerma's views in Rubio, *Los ideales hispanos*, pp. 89–90; these were also the views defended by Spinola in October 1608: see Rodríguez Villa, *Ambrosio Spínola*, pp. 233–4.

[32] Giovanni da Costa, *Ragionamiento sopra la triegua de Paesi Bassi* (Genoa, 1610), pp. 3–4, 14–15.

[33] *Ibid.*, p. 31.

[34] *Ibid.*, pp. 34–6. See also Lipsius, *Los seis libros*, bk. 5, chaps. 5 and 19, and bk. 6, chap. 7.

The regime's answer: peace and Catholicism

The decision by the Spanish rulers to favor a policy of appeasement resulted in the Archdukes' signing of the Twelve Years' Truce on 9 April 1609, later ratified by Philip III on April 14. The agreement was considered provisional, and its temporary character was demonstrated by the fact that neither of the central issues was resolved: the question of the United Provinces' legal status and the status and future of the Catholics in the Dutch Republic.[35] Parts of the agreement did refer to matters of commerce, especially to the question of Dutch participation in the trade with the East and West Indies and with European powers. The Dutch were allowed to trade with all European countries, including Spanish territories in Europe, following concessions made to others (England and France), whereas trade with the Indies was forbidden unless the Spanish monarch gave the Dutch explicit permission.[36]

By 1609 the problem for Philip III and Lerma was not so much the terms of the agreement but how to justify it ideologically when many members of the Spanish elite still perceived the Dutch as "rebels and heretics" and, consequently, might interpret the truce as the action of a king more concerned about the temporal interests of the monarchy than about the spiritual health of his subjects and kingdoms. This attitude had surfaced already during negotiations with England and reemerged during the negotiations with the Dutch. These views were expressed in a memorandum Juan de Ribera, Archbishop of Valencia, sent to the king, the contents of which were discussed in the Council of State on 3 May 1608. Ribera's argument centered on the Peace of 1604 with England and its alarming impact on the religious situation in the Spanish monarchy. Dismissing the economic consequences of peace with England, Ribera focused on the fact that the Protestant English could now travel to the Iberian peninsula and introduce among its inhabitants their "pernicious beliefs." Even more disturbing was the significance of a peace agreement with rulers who persecuted their Catholic subjects and promoted heretical ideas among Europeans. To Ribera, by accepting the peace with England, Spaniards "were deeply offending our Lord and, thus, bringing many ills to the Spanish crown. My fear has increased with time ... thus confirming my belief that making peace with heretics should be forbidden as so many times it is asserted in the Holy Scripture." He made an additional point of reminding Spanish rulers of the conditions that had to prevail for a Catholic king to sign a peace with heretical rulers: the heretics' conversion to Catholicism, something that had not occurred in England, or the overwhelmingly superiority of the enemy forces, which he did not believe to be the case with the English.[37] In this ideological context, Philip III's and Lerma's decision to advocate the opening of peace negotiations

[35] On discontent in Spain and the Dutch Republic over the terms of this truce see Israel, *The Dutch Republic. Its Rise*, pp. 404–5.

[36] The terms of the truce regarding trade with the Indies are reproduced and analyzed by Peter Brightwell, "The Spanish System and the Twelve Years' Truce," *English Historical Review*, 89 (1974), pp. 270–1.

[37] AGS Est., *leg.* 212/n.p., *consulta* of the Council of State on Ribera's memorandum, 3 May 1608.

with the Dutch could be interpreted as the action of rulers who had placed temporal interests above spiritual ones, thus creating possibilities for partisan confrontation and perhaps even attempts by opponents of the truce to foment internal conflict. To prevent such developments, the rulers needed a scapegoat who could help them reinforce their Catholic credentials, and for this they chose the Morisco minority, with whom Lerma had had many contacts when he was Viceroy of Valencia.

Heralded as the culmination of the Christian reclamation of Spain from the Muslim forces that had occupied the territory since the eighth century, the conquest of Granada by the Catholic Monarchs in 1492 forced the Spanish rulers to decide what to do with the Muslim population in the peninsula. Between 1492 and 1609 the debate on this population went through various stages and in general arrived at two mutually contradictory outcomes: conversion of the Muslims to Christianity – the only way to integrate them into the Christian–Spanish community – and the impossibility of their conversion, requiring their expulsion from Spanish territories. Both options remained viable until 1609. The so-called "final solution"[38] (their definitive expulsion) was not inevitable, nor was it the only solution available to the Spanish authorities.[39]

After 1492, all the participants in this debate believed that it was the duty of all Christians to extend their faith and affirmed that, as the holy texts made clear, the conversion of most of the world's inhabitants must antecede the second coming of Christ and the final judgment. This millenarian concept of history had already left its imprint on the first attempts to convert the inhabitants of America, and in many ways the attitudes and the zeal of the missionaries in the Indies were similar to those held by individuals in charge of converting the Moriscos.[40] The conversion of Moriscos and Indians also formed a part of the Christian imperial ideology, of which the Spanish monarchy saw itself as the heir. As Anthony Pagden has written, "In the final transformation of all mankind into the followers of Christ, it was the

---

[38] "Solución final" (final solution) are the words used by Antonio Domínguez Ortiz and Bernard Vincent, *Historia de los moriscos* (Madrid, 1978), p. 160, drawing an implicit analogy between the expulsion of the Moriscos in the early seventeenth century and the Holocaust against European Jews conducted by Hitler and his regime.

[39] A teleological view of the expulsion – the "inevitability" of the expulsion as resulting from "racist" or religious hatred – has been defended by many historians; see, for example, Fernand Braudel, "Conflits et refus de civilisation: espagnols et morisques au XVIe siècle," *Annales*, 14 (1947), p. 408; and Rafael Benítez Sánchez-Blanco and Eugenio Ciscar Pallarés, "La iglesia ante la conversión y expulsión de los moriscos," in Antonio Mestre Sanchís (ed.), *Historia de la iglesia en España. IV: La iglesia en la España de los siglos XVII y XVIII* (Madrid, 1979), p. 254. Domínguez Ortiz and Vincent also believe that Philip III's decision to expel the Moriscos was the result of a long-term conflict between the Christian and Morisco communities and that the expulsion in 1609 resulted from personal changes of mind by Philip III and Lerma in 1608: see Domínguez Ortiz and Vincent, *Historia de los moriscos*, pp. 177, 159–64.

[40] John Leddy Phelan, *The Millennial Kingdom of the Franciscans in the New World* (Berkeley, 1970); Robert Ricard, *The Spiritual Conquest of Mexico* (Berkeley, 1966). See also Antonio Garrido Aranda, *Moriscos e indios: precedentes hispánicos de la evangelización en México* (Mexico City, 1985); and J. M. Headley, "Campanella, America, and World Evangelization," in Karen Ordahl Kupperman, ed., *America in European Consciousness, 1493–1750* (Chapel Hill, 1995), pp. 243–71.

empire which should ensure the dissolution of every cultural, political and confessional difference."[41]

Attitudes regarding the conversion of the Moriscos went through various phases during the sixteenth century. Roughly, until the mid-sixteenth century those charged with their conversion believed in the real possibility of transforming Muslims into Christians. After the 1550s, however, there is substantial evidence of frustration among the Spanish authorities, a sense of failure in their attempts to convert and integrate the Morisco minority into Spanish society, and with it the dissemination of the view that the conversion of the Moriscos was an impossible task because of their refusal to accept Christian values and orthodoxy.[42] Not all Christians believed, however, that the Moriscos themselves were responsible for this failure and placed the blame instead on the inability of the authorities to break the cultural and linguistic barriers that separated them from their Christian neighbors.[43] Nevertheless, after the 1560s, efforts aimed at converting the Moriscos were accompanied by increased coercion as the Inquisition was given a major role in the Morisco communities.[44]

It was also during this period that there emerged an influential image of the Morisco, promoted by those who did not believe in the policy of integration. The Morisco – now depicted as the epitome of all vices in contrast to the good and virtuous Christian – was presented as superstitious, devious, cynical, corrupt, avaricious, greedy, violent, and lascivious. Further portrayed as unable to feel love, friendship, and loyalty – the three basic feelings that permitted the creation of civilized societies[45] – the Moriscos were incapable as well of self-government, proof that they were the descendants of slaves, and thus, in the words of Fray Blas Verdú, "unworthy of ruling and reigning."[46] More important was Spaniards' belief that Muslim characteristics were transmitted from generation to generation as if by a

[41] Anthony Pagden, *Lords of all the World. Ideologies of Empire in Spain, Britain and France* c. *1500–c. 1800* (New Haven, 1995), p. 30; see also pp. 24–37.

[42] For an excellent summary of the evolution of Spaniards' attitudes regarding the conversion of the Morisco population see Ricardo García Cárcel, "The Course of the Moriscos up to their Expulsion," in Angel Alcalá, ed., *The Spanish Inquisition and the Inquisitorial Mind* (Highland Lakes, N.J., 1987), pp. 73–86.

[43] For critiques suggesting that the failure of conversion was due to the Christians' own mistakes see AGS Est., *leg.* 212, fols. 1–3v: proposals for the conversion of the Moriscos, 4 September 1581; fols. 8–24v: reports and proposal by the *Junta de la Instrucción y Conversión de los Moriscos*, 1595–1600; fol. 29v: report of Fray Joseph Cresuelo, n.d.; and BL, Add. 10238, "De los moriscos de España por el padre Ignacio de las Casas" (1605–7).

[44] See Tulio Halperín Donghi, *Un conflicto nacional: moriscos y cristianos viejos en Valencia* (Valencia, 1980), pp. 172–209; Mercedes García Arenal, *Inquisición y moriscos: los procesos del tribunal de Cuenca* (Madrid, 1978); William Monter, *Frontiers of Heresy. The Spanish Inquisition from the Basque Lands to Sicily* (Cambridge, 1990), chaps. 9–10; and García Cárcel, "The Course of the Moriscos," pp. 76–82.

[45] See Miguel Herrero García, *Ideas de los españoles del siglo XVII* (Madrid, 1966), chaps. 20, 22; and Miguel Angel de Bunes Ibarra, *La imagen de los musulmanes y del norte de Africa en la España de los siglos XVI y XVII* (Madrid, 1989), pp. 228–64.

[46] Blas Verdú, *Engaños y desengaños del tiempo, con un discurso de la expulsión de los moriscos de España* (Barcelona, 1612), fols. 145r–v.

degenerative gene. Damián de Fonseca, like many others, believed that among those who practiced false religions the most obtuse were the Muslims, who "do not admit any other reason than to say: my father was a Moor; I myself am a Moor," which explained why there were so few cases of Muslims who truly converted to Christianity – "as they say, no good Christian ever came from a good Moor."[47] Early modern Spaniards believed that to be a Muslim meant the adoption and perpetration of barbaric behavior because Muslim religion made its adherents immune to the beneficial effects of law and culture.[48] According to most Spanish writers, these natural, and thus eternal, characteristics made Muslims completely different from Christians and ultimately "hated by all the nations in the world."[49]

It would, however, be a mistake to assume that these "racist" views were the only factor influencing the debates about the treatment of the Morisco population. Just as important were early modern views on tolerance toward religious minorities. "Let us now say a little about infidel and heretic subjects," Botero wrote in Book 5 of his *Ragion di stato*, because "nothing makes men so different and hostile as opposition or differences between their faiths."[50] After the experiences of the Wars of Religion in France, the rebellion of the United Provinces, and political instability in England, Botero could identify religion as the principal cause of civil conflict and such conflict as the root of the decline of empires. From the point of view of a Christian ruler the best way to prevent the "infidels" from provoking civil instability and destroying his monarchy was to try to convert them to Christianity through religious education (fols. 91v–92v). But given that the characteristics of the "Mohammedans" made true conversion difficult, the ruler should neutralize them by depriving them "of everything that strengthens spirit and daring, such as the pomp of nobility and prerogatives of birth, the use of horses . . . and a militia and warlike exercises" (fols. 94–95v). If all these methods failed and the infidels kept rejecting conversion and conspired against their lord and master, then "they must be dispersed and transplanted to other countries" (fol. 102). Without being as radical, Lipsius also assigned religion a crucial role in the maintenance of internal political stability, which explains his constant pleas to avert a proliferation of many faiths within the monarchy, although he proposed radical measures only against those who practiced a distinct religion in public and provoked the ire of true Christians.[51]

Behind Botero's and Lipsius's views was the notion that the Morisco problem impinged on the security of the state. By the mid-sixteenth century many viewed the Moriscos' reluctance to become real Christians as proof of their political disloyalty and their ultimate determination to undermine the authority of the Spanish empire: this was felt to be demonstrated by their willingness to collaborate

---

[47] Damián de Fonseca, *Justa expulsión de los moriscos de España* (Rome, 1612), p. 173.
[48] Bunes Ibarra, *La imagen de los musulmanes*, p. 229; see also pp. 245–9.
[49] Pedro Aznar Cardona, *Expulsión justificada de los moriscos españoles* (Huesca, 1612), pt. I, fol. 177.
[50] Quotations from the Spanish edition, Botero, *Los diez libros*; references in the text.
[51] Lipsius, *Los seis libros*, bk. 4, chaps. 2–4.

with foreign rulers, first the Turks and later Elizabeth I of England and Henry IV of France. Modern historians have questioned the reality of these claims, which were no doubt exaggerated; however, evidence suggests that a group of discontented Moriscos did conspire with some of Spain's enemies and collaborate with the Algerian pirates as well as celebrating the victories of Spanish enemies and propagating millenarian views maintaining that the "reconquest of Spain" by Muslim forces was a prelude to the end of the world.[52]

This image of the Morisco as a traitor and instigator of internal rebellion was further reinforced as a result of the War of Granada (1568–71), the most important peninsular conflict of the sixteenth century, in which groups of armed Moriscos were able to sustain a prolonged conflict with the army sent against them by Philip II.[53] This war resulted in the defeat of the Morisco army and the removal of the Moriscos from the former kingdom of Granada to other parts of the peninsula, and it also greatly increased the distrust with which they were viewed, leading the authorities to conclude that the politics of conversion had failed and that other measures were needed. This change of attitude became evident in 1582 when, for the first time, an official institution recommended to Philip II that the only solution to the Morisco problem was their expulsion. This advice came from a special *junta* staffed by some of the most prominent ministers of the time – the Duke of Alba, Juan de Idiáquez, Rodrigo Vázquez de Arce, and the royal confessor. In their report the *junta* proposed that to prevent the possibility of rebellion by the Morisco community in Valencia, numerically the most significant in the peninsula, the king should expel all of them – with the exception of all baptized children – and should placate the Valencian lords who made use of cheap Morisco labor by distributing to them the lands and riches taken from the Morisco population.[54]

Although Philip II did not accept the recommendations of the *junta*, after 1582 most of the king's ministers advocated expulsion, and sometimes even the enslavement or killing of the Moriscos. The Council of State, for example, proposed in February 1599 that extreme measures of repression be taken: sending to the galleys all Moriscos between the ages of fifteen and sixty, expelling all who were older than sixty, and reeducating all Morisco children,[55] advice with which many agreed at the

[52] See A. C. Hess, "The Moriscos. An Ottoman Fifth Column in Sixteenth-century Spain," *American Historical Review*, 74 (1968), pp. 1–21; Mercedes García Arenal, *Los moriscos* (Madrid, 1975), pp. 33–42, 57–62, 217–20; Mercedes Sánchez Alvarez, ed., *El manuscrito misceláneo 774 de la Biblioteca Nacional de París. (Leyendas, itinerarios de viajes, profecías sobre la destrucción de España y otros relatos moriscos)* (Madrid, 1982), pp. 45–50; and Francisco Yndurain, *Los moriscos y el teatro en Aragón* (Zaragoza, 1986).

[53] On the Morisco rebellion see Julio Caro Baroja, *Los moriscos del reino de Granada (Ensayo de historia social)* (Madrid, 1957), chaps. 5–6; and Domínguez Ortiz and Vincent, *Historia de los moriscos*, chap. 2.

[54] AGS Est., *leg.* 212/fols. 6v–7v, *consulta* of the *Junta* on Moriscos, Lisbon, 19 Sept. 1582; this report of the *Junta* of Lisbon, as it was called, was published by Pascual Boronat y Barrachina, *Los moriscos españoles y su expulsión. Estudio histórico-crítico*, 2 vols. (Valencia, 1901), vol. I, pp. 300–1.

[55] AGS Est., *leg.* 212/ fols. 25v–26, *consulta* of the Council of State, 30 Jan. and 2 Feb. 1599.

start of Philip III's reign. González de Cellorigo, in a memorandum (dated 1600) he prepared on the restoration of Spain, declared that one of the ways to achieve this goal was by killing or expelling the Moriscos,[56] and Alamos de Barrientos depicted the Moriscos as one of the most committed enemies of the Spanish monarchy and warned that they could become a powerful internal ally of Spain's external adversaries.[57]

In conjunction with a growing concern about the Morisco problem as a matter of state, the Spanish government started to promote a discourse that presented the monarchy as a polity whose *raison d'être* was not to fight other Christian powers but to protect Christian Europe against the Turks. This policy required that increased attention be paid to the situation in the Mediterranean and the promotion of an anti-Islamic ideology.[58] The construction of the anti-Islamic credentials of Philip III became evident in 1601 when he ordered the creation of a special force to attack and conquer Algeria. Although this campaign was a total failure,[59] attempts to control Algerian pirates and to stop the expansion of Turkish power in the Mediterranean continued throughout the entire reign and became the ideological and strategic alternative Lerma and his supporters used against those who advocated the monarchy's involvement in European conflicts.[60]

It was during these years (1602–5) that a growing number of ministers began to favor the expulsion of the Moriscos, including Juan de Idiáquez and the Count of Miranda, who proposed it at a meeting of the *Junta de Gobierno* held in January 1603. Although Lerma opposed this measure, observing that the Moriscos were officially Christians and it was impossible to treat them as infidels, Philip III tended to favor the position taken by Idiáquez and Miranda and ordered his ministers to start preparations for the expulsion.[61] The influential Archbishop of Valencia Juan de Ribera also championed drastic measures, and in two memoranda addressed to the king he recommended the expulsion of all Morisco communities, which he portrayed as eternal enemies of the Christian community.[62] It was Jaime Bleda, another cleric working in Valencia, who, in several written opinions sent to Philip III and Lerma, provided stronger legitimating support by emphasizing the dramatic moment in which they were living, reminding them that as reward for both the conquest of Granada and the expulsion of the Jews in 1492 the Catholic Monarchs received from God the prize of a "New World," whereas as a punish-

---

[56] González de Cellorigo, *Memorial de la política*, p. 57.

[57] Alamos de Barrientos, *Discurso político*, p. 50.

[58] On this topic, see Miguel Angel Bunes Ibarra and Mercedes García Arenal, *Los españoles y el norte de África, siglos XV–XVII* (Madrid, 1992), pp. 122ff.

[59] On the importance Lerma gave to this "jornada" and his disillusionment about the outcome (considered by Lerma as God's desire), see BL, Add. 28424: Borja to Lerma, 15 Sept. 1601, and Lerma's answer, 19 Sept. 1601, fol. 138.

[60] On a summary of some of these initiatives see AGS Est., *leg.* 249/n.p., *consulta* of the Council of State, Sept. 1612; Bunes and García Arenal, *Los españoles y el norte de África*, pp. 122ff.

[61] AGS Est., *leg.* 208/n.p., *consulta* of the *Junta de Gobierno*, 3 Jan. 1603.

[62] AGS Est., *leg.* 212/fols. 31–41, memoranda of Fray Ribera to the Council of State, 1601–2.

ment for their inability to solve the Morisco problem, the recent Spanish monarchs had suffered many defeats and punishments. To Bleda, now was just the moment to revitalize the monarchy by expelling all Muslim enemies.[63]

Until 1607 the situation remained ambivalent: a growing number of ministers supported the banishment of the Moriscos, a measure opposed by Lerma.[64] But the circumstances changed radically when it became clear that there was a possibility of establishing a peace agreement with the Dutch. In 1608 the king ordered the Council of State to collect all documents written on the Morisco problem from 1582 onward,[65] and some royal ministers made even more clear their pro-expulsion views. Juan de Idiáquez, perhaps the most effective pro-expulsion theorist of all, spoke at a meeting of the Council of State held in 1608 that Lerma also attended. The Morisco problem, Idiáquez asserted, was one of "conscience" and one of "obligation for the security of the state." Regarding the latter, Idiáquez noted that the Moriscos had greatly increased in number and sooner or later would overpower and endanger the Christian domination of the Spanish monarchy, and, furthermore, Moriscos were loyal to "foreign" powers set upon destroying the Spanish empire. But the Morisco problem was also religious, and its resolution was one of the king's sacred duties in his role as *Defensor Fidei*. Christians had offered them salvation and civil integration through conversion, which most of them had rejected; now was the time to take more radical measures.[66] After a debate that took place over several months, paralleling the ongoing deliberations on the truce with the Dutch, the Council of State finally recommended that the king expel the Moriscos, giving justifications similar to those put forth by the *junta* organized in 1582 to discuss the Morisco question. Philip approved this recommendation on 14 April 1609, the same day he approved the Twelve Years' Truce. He did not, however, make public his decision until September when the first decree ordering the deportation of all Moriscos from Valencia was first published, thus initiating a long process of repression and expulsion of more than 300,000 Moriscos from 1609 to 1614. In his justification for adopting such a measure, Philip III adduced his duty to "protect his subjects and kingdoms against everything that could scandalize and hurt them ... destroy everything that could destroy the state, and especially everything that offends and displeases God."[67]

The fact that the timing of the expulsion coincided with the signing of the Twelve Years' Truce suggests that the expulsion of the Moriscos was used by the Spanish rulers to mitigate the potential consequences of the truce with the

---

[63] AGS Est., *leg.* 212, Father Bleda's memorandum, 10 Apr. 1605, fols. 43v–44r.

[64] AGS Est., *leg.* 208/n.p., *consulta* of the *Junta de Tres*, 29 Sept. 1607.

[65] AGS Est., *leg.* 212, fols. 1–48: "Papeles que el señor comendador mayor de Aragón envio al secretario de Estado Antonio de Prada."   [66] AGS Est., *leg.* 212/n.p., *consulta* of the Council of State, 1608.

[67] BNM, Mss 11773, "Orden de Juan de Mendoza, marqués de San Germán, sobre la expulsión de los moriscos de la provincia de Andalucía, reino de Granada y villa de Hornachos," 12 Jan. 1610, fols. 623r–v. On the technical aspects and economic consequences of the expulsion, see Domínguez Ortiz and Vincent, *Historia de los moriscos*, chaps. 9–11.

"heretic" Dutch Republic and to protect themselves from having their Christian credentials questioned. Lerma himself gave this interpretation in 1617, in a meeting of the Council of State in which the counselors discussed what to do about the conflict with the Duke of Savoy – a dispute that was becoming a serious embarrassment for Spain. Lerma proposed that to avoid criticism concerning the peace signed with Savoy the monarchy should attack the Venetian Republic, a traditional enemy of Spain's presence in Italy, believing that this would evoke a patriotic response and reduce the apparent significance of the peace agreement. By doing so, Lerma continued, they would be following the precedent set in 1609 when Philip III decided to decree the expulsion of the Moriscos to reduce possible "humors" of opposition and discontent generated by the truce with the Dutch Republic.[68]

The expulsion of the Moriscos indeed became central to the politics of propaganda aimed at presenting Philip III and Lerma as champions of the Catholic faith and protectors of the community; the expulsion itself was presented as a deed inspired and ordered by God. Philip III was compared to Don Pelayo, the historical ruler who because of his divinely inspired valor had begun the fight for Spain's restoration from her Muslim occupiers. Damián de Fonseca in *Justa expulsión de los moriscos de España*, dedicated to Francisco de Castro, Count of Castro, ambassador to Rome and Lerma's nephew, depicted Philip III as the unique successor to Hercules and compared him to other historical liberators: Moses, Saul, David, and Solomon. These individuals, like Philip III, had not only liberated God's chosen people but also protected them against being infected by evil religions. The conservation of the true faith, Fonseca wrote, had been throughout history the bond that had kept the chosen people united.[69] In 1619 Juan de Salazar expressed the views of many of his contemporaries on the expulsion of the Moriscos, which he claimed was decreed by a wise king who had understood that the Moriscos' mission had been to destroy Spain, allowing him to conclude that:

among all the things that will make Philip III famous and immortalize his memory is the heroic deed of conserving the purity and faith of his [peninsular] kingdoms (head of his monarchy) ... by expelling all the Moriscos, heretics, and apostates of our holy faith. By not worrying about the losses that the expulsion of such a large number of subjects would entail, he purged Spain of this incorrigible and vile horde, who put in serious danger all Christians, whose faith, if not lost, would be at least weakened.[70]

[68] BNM Mss 5570, "Copias de los pareceres que el Sr. duque de Lerma ha dado en las consultas que se han hecho a Su Majd. desde el 22 de junio de 1613," vote of the Duke of Lerma in the meeting of the Council of State celebrated on 8 Apr. 1617, fols. 164r–v. On the Italian conflicts in 1615–17 see below, chap. 12.

[69] Fonseca, *Justa expulsión*, pp. 169–74; see also Marco Guadalajara y Xavier, *Memorable expulsión y justísimo destierro de los moriscos de España* (Pamplona, 1613).

[70] Juan de Salazar, *Política española* [1619], ed. Miguel Herrero García (Madrid, 1945), pp. 70–1. On this campaign of propaganda see Miguel Angel de Bunes Ibarra, *Los moriscos en el pensamiento histórico. Historiografía de un grupo marginado* (Madrid, 1983), pp. 31–55. On the popularity of the expulsion in the so-called "literatura de cordel," cheap and popular publications, see María Cruz García de Enterría, *Sociedad y poesía de cordel en el barroco* (Madrid, 1973), pp. 224–7.

The propaganda campaign centered on the expulsion of the Moriscos could not hide the fact that the signing of the Twelve Years' Truce with the Dutch Republic signified an important change in the role of the Spanish monarchy in Europe. Although some historians have defined the period beginning in 1609 as the era of the "pax Hispanica," and thus as a period of Spanish prominence, in reality the Twelve Years' Truce indicated Spain's declining influence. This is not to say that by 1609 Spain had ceased to be the most powerful European monarchy; in fact, many Europeans still believed that Spain aspired to, and could, become a "universal monarchy."[71]

But European fears about Spain's desire to dominate the world seemed to many Spaniards a reflection of its glorious past rather than its present-day reality. Although at the beginning of Philip III's reign some authors had written books in an attempt to demonstrate that Spain was destined by God to become the last monarchy before the second coming of Christ, such messianic views almost disappeared during Philip III's reign,[72] and by 1609 "confidence in both the possibility and the desirability of a universal Spanish or Habsburg empire for the defense of Europe" had dissolved.[73] After the signing of the Twelve Years' Truce, King Henry IV and the Duke of Savoy, for example, also began to express views indicative of their belief that it was now possible to threaten Spanish power, especially in Italy.

To Lerma and some of his supporters the truce with the Dutch represented the crossing of the Rubicon towards retrenchment. Lerma appeared to have decided to follow the advice Alamos de Barrientos had given at the start of the reign: never to start a new war that could not be finished with a victory and never to succumb to pressure from others for involvement in new conflicts. When making decisions, a ruler should bear in mind only today's realities, not the possibility of future ills. Peace, Barrientos proposed, was the only road to recovery, and it would permit Spain to restore its lost forces and conserve itself.[74] The only feasible strategy, given that the Spanish empire was short on friends and money and long on enemies, was to make peace with some, buy the will of others, and "attack the weakest and easiest to defeat."[75] The Venetian ambassador in England, Antonio Foscarini, best summarized the Spanish regime's views when in 1612 he stated that

it suits the Duke of Lerma not to embroil the King of Spain in war so as to allow himself the opportunity of turning to account a large part of that money which would otherwise be spent

---

[71] *CSPVen*, vol. XI, p. 84, report of the Venetian ambassador to England; on Europeans' fears that Spain could still become a universal monarchy in the first decades of the seventeenth century see J. M. Headley, *Tommaso Campanella and the Transformation of the World* (Princeton, 1997), chaps. 6–8.

[72] See Fernández Albaladejo, *Fragmentos*, pp. 93–111; and Donatella Montalto Cessi, "L'immagine dell'imperio e della Spagna nella circolazione delle idee politiche in Spagna dal XVI al XVII secolo," in Massimo Ganci and Ruggiero Romano, eds., *Gobernare il mondo. L'imperio spagnolo dal XV al XIX secolo* (Palermo, 1995), pp. 421–39.   [73] Tuck, *Philosophy*, pp. 73–4.   [74] See above, chap. 7.

[75] Alamos de Barrientos, *Norte de príncipes*, pp. 97–8.

on the army, but on the other hand he has to maintain the reputation of so great a prince, and this he does by small and safe conquest.[76]

This peace took Philip III and Lerma eleven years to accomplish, however, and many believed that it came too late. The truce with the Dutch, which was not excessively criticized in public, was nevertheless perceived by Lerma's opponents as an act of capitulation, a clear sign that the Spanish monarchy under his command was renouncing its influence and power in Europe. These views became more widespread later during the conflicts with the Duke of Savoy, conflicts that ended with the Peace of Asti (1615), which was strongly criticized at the time and viewed as a complete defeat for Spanish authority. This interpretation of Lerma's policies permitted the rise of an incipient court faction that, by defending a more militant policy toward other European powers, was able to take control of the decision-making process during the last years of Lerma's *privanza*.[77]

[76] *CSPVen*, vol. XII, p. 284, Antonio Foscarini to the Venetian senate, 9 Feb. 1612.
[77] On these topics see below, pt. IV.

PART IV

Reversal of fortune

Introduction

One of the paintings Giorgio Vasari designed to decorate his house in Arezzo depicted "Virtue trampling on Envy and seizing Fortune by her hair, hitting both with a stick." The most intriguing aspect of this painting, Vasari wrote, was that when one "walks around the room, it sometimes looks as if Envy were above Fortune and Virtue, and then Virtue above Envy and Fortune, just as it often happens in real life."[1] Although Lerma's fate during his *privanza* was no doubt more complicated, Vasari's painting summarizes it fairly well. In his triumphal moments he was portrayed as a man of Virtue, in control of Fortune and victorious over Envy, while during moments of crisis and before his downfall he seemed to his admirers and, no doubt, to himself a victim of Envy and Fortune. By presenting himself as a virtuous servant of the king, Lerma tried to protect himself against attacks by opponents whom he and his followers tried to portray not as adversaries of the *privado* but as enemies of the king.

Not all observers accepted this idealistic vision of the powerful favorite. Indeed, a competing public image of Lerma and of the role a favorite should play in the government of the monarchy began to acquire prominence, particularly after 1607. Unlike Lerma's supporters, those who opposed him viewed his *privanza* as a political farce with dreadful consequences for the entire kingdom: an unprecedented spread of corruption and the destruction of the political foundations of the Spanish monarchy. The proponents of these negative views were careful to present themselves as good counselors to the king with a mission to liberate him and his kingdoms from the insufferable and corrupt influence of Lerma and his followers. They did not stress their opposition to Lerma or the king's decision to have a favorite, but they assailed the theoretical principles employed to justify Lerma's role in government and called for vindication of the "traditional" constitution of the monarchy in which all authority belonged to the king, who should rule in collaboration with his counselors. As Lerma had done in the first half of the reign, his opponents claimed that they were not a threat to the king's power but genuine sustainers of it.

Despite the increasing ideological debate after 1607, Lerma's grip on power held solid and his faction remained more or less intact until 1611. Thereafter, however,

---

[1] Cf. E. H. Gombrich, "Getting the Picture," *New York Review of Books*, 40/5 (1993), p. 19.

his monopolistic control over the king's favor was challenged by other courtiers, especially by his eldest son, the Duke of Uceda, and Fray Luis de Aliaga, the king's confessor since 1608, making possible what in the first half of Philip III's reign had seemed unthinkable: the destruction of Lerma's dominion over the king's favor. Time and again the fight for power demonstrated that those with open access to the king were in an advantageous position. Ultimately Uceda and Aliaga succeeded in winning Philip III's favor and stripping Lerma of his former power, precisely because of their ability to become members of the king's inner circle.

Uceda's involvement in a faction dedicated to banishing his father from the court also reminds historians that kinship did not guarantee absolute loyalty. Indeed, his behavior challenges traditional historiographical interpretations of early modern society which claim that the principal concern of the nobility was to protect family fortune, honor, and power through a grand "family strategy." Uceda's leadership of the anti-Lerma faction demonstrates that individual ambition could take precedence over kin solidarity. Few historians have made this point more succinctly than Jaime Contreras who wrote that in early modern Spain

> Groups did not obliterate individuals; the objective existence of group forces did not prevent the exercise of a personal trajectory. Families ... deployed their strategies to widen their spheres of solidarity and influence, but their men also played their roles individually. If the call of blood and the pull of lineage were intense, so too were the desire and the opportunity to create individual spaces.[2]

The political context of Lerma's fall from power displays other interesting theoretical and practical elements as well. In one of his essays, "Of Faction," Francis Bacon developed an acute analysis of the rise and fall of court factions, stressing, among other issues, the complexity of the motives behind political alliances and conflicts in early modern courts. According to Bacon, for example, in power struggles "those that are seconds in faction many times, when the faction subdivides, prove principals."[3] This description well characterizes the situation at Philip III's court immediately before and after Lerma's fall. In their attempt to break Lerma's hold on the king's favor, Uceda and Aliaga sought the assistance of courtiers and royal ministers who had not belonged to Lerma's faction and who had for years disagreed with his international policies. Two men – the Duke of Osuna, Viceroy of Sicily and Naples during the 1610s, and, most importantly, Baltasar de Zúñiga, former ambassador to France and the empire and, from 1617, the most influential counselor of state – assisted Uceda and Aliaga in their initial efforts to displace Lerma. After Lerma's fall on 4 October 1618, however, these same men, originally of secondary importance in the faction opposed to Lerma, rose to

---

[2] Cf. Roger Chartier, *On the Edge of the Cliff. History, Language, and Practices*, trans. Lydia G. Cochrane (Baltimore, 1997), p. 16.

[3] "Of Faction," in *Francis Bacon: A Critical Edition of the Major Works*, ed. Brian Vickers (Oxford, 1996), p. 440.

prominence through their support of a radical change in the international policies of the monarchy and eventually displaced Uceda and Aliaga. Lerma's downfall, ironically, coincided with Philip III's acceptance of Zúñiga's interventionist position on the rebellion in Bohemia that initiated the Thirty Years War.

Because of the diversity of political views among Lerma's opponents, his fall from power in the early days of October 1618 did not result in the creation of a monopolistic faction led by a sole favorite; rather it signified the beginning of a war of all against all. The most important consequence of these factional conflicts was the intensification of political and ideological debate. Hundreds of pamphlets, treatises, poems, and memoranda on the problems of the monarchy and possible solutions for the crisis provoked by Lerma and his followers inundated the court. At the same time, between 1618 and 1621, Philip III increasingly saw himself being displaced by his son and heir Prince Philip, who was by then surrounded by men such as Zúñiga and his nephew Gaspar de Guzmán, the future Count-Duke of Olivares, both of whom ultimately became the leaders of the new regime constituted after the king's death in March 1621.

10

Ideological confrontation and factional division

The truce with the United Provinces and the decision to expel the Moriscos seemed to put Lerma's *privanza* on an ideal footing, despite the fact that both decisions involved political risks for the king and his favorite. As noted in Chapter 9, as a result of the truce with the Dutch Republic the Spanish rulers could now be accused of renouncing lands that were part of the inheritance left by Charles V and, worse, of abandoning the Spanish king's sacred duty to fight the enemies of Catholicism. Nevertheless, the truce provided a financial and political respite, if temporary, for the Spanish monarchy. The expulsion of the Moriscos led to a significant decrease in the population, but at the same time it could be presented as an advancement of the religious homogenization of the Spanish kingdoms.

To these "successes" the regime was able to add another, a fortuitous one, namely the assassination of Henry IV of France on 14 May 1610. Despite the Peace of Vervins, the increasingly active French monarch had given cause for much concern to Madrid. He had continuously supported actual and potential rebels against Spain, specifically the rebels in the United Provinces and the peninsular Moriscos, thus increasing political tension between the two monarchies and fear among the Spanish authorities that a general conflict with France was imminent.[1] Henry's policies were motivated, as Roland Mousnier has asserted, by his belief that "any reconciliation with Philip III ... would be tantamount to giving the Habsburg a free hand in Europe."[2] The situation became extremely critical in 1609–10, a few months before Henry's assassination, when, with some of his allies, he plotted an attack on Habsburg possessions in the empire and Italy. First, he entered into an agreement with various German princes to take the Duchy of Jülich-Cleves from the control of the Austrian Habsburgs.[3] Next, on 20 April 1610, Henry signed a pact with Charles Emmanuel, ruler of Savoy, in which they agreed on a matrimonial alliance and the creation of an army (with 14,000 to 20,000 French

---

[1] See, for example, Cioranescu, *Le Masque et le visage*, pp. 15–17; Antonio Eiras Roel, "Desvío y 'mudanza', de Francia en 1616," *Hispania*, 100 (1965), pp. 521–4; Roland Mousnier, *The Assassination of Henry IV*, trans. Joan Spencer (New York, 1973), pp. 125–6; and Mark Greengrass, *France in the Age of Henry IV. The Struggle for Stability* (London, 1984), chap. 8, "Pax Gallicana."

[2] Mousnier, *The Assassination of Henry IV*, p. 121.

[3] *Ibid.*, pp. 132–7; Eiras Roel, "Política francesa de Felipe III," pp. 309–11; Victor Lucien Tapié, *France in the Age of Louis XIII and Richelieu* (Cambridge, 1984), pp. 65–7; Greengrass, *France in the Age of Henry IV*, pp. 195–7; and Geoffrey Parker, *The Thirty Years' War* (London, 1984), chap. 1.

soldiers) to attack and conquer Milan as a first step toward ending Spanish preeminence on the Italian peninsula.[4] The killing of Henry IV by François Ravaillac, a self-declared friend of Spain, curtailed these plans: the Habsburgs defeated the forces that attempted to conquer the Duchy of Cleves, Milan was spared, and the Duke of Savoy was obliged to ask for Philip III's mercy and to halt, for the moment, his plans to become the leader of the Italian rulers against the Spanish crown.[5]

More importantly, after Henry's death the political situation in France deteriorated,[6] giving Spain the opportunity to impose upon the queen regent, Marie de Medici, a double matrimonial alliance: the wedding of Louis XIII to Anne of Austria, Philip III's daughter, and that of Prince Philip, the Spanish heir, to Isabelle of Bourbon, Louis XIII's sister. This agreement was signed by representatives of both monarchies on April 1611, less than one year after Henry IV's assassination.[7] The hope that this turn of events brought to the Spanish authorities was very well expressed by Cabrera de Córdoba who believed that the killing of Henry would "bring total peace to Christendom."[8] If not total peace, Spanish rulers believed that now at last it would be possible to solve some of their most pressing internal problems. This hope, as they were soon to find, was an illusion, an impossible dream.

There were structural reasons why the Spanish authorities could not solve the problems confronting the monarchy. As modern historians have shown, by the early 1610s Castile, the economic and financial mainstay of the Spanish monarchy, was being adversely affected by a number of social and economic developments. Its population was steadily decreasing, especially in the urban centers, and with it the kingdom's productive capacity, thus reducing the size of the fiscal pool.[9] The consequences of these social and economic crises in Castile convinced the members of the councils that the kingdom could not bear any additional fiscal pressure. The Council of Finance, for example, in a *consulta* sent to Philip III dated 13 May 1609,

---

[4] Antonio Bombín Pérez, *La cuestión de Monferrato (1613–1618)* (Vitoria, 1975), pp. 11–18.

[5] *Ibid.*, p. 19. [6] Tapié, *France in the Age of Louis XIII*, pp. 68–88.

[7] Eiras Roel, "Desvío y 'mudanza' de Francia en 1616," pp. 525–33. The agreement was kept secret in France until January 1612 when it was approved by the Royal Council; the agreement stipulated that the wedding between Anne and Louis XIII would take place in 1613, but because of internal opposition and political unrest in France, the wedding was delayed until 1615. On the debates in France surrounding the agreements with Spain see Michel Bareau, "Thèmes et métaphores dans la polémique sus les Mariages espagnols," in Carlos García, *La oposición y conjunción de los dos grandes luminares de la tierra, o la antipatía de franceses y españoles* [1617], ed. Michel Bareau (Alberta, 1979), pp. 304–31.

[8] Cabrera de Córdoba, *Relaciones*, p. 407. See also Vega Carpio, *Epistolario*, vol. III, pp. 22–6. Philip III officially proposed a matrimonial alliance to James I of England about the same time by suggesting a marriage of the English heir, Prince Henry, to one of his daughters.

[9] On these social and economic trends see Bartolomé Yun Casalilla, *Sobre la transición al capitalismo en Castilla* (Salamanca, 1987), chaps. 6–8; the articles collected in I. A. A. Thompson and Bartolomé Yun Casalilla, eds., *The Castilian Crisis of the Seventeenth Century: New Perspectives on the Economic and Social History of Seventeenth-Century Spain* (Cambridge, 1994); and Gelabert, *La bolsa del rey*, esp. chap. 4.

Auec priuilege du Roy. 1612.   I. le Clerc excud.   L. Gaultier sculp.

CHRISTVS honoratæ Pacis mutatus in ora,
Protegit has Gentes, æterno fœdere iunctas;
Vt dum concordes fuerint, non viribus vllis
Vinci, sed valeant Atlantis voluere pondus.

De ces Peuples guerriers DIEV prenant la defence,
Les vnit sainctement, se transformant en Paix;
Afin qu'estans d'accord, nul effort les offense,
Mais qu'eux du grand Atlas puissent porter le faix.

11   Louis Gaultier, *Allegory of the Wedding between Louis XIII of France and Anne of Austria, Daughter of Philip III of Spain.* One of the engravings celebrating the matrimonial alliance between the Spanish and the French monarchies through the weddings of Louis XIII to Anne of Austria and Prince Philip (the future Philip IV) to Isabelle of Bourbon.

insisted that the situation of the Castilian cities, towns, and villages was difficult, and referred to their constant petitions to reduce their fiscal contributions to the crown.[10] The deplorable condition of Castile was discussed in 1610 by an anonymous writer who spoke of depopulation and impoverishment, debts and social discontentment. More important were the consequences the state of Castile could have for Spain, now depicted like a giant "with a head of gold and a torso of silver" but with feet of mud and hence condemned to total ruin within forty years unless the rulers were able to halt the decline.[11]

Given these appraisals of conditions in Castile, the dialogue between the king's financial ministers and the representatives of the kingdoms took on a familiar tone.[12] The king and his favorite appealed to the counselors for funds to cover the military costs in Italy, to assist the rulers of the Low Countries, and to pay the salaries of royal servants. Lerma, in turn, took it upon himself to declare that if the royal ministers were unable to provide the king with the funds he required, it was not for lack of resources but because they deliberately hindered the implementation of the king's orders or because the funds destined for the king were appropriated by corrupt officials. Both Philip III and Lerma continuously reminded the members of the Council of Finance of their obligation to serve the king and his policies and of their duty to find the means (extraordinary if necessary) to meet his urgent fiscal needs.[13]

The financial ministers, however, countered the king's claims by maintaining that they, above all, were the defenders of the "public cause" and the interests of the king's subjects. They insisted that the solution to the monarchy's fiscal mess lay neither with the kingdom nor with themselves but solely with the king. Divine law, wrote the counselors of finance, prohibits the king from taking the property of his subjects without their consent; and by not paying his debts, the monarch was doing just that. Since the Council of Finance was constituted to protect the interests of the king's subjects and to "defend the rights of those [to] whom the monarchy owes money," the council now attempted to deal with the fiscal shortfall by proposing that the king should radically reduce expenses rather than increase taxes or suspend the payment of debts. Everything superfluous must be eliminated, and even necessary and unavoidable expenses had to be substantially reduced.[14] The king had no alternative but to reduce the number of his servants and the number of those who received benefits from the royal treasury and to further reduce the Spanish

---

[10] AGS CJH, *leg.* 488/fol. 134, *consulta* of the Council of Finance, 13 May 1609.
[11] Cf. Luis Perdices, *La economía política de la decadencia de Castilla en el siglo XVII* (Madrid, 1996), pp. 39–40. [12] See above, chap. 9.
[13] See Lerma's answer to a *consulta* of the Council of Finance dated 24 Apr. 1610, in AGS CJH, *leg.* 493/fol. 114. See also Philip III's answer to a *consulta* from the Council of Finance (25 Oct. 1610) in which the king accused his ministers of hiding information regarding the real number of ducats that the king could use to pay for special engagements: AGS CJH, *leg.* 493/fol. 308.
[14] AGS CJH, *leg.* 511/fol. 290, *consulta* of the Council of Finance, 17 Oct. 1612.

monarchy's presence in Europe.[15] As before, Lerma tried to take political initiatives to increase the funds available to the monarch by, for instance, attempting to control the institutions in charge of collecting and distributing Castile's taxes, but this and other initiatives failed to improve the financial situation, which continued to worsen as the reign approached its end.[16]

Philip III and Lerma had no better luck in their attempts to increase fiscal pressure on other kingdoms, though perhaps in this respect their failure was due to a lack of political will. Nevertheless, they tried to promote the idea that the monarch had the same authority in these kingdoms as in Castile. This, at least in theory, gave the monarch quasi-absolute powers that could be used to impose new taxes without the consent of his subjects. Pedro Franqueza had defended such views in relation to Catalonia and Juan de Borja with regard to Portugal in the first years of the reign,[17] and the regime promoted them again in the 1610s. Diego de Silva, for example, Lerma's ally and one of the most influential royal ministers in the Council of Portugal, declared in a memorandum sent to Lerma that in Portugal the Spanish king had absolute power and thus the right to impose new taxes without consulting his subjects.[18] But, as Moura pointed out in 1613, if Philip III wanted to impose new taxes or increase existing ones, then he needed to visit Portugal to persuade its elites to collaborate in the defense of the monarchy.[19] Once again, Philip III disregarded Moura's advice; he did not visit Portugal until 1619, almost a year after Lerma's fall from power.[20]

The only other kingdom targeted for a tax increase at this time was Naples. Two factors made Naples the focus of Philip III's and Lerma's attempts to integrate the non-Iberian kingdoms in the defense of the monarchy. In Naples, as in the other Spanish possessions on the Italian peninsula, the king's subjects were used to his absence, and the Spanish viceroy had been granted powers (including the right to summon parliament in the name of the king) that gave him a more active role in the mobilization of the Neapolitan political elite.[21] In addition, from the start of the reign Lerma and his allies had attempted to create a strong pro-Spanish faction in

---

[15] AGS CJH, *leg*. 493/fol. 308.

[16] Between 1608 and 1617, the *Cortes* of Castile were summoned only on two occasions: from December 1611 to April 1612 and from February to June 1615. During this period, 1608–17, the crown was able to impose its policy regarding the collection of the financial duties approved by the *Cortes* mainly by introducing some of Lerma's clients as members of the "Comisión de Millones," charged with the important task of controlling payment to the king of the amount approved by the *Cortes* in the agreement of the *millones*. On these topics see Charles Jago, "Fiscalidad y cambio constitucional," pp. 117–32. On the financial problems toward the end of the reign see below, chap. 12.

[17] See above, chap. 7.   [18] Salinas, "Dictamen," p. 378.

[19] AGS CJH, *leg*. 520/fol. 12, *consulta* of the *Junta de Hacienda*, 17 Apr. 1613.

[20] Philip III and Lerma accepted invitations to visit the kingdoms of the Crown of Aragon in 1608 and 1616, but on both occasions the royal journeys were canceled because of lack of funds to pay for their costs; see AGS Est., *leg*. 262/n.p., *consulta* of the Council of State, 10 Sept. 1616.

[21] On Naples under the Spanish monarchy, see Rosario Villari, *The Revolt of Naples*, trans. James Newell (Cambridge, Mass., 1993); and Giuseppe Galasso, *Alla periferia dell'impero. Il regno di Napoli nel periodo spagnolo (secoli XVI–XVII)* (Turin, 1994).

Naples. Lerma demonstrated his interest in Naples – a kingdom valued for its geopolitical importance, its wealth, and its centrality to the conservation of the Spanish monarchy – by appointing his own brother-in-law, Francisco Ruiz de Castro, Count of Lemos, as its viceroy at the end of 1598. His death in 1600 led to the promotion of Fernando de Castro y Sandoval, Lemos's son and Lerma's nephew, as Naples's interim viceroy. Lerma's continued interest in Naples was reaffirmed in 1607 when he proposed that his other nephew, Pedro Fernández de Castro, the new Count of Lemos and, without doubt, Lerma's favorite among his relatives, be made the new viceroy of Naples. Although Lemos did not take up the post until 1609, by 1607 he was involved in debates regarding the situation in Naples. It was, in fact, Lemos who in 1607 proposed a radical plan for improving the financial situation of the monarchy which, had it been implemented, would have made Naples, of all Spanish kingdoms, one of the most important contributors to the royal treasury. In a report sent to the Council of State, Lemos proposed the introduction of a series of *arbitrios* (fiscal expedients) – taxes on the consumption of salt, the selling of public offices, the creation of a royal bank, and so on – to force Naples to pay for its own expenses and defense. The Council of State rejected Lemos's proposals because the counselors believed that such a sweeping fiscal program would provoke a general rebellion in the kingdom.[22] But when Lemos became viceroy in 1609 he implemented a similar program that led to a gradual increase in the revenues the monarchy received from the kingdom – from 3,200,648 ducats in 1605 to 4,299,638 ducats in 1616 (his final year of service in Naples), a 34 percent increase, whereas expenses in the kingdom increased by a mere 1 percent, from 4,277,205 ducats in 1605 to 4,335,590 in 1616.[23] Lemos's successes in Naples, however, were unimportant compared to the general opinion, promoted by the Council of Finance and the *Junta de Hacienda*, that immediate solution of the financial crisis was impossible.

From Lerma's point of view the most critical aspect of the debates on the state of the royal treasury was the divisiveness emerging in his own faction. Maintaining factional unity became difficult after 1606. In that year Juan de Borja, perhaps Lerma's most trusted ally and relative, died. Although Lerma promoted other allies and relatives to occupy Borja's offices, his successors (Sancho de la Cerda, Marquis of La Laguna and Lerma's brother-in-law, as the *mayordomo mayor* to the queen, and Diego de Silva, Count of Salinas, as the principal member of the Council of Portugal), lacked Borja's political weight, which made dissidence in the Council of Portugal possible and led to increasing activity of a party organized around the queen and her confessor.[24]

A more serious threat to Lerma's control of the political machinery came in 1608

---

[22] AGS Est., *leg.* 187/fol. 215, *consulta* of the Council of State, 30 Jan. 1607.
[23] Antonio Calabria, *The Cost of Empire. The Finances of the Kingdom of Naples in the Time of Spanish Rule* (Cambridge, 1991), tables 1 and 6, pp. 134, 142; see also Galasso, *Alla periferia dell'imperio*, pp. 157–84. [24] On this topic see Sánchez, *The Empress, passim*.

when Baltasar de Zúñiga – a member of the Guzmán family and the uncle of the Count of Olivares, the future favorite of Philip IV and Lerma's mortal enemy – was appointed ambassador to Emperor Rudolf II. Zúñiga's appointment to this important office resulted not from connections with Lerma or Lerma's faction but from his diplomatic experience. Although Zúñiga never publicly opposed the policies adopted under Lerma's *privanza*, he thought they indicated the absence of political will at the center, an opinion he expressed when he returned to court in 1617 and became the most influential counselor of state.[25]

Lerma's political problems increased substantially in 1608 when he lost one of his most loyal and powerful allies, the Count of Miranda, who retired from public life in April 1608, owing to his deteriorating health and advanced age (he was seventy-seven years old). A few months later, Miranda died, causing great consternation to the king, Lerma, and other members of the court.[26] Despite rumors of disagreements between them, Lerma had lost an important ally and the support and advice of one of the best royal ministers, and he was to pay dearly for this loss in years to come.[27] Although Lerma was able to secure the appointment of his own clients to the important post of President of the Council of Castile, the men he promoted were unable to achieve the same level of political control as Miranda. In April 1608 the king appointed Juan Bautista de Acevedo, Bishop of Valladolid and Inquisitor-General, to the presidency, and after Acevedo's death three months later, Pedro Manso, head of the Chancellery of Valladolid. Neither had the experience, authority, or prestige of Miranda. Perceived as minor characters and Lerma's puppets, they came from the ranks of the provincial low nobility (Acevedo) and the *letrados* (Manso), origins that further reduced their ability to impose authority on the grandees and other members of the nobility in a society dominated by concepts of honor and hierarchy. In the three months he served as the President of Castile, Acevedo caused more problems than he solved in his concern to establish new forms of etiquette to elevate his social prestige and cover up his lack of political experience.[28] Manso's presidency was no more successful. His appointment came as a big surprise to court observers, not only because of his humble origins but because there were other more qualified candidates, much more experienced in matters of government and higher in social status, both essential qualities for the holder of so elevated an office.[29]

Although continuing to control some of the most important political and administrative offices, by 1608–9, Lerma was clearly beginning to lose his grip on the monarchical machinery and, even more importantly, his monopoly over the king's favor and confidence. The first sign of weakness came with the appointment of Fray

---

[25] On Zúñiga's career and views see Elliott, *The Count-Duke*, pp. 40–5; Sánchez, *The Empress*, p. 89; and below, chap. 12.

[26] The impact of Miranda's death for Lerma is best expressed in a letter of Sor Margarita de la Cruz to Rodrigo Calderón, 20 Sept. 1608: Serrano i Sanz, *Apuntes*, vol. I, p. 91.

[27] Vitrián, *Memorias*, vol. II, p. 350.   [28] See Cabrera de Córdoba, *Relaciones*, p. 338.

[29] *Ibid.*, p. 346.

Luis de Aliaga as Philip III's confessor in 1608.[30] Aliaga's appointment, in the main, followed precedent except that, unlike Philip III's former confessors, Aliaga owed his career and rise not to Lerma but to his protector, Fray Gerónimo Javierre, royal confessor from 1606 to 1608.[31] As the spiritual counselor of the king, Aliaga soon acquired enormous influence that was further enhanced by his office as a counselor of state and his membership together with Juan de Idiáquez in the *Junta de Dos*, which continued the work of the *Junta de Gobierno*.[32] It is difficult to ascertain from the *consultas* of this *junta*, or those signed by Aliaga, if the new confessor disagreed with Lerma's policies, but he became one of the king's advisers on financial affairs, collaborating with and sharing the views of Juan de Acuña and Cristóbal de Ipeñarrieta in these matters. Furthermore, soon after his appointment, Father Aliaga began to express his desire to disassociate himself from Lerma, apparently believing that both the king and the monarchy would benefit if Lerma were to lose his power and influence.

Lerma's decision to appoint his son-in-law and nephew, the Count of Lemos, as Viceroy of Naples in 1609, left vacant the presidency of the Council of the Indies, which Lemos had occupied since 1604. The person selected to fill this position was Juan de Acuña, President of the Council of Finance, a minister not very well liked by Lerma because of his position on financial matters. In addition, Acuña had become a part of the governing faction not through his connections to Lerma but through Lerma's son, the Duke of Uceda. Acuña's appointment in turn left vacant the presidency of the Council of Finance to which the king appointed Fernando Carrillo, who had been in charge of the investigations and trials against Franqueza and Alonso Ramírez de Prado and who, like Acuña, had strong ties to Uceda.

Although Lerma did not need to control each and every royal minister to keep his faction united and to preserve the king's confidence, by 1608 conflict within Lerma's faction began to emerge and ultimately led to a new regrouping at court. Lerma's eldest son, Cristóbal Gómez de Sandoval, better known as the Duke of Uceda, began to play an increasingly active role in court politics and to collaborate with Aliaga, Acuña, and Carrillo. The motives behind Uceda's alignment with courtiers who opposed his own father are uncertain, but many accounts of tensions between father and son began to circulate from 1606–7. These tensions were reported as early as 1606 when the emperor's ambassador to Madrid, Johann Khevenhüller, predicted to his master that with time "the *lermenses* [members of

---

[30] On Aliaga's appointment as Philip III's confessor see AGPR Ex. Per., 28/42; he was sworn in on 6 Dec. 1608. On the same day he was appointed a counselor of state. See also J. Navarro Latorre, *Aproximación a Fray Luis de Aliaga, confesor de Felipe III* (Zaragoza, 1981), p. 13.

[31] On the relationship between Javierre and Aliaga see *ibid.*, pp. 10–11.

[32] On Aliaga's role as a personal counselor of the king and Lerma, see BNM, Mss 1923, "Papeles del padre confesor Fray Luis de Aliaga tocantes a diversos negocios de los que se le ha pedido su parecer," 1610. See also AGS Est., *leg.* 258, where there are many *consultas* from the *Junta de Dos*; all these *consultas* are from the years 1610 and 1611.

Lerma's faction] will destroy themselves by internal feuding." As support, he referred to the growing tension between Lerma and the Duke of Uceda, the result apparently of Lerma's preference for his nephew and son-in-law, the Count of Lemos. There were, as well, other matters, questions concerning Uceda's rights as the sole inheritor of the Sandoval legacy.[33] Lerma himself, however, gave his son an important political role when he named Uceda as his substitute to attend to those who asked for the king's patronage, a function Uceda performed temporarily until 1612 and permanently thereafter.[34] Using this position as a platform for enhancing his influence, Uceda began to be depicted as "the left hand of the king," always ready to assist Philip III and to share the position of his father, "the king's right hand."[35] Uceda's decision to align himself with Aliaga and Acuña increased the tensions within Lerma's faction, strains that became quite apparent in October 1610. The retirement of Pedro Manso, Lerma's creature, as President of the Council of Castile, forced the king to select his replacement at a time when the rivalry between Lerma and Aliaga and Uceda was intensifying. Lerma had his own candidate, Gabriel de Trejo y Paniagua, who was "a relative and creature" of Rodrigo Calderón.[36] Aliaga and Uceda, in turn, championed Juan de Acuña. In a decision that surprised many of his contemporaries, Philip III selected Acuña, who occupied the presidency of Castile until his death in December 1615.[37]

These incidents demonstrate that Lerma could no longer count on the support of a unified faction or Philip's total confidence. The increasing ideological debate on the nature of his government was of essential concern to those who held power and to those who aspired to gain it. Success for Lerma's opponents lay in their ability to prove that they did not oppose the king but wanted to help him restore good government and save the monarchy from decline. Their central message was very clear: the urgent object of royal concern was to attend to the common good; therefore, the king's obligation was to reestablish a mixed form of government that returned to the councils the power and prerogatives that the royal favorite had

[33] "Relación que hace el conde de Franquenburg al emperador," in BNM, Mss 2751, "Historia de Johann Khevenhüller, conde de Franquenburg," 1145–6. Among the papers taken from Rodrigo Calderón after he was detained in 1619 were many letters from Lerma discussing his conflicts with Uceda; see AGS CC DC, *leg.* 35/1, *exp.* 7, n.p.; see also BNM, Mss 722, "Advertencias que se dieron a Don Rodrigo Calderón," fol. 165v.

[34] "Relación que hace el conde de Franquenburg al emperador," in BNM Mss 2751, "Historia de Johann Khevenhúller," p. 1146, and Cabrera de Córdoba, *Relaciones*, pp. 212–13.

[35] Márquez Torres, *Discursos consolatorios*, fols. 82r–83v; on Uceda as Lerma's lieutenant in handling affairs of state, see BNM, Mss 11569, "Memorial del pleito contra el duque de Uceda," fols. 214r, 230v–231r.

[36] Cabrera de Córdoba, *Relaciones*, p. 492; in reality Gabriel de Trejo y Paniagua was a relative of Calderón's wife; Trejo's administrative experience included royal attorney (1607) and *oidor* [judge] (1608) of the Chancellery of Valladolid, royal attorney at the Council of the Military Orders (1609), and counselor of the Inquisition (1610). In 1613 he became a counselor of Castile, and in December 1616 he was named cardinal by Paul V.

[37] On the appointment of Juan de Acuña see AHN CS, bk. 724, fols. 90r–v; on the defeat of Lerma's candidate see Mateo Escagedo y Salmón, ed., "Los Acebedos," *Boletín de la Biblioteca Menéndez y Pelayo*, 5–9 (1923–7), 6, p. 238.

usurped by acting as the king's prime minister.[38] It is not clear whether the writers who published these views between 1609 and 1612 were, in fact, supported by the leaders of the emerging anti-Lerma faction, but they could hardly have made their views public had Lerma not begun to lose political power.

The first critical treatise against Lerma and his regime was written by the Jesuit Fray Juan de Mariana, who had connections neither with Lerma nor with the group of ministers who questioned his power. Famous for his defense of tyrannicide,[39] Mariana returned to the center of political debate in 1609 after he tried to publish a Spanish translation of a short treatise entitled *De monetae mutatione*.[40] The central theme of *De monetae* was a critique of the devaluation of the coinage and, more specifically, the rulers' decision to mint *vellón*, a topic that, however, had lost urgency by the time the book was published because of the agreement between the crown and the *Cortes* to halt the coining of *vellón* in 1608.[41] The fact that devaluation of the coinage was no longer a pressing issue only increased the importance of the other ideas and proposals expressed in the treatise. Mariana's principal intention, in fact, was not to denounce the regime's monetary policies or their legal and political consequences but to use this case as an exposition of what he considered to be the terrible state of the kingdom.

The foundations on which his criticism rested were the theories he had discussed in his *De rege*: that monarchical power had limits which were established through a covenant between the king and the kingdom and that those who wanted to eliminate them aimed to make royal power absolute and transform the king into a tyrant. For Mariana the coining of *vellón* was an example of tyrannical behavior because the devaluing of coins in circulation allowed the king to rob his subjects of their property and indirectly impose new taxes without their consent. The king could use no legal argument – certainly not the principle of "necessity" as defenders of reason-of-state theories claimed – to support what was simply robbery. To reestablish the health of his kingdom, the monarch should not resort to tyrannical measures but should institute a new program of political and financial austerity. Concurring with the measures proposed by the Council of Finance and the *Junta de Hacienda*, Mariana also urged the monarch to order an immediate and radical reduction of expenses – in the royal household and also by reducing the number of *mercedes* with grants attached. In addition, Mariana advocated the

---

[38] On the character of political opposition in early modern states see Quentin Skinner, "The Principles and Practice of Opposition: The Case of Bolingbroke versus Walpole," in Neil McKendrick, ed., *Historical Perspectives. Studies in English Thought and Society in Honour of J. H. Plumb* (London, 1974), pp. 109–13; on the methodological implications of studying ideological debates, see pp. 94–108.   [39] See above, chap. 1.

[40] This treatise was included in a collection of seven treatises published in Latin in Cologne under the title *Septem Tractatus Joannis Marianae e Societatis Jesu*; on this collection and its contents see Christian Hansen Roses, *Ensayo sobre el pensamiento político del padre Juan de Mariana* (Santiago de Chile, 1959), pp. 105ff. I use the Spanish translation published in Fray Juan de Mariana, *Obras del Padre Juan de Mariana*, ed. F. Pi y Margall, 2 vols. (Madrid, 1950), vol. II, pp. 577–93. Further references in the text.   [41] On this topic see above, chap. 7.

reduction of the monarchy's involvement in European conflicts, claiming that nothing, especially not the Low Countries, was important enough to compromise the future of the monarchy.

Up to this point, Mariana's proposals and analysis of the monarchy's predicament did not differ substantially from the views of many of his contemporaries. But he went on to develop a topic that, since the detention of Franqueza and Ramírez de Prado, had been a constant and important subject of the contemporary political debate: corruption. To Mariana, the detention of several ministers demonstrated that those who helped the king rule were infected by an epidemic of corruption that threatened the stability of the monarchy. To put an end to this situation it was necessary to move beyond punitive measures: it was no longer enough to detain those found guilty; now measures must be established to prevent the spread of the disease. Before taking office, all royal ministers must be ordered to present inventories of their fortunes for eventual comparison with inventories they would present when they left their ministerial posts. Mariana ended his treatise by discussing the progressive decline of the Spanish monarchy since the death of Philip II. Formerly, he wrote, the Spanish monarchy, with fewer financial resources than those available to Philip III, had conquered numerous kingdoms. Now, the monarchy appeared completely paralyzed and unable to defend itself and its territories. Furthermore, he did not believe that this decline was the inevitable result of the "natural aging" that all bodies experienced; he remained committed to a more personal, and thus political, explanation: "It is men . . . who are bringing this monarchy down" (p. 593).

That Mariana's critique profoundly disturbed Lerma is demonstrated by the immediate reaction, first against the book and then against the author himself. On Lerma's orders the President of the Council of Castile, Pedro Manso, carefully examined the contents of *De monetae mutatione*.[42] In his report, he showed no concern over Mariana's critique of the coining of *vellón* or his radical views on royal power. What concerned Manso were several passages in which Mariana dealt with the expenses of the royal household, the charges that all offices were sold or given to people whose only merits were "to be relatives or clients of courtiers serving in the royal household," and accusations that all ministers in charge of royal finances had agreements with bankers and others who conducted business with the royal treasury. The most damaging passages, however, were those in which Mariana claimed that following Philip II's death the Spanish monarchy had been in continual decline. According to Manso, the acerbic Jesuit was implicitly saying that "when Philip II died, everything died." This accusation convinced Manso that the only prudent and legal thing to do was to prohibit the circulation of the book in the Spanish kingdoms. Mariana himself encountered a similar fate. Almost immediately

---

[42] Manso's report, indicating what parts should be taken from Mariana's treatise, because it went against "the authority of the pope, the king and his ministers," in BNM, Mss 12179: "Consultas originales de Estado," fols. 138r–v, 141r. Manso wrote his report in 1609.

after Manso's report was released, he was arrested on charges of having committed a crime of treason, although he was freed in 1611 as a result of the opposition of Rome to the persecution of a Jesuit.[43]

Despite the repressive measures against Mariana and other critics of the regime, by 1609 Lerma and his allies were losing control over what was said and written about the state of the monarchy, and between 1609 and 1612 some very critical analyses of the dominant political theories appeared in print. The first to be published appeared under the false authorship of Benito Arias Montano, a famous humanist during the reign of Philip II. The title of the book, with explicit references to Tacitus, initially created expectations that it had been written in defense of theories of reason of state advocated by Lerma and his allies: *Aforismos sacados de la historia de Publio Cornelio Tácito por el doctor Arias Montano, para la conservación y aumento de las monarquías.*[44] The contents, however, offered the exact opposite: a radical critique of reason of state and its practical consequences for the ruling of the monarchy. Reaffirming traditional theories regarding the power and place of the monarch, the anonymous author noted, for example, that the ruler was the holder of a public office, and, hence, was obliged "to serve" the people and the common good. All attempts to transform the king's power into absolute power were a recipe for disaster (fols. 4v, 26r–v). It was, however, the author's view that the monarch had the obligation to rule alone that became political dynamite in the context of the increasing opposition to Lerma's monopolistic *privanza*. According to the author, the worst thing for a kingdom was to have a weak monarch who lacked courage (*gallardía*). Inevitably, he would be dominated by a *privado*, who would use every tactic, even promoting the king's privacy and persuading the king to live in the countryside ("*una vida tranquila de aldea*"), in order to usurp royal power and prerogatives. The author went on to claim that there are "many princes who have little will and understanding and who are king only in name while the force and authority of the state is in the hands of a *privado* who rules on his own." He ended with the prediction that a *privado* with such power would provoke envy and hatred among the king's subjects who would come to view the monarch as the one ultimately responsible for their discontent because of his decision to uphold such a favorite (fols. 2, 31, 84v–5).

Attacks on the absolute power of a monopolistic favorite and the defense of a system of mixed monarchy were even more sharply expressed in three treatises published in 1611 and 1612 by Agustín de Rojas Villandrando (*El buen repúblico*), Fray Jerónimo Gracián de la Madre de Dios (*Diez lamentaciones del miserable estado de los ateístas de nuestro tiempo*), and Fray Juan Márquez (*El gobernador christiano deducido de las vidas de Moisés y Josué, príncipes del pueblo de Dios*), all of whom presented a radical critique of reason-of-state theories.[45] Very little is known of the

---

[43] Roses, *Ensayo*, pp. 109–12. [44] (Barcelona, 1609). Further references in the text.
[45] Agustín de Rojas Villandrando, *El buen repúblico* (Salamanca, 1611); Jerónimo Gracián de la Madre de Dios, *Diez lamentaciones del miserable estado de los ateístas de nuestro tiempo* [1611], in *Beatus vir, carne*

authors' motivations, although there are certain indications – at least in the case of Gracián and Márquez. They wrote in response to the political presence of Lerma as the king's chief minister and as critics of the forms of rule he had promoted in the first part of the reign. Fray Juan most clearly posed the central theme in this ideological debate: how to reconcile, from a Christian point of view, "the contradictions between what is useful and what is honest" in governmental matters, and how this understanding should influence the political decisions of a Christian ruler.[46] The difference between the useful and the honest and the limits upon a Christian ruler were indeed central topics in all three treatises. Fray Jerónimo Gracián made his point simply, stating that there were only two kinds of monarchs – good and bad. The former in both their personal and their public lives followed Christian principles, upheld as their ultimate goal the defense of the true religion, and created a just government always following "the advice of the wisest and the elders, and the good counsel and decisions of their ancestors."[47] In contrast, bad monarchs were sinful and believed that personal power was more important than their duty to defend God and Catholicism. To accomplish their debased goals "these rulers closed their eyes to all divine reason and ruled following only [their] reason of state, accepting the terrible doctrine that argues that all good things must be shunned to pursue temporal and earthly pretensions."[48]

That a monarch should value the useful rather than the honest was, as mentioned earlier, a central tenet proposed by Botero, Lipsius, and Alamos de Barrientos, authors who had influenced the policies of the current regime. In the eyes of Márquez, Gracián, and Rojas, such evil advice would ultimately drive the Spanish monarchy to total ruin. Márquez defined utility, the determining principle of reason-of-state doctrines, as a "narrow and wrong path" and claimed that monarchs can only triumph by following "the truth and the Gospels."[49] According to these writers, the ascendancy of theories of reason of state had prompted rulers to abandon their duty to defend all Catholics living in lands controlled by heretics, an indirect critique, no doubt, of peace agreements with England and the Dutch Republic. There were internal consequences as well. Rojas, for example, believed that the principal cause of the monarchy's decline was that the king followed and gave his favor to advisers who promoted reason of state in order to advance their own interests without considering the needs of the king and the kingdom.[50] The immediate result was the surge of political corruption to a level previously unknown, thus demonstrating once again that bad and weak monarchs were friends of "thieves and all those who wished to receive unjust and corrupting bribes."[51]

---

de hoguera, ed. Emilia Navarro de Kelley (Madrid, 1977); Juan Márquez, *El gobernador christiano deducido de las vidas de Moisés y Josué, príncipes del pueblo de Dios* (Salamanca, 1612).

[46] Márquez, *El gobernador cristiano*, dedication: "*las contradicciones de lo útil con lo honesto, el peso que han de tener las cosas no tan buenas, o los medios humanos que exceden de su límite.*"

[47] Gracián, *Diez lamentaciones*, pp. 328, 332.   [48] *Ibid.*, p. 328.

[49] Márquez, *El gobernador christiano*, p. 73.   [50] Rojas, *El buen república*, pp. 272, 273–4, 275.

[51] Gracián, *Diez lamentaciones*, p. 336.

As before, these references to political corruption invoked actual political events and debates. Certainly, the cases of Franqueza and Ramírez de Prado served to remind Lerma's contemporaries of the level of corruption during his *privanza*. In addition, after Franqueza's and Prado's downfall, Lerma's unpopularity, no longer simply the result of his failure to contain the fiscal crisis or to develop support for his foreign policy, also stemmed from the increasing opposition to Rodrigo Calderón. Although officially pardoned by the king in 1607, Calderón (see Chapter 8) remained at the center of court confrontations, surrounded by an expanding number of enemies. Although the royal sentence of 1607 had forced him to resign his offices, Calderón continued to accumulate power, political influence, titles, and riches thanks to Lerma's favor, even while his enemies actively pursued ways to undermine his influence and, at the same time, used him to attack the royal favorite. Immediately after the king's pardon, for example, Francisco de Mendoza, Admiral of Aragon and a member of the powerful house of the Dukes of Infantado, initiated such a campaign. Mendoza's criticism was based on allegations by Francisco de Gamboa, Calderón's former secretary, who accused him of using royal funds to his own benefit, accepting bribes from courtiers and foreign ambassadors, and persecuting all who dared to criticize him and his patron. Mendoza sent his report to Fray Luis de Aliaga, Philip III's confessor, but once again Calderón received Lerma's support, and in June 1609 Francisco de Mendoza was detained and accused of treason.[52]

Calderón's problems did not end with Mendoza's detention, however, because the queen herself and some of her allies took up the denunciation of Calderón, apparently in an attempt to tighten the circle of opposition around Lerma. Documents seized from Calderón in 1619 make it clear that he and Lerma knew of the activities of the queen and her allies, and were convinced that only Lerma's support had prevented Calderón's detention and official persecution.

Although the queen was unable to influence Calderón's fate when she was alive, her death made Lerma's and Calderón's opponents bolder in their critiques of the regime. The queen's opposition to Calderón had been so public that immediately after her death on 3 October 1611 there began to circulate rumors that he had plotted against her life. Sir John Digby, the English ambassador, informed John Holles that the late queen "a little before her death took many distastes against this Don Rodrigo Calderón and complained of him to the king, since which time his enemies have followed him so closely; and (as it is said) some such information has been found by the king in a cabinet of the queen."[53] Although the queen had in fact

---

[52] On Mendoza's attacks against Calderón, see RAH CLSC, N-71, fols. 129–130r; on the detention of the Admiral of Aragon, see Cabrera de Córdoba, *Relaciones*, p. 370; on the charges against the Admiral and his defense see RAH CLSC, N-71; on Calderón's participation in the Admiral's detention see BNM, Mss 6713, "Descargos de don Rodrigo Calderón," fol. 31v.

[53] Sir John Digby to Sir John Holles, 29 Nov. 1611, in Holles, *Letter book*, pp. 103–4.

died of complications following childbirth, the rumored allegations transformed Queen Margaret, in the words of Calderón's enemies, into a "martyr of Jesus Christ." An anonymous author of one of the pamphlets that circulated at the court after Margaret's death wrote, for example, that the queen

moved by the outcries of the people and the advice of wise and virtuous persons ... felt obliged to confront the ill intentions of those who without doubt have caused her death. Her goal was to serve our Lord by promoting justice in the distribution of *mercedes*, appointments of good ministers, and the elimination of bribes, simonies, the sale of offices, and the promotion of unworthy and inept persons.[54]

Fray Gerónimo de Florencia similarly addressed the late queen's aspirations in a sermon preached before the king in a funeral mass held on 18 November 1611. Speaking on the queen's behalf, Florencia reminded Philip III that

a king has two wives, the queen and the community.... The offspring of the first marriage should be children. The offspring of the second marriage should be prudent laws, the appointment of good ministers, *mercedes* to those who deserve them, the punishment of criminals, audiences to all your subjects, dedication to affairs of state, and the consolation of the afflicted. To repay God for the abundant offspring from the first marriage Your Majesty has to comply with your duties towards your second wife.[55]

Fray Gerónimo was reminding Philip III of his duty to govern as the sole ruler of the Spanish monarchy, a responsibility that an increasing number of his subjects believed he had forsaken and delegated to an incompetent and corrupt favorite. A few months after Queen Margaret's death, a series of very critical poems appeared at court accusing Lerma, Calderón, and some of their allies of using royal favor and power to enrich themselves, their relatives, and clients, and specifically charging Lerma – depicted as "Archduke Lerma" – of usurping the king's authority.[56]

Despite the accusations against Calderón, Lerma continued to support his favorite as he had done in 1607 and 1609.[57] Although rumors of Calderón's imminent departure from the court to his country estate persisted, few seem to have believed them.[58] Lope de Vega, for example, reported to Sessa in November 1611 that, despite attacks, Calderón continued to be Lerma's favorite and that Lerma would never let Calderón be detained.[59] But at court the situation was

---

[54] BNM, Mss 20260/30, Anonymous: "Sobre la muerte de la Reina," fol. 194r–v. After his detention in 1619, Calderón was indeed prosecuted for having procured the death of the queen; in the final sentence against him this charge was dropped.

[55] Gerónimo de Florencia, *Sermón que predicó a la Majestad del rey don Felipe III en las honras que su Majd. hizo a la serenísima reina doña Margarita su mujer, en San Gerónimo el Real de Madrid a 18 de noviembre de 1611* (Madrid, 1612), fols. 17r–v; I thank Dr. Magdalena Sánchez for providing me with a copy of her notes on this sermon.   [56] BNM, Mss 9087, "Sátiras políticas," 1612.

[57] See BNM, Mss 6713, "Descargos de don Rodrigo Calderón," fol. 213r.

[58] In a letter to his patron, the Duke of Sessa, written between 22 and 30 October 1611, Lope de Vega echoed these rumors and the general disbelief: Vega Carpio, *Epistolario*, vol. III, p. 71.

[59] *Ibid.*, vol. III, pp. 73–74.

becoming more and more difficult, and Lerma's support was no longer enough to protect Calderón. As an anonymous follower warned Calderón in a letter early in 1612, "You have too many enemies, some of them very important, including the king himself who is against you and who has decided to banish you from his side."[60] Calderón's only friend, he continued, was the Duke of Lerma, but he could change his mind as he did with Franqueza in 1607. Under these circumstances, Calderón would be well advised to leave the court, but before going, "[you should] woo (*cortejar*), flatter, serve, and buy with a thousand gifts and good words the support of the Duke of Uceda and declare yourself his creature." In September 1612, Calderón did leave the court to serve as an ambassador extraordinary to the archdukes in Flanders, an appointment that turned out to be a short retreat, for he returned to Madrid in January 1613 as if nothing had happened.[61]

By 1612 Calderón's fate had become a thermometer by which to measure the political temperature at the court. At the time of Calderón's departure for Flanders, the group led by Aliaga and Uceda decided to step up their attacks against Lerma. Their position of power was now impressive. In addition to Uceda and Aliaga, who as royal confessor had free access to the king, this group included some of the most important office holders in the monarchy: Acuña was President of the Council of Castile, Carrillo was President of the Council of Finance, and Agustín de Villanueva was the powerful secretary of the Council of Aragón. Using Calderón's reputation and the public outcry over corruption among Lerma's clients as justification, they charged Aliaga, the king's spiritual advisor, a man of tremendous influence over the pious king, with the task of addressing Philip and offering him advice on how to rule the monarchy: "by yourself with the sole help of your Councils," the only respectable path a good king should follow.[62]

In response to Aliaga's challenge, Lerma ordered the President of the Council of Castile, Juan de Acuña, to investigate Aliaga's past and activities, to uncover evidence to justify a petition asking the king to dismiss Aliaga. Acuña's refusal to follow Lerma's order to open an investigation against Aliaga, his political ally, clearly showed that Lerma's grip on court power was diminishing. But he was not yet finished. In response to Acuña's noncompliance, Lerma asked Philip III to remind all councils of their duty to obey Lerma's orders as if they were his own, an

---

[60] BNM, Mss 722, "Advertencias que se dieron a Don Rodrigo Calderón, marqués de Siete Iglesias, nombrado para la embajada de Venecia: ¿Cuál le es mejor a vuesa señoría, quedarse en su oficio o irse a su embajada?" fol. 165r.

[61] On Calderón's return to the court and Philip III's friendly reception see Cabrera de Córdoba, *Relaciones*, p. 506. Luis Cabrera de Córdoba reported soon after Calderón's return that he "continues to assist the Duke of Lerma … who communicates with [his favorite] the most important affairs of state" (p. 508). Calderón returned to the court haughtier than ever, declaring that, while in Flanders, he had found papers demonstrating that he was a natural son of the famous Duke of Alba. This was a signal that Calderón wanted to become a grandee of Castile, a title that "Lerma had allegedly promised him": Lope de Vega to the Duke of Sessa, Jan. 1613, in Vega Carpio, *Epistolario*, vol. III, p. 166.   [62] Cabrera de Córdoba, *Relaciones*, p. 494, 20 Sept. 1612.

order sent by the king to all councils in October 1612, and known as the "*decreto de delegación de la firma real.*"[63]

But the same month, Lerma made another decision, one that increased his political isolation: he retired completely from giving public audiences. In a letter to the king's secretary Juan de Ciriza, he justified his decision by asserting that attending to private memoranda and public audiences "impedes me from attending to the more important matters of His Majesty, [and for this reason] I implored Him that from now on this task should be given to secretary don Bernabé de Vivanco, and His Majesty has agreed."[64] It is impossible to know exactly why Lerma decided to take this step, which increased Uceda's political influence by transforming him into the king's public representative in charge of listening to the complaints and petitions of the king's subjects and of receiving foreign ambassadors. From then on, many at the court began to view Lerma simply as one of the many players who competed for the king's favor and confidence. Although his power and influence were still apparent, his political machine was beginning to show signs of weakness.

Contemporary interest in Lerma's future extended far beyond Spain. Edward Grimston, for example, in his English translation of Louis de Mayerne's *The General Histoire of Spaine* (published in 1612 and probably affected by the events of 1607), speculated about the likely fortunes of the Duke of Lerma, whose *privanza* Grimston believed was approaching a dramatic end. To support his prediction, Grimston invented an account of a play performed by the "people of Valladolid," an imaginary play with the following cast: the king, Lerma, the Constable of Castile, and the people. The plot was quite simple: "the complaints and insolence of the Duke of Lerma; the Catastrophe, and the Duke of Lerma's death who was torn to pieces by the furious multitude."[65] Nothing so dramatic happened to Lerma, although after 1612 many of his political initiatives, his monopoly over the most important offices of the monarchy, and his control of the political discourse began indeed to be "torn to pieces."

---

[63] On this decree see above, chap. 6; on the connections between this decree and the political feuds between Lerma and Aliaga see Cabrera de Córdoba, *Relaciones*, p. 501, Oct. 1612.

[64] AGS Est., *leg.* 247/n.p., Lerma to Juan de Ciriza, 29 Oct. 1612.

[65] Mayerne, *The General Histoire of Spaine*, p. 1295.

11

Fall from power

By the end of 1612, many court observers were discussing the intensifying struggle for power and Lerma's growing loss of control. In one of his letters from Madrid, Pedro García do Valle, for example, informed his patron the Count of Gondomar, Spanish ambassador in London, of the king's decision to exile eight Portuguese from court because they had aligned themselves with the royal confessor, Aliaga, and some members of the Council of Portugal in order to talk with Philip III about the increasing discontent in the realm. Criticized by Calderón for trying "to disturb the peace in the kingdom," the Portuguese were banished from court after stating that the only hope left for them and for the kingdom was to wait for better times and for a change of those who controlled power and the king's grace. In the same letter, Do Valle communicated to Gondomar an account of an incident that everyone regarded as representative of the state of affairs at court. A group of palace guards – whose captain at the time was Calderón – had fought with the officials in charge of keeping peace and order at the court (*alcaldes de casa y corte*) and had killed one of them. Some of the guards were imprisoned, but a few hours later their comrades attacked the court jail and liberated them: this incident made many wish for the end of Lerma's regime.[1] A few months later, on 1 December 1613, Do Valle once again referred to the political situation: "the court is full of rumors against the Duke [of Lerma] and his underlings (*secuaces*)," criticisms so strong in tone that he did not dare to include them in his letters.[2]

Such references to the discontent with Calderón and Lerma were accompanied by public acknowledgment of the growing factional divisions. It was public knowledge that Aliaga maintained his distance from the royal favorite and that he was now trying to undermine the king's confidence in Lerma. Uceda's situation was somewhat different; few knew the nature or the source of the conflict between him and his father. The tension was publicly addressed for the first time in 1614 in the dedication to Uceda of a book written by Cristóbal de Fonseca, *Discursos para todos los evangelios de Cuaresma*, in which the author tried to justify Uceda's decision to criticize and confront the king's favorite, who happened to be his own father and to

---

[1] Pedro García do Valle to Gondomar, 10 July 1613; BNM, Mss 18149, "Correspondencia de Pedro García do Valle con el Conde de Gondomar," 1613–16, fols. 25r–v, 26r.
[2] *Ibid.*, fol. 37r.

whom, at least in theory, he owed absolute obedience and loyalty.[3] Comparing Uceda to Abraham's son, Fonseca claimed that, as an example of extreme obedience, Uceda was prepared to accept his sacrifice at the hands of his own father to avoid conflicts that could divide the court and harm the common good of the republic. But there came a time when sons could no longer be loyal to their fathers. Uceda had reached this point, according to Fonseca, not through lack of virtue but because his father had asked him to reward and favor men – an implicit reference to Calderón – of such low quality and nature that he had to confront his father even if it meant a clear and public clash of wills.

When Fonseca published his book, the struggle for control over the decision-making process had become fierce, and in 1614–15 many of the familiar concerns and new circumstances coalesced, all of which significantly influenced the remainder of Lerma's *privanza*. Intense debate on the regime's international policies resurfaced as a result of renewed conflicts with Savoy. Prince Philip's household, in which both factions had placed their members, was under scrutiny, and so was Uceda's growing political and public presence. The first publications raising fundamental questions about the political theories promoted by Lerma's faction now appeared.

After the assassination of Henry IV of France,[4] Lerma's main goal in international affairs was to maintain peace in northern Italy at all costs by isolating Savoy and by tightening control over Milan. To accomplish the latter, Lerma believed that it was crucial to appoint to the governorship of Milan a member of his own faction who shared his pacifist views. In June 1611, he selected his relative and ally Juan Hurtado de Mendoza, Marquis of San Germán and Hinojosa, as Milan's governor. His main duties were to avoid new conflicts and expenses and to increase Milan's contributions to the defense of the empire by following the model Lemos was implementing in Naples.[5]

Relative tranquility in northern Italy ended, however, in 1612 when the Duke of Mantua, Francesco II Gonzaga, an ally of Spain but also the Duke of Savoy's brother-in-law, died without an heir, creating an unstable and explosive situation both in the duchy and in the Italian peninsula by affecting the relationships between Savoy and Spain. The Duke of Savoy, Charles Emmanuel, reacted with celerity, and in April 1613 he and his allies attacked Monferrato, capturing several cities and dividing the duchy into two separate parts. Hinojosa's reaction, in line with Lerma's policies, was to avoid direct conflict, opting to negotiate a settlement

---

[3] Fray Cristóbal de Fonseca, *Discursos para todos los evangelios de Cuaresma* (Madrid, 1614), dedication, n.p.

[4] On Spain's policy towards France and its attempts to reduce tensions and neutralize its enemy by proposing a matrimonial alliance see Eiras Roel, "Desvío y 'mudanza' de Francia en 1616," pp. 528–38.

[5] On this appointment see Bombín Pérez, *La cuestión de Monferrato*, p. 24; on Hinojosa's mission see Fernández Albaladejo, *Fragmentos*, p. 224.

with Charles Emmanuel for the return of the conquered territory to Mantua.[6]

At the first meeting of the Council of State after Charles Emmanuel's attack on Mantua, with Philip III presiding, Lerma expressed his pessimism regarding Spain's ability to force Savoy to return the territories it had conquered and his belief that Savoy was ready to collaborate with all the crown's enemies to keep its conquests and to destabilize Italy. He also seemed convinced that the Spanish crown was utterly isolated and that no one would come to its aid in defense of Mantua. In these circumstances, he proposed to the king to order Hinojosa to begin immediate negotiations to end the war; otherwise, he warned, hostilities would carry on for some time, forcing the king to spend an enormous amount of money without obtaining "any fruit or reputation," perhaps provoking a total war in Italy, and maybe even in Europe.[7]

In subsequent meetings Lerma cited the perennial lack of funds to explain his reluctance to advocate a more aggressive policy, but by September 1613 he acknowledged that the Italian conflict involved considerations of broader concern to the Spanish monarchy. Even then, he continued to maintain that the only answer to the conflict was peace as soon as possible. In the meeting of September 1613, Lerma made a long speech in which he summarized his views on Spain's role in "foreign" conflicts. Before considering a more activist position in the conflict between Savoy and Mantua, Lerma noted, the monarch had to remember that the Spanish monarchy was like a sick person in a period of painful convalescence, and the king's obligation was to care for the recovery of the monarchy. At a time when the monarch had ordered a radical reform of all expenses, he further noted, and had achieved peace with England, Holland, and other powers, it would be unfortunate to become involved in a new conflict.[8]

Lerma began to change his position only when it became clear that Spain's inability to end Savoy's attempts to control northern Italy was a weapon that other European powers could use against the Spanish monarchy and equally clear that his internal opponents had begun to cite his and Hinojosa's attitudes as proof that the *valido* had persuaded the king to abandon all the monarchy's duties and responsibilities. In the meeting of the Council of State held on 28 December 1614 Lerma finally began to criticize Hinojosa, whose handling of the conflict had resulted in a serious weakening of Philip's international and internal reputation.[9] In a radical change of his views on the conflict, he asked the king to take personal control of the situation by traveling to Italy and leading the Span-

---

[6] On this conflict, see Bombín Pérez, *La cuestión de Monferrato* and Fernández Albaladejo, *Fragmentos*, pp. 225–8; David Parrott, "The Mantuan Succession, 1627–31: A Sovereignty Dispute in Early Modern Europe," *English Historical Review*, 112 (1997), pp. 33–7.
[7] Lerma's vote in the meeting of the Council of State held on 22 June 1613 in BNM, Mss 5570, "Copia de los pareceres que el Sr. Duque de Lerma ha dado en las consultas que se han hecho a Su Majd. desde el 22 de junio," fols. 19–21v.
[8] *Ibid.*, meeting of the Council of State, 8 Sept. 1613, fols. 36v–37.
[9] *Ibid.*, meeting of the Council of State, 28 Dec. 1614, fols. 47–52v.

ish army against Savoy. "A great king," he stated, "has to follow [such a course], not only to conserve his kingdoms but to avoid losing his reputation."[10]

Immediately after reversing his position, Lerma attacked Hinojosa directly, accusing him of being pusillanimous in the resolution of the conflict. This attack took place in the meeting of the Council of State held on 28 February 1615,[11] when Lerma claimed that the war against Savoy could not be solved the way the crown would have liked because it lacked funds, but that a prompt solution was now necessary, either through negotiation or through increased military effort against Savoy. If the king were to adopt the latter course of action, then Hinojosa must be told to act more forcefully, and if he failed to comply, he would be accused of treason and forced to resign. Rodrigo Calderón and others joined Lerma in criticism of Hinojosa, and, more importantly, public opinion had become increasingly radicalized because of the conflict with Savoy. In a letter to Hinojosa on 16 January 1615, Calderón noted the escalating accusations against Hinojosa for his alleged military incompetence and referred to the detention of Hinojosa's agent at court, Juan de Urbina. He also deplored the changing mood at court, especially the growing criticism of all royal officials linked to the government: "by God I have to tell you that I am on the verge of losing my mind because no one has seen, not in a thousand years, a situation in which everyone, including the greengrocers (*las verduleras*), is talking about [affairs of state]."[12] The Marquis of Piovera expressed similar sentiments in a letter to Juan de Vivas, ambassador to Genoa, sent just five days after Calderón's letter to Hinojosa: "Never before," he wrote, "have we seen royal ministers attempting to do all they can" to solve the problems of the kingdom being pressed by the people's new-found aversion to political inertia. The renewed activism of the royal officials was matched by the king who "is also giving signs that he is a real king; it seems that the blood in his veins is running again and that he is no longer going to endure all the ignominies" that he has suffered until now.[13] Piovera's statement appears to be an announcement that Lerma was losing his ability to control Philip III, who was liberating himself from the "magic spell" of his favorite. During the summer of the same year the usually well-informed Pedro García do Valle, Gondomar's agent in Madrid, informed Gondomar that an unknown individual had given the king a memorandum denouncing Calderón and Lerma and that, on hearing of it, Lerma had become extremely depressed.[14]

The "ignominies" the Spanish monarch had to suffer reached their height in June 1615 when Hinojosa signed a treaty with the Duke of Savoy. The Peace of Asti restored to Savoy all of the territories it had lost to Spain and left the future of

[10] *Ibid.*, fol. 50. No one else at the Council of State supported Lerma's proposal.
[11] *Ibid.*, fols. 52v–57.
[12] Calderón to Hinojosa, Madrid 16 Jan. 1615, in BNM, Mss 1174, "Cosas curiosas sucedidas en el tiempo y vida del rey Phelipo Tercero, así de su gobierno como de su vida," fols. 37r–v.
[13] Piovera to Vivas, 21 Jan. 1615, in *ibid.*, fols. 39r–v.
[14] Pedro do Valle to Gondomar, 12 Aug. 1615; in BNM, Mss 18149, "Correspondencia de Pedro García do Valle con el Conde de Gondomar," fol. 132.

Mantua undecided, thus an opportunity for further conflicts. After two years of fighting, the Spanish monarch obtained only a loss of political reputation, and the treaty convinced other European powers that Spain's control of Italy was weakening.[15]

When news of the agreement between Charles Emmanuel and Hinojosa reached Spain, Lerma tried to distance himself further from the Governor of Milan as the only way to save his policies, if not his *privanza*, now under general attack. He was one of the most critical members of the Council of State against Hinojosa and the Peace of Asti and asked that Hinojosa be detained and judged for high treason, that the agreement be repudiated, and that "we prepare ourselves for a major conflict."[16] His was the advice Philip III followed, ordering Hinojosa to stand trial and officially repudiating the agreement of Asti. To complement these measures, Philip III appointed, as Hinojosa's replacement, Pedro Alvarez de Toledo and Ossorio, Marquis of Villafranca, who supported a more aggressive stance for the Spanish monarchy in Europe,[17] initiating a new round of conflicts that lasted two years and were, from a political and military point of view, as David Parrott has asserted, "futile and inconclusive."[18]

Lerma, however, lost the most as a result of the Peace of Asti, which led many to question the validity of his European policies, his criteria for selecting those who helped him rule, and his tendency to decide by himself the policies intended for the king's consideration. Asti, indeed, convinced his opponents that the ultimate consequence of the pacifist policies promoted during Lerma's *privanza* meant a complete "discrediting and loss of reputation" of the Spanish monarchy.[19] Although Lerma did not lose total control of international affairs in 1615, the Peace of Asti constituted the first important crisis that allowed other royal ministers, including the Dukes of Osuna, Alba, and Infantado, and Baltasar de Zúñiga, to call for a radical change in the monarchy's policies and to champion a more active role for Spain in European politics following the model set by Philip II.

Before the conflict with Savoy became again central to the political struggle at court, 1615 was an important year in the history of Lerma's *privanza* for other reasons. This was the year when, as mentioned in Chapter 10, Aliaga and Uceda broadened their influence in political affairs, and Fray Juan de Santa María presented the most radical critique of the theories and images of royal favorites that had been created to legitimize and institutionalize the power of the Duke of Lerma.

---

[15] On the Peace of Asti and its consequences see Bombín Pérez, *La cuestión del Monferrato*, pp. 154–63; Fernández Albaladejo, *Fragmentos*, p. 226; and Parrott, "The Mantuan Succession, 1627–31," p. 36. For satirical comments on the Peace of Asti both in Spain and Italy see the Duke of Alcalá to a friend, Aug. (?) 1615; in BNM, Mss 1174, "Cosas curiosas sucedidas en el tiempo y vida del rey Phelipo Tercero," fols. 64–67v.

[16] Lerma at the meeting of the Council of State, 11 July 1615, in BNM, Mss 5570, "Copia de los pareceres que el Sr. duque de Lerma," fols. 73v–77v.

[17] Bombín Pérez, *La cuestión del Monferrato*, pp. 162–5, 186ff; and Fernández Albaladejo, *Fragmentos*, pp. 226–8.   [18] Parrott, "The Mantuan Succession," p. 36.

[19] Fernández Albaladejo, *Fragmentos*, p. 226.

That Uceda and Aliaga had succeeded in dividing the court into two camps and that Philip III no longer relied solely on Lerma's advice is epitomized by appointments to Prince Philip's household in October 1615. From his own experience Lerma knew that he needed to dominate the entourage of the heir to the crown to maintain his position as Philip III's sole favorite, and in January 1611 he succeeded in persuading Philip III to appoint him as Prince Philip's governor and *mayordomo mayor*.[20] From 1611 to 1615, Lerma was the only major servant attending to the prince's needs, but the planned wedding of the prince to Isabelle of Bourbon, Louis XIII's sister, compelled Philip III to establish his heir's household. The king retained Lerma as the prince's chief servant, but he also appointed Uceda as *sumiller de corps* and the Count of Saldaña, Lerma's youngest son and a supporter of his father, as *caballerizo mayor*. As *gentileshombres de la cámara*, Philip III named two of Uceda's allies, the Count of Olivares and the Count of Lumiares,[21] and two of Lerma's relatives and supporters, the Count of Santisteban and Fernando de Borja.[22] Although direct testimony from the king is lacking, it seems clear that he was aware of the intra-factional conflict and probably thought it beneficial for himself to allow the development of the Uceda–Aliaga faction while allowing his old favorite to retain a part of his previous influence.

These were some of the men who accompanied the king and his heir on their journey to the Franco-Spanish border to seal the matrimonial alliance between the two monarchies through the celebration of the weddings of Louis XIII and Anne of Austria, Philip III's daughter, and Prince Philip and Isabelle of Bourbon. The king designated Lerma as his representative in the negotiations between the monarchies regarding etiquette, ceremonial, and the future of their alliance, as stipulated in a decree signed by the king on 30 July 1615.[23] Lerma, as was his custom, used his role to promote himself, and between Madrid and Burgos he staged ceremonies, banquets, and festivities celebrating his accomplishments as the king's *valido*.[24] On 25 October 1615, however, when the royal retinue left Burgos to continue its journey toward the Franco-Spanish border, Lerma declared that he was feeling ill and chose to remain behind. His son, the Duke of Uceda, replaced him as Philip III's representative, and he, together with Aliaga, took charge of the royal progress to Hendaye, taking full advantage of the opportunity to be close to the king in Lerma's absence.[25] Strangely, perhaps, Lerma was not really ill: in a letter to Calderón he reveals that he had decided to "fake his ailment" and remain behind

[20] Lerma was appointed on 21 Jan. 1611; see AGPR Ex. Per., 50/24, 548/4.
[21] See Juan Antonio de Vera y Figueroa, "Fragmentos históricos de la vida de don Gaspar de Guzmán," *Seminario Erudito de Valladares*, 2 (1787), pp. 153–4, 157; and Escagedo y Salmón, "Los Acebedos," 8, pp. 243, 338.
[22] All of these appointments were made in October 1615; see AGPR Sec. His., caja 113: "Casa que tuvo don Felipe IV siendo Príncipe."
[23] Royal order, 30 July 1615. For a copy see Pedro de Mantuano, *Casamientos de España y Francia* (Madrid, 1618), pp. 21–2.
[24] For all the ceremonies and festivities organized by Lerma during the journey from Madrid to Burgos see *ibid.*, pp. 124–39.   [25] *Ibid.*, pp. 88–9.

because he could not stand the French, whom he viewed as the principal cause of the anti-Spanish movements in Italy.[26]

Lerma's unwillingness to remain close to Philip at all times paralleled his and his followers' inability to control public discourse. This failure became manifest with the publication of Fray Juan de Santa María's *República y policía christiana* in 1615, the finest and most influential attempt by Lerma's opponents to challenge the political discourse he had promoted. Other authors who had published their works before 1615 had expressed similar views, but Santa María's astounding ability to dismantle the arguments in support of the *valido* as the king's friend, together with the fact that Lerma's power was now questioned at court, gave his book a relevance others lacked.[27]

Santa María began his book with the assertion that the ideal government was a mixed government, a combination of monarchical and aristocratic elements. As seen before, these views translated into a defense of the king's duty to rule with his councils, whose obligation in turn was to "temper (*templar*) the king's power to prevent the monarch from becoming a tyrant" (p. 18). The king could ask for advice from whomever he wished, but in the ruling of the monarchy and in the implementation of royal policies he was obliged to rely on the councils, and not, for example, on *juntas* which, according to Santa María, were created to promote and defend the specific interests of their members and of the king's favorite (pp. 47, 55, and 100–3).

If the presence of the *juntas* seriously threatened the well-being of the community, the extraordinary spread of corruption among the king's closest advisers signaled a profound deterioration in the ethos of public service among the king's servants. Santa María viewed corruption as a cancer slowly damaging every component of the body politic, demoralizing the entire republic, and driving it to decline. To emphasize his views, he noted that bribery of royal ministers had become "natural and more used today than in any other period in the history of Spain," and to stop this situation he proposed (following Mariana's advice) that the king's ministers must present inventories of their wealth before they accepted an office and after they resigned.

But perhaps most damaging were his attacks against the arguments Lerma and some of his allies commonly employed to justify their enrichment. Although many recognized that the favorite and his allies had received "gifts," they also claimed that these gifts were exchanges of "love and friendship" between the givers and the

---

[26] AGS CC DC, *leg.* 35/1, *exp.* 7, 28 July 1619 n.p.: report of the judges in charge of investigating Calderón.

[27] Fray Juan de Santa María was confessor of the Infanta Margarita, Philip III's daughter, and active in the opposition to Lerma before and after 1618. Although the original edition of his *República y policía christiana* was published in Madrid in 1615, I use the edition published in Naples in 1624; further references in the text. On Santa María's book as an attempt to revise "the concept of the royal favorite imposed during Lerma's *privanza*" see Jean Vilar, "Conciencia nacional y conciencia económica," in Sancho de Moncada, *Restauración política de España* [1618], ed. Jean Vilar (Madrid, 1974), p. 18.

receivers without any intent to use public offices and jurisdictions for private interests. To Santa María such arguments were an *ex post facto* justification of behavior that was purely and simply illegal. No less corrupt, and perhaps even more dangerous, was the behavior of those in the king's intimate circle who (like Lerma on many occasions) defended their acceptance of gifts from courtiers, royal ministers, and foreign ambassadors by asserting that they had "the king's permission," which to Santa María was impossible and devilish because "there could not be a Christian king who would willingly permit such acts against the common good" (pp. 74–7).[28]

Santa María also analyzed the character of a good monarch and explained how he should rule. Kingship was an office, a duty, the most difficult of all, and to be a king implied great responsibilities and required a genuine royal character (p. 29). The ideal ruler "guides his kingdom to perfection" and "manages on his own the affairs of state, has courage and fortitude during moments of danger, is wise and prudent in his deeds and, above all, has a free will and is determined to carry out his own decisions" (p. 43). Charles V and Philip II were monarchs whose conduct always showed them to be "free and real kings, not only in their external appearance but also internally, because the proper state of monarchs is to rule and not to be ruled, to administer their kingdoms by their own will and not by the will of others" (p. 318). The antithesis of this ideal king – and here many of Santa María's readers could see a direct criticism of Philip III – was one who retired from public view and delegated his power to others (pp. 127–9), as did the ancient French kings who were dominated by "their *mayordomos* or favorites." In their time, the "royal majesty had only the name of a king because the real rulers were their *privados* who dominated and oppressed the king and his subjects" (p. 29).

Any doubt that Santa María was criticizing the state of affairs during Philip III's reign was dispelled when he turned to the direct dismantling of the claim that the favorite was the king's friend, the theoretical foundation that permitted the consolidation and legitimation of Lerma's role as Philip III's chief minister.[29] Given that *privados* were products of the king's grace, Santa María noted, "the favorite naturally becomes a friend of the king. But friendship can only exist between two equals and for this reason it seems to me impossible that one of the king's subjects could be his friend" (pp. 281–2). If a king has a friend–favorite, the king and the kingdom face two dangers, both with deadly consequences for the entire body politic. In having a friend, the king "lowers himself to the level of his subject, making him his equal. But the king is and should be the head of the body politic, and he cannot diminish the sovereignty God has given him by becoming equal to anyone else" (p. 282). Alternatively, if the king has a friend–favorite, he might "aggrandize his friend" and, thus, create a monster, a body politic with two kings,

---

[28] Lerma himself and some of his supporters had used precisely this argument – that they had the king's permission to receive "gifts" – to justify what others viewed as corrupt practice; see above, chap. 8.

[29] On the theories of the favorite as the king's friend see above, chap. 6.

which would threaten the foundations of the monarchy in which power could only be in the hands of one (p. 281). To avoid this horrifying fate Santa María, making a point repeated by many writers who published their works in the last years of Philip III's reign and during the reign of Philip IV, advised the king to have many favorites, selected, following biblical examples, not because they were seeking the king's pleasure but because they were willing to serve the interests of the community. These favorites could help the monarch, but he should never let them have any say in matters of justice and government. A Christian king had always to remember that the advice of royal favorites was much less important than that of "your wise counselors and councils" (p. 295). In a clear reference to Lerma's behavior, Santa María went on to argue that all favorites tended to promote – both to the government and the royal household – their relatives and creatures, a clear indication of the need to eliminate the favorites' control over royal patronage. Otherwise they would isolate the king from his vassals and subject him to "their tyranny in which only the favorites' interests would be defended and implemented" (pp. 314–15). Favorites, Santa María claimed, needed only one goal: to serve the king and the community; otherwise, their presence would motivate the decline, even the destruction of the kingdom (pp. 288–9).

It should not surprise anyone that Lerma tried to impede the distribution of Santa María's book. In the end, however, his actions turned out to be counterproductive. As Juan de Vitrián pointed out, Lerma's attempts to silence both Mariana and Santa María merely "increased the fame of these authors" and transformed their writings into theoretical and practical inspiration for many others.[30] Mariana acquired the image of a political martyr, whereas Santa María was asked to become a member of the various factions that, before and after 1618, criticized Lerma and his clients, while his book, a bestseller of the period, was published in Madrid (1615), Barcelona (1617, 1618, 1619), Valencia (1619), Lisbon (1621), and Naples (1624), and was translated into English in 1632, during Charles I's personal rule, under the title *Christian Policie*.

But even if Lerma had been successful in silencing Santa María, other books and pamphlets soon followed, in which other authors claimed that the presence of a single favorite challenged the very existence of the monarchical regime. Mateo López Bravo in his *Del rey y de la razón de gobernar*, published in 1616, also advised the king to be careful with "your favorite, who will seduce you and convince you to abandon your duties as a monarch." To comprehend the devastating consequences of an inaccessible king and an all-powerful favorite, the king should bear in mind the example of the tyrant Tiberius, who favored the villain Sejanus and brought despair and tragedy to the entire commonwealth.[31] In 1616 Francisco de Quevedo also completed parts of one of his most forceful works, *Política de Dios y gobierno de*

[30] Vitrián, *Las memorias de Felipe de Comines*, vol. II, p. 414.
[31] Mateo López Bravo, *Del rey y de la razón de gobernar* [1616], ed. Henry Mechoulan (Madrid, 1977), pp. 226–8.

Cristo, in which he explicitly attacked weak monarchs and "evil favorites."[32] All monarchs, claimed Quevedo, and especially weak ones, should remember that Christ did not let "one of his followers be superior to the rest." Christ had not "favorites, but disciples," and accordingly a king should have not favorites, but simply subjects (pp. 50, 81). Quevedo also reminded would-be favorites "that a servant who imitates the greatness of his master not only tries to become the king's equal but his superior, and in doing so he is no longer a servant, a minister of the king, but a tyrant who aspires to possess the king's crown and power" (p. 102).

The struggle to dominate public discourse and, ultimately, the king's favor was not over, however. During 1616 and the first half of 1617, there was a sort of stalemate in which neither faction was able to eliminate the other. Aliaga and Uceda continued to place their men in important offices, within and without the peninsula, but so did Lerma. In 1616, for example, the Count of Lemos returned to Madrid from his office at Naples and was appointed president of the Council of Italy. Uceda and Aliaga were, however, able to persuade the king to appoint the Duke of Osuna, Pedro Téllez Girón, to replace Lemos as the Viceroy of Naples.[33] One year later, on 27 August 1617, Uceda obtained a royal decree appointing him official in charge of communicating directly with Spanish institutions and officials in Naples, an obvious attempt by Uceda, Aliaga, and Osuna to circumvent Lemos's jurisdiction.[34] Given these events, it is not surprising that in February 1616 Francisco de Quevedo wrote to his patron, the Duke of Osuna, that "the Duke of Uceda is giving public audiences ... and it seems that the Duke of Lerma has retired from public affairs."[35] Fray Martín de la Mariana y Vergara made a similar observation in reference to Aliaga in a letter to his patron, the Count of Gondomar, dated November of the same year: "Fray Luis de Aliaga is moving ahead in his *privanza* with the king," and everything seemed set for the fall of the old favorite.[36] But Lerma's dismissal was more desired than attained, and he continued to handle state affairs with the king.[37]

The continuing importance of Lerma's public role was demonstrated in October

[32] Francisco de Quevedo y Villegas, *Política de Dios y gobierno de Cristo*, ed. James O. Crosby (Madrid, 1966), pp. 27–131; the first part of this work was written according to Quevedo himself in 1616 although it was not published until 1626 when it was dedicated to Philip IV and the Count-Duke of Olivares. Further references in the text.

[33] The dukes of Osuna and Uceda had signed in 1608 a matrimonial agreement according to which Osuna's heir, the Marquis of Peñafiel, would marry Uceda's daughter. The wedding was celebrated in 1617. From 1608 to 1617 Peñafiel lived in the house of Uceda. On the relationships between Osuna and Uceda, including Uceda's and Aliaga's maneuvers to make Osuna Viceroy of Naples, see BNM, Mss 11569, "Memorial del pleito contra el duque de Uceda," fols. 214ff.

[34] A copy of this royal decree in *ibid.*, fol. 215.   [35] Quevedo, *Epistolario*, p. 36.

[36] Fray Martín de la Mariana y Vergara to the Count of Gondomar, 30 Nov. 1616, in Diego Sarmiento de Acuña, "Cartas escogidas de las escritas a don Diego Sarmiento de Acuña, conde de Gondomar, o reunidas por éste," *RABM*, 5–6 (1901–2), 5, p. 495.

[37] BNM, Mss 18419, Pedro García do Valle to Diego Sarmiento de Acuña, Count of Gondomar, 23 Feb. 1616, fol. 190v, saying that Uceda was giving public audiences, while Lerma was still in charge of handling public affairs.

1617 on the occasion of several festivities he organized in the town of Lerma, where, assisted by some of his allies, he continued to promote himself as the king's *alter ego* and the co-architect of Philip III's policies. These festivities commenced on 6 October with fireworks that announced the entry of a triumphal chariot adorned with Lerma's coat of arms and carrying four statues representing Mars, Neptune, Jupiter, and Fortune. These statues supported a throne where a statue of "Love" was placed to symbolize that "the love that the Duke of Lerma has for His Majesty is more powerful than anything else in this world."[38] During the following three weeks Lerma's guests attended numerous events, bullfights, dances, and plays, many of them commissioned by the Count of Saldaña, Lerma's youngest son, and the Count of Lemos, Lerma's nephew and son-in-law. Perhaps the most significant event took place on 17 October just before the performance of one of Mira de Amescua's plays commissioned by Lemos. In a theater built specifically for these festivities the guests sat on two sides while opposite the stage on an elevated platform "sat Philip III, Prince Philip, heir to the crown, and the Duke of Lerma" (fol. 47r). Before the play, the actors performed a series of intermezzos introduced by a character named "Fame," who at the end addressed the king and declared before the entire court: "It must be a great happiness for Your Majesty to have at your side so great a man as the Duke of Lerma, who helps you to support the weight of this monarchy. In this, no doubt, Your Majesty is imitating Alexander the Great who justly favored Hephaestion" (fol. 6or). The characters introduced by Fame all claimed that the duke had inspired the king to choose some of the policies that were recognized as the regime's greatest accomplishments: peace with England and the Dutch Republic, the matrimonial matches with the French, the expulsion of the Moriscos, the maintenance of peace and tranquility in the kingdoms, and the conservation of the territorial power of the Spanish monarchy. Many of those present could well have believed that Lerma alone, and not Philip, ruled the monarchy because he received greater compliments than those bestowed on the king.

It is difficult to determine whether this campaign for Lerma's public glorification in the presence of the king and most of the courtiers and royal servants was part of a deliberate effort to contain the attacks against Lerma, to present a united front by Lerma's faction, and to claim that he remained in control of both the government and the king's favor. But these ceremonies were not the product of Lerma's strength so much as an attempt to reverse, or at least decelerate, his loss of power at court.[39] Philip III himself seemed content with the festivities in the city of Lerma

[38] Pedro de Herrera, *Traslación del Santísimo Sacramento a la iglesia colegial de San Pedro de la villa de Lerma* (Madrid, 1618), fols. 15r–v; further references in the text. For a summary of these festivities, see Shergold, *A History of the Spanish Stage*, pp. 255–8.

[39] By the summer of 1617 Uceda started to sign an increasing number of *billetes*, following the model of those sent by Lerma, ordering various councils to execute the king's orders; see, for example, AGS Est., *leg.* 263: Uceda's *billetes* to Juan de Ciriza and Aroztegui, secretaries of the Council of State, ordering, for example, the Council of State to hold special meetings to speed up the resolution of

and believed that it was he and not his favorite who was being honored.[40] It is, therefore, difficult to discern whether by 1617 the king had already lost confidence in Lerma and was simply waiting for the right moment to dismiss him without causing a political upheaval. In any case, between August 1617 and August 1618 the political situation and Lerma's personal standing changed radically, ultimately creating the conditions for his fall. The debate concerning the conflicts in Italy continued, new conflicts were emerging in Bohemia, and the factional struggle continued to intensify, leading to the dismissal of some of Lerma's allies, among them Lemos, events that permitted Aliaga and Uceda to consolidate their power and take control of the king's inner circle. Lerma's personal circumstances also changed.

At least since 1612, Lerma had expressed his desire to become a cardinal of the Roman Church, a dignity he received on 26 March 1618 when Pope Paul V appointed him Cardinal of San Sisto.[41] News of his appointment reached Lerma on 10 April, and from then on his influence at the court waned rapidly.[42] As Lerma himself wrote, "given my new condition (*respecto de la mudanza de hábito en que me hallo*)" he could no longer attend to his duties as a palace servant. Forced to resign his offices of *sumiller de corps* and *caballerizo mayor* to the king and *mayordomo mayor* to the prince, Lerma transferred them to Uceda, who became, at least in theory, the most influential person in the kingdom,[43] and who appeared in public determined "to divest his father of all power (*despojar a su padre de raíz*)."[44]

Lerma's renunciation of the palace offices that once had given him control over access to the king was accompanied by his loss of control over the decision-making process regarding Spain's role and policies in Europe. After Philip III made his decision to continue the conflict with Savoy and to reject the Peace of Asti, a limited "but futile conflict" between Spain and Savoy for the control of northern Italy took place between 1615 and 1618.[45] Although Lerma made occasional, rather radical, statements in support of extreme military efforts to crush Savoy, he clearly leaned toward measures similar to those he had advocated with regard to England and Holland; he continued to believe firmly that the Spanish monarchy did not have the military or financial capacity to maintain any major conflict.

various affairs (17 July 1617) and ordering the same council to study various *consultas* from the Council of Castile (17 Aug. 1617).

[40] Felipe III, *Cartas de Felipe III a su hija Ana, Reina de Francia (1616–1618)*, ed. Ricardo Martorell Téllez-Girón (Madrid, 1920), p. 30.

[41] On Lerma's intentions and his insistence and pressure to obtain the cardinalate, see González Dávila, *Historia de la vida*, p. 203, and Pérez Bustamante, "Los cardenalatos del duque de Lerma," pp. 150–5.

[42] In a letter to his daughter Queen Anne of France, Philip III informed her that "your godfather Lerma looks quite good in his new robes; I am sure you would not recognize him if you saw him now. He wanted this dignity, and I believe God will help him," 6 June 1618, in Felipe III, *Cartas*, p. 47.

[43] AGPR Ex. Per., 450/24, 1048/26.

[44] BNM, Mss 18430/1: "Apuntaciones de varios libros de correspondencia del conde de Gondomar, embajador de Felipe III en Inglaterra," fol. 2v, news dated 12 May 1618.

[45] Parrott, "The Mantuan Succession," p. 36.

12   Anonymous seventeenth-century Valladolid artist, *The Cardinal-Duke of Lerma*. The appointment of Lerma as Cardinal of San Sisto by Pope Paul V in 1617 presaged Lerma's fall from power in October 1618. This portrait was completed when Lerma was living in Valladolid, exiled from the court.

Defending these views, Lerma was again victorious in convincing the king and his ministers that the only alternative to "losing everything"[46] was to reach a peace agreement with the Duke of Savoy, and on 9 October 1617 representatives of Spain, Savoy, and Venice signed the Peace of Pavia, the terms of which were not radically different from those contained in the Peace of Asti.[47] For a while this agreement appeared to have reduced tensions and demonstrated that Lerma was still a political force to be taken seriously. Even Philip III seemed to agree that the best solution to the conflict had been reached, as he himself wrote in a letter to his daughter the Queen of France one year later on 18 August 1618. But in the same letter he also expressed a clear sense of pessimism, declaring that "what worries us now are the events in Germany; let us hope God will help us handle them well."[48]

Philip III was referring to the conflict provoked by the rebellion in Bohemia on 23 May 1618, the event that initiated the Thirty Years War.[49] News of the Bohemian rebellion reached the court in the first week of June and reopened the debate on "the nature and best means of defense of the Spanish monarchy."[50] In the context of the political feuds at court, the debate on Bohemia showed that Lerma and his policies were questioned not so much by the Aliaga–Uceda alliance as by another faction headed by Baltasar de Zúñiga, which had increased its influence, at least on international issues. As Brightwell has noted, two meetings of the Council of State held on 6 June and 14 July 1618 were crucial in persuading Philip III to intervene in support of Emperor Matthias against the Bohemian rebels.[51] Members of the council were divided in support of two positions. Lerma's arguments were supported, at least partially, by a group composed of Lerma himself, Fray Luis de Aliaga, the Duke of Infantado, and Agustín de Messía. The other position was supported by Zúñiga, who at the start of the debate appeared to be alone. In the first of the two crucial meetings, that of 6 June 1618, which Lerma did not attend, the entire Council of State agreed on the urgency and gravity of the events in Bohemia. The rebellion, they advised the king, brought into question the survival of the Catholic faith in the German empire and of Habsburg influence over it. Even more importantly, if the Protestant rebels were to gain control of the empire it would become impossible for the Spanish monarchy to conserve its Italian territories. This serious matter deserved the full attention of the king and his ministers. Zúñiga and the other counselors also realized that Spain's intervention could provoke an extension of the conflict, and for that reason the Council of State recommended

---

[46] BNM, Mss 5570, "Copia de los pareceres que el Sr. Duque de Lerma ha dado en las consultas que se han hecho a Su Majd. desde el 22 de junio de 1613," fol. 143.
[47] Bombín Pérez, *La cuestión de Monferrato*, pp. 250–1.   [48] Felipe III, *Cartas*, p. 51.
[49] On the Thirty Years War see Parker, *The Thirty Years' War*; and Ronald G. Asch, *The Thirty Years War. The Holy Roman Empire and Europe, 1618–48* (New York, 1997). To appreciate how the conflict was understood during its first months at the Spanish court and the debates on what to do regarding the rebellion of Bohemia see Peter Brightwell, "The Spanish Origins of the Thirty Years' War," *European Studies Review*, 9 (1979). The discussion here closely follows Brightwell's arguments and analyses.   [50] *Ibid.*, p. 414.   [51] *Ibid.*, p. 422.

that the king send adequate funds to the Count of Oñate, the Spanish ambassador to the emperor, to help him contain the rebellion. The counselors voted, however, against the dispatch of Spanish troops because "if the king's troops intervene directly in Germany we are sure that the Dutch and all the Protestant princes will oppose such action with all their forces, and even France, and the actual conflict would be transformed into a religious war within Germany, something that we have always viewed as very pernicious." In accord with this evaluation, the counselors also recommended that the king order Oñate to make every attempt to resolve the conflict "through diplomatic means" to avoid further complications and to localize it.[52]

In the meeting held by the council one month later on 14 July the debate initially proceeded along the same lines as the earlier meeting.[53] Fray Luis de Aliaga, Bernardo de Sandoval, Agustín de Messía, Baltasar de Zúñiga, and the Duke of Infantado were especially concerned about the need to gain allies – particularly the Pope – and to make the French king understand that the rebellion in Bohemia must not be transformed into an opportunity to weaken Habsburg influence in the empire. The tone of the debates, however, changed radically after Lerma joined the meeting. He agreed with the other counselors about the potential consequences of the Bohemian rebellion, that it could seriously damage Spanish power and the Catholic faith. The rebels, Lerma claimed, could not have taken this initiative without explicit or tacit support from other German "Protestant princes," who had designs to take the empire from the Habsburgs. At the same time, Lerma believed, the king had to help the emperor, otherwise Germany and Italy would be lost and the Protestants in the Low Countries would use this opportunity to break the truce. Lerma was not making a case for direct intervention but rather for a quick end to the crisis. Spain, he thought, should persuade the emperor to negotiate with the rebels and their supporters. According to Lerma, the Spanish king also had to consider important internal affairs. He reminded the council of the ruinous state of the royal treasury and asked them to recall how the crown's finances had "forced us to sign the truce with the Dutch and the peace with Savoy in Italy although everything could have been different under other circumstances." Lerma went on to emphasize that before intervening in "alien causes," the king should invest money and effort to secure the defense of his own kingdoms, for example, from the north African pirates who were attacking the peninsular coasts. After this introduction Lerma vehemently argued against intervention in the Bohemian conflict and maintained that an allocation of 100,000 ducats to Oñate, as other counselors had proposed,

will convince the emperor and his men that Spain is ready and willing to send further help. This belief in turn will move them to promote war in order to retake control of Bohemia, but

---

[52] AGS Est., *leg.* 711/fols. 201–2.
[53] *Ibid.*, fols. 204–9; see also Brightwell, "Spanish Origins," p. 422.

then we will not have additional financial resources to help them: this will soon all be true. By then, however, the emperor will have become involved in a war impossible to stop, as now at the start of the conflict it is not.

Lerma's intervention provoked an immediate response from the other counselors. A majority, including Infantado, Aliaga, and Messía, agreed with most of the important elements in Lerma's plan: that the royal treasury was completely empty and that it was important to attend to other strategic needs. They thought it important to order Oñate to convince the emperor to reach an agreement with the rebels, even if, in the words of Messía, "that agreement is not as good as we all would like. The important thing is to stop this conflict, because the emperor and the king of Bohemia do not have many resources to continue it, and Your Majesty has little more with which to support them." But they disagreed with Lerma about sending money to Oñate. They believed that 100,000 ducats should be sent to Oñate to pay the Spanish troops, which should be ready for any possible turn of events.

The counselor who disagreed the most with Lerma was Baltasar de Zúñiga. Although he also recognized the desperate state of royal finances and the difficulties the monarchy would face with involvement in a new conflict, he insisted that Philip III could not ignore the Bohemian rebellion because of its strategic importance for the Spanish monarchy and the critical need to maintain Habsburg control over Germany. Zúñiga also agreed that the emperor and his allies should look for a diplomatic resolution of this conflict, but should they fail, it would then be the king's duty to assist the emperor. Regaining control of Bohemia, he concluded, should be a priority for the Spanish monarch.

By the next meeting of the Council of State it was clear that Zúñiga's argument had prevailed, and on 18 July the council advised the king to make the rebellion in Bohemia "the most important matter this crown has to confront at this time." The *consulta* the council sent to the king on 21 August 1618, which was a copy of a report written by Zúñiga a few days earlier, made it clear that the decision to intervene was now supported by the majority of the counselors and officially approved by the king.[54]

The factional conflicts at court were also affected by the outcome of the Bohemian debate and the king's decision to support Zúñiga's proposals. Overruled in the debate, Lerma had become more vulnerable in the struggle between his faction and that of Aliaga and Uceda. Hurt by his loss of influence over Philip III, Lerma had tried to win the favor of the prince by "wooing him with constant attention and gifts" as he had wooed Philip III during the reign of Philip II.[55]

[54] AGS Est, *leg.* 711/fols. 210, 214–15, 217; see also Brightwell, "Spanish Origins," p. 425. The total triumph of Zúñiga's position came in 1619 after Lerma's fall; see Peter Brightwell, "Spain and Bohemia: The Decision to Intervene, 1619," *European Studies Review*, 12 (1982).

[55] BNM, Mss 2349: "Resolución que tomó su Majd. acerca de algunas cosas que importan a su monarchía por septiembre de 1618," fol. 192r.

Helping Lerma was his son-in-law Lemos and Lemos's cousin Fernando de Borja, who together "tried to foster Lerma's influence by talking privately with the prince and accentuating (*catequizándole*) the good qualities and wisdom of the Cardinal-Duke of Lerma and the shortcomings of Uceda and even the king himself."[56] The Duke of Uceda, aware of these activities, reported Lerma's machinations to Philip III, who immediately ordered Fernando de Borja to return his key to the prince's privy chamber and to leave the court to serve as Viceroy of Aragon. To complicate matters further, the Count of Lemos resisted the king's order to expel Borja from court and threatened to resign his office as President of the Council of Italy if Philip III did not rescind his mandate. Unable to persuade Philip, Lemos resigned on 7 September 1618 and departed immediately for his estates in Galicia.[57]

Within a matter of weeks following these events, known as the "Revolution of the Keys," Lerma's *privanza* came to an end. Between Lemos's resignation and his own fall from power, Lerma tried vainly to postpone what seemed inevitable.[58] He even stooped to asking Fray Gerónimo de Florencia, a well-known opponent, to intercede with the king on his behalf. The answer Philip III gave to Florencia showed the king's increasing impatience with his favorite. "Did not you," Philip III allegedly asked Florencia, "preach to me that it was good that not only the lion and the bull, but even the lamb should sometimes roar? Is it not true that you told me that it was sometimes necessary for a king to show his wrath and punish evil deeds and those who committed them?" (fol. 191r). He had given Lerma one week to leave the palace and the court, and if the former favorite did not comply with his order, "I will be obliged to use violence against him" (fol. 191v). The week expired on 2 October, when Lerma had his last meeting with the king, a meeting that left the cardinal-duke "in tears (*lloroso*)" (189r). Lerma spent the next two days giving audiences to all who wanted to see him, and in the afternoon of 4 October 1618, after bidding goodbye to his sister, the Countess of Lemos, to the prince, and to several of his former clients, he took the road to exile without being able to say goodbye to the king, who remained invisible and inaccessible to his former favorite (fol. 189v).

---

[56] *Ibid.*; the Count of Lemos referred to these events in a letter to his cousin Francisco de Borja, Prince of Esquilache, 15 Mar. 1619, in Antonio Paz y Meliá, ed., "Correspondencia del conde de Lemos con don Francisco de Castro, su hermano, y con el príncipe de Esquilache (1613–1620)," *Bulletin Hispanique*, 5 (1903), pp. 355–6.

[57] The Count of Lemos's resignation and the Council of Italy's attempts to convince Philip III not to accept Lemos's decision in AGS SP, *leg.* 13/n.p., *consulta* of the Council of Italy, 7 Sept. 1618. The Count of Lemos defended his behavior in a letter to his cousin the Prince of Esquilache, asserting that once Fernando de Borja was dismissed, "I did everything I possibly could to reverse the king's decision, but when I realized I could not change anything, I decided to support [Fernando de Borja] and fall with him (*perderme con él*)." See Paz y Meliá, "Correspondencia del conde de Lemos," pp. 355–6. For a summary of the "Revolution of the Keys" see Elliott, *The Count-Duke*, pp. 35–6.

[58] The following summary is based on a document that narrates what happened in the last days of Lerma's *privanza*; BNM, Mss 2349, "Resolución que tomó su Majd. acerca de algunas cosas que importan a su monarchía." Further references in the text.

12

In search of culprits

Although it took twenty years, Lerma's banishment seemed to many a confirmation that those who sought to rise were destined to fall, that *privados* could maintain their power and influence only until the king opened his eyes and saw the evils brought about by those who wanted to promote their own interests over those of the king and the kingdom.[1] Regardless of the moral reflections provoked by Lerma's fall, his dismissal from power certainly inaugurated a period of political instability. Those who had fostered his expulsion began to fight among themselves and transformed the court into a place of constant conflict and political uncertainty; all sought the favor of Philip III and/or Prince Philip, rivalry which greatly complicated Uceda's and Aliaga's quest to become the king's undisputed favorites. On 30 October 1618, for example, an observer reported that "in matters of *privanza* I cannot tell you anything because nothing is certain."[2] A few days later the same observer wrote: "No one knows what is happening; we do not know if we are following the general [the king], a lieutenant [one of the candidates to become a favorite], or merely a shadow."[3]

One reason for political uncertainty was the new attitude of Philip III, who, after Lerma's downfall, devoted most of his time to state affairs.[4] The king "works courageously," a contemporary witness observed, "and controls all affairs; when Lerma was in power, those who attended the public audiences of the king were just a dozen, now there are so many that there is no empty space in the hall where the king receives."[5] Aware that criticism of Lerma had affected his own image, the king made every attempt to demonstrate that Lerma's downfall signaled a change in the way he ruled.[6] Although he publicly recognized Uceda as his favorite, Uceda's role in the government was to be radically different from his father's. In an order Philip III sent to all councils on 15 November 1618 he stated that even though the Duke of

---

[1] BNM, Mss 4072, "Memorial de cosas sucedidas en España y a sus gentes," fol. 160r.
[2] BNM, Mss 1858, "Relaciones de 1618 a 1621," fol. 14v. This manuscript, with dozens of reports in the form of letters (author and addressee(s) are unknown), is one of the best sources of information about the Spanish court from October 1618 through to August 1621.
[3] *Ibid.*, 27 Nov. 1618, fol. 20v.   [4] *Ibid.*, 24 Oct. 1618, fol. 13r.   [5] *Ibid.*, 20 Nov. 1618, fol. 25r.
[6] When reminding Philip III of how badly Lerma's active role in the government of the monarchy had affected his image Juan de Santa María told him "it is a pity that Your Majesty could go to hell for not having been a king (*Vuestra majestad considere que es grande lástima que como otros por reinar se han ido al infierno, vuesa Majestad se vaya por no reinar*)," in *ibid.*, 27 Nov. 1618, fol. 28v.

Uceda had signed some of the royal orders after the Cardinal-Duke left court, he wanted to make it clear that

I, and not any other person, will sign everything concerning universal orders, *mercedes*, and other important matters, the resolution of which belong to me. With this I end the former way of conducting state affairs through orders that [Lerma] signed in my name. All decrees I sent declaring your duty to obey Lerma and to answer all his queries should be collected and sent to me immediately.[7]

Philip III's definition of Uceda's role in government was viewed at court as a "disfavor to Uceda,"[8] who soon realized that he "has not as much power as he thought he would have" after his father's exile from the court.[9] Fray Luis de Aliaga was having his own difficulties. More interested in his duties as a counselor of state and Inquisitor-General, he neglected his obligations as royal confessor, giving others, especially Fray Juan de Santa María and Fray Gerónimo de Florencia, an opportunity to become close to the king and to conspire to oust both Aliaga and Uceda.[10] As one contemporary described the situation, "Here are the preachers [Santa María and Florencia] conspiring against the son [Uceda] . . . I think they are going to be powerful enough to separate him (*descomponerlo*) from the king. . . . Perhaps [Uceda] deserves this punishment."[11] Moreover, both Aliaga and Uceda were criticized for the way in which they handled public affairs, and many even began to miss Lerma's government. "The populace," wrote an agent of the Count of Gondomar, "are starting to say that the government was good under Lerma's *privanza* and criticize the new favorites."[12] That the Count of Gondomar was among these critics is clear from a letter in which Gondomar complained to Uceda about the way he had been treated and warned Uceda that if he treated others as badly, he "should not be surprised at having so few followers."[13]

---

[7] There are dozens of copies of this order; see, for example, *ibid.*, fols. 24v–25r; Gerónimo Gascón de Torquemada, *Gaceta y nuevas de la corte de España desde el año 1600 en adelante*, ed. Alfonso de Ceballos-Escalera y Gila (Madrid, 1991), p. 57, and Tomás y Valiente, *Los validos*, p. 158. That Philip III was more active in handling state affairs after Lerma's downfall is demonstrated by the increasing number of *billetes* sent to the councils signed by the king; for a few examples, see AGS Est., *leg.* 437/fols. 54, 55 (1618); fols. 30, 35, 37, 50 (1619), and fols. 6, 13, 19, 21, 23 (1620).

[8] BNM, Mss 17858, "Relaciones de 1618 a 1621," 20 Nov. 1619, fol. 25r; and González Dávila, *Historia de la vida*, p. 204.

[9] The Count of Lemos to his cousin the Prince of Esquilache, 14 Mar. 1619, in Paz y Meliá, "Correspondencia del conde de Lemos," p. 353.

[10] On the increasing influence of Florencia and Santa María see BNM, Mss 17858, "Relaciones de 1618 a 1621," fols. 27v–29v, 103v, 105v; see also Escagedo Salmón, "Los Acebedos," 8, pp. 22, 23, 26, 28–9, 159. On Santa María's active role during these years, see Vilar's introduction in Moncada, *Restauración política de España*, pp. 17–18.

[11] BNM, Mss 17858, "Relaciones de 1618 a 1621," fol. 53v.

[12] BNM, Mss 18430/1, "Apuntaciones de varios libros de correspondencia del conde de Gondomar, embajador de Felipe III en Inglaterra," 12 Oct. 1620, fol. 6r–v. See also the report of the Genoese ambassador Giovanni Battista Saluzzo, 25 Oct. 1622, in Raffaelle Ciasca, ed., *Istruzioni e relazioni degli ambasciatori genovesi*, vol. I: *Spagna, 1494–1617*; vol. II: *Spagna, 1619–1635* (Rome, 1955), vol. I, pp. 161–2; Saluzzo began his term of office in 1617.

[13] The Count of Gondomar to Uceda, 8 Jan. 1620, in Diego Sarmiento de Acuña, *Correspondencia oficial*

The inability of Uceda and Aliaga to consolidate their influence increased the number of candidates seeking the king's favor, including, paradoxically, Prince Philibert of Savoy (the son of the Duke of Savoy who had been educated at the Spanish court and who was supported by Juan de Santa María) and the Duke of Infantado, the king's *mayordomo mayor*. Olivares and his uncle Baltasar de Zúñiga, on the other hand, concentrated their efforts on Prince Philip.[14] The political situation had become so unpredictable that even individuals with only the slightest chance of becoming the king's favorites decided to prepare themselves in the event of an opportunity to advance themselves. The Duke of Sessa, for example, requested the advice of none other than Juan de Mariana, whom he asked to write two "papers, one on how to rule my own vassals and the other on how a man of my position should behave if I should become the king's favorite."[15] With so many courting the king's favor, this was a period of total conflict, a sort of courtly guerilla war, "a very turbulent time, when past royal favorites [Uceda and Aliaga] resisted as best they could and future favorites [all the rest] did not yet possess what they desired."[16] It is no wonder that satires attacking former, new, and would-be favorites flourished as never before. "Every day there are more satires," wrote one of Olivares's supporters; "many of them are so filthy that I do not dare reproduce them. The last one, the worst, attacks our Count of Olivares, something that has made me very unhappy."[17]

But the political debate in 1618–21 was not only about the individual aspirations of favorites and would-be favorites. This was also a period of "spiritual and intellectual upheaval"[18] when Spaniards viewed the past as a time when public virtue flourished, and sought ways to recreate that past. Many of them found the mythical golden age not in the remote past but in the reigns of the Catholic

de don Diego Sarmiento de Acuña, conde de Gondomar, ed. Antonio Ballesteros y Beretta (*Documentos inéditos para la historia de España*, vols. I–IV (Madrid, 1936–45), vol. II, pp. 236–8). Gondomar also sent a letter to Lerma complaining of Uceda's behavior and expressing his loyalty to his former patron, see *ibid*.

[14] On Philibert of Savoy see BNM, Mss 17858, "Relaciones de 1618 a 1621," fols. 139v–146r and 155–7, and Escagedo y Salmón, "Los Acebedos," 8, pp. 23–4; on the conflicts of Uceda and Aliaga with the Duke of Infantado see *ibid.*, 8, pp. 16–17; on the increasing influence of Zúñiga and Olivares see Elliott, *The Count-Duke*, pp. 38–42.

[15] The Duke of Sessa to Juan de Mariana, Feb. 1619?, in Vega Carpio, *Epistolario*, vol. II, p. 280. To overcome Mariana's scruples against writing something favorable about royal favorites, Sessa insisted that he was asking Mariana's advice as "a courtier who lives outside the court," and who "wants to recover the ancient faith, now lost," a faith necessary to solve the demanding problems of the times. Mariana, despite Sessa's insistence, never responded.

[16] Escagedo y Salmón, "Los Acebedos," 8, p. 254.

[17] BNM, Mss 17858, "Relaciones de 1618 a 1621," 5 Dec. 1618, fol. 31v, and 3 Dec. 1619, fol. 108r; on the increasing number of satires and pamphlets against former and new favorites see Teófanes Egido, *Sátiras políticas de la España moderna* (Madrid, 1973), pp. 22–7, 81–104; see also Jean-Marc Pelorson, "La Politisation de la satire sous Philippe III et Philippe IV," in *La Contestation de la société dans la littérature espagnole du siècle d'or* (Toulouse, 1981), pp. 95–107.

[18] Ruth Lee Kennedy, "The Madrid of 1617–25. Certain Aspects of Social, Moral, and Educational Reform," in *Estudios Hispánicos en Homenaje a Archer M. Huntington* (Wellesley, Mass., 1952), p. 276.

Monarchs and Philip II. Under these rulers, they believed, Spain had reached the apex of its power because of the virtue of its rulers and the good conduct of its citizens.[19] In contrast, the 1610s were viewed as a time of general decline as witnessed by a court that had become a theater of corruption and sins, "the New Babylon of confusion."[20] The general decline and the corrupt moral standards of those who served the king were forcefully evoked by the Count of Gondomar in a letter sent to Philip III on 28 March 1619.[21] He began his letter by pointing to some indicators of decline: further decline in the population of Castile, the economic crisis, and the lack of confidence among the king's subjects regarding the ability of royal officials to offer stability, tranquility, and prosperity. Everyone was indebted, and no one, Gondomar noted, thought about the future or cared about the public good. Royal officials were utterly irresponsible in the implementation of royal orders because relatives and clients of those who controlled royal patronage had taken over the administration of the monarchy (pp. 137–8). Here Gondomar was pointing to an insoluble dilemma created by a system that promoted patron–client networks to assist the monarch and his most intimate counselors, a system that was, at the same time, a source of corruption because it permitted the encroachment of private interests upon the public good.[22] According to Gondomar, negotiation – his word for the practice of accepting bribes – had become so prevalent among royal officials that it would in time lead irremediably to the decline and death of the republic (p. 140).

In the search for lost public virtue and the means of restoring Spanish power, many directed their attention to the relationship between the king and the kingdom and, more specifically, to the way in which the king should be counseled. It was commonly believed that the restoration of the glory of the Spanish monarchy depended on the renewal of harmony between the various members of the *corpus misticum*, a goal that could be achieved only by the revival of the role played by the royal councils. Soon after Lerma's downfall, this position was stated in the *consulta* sent by the Council of Castile to Philip III on 1 February 1619, a report that represented the culmination of a debate begun in 1615 when the Council of State advised the king to order the Council of Castile to recommend remedies for the decrease in population and the lack of fiscal resources. Following this recommendation, Philip ordered the Council of Castile to address these issues, but nothing was done. In a *consulta* dated 28 February 1618, the Council of State returned to these matters and asked the king to order the President of the Council of Castile to appoint a few counselors to prepare a report on the ills of the realm.[23] In response,

[19] On this topic see *ibid.*, *passim*; Elliott, "Self-perception and Decline," in his *Spain and its World, passim*; and Pedro Sainz Rodríguez, *Evolución de las ideas sobre la decadencia española* (Madrid, 1962), chap. 3.   [20] Liñán y Verdugo, *Guía y avisos de forasteros*, pp. 49, 97.
[21] Sarmiento de Acuña, *Correspondencia oficial*, vol. II, pp. 131–45. Further references in the text.
[22] On this topic see J. G. A. Pocock, "Machiavelli and the Rethinking of History," in *Rivista di Storia delle Idee Politiche e Sociali*, 27 (1994), pp. 229–30.
[23] AGS Est., *leg.* 264/fol. 154, *consulta* of the Council of State, 28 Feb. 1618.

Philip III instructed the President of Castile, through a *billete* signed by Lerma on 6 June 1618, to find solutions for the "conservation of Spain" and to offer specific recommendations for halting the "increase in existing ills."[24]

The council responded on 1 February 1619 after it discussed and approved a report prepared by one of its members, Diego Corral y Arellano. This report addressed the ills of the kingdom: the further decline in the population of Castile (attributed to excessive taxation, large numbers of individuals living at court, and the creation of too many religious foundations and communities); the crisis in agriculture (from the depopulation of the countryside); the fiscal crisis (provoked by, among other factors, the excessive number of financial *mercedes* awarded by the king); and the destruction of justice and increasing corruption in the administration of the kingdom (represented by the sale of large numbers of local and territorial offices). The Council of Castile considered the current crisis to be without precedent, one which only radical measures could solve:

> The sickness [of the monarchy] is grave indeed ... [so grave that] it cannot be cured by ordinary means. Bitter remedies are usually the healthiest for those who are ill, and in order to save the body sometimes it is necessary to cut off the arm, and cancer can only be cured with fire (pp. 29–30).

This *consulta* opened an important debate on the monarchy's ills and between 1619 and 1625 many other memoranda, books, and royal decrees appeared, all addressing the monarchy's problems and offering numerous solutions.[25] The *consulta* of the Council of Castile was also influential in its suggestion that the origins of the monarchy's difficulties were mainly political. The counselors of Castile knew that "cities, kingdoms, and monarchies perish as do men and other beings," but the decline of the monarchy could be avoided if it returned to "the same path taken when it was founded, which was very different from that which rulers are following today" (p. 30). The correct course to restore past glory, the counselors believed, was intimately connected with the way the king received counsel. Certainly, the counselors of Castile accepted that the king was "the heart of the commonwealth because the king as the heart can only be one, and, as the heart, the king communicates strength and life to all members of the body" (p. 15). But if the king was the heart, the counselor was "a patrician, the father of the king ... and, thus,

---

[24] Lerma's *billete* is summarized in the beginning of the *consulta* of the Council of Castile 1 February 1619; this *consulta* has been edited many times and has been the subject of many commentaries by contemporaries and modern historians. I use the copy of the *consulta* published by González Palencia, *La Junta de Reformación*, pp. 12–30; further references in the text. For another copy see Fernández Navarrete, *Conservación de monarquías*, pp. 9–30. For an analysis of this *consulta* see Gordon, "Moralidad y política en la España del siglo XVII. El pensamiento de Pedro Fernández Navarrete," in *ibid.*, pp. ix–xxvii. For concise summaries in English of this *consulta* see Kennedy, "The Madrid of 1617–25," p. 277 n. 5, and Elliott, *The Count-Duke*, pp. 98–100.

[25] On the literature on the ills of the Spanish monarchy in this period see Kennedy, "The Madrid of 1617–25"; Elliott, "Self- perception and Decline," in his *Spain and its World*; and Vilar, "Conciencia nacional," in Moncada, *Restauración política*.

Your Majesty has to listen to and follow the advice of your counselors . . . because a monarch has to remember that the office of the king was created to serve the kingdom and that the kingdom was not created to serve the king" (pp. 18–19). The views of the Council of Castile appeared at a moment when contemporary political discourse again favored the traditional paradigm of the monarchy as a mixed government. In *Del senado y de su príncipe* (1617),[26] for example, Madariaga described the monarchy as a *corpus mysticum* composed of king and counselors who shared royal power (*potestad suprema*). Like the counselors of Castile, Madariaga recognized the preeminence of the king in the body politic, but he also indicated that the head was "the more restless part of the body," whereas the senate (the union of all councils) was "the better balanced member of the body, the heart of this immense *corpus mysticum* of the Spanish monarchy, the one in charge of communicating life to the head [the king] and to the rest of its members [the king's subjects]." Juan de Salazar's influential book, published in 1619, emphatically maintained that the Spanish monarchy could be conserved only if rulers reestablished a mixed government (*gobierno mixto*),[27] an opinion shared by the President of the Council of Castile, Fernando de Acevedo, who believed that Lerma's downfall had ended "government by decree that had already begun during the reign of Philip II" and had led to the fortunate restoration of good government in which the councils had regained their lost power that "never before has been so absolute."[28]

The political system which gave the king, his favorite, and the favorite's clients control of the decision-making process was not the only aspect of Lerma's *privanza* under examination during these years of transition. Lerma's pacifist policies towards Europe were also contested. Zúñiga and his allies from the Council of State and also men like Gondomar claimed that the peace with England and Holland had not helped Spain but had benefited Spain's enemies, including France. The conflict with Savoy, in turn, had exposed Spain's weaknesses without resolving the disagreements that had provoked the conflict in the first place. These ministers agreed that in the coming years the Spanish monarchy would have to confront important conflicts, as already suggested by the rebellion of Bohemia; therefore, Spain should get ready as soon as possible. Gondomar further believed that Lerma's policies had caused the loss of Spanish military advantage; other European powers, especially England and Holland, were now in "control of the sea." Spain's enemies had been working during all these years of peace, he wrote, while "we just slept."[29]

According to those who participated in the political debates of the time, Spain

---

[26] Juan de Madariaga, *Del senado y de su príncipe* (Valencia, 1617); all references from the dedication, n.p.
[27] Salazar, *Política española*, pp. 125–6.
[28] Escagedo y Salmón, "Los Acebedos," 7, p. 185, and 8, p. 156. This was in effect one of Uceda's arguments in his own defense after he was detained in 1621; see BNM, Mss 11569, "Memorial del pleito contra el duque de Uceda," fols. 231–232v.
[29] Sarmiento de Acuña, Count of Gondomar, to Juan de Ciriza, secretary of state, 21 Nov. 1619, in Sarmiento de Acuña, *Correspondencia oficial*, vol. II, p. 228. See also Gondomar to the king, in *ibid.*, vol. II, p. 145.

had to recover the ideological principles promoted by Philip II: the defense of a "real reason of state" identified with the preservation of the Catholic religion over all other interests. The book that forcefully argued for the centrality of this principle over all other tactical considerations was Juan de Salazar's *Política española*, published in the last months of 1619.[30] Salazar, in the tradition of other late sixteenth- and early seventeenth-century writers, claimed that Spain was destined to become a universal monarchy given its religious and historical credentials and the extension of its territorial power. In this context, the history of the Spanish Catholics was seen as an exact replica of the history of the Israelites, God's chosen people (pp. 23–37, 74–89), with various Spanish monarchs reproducing the behavior of David, Solomon, and others. Salazar indeed tells a story of a polity populated by *conquistadores* and generals, none of them from the reign of Philip III; he tells instead of rulers such as the Catholic Monarchs, Charles V, and Philip II (with Philip III mentioned only for his decision to expel the Moriscos), who were victorious precisely because they defended the Catholic faith and spread it to new territories (pp. 44ff). The main goal of a Christian monarch, he insists throughout the entire book, is not to conserve his power, as claimed by the defenders of reason of state, but to uphold Catholicism everywhere (pp. 59–70), an ideal embraced by the "new powerful men," particularly Zúñiga, who successfully persuaded the king to take a more active role in European conflicts such as the rebellion in Bohemia.[31]

In many ways the political debate taking place in the last years of Philip III's reign resembles the one that occurred at the end of his father's reign. In 1598, two groups had competed for power at court, one led by the favorite of the prince (Lerma) and the other by the favorites of the old king (Moura and others). Once again, in 1621, two factions were vying for power and influence, one led by Zúñiga and his nephew Olivares (favorites of the prince) and the other by Aliaga and Uceda (favorites of Philip III). The popular views in 1598 and in 1621 were also rather similar. At both times, many claimed that the ills of the monarchy were not fiscal but political and that royal favorites had monopolized and corrupted the counsel of the king, making it necessary to restore traditional forms of government. Those supported by the prince (Lerma in 1598 and Zúñiga and Olivares in 1621), in turn, believed that the monarchy could be saved only by strengthening the power of the king. The two periods are distinguished by contrasting views on how to resolve the problems afflicting the Spanish monarchy. In 1598 many thought that the only way to strengthen the crown was by a policy of retrenchment to avoid the many conflicts that were weakening its economic strength. In 1621, however, everyone seemed to agree that the Spanish monarchy and its influence could be restored only if the king were to take an active role in European politics in defense of Catholicism and of Spanish preeminence.

---

[30] Salazar, *Política española*; further references in the text. Salazar finished his book in the fall of 1617, and it was officially approved in December 1618, but its printing was not completed until at least mid-September 1619 (pp. 3–14).   [31] See Brightwell, "Spain and Bohemia," pp. 135–7.

These debates gained momentum in March 1621 when Philip III fell ill. During his illness his contemporaries believed that the ailments of their king were not physical but spiritual, as revealed by his melancholy and regret for having failed as a good king. "If Heaven gives me life," he allegedly said, "I will rule in a completely different manner." His words echoed those of his father, who on his deathbed told one of his favorites that Prince Philip "will be not the ruler, but the ruled."[32] A few days later, on 31 March 1621, King Philip III died, leaving behind what many contemporaries viewed as a very poor legacy: a monarchy controlled by corrupt ministers, with royal prestige diminished by the delegation of too much power to his favorites, Spain's international reputation damaged by agreements reached with rebels and heretics, and worst of all, a general feeling that the Spanish monarchy was no longer invincible.

The death of Philip also brought a reorganization of court factions, the establishment of a new political scene, and the rise of new favorites. Commenting on the increased influence of the Duke of Buckingham, the favorite of James I of England, after he had eliminated other competitors for the king's grace, James Howell noted that "there is rising and falling at Court; and as in our natural pace one foot cannot be up till the other be down, so it is in the affairs of the World commonly, one Man riseth at the fall of another."[33] The same could be said about Spain after March 1621. Those at the pinnacle of power and influence as a result of the old king's favor saw their fortunes fall immediately after their master's death, while those who had placed their hopes in the new king rose to power, influence, and riches. And no one was in a better position to take advantage of the changing circumstances than the Count of Olivares, who – confident of his power as the favorite of the new king – immediately after Philip III's death declared, "Now everything is mine."[34] Nevertheless, there were ways in which the transition from one reign to another was characterized by continuity rather than change. Despite the new favorites and new faces in the corridors of power, it all seemed rather familiar to those who had witnessed the start of Philip III's reign. After the death of Philip II, the Sandovals, headed by Lerma, rose to prominence and wealth, whereas now the faction led by Olivares and his uncle Baltasar de Zúñiga monopolized benefits, offices, and rents just as the "Sandovals had done in old times (*a los Guzmanes comenzó a lucirles como a los Sandovales en la ley vieja*)."[35]

Life at court no doubt demanded familiar behavior from all who tried to conquer and dominate power, even to the advice the new favorites received from their allies regarding what to do with the fallen favorites. "The first law of the favorite (custom and necessity of all those who are newly in power)," wrote the Count of La Roca,

---

[32] On Philip II's words see above, chap. 1; on Philip III's last moments see a summary in Elliott, *The Count-Duke*, pp. 3–6, 40–2. Philip III died on 31 March 1621 at the age of forty-two.

[33] James Howell to his father, 22 Mar. 1622, in James Howell, *Epistolae Ho-Elianae. The Familiar Letters of James Howell*, ed. Joseph Jacobs, 2 vols. (London, 1892), vol. I, p. 145.

[34] Cf. Elliott, *The Count-Duke*, p. 42.   [35] BNM, Mss 17858, "Relaciones de 1618 a 1621," fol. 326v.

Olivares's biographer and close ally, "is to banish from the palace and the court all those who could thwart the new disposition of matters." The new favorite should advance his own relatives, allies, friends, and supporters because "one of the laws of the *privanza* and the favorite's reason of state (*la razón de estado del favorito*) is to determine who will be close to the king." Preservation was the key. Olivares's career demonstrated the danger of promoting persons of dubious loyalty to high places. The Duke of Uceda, in his attempt to create his own factional opposition to his father, had placed Olivares in the household of Prince Philip, a position that Olivares used to win Philip's favor and displace Uceda. "Past events teach us how to cope with future menaces," noted the Count of La Roca, and Olivares, as Lerma had done before him, acquired for himself some of the most important palace offices and promoted his relatives, allies, and creatures to many others.[36]

But Philip IV's reign began in a political environment distinctly different from his father's. In 1598 the repression of former favorites was viewed not only as a necessary step Lerma had to take to consolidate his influence but also as a vendetta by Lerma and Philip III for the way Philip II's ministers had treated them during the last years of the reign.[37] In contrast, Olivares and his supporters were committed to a program of radical political and administrative reform, which they believed should start with punishment of former favorites in symbolic demonstration of the new king's courage and political will and proof of his commitment to restore the greatness of the Spanish monarchy.[38]

The need to take prompt measures against former favorites was clearly articulated by Fray Juan de Santa María in a memorandum sent to the new king only six days after Philip III's death.[39] The monarchy and the kingdom were on the verge of complete destruction because of the "wickedness and inadequacy of those who have governed it," he wrote. The malevolence of Philip III's favorites was so extreme that "the late king in his last moments confessed that he had lived in a state of deception during many years and that the realization of this truth and the difficulty in reversing the situation had killed him." Unlike his father, Philip IV should show himself to be a real king, and he must not shrink from the Herculean task of restoring his monarchy. To have any success in this task, he must discharge as

[36] Vera y Figueroa, "Fragmentos históricos," pp. 164, 167; the Count of La Roca finished this work in 1628. Olivares, following Lerma's example, became *sumiller de corps* and *caballerizo mayor* to Philip IV and counselor of state; on the offices accumulated by Olivares and his strategy to promote his relatives and allies see Elliott, *The Count-Duke*, *passim*, and Antonio Feros, "Lerma y Olivares: la práctica del valimiento en la primera mitad del seiscientos," in John H. Elliott and Angel García Sanz, eds., *La España del Conde-Duque de Olivares* (Valladolid, 1990), pp. 205–9, 221–2.

[37] See above, chap. 3.

[38] See BNM, Mss 4072, Gabriel de Peralta: "Memorial de cosas sucedidas en España y a sus gentes," fol. 163r; on the political environment during the first months of Philip IV's reign, see Elliott, *The Count-Duke*, pp. 101–15, and I. A. A. Thompson, "The Government of Spain in the Reign of Philip IV," in his *Crown and Cortes*, chap. 4, pp. 1–13.

[39] AHN Est., bk. 832, fols. 323–8, "Lo que su Majd. debe executar con toda brevedad, y las causas principales de la destrucción de la Monarchía. Diole a su Majd. el padre fray Juan de Santa María, en 6 de abril de 1621." For a summary of this document, see Elliott, *The Count-Duke*, p. 102.

many officials appointed by Philip III as possible, and at the very least he must "purge the heads of the tumors" that have corrupted the realm. To be effective, the new king has to act quickly when everyone was expectant and hesitant, because it was in these first moments of the reign that the new king could apply remedies to extirpate the cancerous influence of those who previously held power. But there was also a more practical reason for the swift punishment of former favorites: "each of them has palace offices and so many creatures and confidants that the king and his good servants (*los buenos*) could easily become isolated," making it possible for the former favorites to return to power.

With Lerma still exiled in Valladolid those whom Fray Santa María designated as prime candidates for distinctive punishment included Fray Luis de Aliaga; Diego de Guzmán, Patriarch of the Indies; Fernando de Acevedo, President of the Council of Castile; Juan de Ciriza, Secretary of the Council of State; and the Duke of Uceda. All of them, Santa María wrote, "in order to fulfil their insatiable greediness, oppressed and deceived the late king, thus preventing him from recovering his power after he had thrown out the Duke of Lerma." Following Fray Santa María's recommendations, Philip IV and Olivares moved quickly. They stripped Aliaga of all his offices and exiled him to a little town in Aragon where he remained until his death in December 1626.[40] The new rulers also removed Acevedo from the presidency of the Council of Castile and sent him to Burgos to serve as archbishop. Juan de Ciriza got off more lightly. Although he lost his political influence, he managed to hold on to his office in the Council of State. The Duke of Uceda presented a more delicate case. Fray Juan de Santa María feared that any punishment of Uceda might spark some opposition among his extended kin network (*parentela*), but his relatives remained quiet after he was judged and found guilty of corruption. He was subsequently banished from court and died in the town of Alcalá de Henares in May 1624.[41] Others who had gained power under Philip III experienced a similar fate. "Every day," a courtier wrote, "there are royal orders dismissing all those who were nurtured by Lerma and Uceda (*no dexan en peu a ningú que si a estat criat de Lerma ni de Uzeda*)."[42] The accuracy of this information is confirmed by the dismissal of many of Lerma's creatures and relatives from their offices in the royal palace and in the councils.[43]

[40] On the measures taken against Fray Luis de Aliaga see AGS GJ, *leg.* 621; and Navarro Latorre, *Aproximación a Fray Luis de Aliaga*, pp. 65–71.

[41] Diego de Guzmán did not receive any kind of punishment; on the fate of these members of Philip III's regime see Pérez de Bustamante, *La España de Felipe III*, pp. 176–9, and Elliott, *The Count-Duke*, pp. 102–4.

[42] Alonso de Aguado in a letter to Jeroni Pujades at the end of May 1621, in Jeroni Pujades, *Dietari de Jeroni Pujades*, ed. Josep Maria Casas Homs, 4 vols. (Barcelona, 1975–6), vol. III, p. 302. See also BNM, Mss 17858, "Relaciones de 1618 a 1621," fols. 267r, 269v, 295r–v, 306r–v.

[43] Those who lost their offices because of their connections to Lerma included Tomás de Angulo, royal secretary; Antonio Bonal and Pedro de Tapia, counselors of Castile; the Count of Saldaña, Lerma's youngest son and Philip IV's *caballerizo mayor*; the Count of Altamira, Lerma's brother-in-law and Queen Isabella's *caballerizo mayor*; and the Countess of Lemos, Lerma's sister and Queen Isabella's *camarera mayor*.

None, however, suffered a fate as dramatic as that endured by Rodrigo Calderón, Lerma's most famous favorite. On 20 February 1619, Calderón, who had already been detained a few months after Lerma's fall from power, was made into a vivid example of the immorality and corruption associated with Lerma's *privanza*. A civil lawsuit accused him of accumulating dozens of offices, titles, pensions, and possessions, all of which were considered proof that, while acting as one of the king's servants, Calderón had let arrogance and greed guide his behavior.[44] Other charges included Calderón's unwarranted intervention in state affairs, the perversion of justice, and the receipt of numerous bribes.[45] But the worst allegations brought against him were those included in his criminal trial. He was indicted for arranging and causing the death of Queen Margaret and for using exorcism and magic potions to bewitch Fray Luis de Aliaga, the Duke of Uceda, and Prince Philip. Finally, he was accused of having arranged the murder of five individuals who had dared to criticize both him and Lerma.[46]

Calderón's connections to Lerma had left his fate uncertain until Philip III's death in March 1621. But when Calderón heard the bells announcing the death, he knew that his own time had come: "The king is dead, and I am dead," he allegedly said.[47] For the new rulers Calderón was a gift from heaven, one who symbolized the moral degradation permitted, if not promoted, by Lerma. Calderón's close association with Lerma and, indeed, his real crimes transformed him into the propitiatory example of the new king's commitment to justice and the restoration of the monarchy's former glory. Consequently, Philip IV ordered Calderón's judges to end the trial as quickly as possible. In their sentence, announced on 9 July 1621 less than three months after Philip III's death, Calderón's judges dismissed many of the charges presented against him, including those accusing him of killing the queen and bewitching Aliaga and Uceda. The court, however, found him guilty of all civil charges and of the murder of Francisco Juara, killed on Calderón's orders because he possessed information about Calderón's misdeeds. The judges condemned Calderón to death and gave explicit instructions as to how his punishment was to be

---

[44] The civil charges against Calderón in BNM, Mss 6713: "Cargos y sentencia de Don Rodrigo Calderón," fols. 28–185; the criminal charges in José Martí y Monsó, "Los Calderones y el monasterio de Nuestra Señora de Portaceli," *Boletín de la Sociedad Castellana de Excursiones*, 83–5 (1908–10), 85, p. 555, doc. 67. On Calderón's trial see Angel Ossorio y Gallardo, *Los hombres de toga en el proceso de Don Rodrigo Calderón* (Madrid, 1918), *passim*.

[45] Among those who bribed Calderón were the Grand Duke of Tuscany, but also Philip IV's favorites, the Count of Olivares and his uncle Baltasar de Zúñiga, and aristocrats such as the Dukes of Osuna and Infantado and many others. As in the cases of Franqueza and Prado, the official sentence against Calderón does not reveal the names of those who bribed him; their names are included in an internal document prepared by Calderón's judges and preserved in AGS CC DC, *leg.* 35/1: "Visita."

[46] *Ibid.*, fols. 1–10: "Resumen de las manifestaciones de los testigos sobre los diversos cargos que se imputan a Rodrigo Calderón"; and *leg.* 35/2, *exp.* 7: "Consultas hechas por los jueces del marqués de Siete Iglesias." Experts on witchcraft testified that Calderón possessed "artifacts used by sorcerers and witches to attack their enemies, acquire friends, and win the will of others." They even suggested that these artifacts proved that he had "a pact with the Devil."

[47] Cf. Elliott, *The Count-Duke*, p. 6.

carried out: he was to be led from his cell to the Plaza Mayor, Madrid's ceremonial center, where the executioner was to cut his throat and leave him on the scaffold "until he dies naturally."[48] After an unsuccessful appeal, Calderón was executed on 21 October 1621. Calderón's death did not, however, have the effect that Philip IV and Olivares had intended because the new rulers failed to follow seventeenth-century writers' advice that a new monarch should begin his reign with an emphasis on his magnanimity and mercy rather than his power to punish. John H. Elliott has well described the reaction of Olivares's contemporaries' to Calderón's death. "Instead of the approval it had so confidently expected," he writes, "the ritual murder planned by the new regime to serve as a symbol of cleansing and regeneration brought only a massive condemnation. The Duke of Alba wrote to Olivares that he had watched the death not simply of a Roman, but a Roman and an apostle."[49] Despite the unanticipated consequences of Calderón's execution, the accusation and trial of some of Philip III's most prominent ministers served to portray the former reign as a dark age and to advance the notion that restoration of the monarchy to its previous glory required the eradication of Philip III's legacy, if not the memory, of a period depicted by the new rulers as a time of lost opportunities, decline, and utter political corruption.

But what to do with the Duke of Lerma? Despite his banishment from court and his loss of power three years earlier, Lerma remained a cause of pressing concern to the new regime. Undoubtedly the ultimate symbol of the former regime, he was in the eyes of the new rulers the person responsible for the ills of the monarchy. If they let him go unpunished, it would appear that the new regime was unable to conduct a thorough cleansing of the realm. The new rulers' principal dilemma was to decide what measures to take against a fallen favorite who was also a cardinal and, thus, endowed with immunity from royal jurisdiction. To demonstrate that his ecclesiastical status would serve as his protective shield, Lerma could always refer to a letter from Pope Paul V in August 1621: "From your letter I became aware of the dangers that threaten you.... I have assigned your cause and protection to the Catholic king, and I have asked him to seek and protect the truth [about you and your affairs], which is being hounded by the envy of the envious (*acosada por las envidias de los envidiosos*)."[50]

Consequently, Philip IV and Olivares adopted a strategy previously proposed by Fray Juan de Santa María: to sequestrate Lerma's estate, but otherwise treat the Cardinal-Duke leniently, owing to the support he still enjoyed at the court and his papal protection. The opportunity to adopt stronger measures against Lerma

---

[48] Martí y Monsó, "Los Calderones," 85, pp. 554–5. For a summary of the judges' debate about Calderón's sentence see Elliott, *The Count-Duke*, p. 107.

[49] *Ibid.*, p. 108. Diego de Saavedra y Fajardo, one of the most influential seventeenth-century Spanish writers and, ironically, a supporter of Olivares, viewed Calderón's death as an example of the redemptive force of repentance. See Diego de Diego de Saavedra y Fajardo, *Idea de un príncipe político-cristiano representada en cien empresas* [1642], facsimile edn. (Murcia, 1985), *empresa* 33.

[50] Pope Paul V to Lerma, 22 Aug. 1621, in BNM, Mss 2352, "Sucesos del año 1621," fols. 509r–v.

would soon come, Santa María wrote; the king should let time go by until Lerma's supporters were divided and began to fight among themselves.[51] Following Santa María's recommendation, Philip IV placed a sequestration order on Lerma's estate[52] and initiated an exhaustive investigation of the distribution of *mercedes* during Philip III's reign. This inquiry started with the premise that every *merced* awarded both to Lerma and his allies was unlawful to the extent that it had been granted not on the basis of the merit of the recipient but as a result of Lerma's unrestricted, unlawful, and corrupt control over the distribution of royal patronage.[53]

This course of action was also necessary because Lerma's public image was still viewed favorably by some Spaniards and foreigners alike. Writing in 1622, for example, the Genoese ambassador, Giovanni Battista Saluzzo, depicted Lerma's government as one of "great sophistication" owing to Lerma's exquisite "courtesy" in dealing with affairs and persons.[54] Lerma was also depicted as a proud man who coped with the attacks of the new rulers with disdain and irony. Howell, for example, reported that "The Duke of Uceda, his son, finding himself out of favor at the court, had retired to the Country, and dying soon after of discontentment: during his sickness the Cardinal wrote this short weighty letter unto him: *Dizenme que moreys de necio; por mi, mas temo mis años que mis Enemigos* (They tell me that you are dying as a result of your foolishness; I myself fear more my age than my enemies)."[55] Lerma himself, in a memorandum he sent to Philip IV in response to the king's order sequestrating his estate, congratulated the monarch on his actions, proving "his sanctity and wisdom," qualities for which he had to thank his former tutor, the Duke of Lerma.[56]

A favorable image of the Duke of Lerma also appeared in several plays written in the first years of Philip IV's reign by Mira de Amescua, a former client of the Count of Lemos, who used a completely recreated history of Alvaro de Luna as an analogy to reflect on Lerma's *privanza*. In a play performed in 1624, *Adversa Fortuna de Don*

51 AHN, Est., *leg.* 832/fols. 323–8, "Lo que su Majd. debe executar con toda brevedad, y las causas principales de la destrucción de la Monarchía."
52 The process of stripping Lerma and his heirs of the royal rewards he received during his *privanza* took, however, many years, and continued at least until the 1650s. See "Memorial de Juan de Chumacero de Sotomayor a Felipe IV sobre las mercedes del duque de Lerma," published by Pérez Bustamante in "Los cardenalatos," pp. 524–32; Gómez de Sandoval Manrique de Padilla, *Memorial*; and *Memorial de los artículos*.
53 See BNM, Mss 8512, "Felipe IV a Domingo de la Torre," 8 Apr. 1621, fols. Br–v; and "Orden de Felipe IV a Fernando Carrillo," 23 Apr. 1621, fol. C, on orders to revise all *mercedes* granted from 1596 through 1621. "The revision of *mercedes*" became, in fact, a pivotal element of Olivares's policy; he considered that the restoration of the monarchy required, among other things, strict control over the number of monetary *mercedes* granted by the monarch. The first memorandum of advice that Olivares sent to Philip IV was precisely about this matter; see "Memorial de las mercedes" [1621], in Elliott and de la Peña, *Memoriales*, vol. I, pp. 3–11.
54 Report of Giovanni Battista Saluzzo, 25 Oct. 1622, in Ciasca, *Istruzioni e relazioni*, vol. I, pp. 161–2.
55 James Howell to Sir James Crofts, 21 Aug. 1623, in Howell, *Epistolae Ho-Elianae*, vol. I, p. 184.
56 BNM, Mss 8512, "Memorial del duque de Lerma a Felipe IV," 12 May 1621, fol. Bv; see also Pujades, *Dietari*, vol. III, pp. 275–6.

Alvaro de Luna, for example, Amescua presents Luna as an honorable favorite defeated by envious enemies with the help of his intimate servants.[57] Amescua did not portray Alvaro de Luna as a loser but as a moral victor, a tragic hero who throughout the play remained the virtuous and noble servant of King John II, his master and friend. In a clear reference to Lerma, Alvaro de Luna is shown answering graciously the king's order to sequestrate his annuities and possessions, even though Luna believed that these were well-deserved payments for his many services to the king. He appears as a stoic favorite who endures the time of troubles with constancy and resignation in the full understanding that his fall is a sacrifice he has to endure to protect the power of the king and the stability of the kingdom. The real loser in the play is King John II. In an emotional conclusion Amescua depicts a solitary and rejected John II, who sadly admits his failure as a king not because he had a favorite but because he did not possess the will and presence of mind to support his most loyal servant and friend against envious and discontented enemies. Having been forced to sign the death penalty by Alvaro de Luna's foes, John II deeply regrets his pusillanimity and implores his descendants "never to destroy your creatures, never abandon those whom you have selected as your favorites."[58]

Lerma himself also attempted to defend his record and actions. In a codicil he added to his testament on 21 October 1622 Lerma addressed two of the charges the new rulers were pressing against him: his actions as the king's chief minister and the number of *mercedes* he had received from Philip III.[59] "Firstly, I declare," he wrote, "that in the administration of justice and the provision of public offices, duties I assumed by order of His Majesty, I never knowingly committed any injustice." He went on to note that he had administered justice equitably and that in attending to his duties he was only guided by his desire "to serve our Lord, protect the well-being of the commonwealth, and fulfill the confidence the king had conferred on me." Lerma also acknowledged that throughout his long *privanza* he had received numerous *mercedes*, but he did not understand the commotion the new rulers were making about them. After all, he had served Philip II, Philip III, Queen Margaret, Prince Philip, and other members of the royal family for many years with love, loyalty, and purity. The only way to repay all these services was for the king to protect Lerma's household by ordering his ministers to leave his annuities and properties alone, or at least to leave him enough to be able to attend to his debts and distribute alms after his death.

But the new king did not answer Lerma's call for help; he stripped the former favorite of all the annuities and possessions he had received during Philip III's reign. Lerma was spared further legal and political persecution by his death on 17

---

[57] Antonio Mira de Amescua, *La segunda de don Alvaro (Adversa Fortuna de don Alvaro)*, ed. N. E. Sánchez-Arce (Mexico City, 1960).

[58] *Ibid.*, verses 3054–65.

[59] BPR, Mss III/6467, *exp.* 11: "Autos que se hicieron para abrir el codilicio que se otorgó con el testamento del Excelentísimo Señor cardenal duque de Lerma." References are to fols. 3–4.

May 1625 in his house in Valladolid. By then, however, he was no longer a pressing concern to the new king and his favorite because his influence at court was forever gone. Those who did not forget Lerma were the Dominicans, an order patronized by Lerma from the first days of his *privanza*. As a tribute to their patron, the head of the order, Fray Juan de Berrio, ordered the celebration of masses in Lerma's honor immediately after his death and commanded that in every church of the order sermons be preached to praise the Christian virtues of their famous protector. One of these masses was held in Plasencia on 22 June 1625 with the Bishop of Córdoba attending the celebration.[60] Fray Fernando de Araque, who was in charge of eulogizing Lerma, began his sermon by recalling that the most important virtue among humans should be gratitude, and that if anyone deserved the gratitude of almost everyone, it was Lerma, without doubt the most liberal royal servant in the history of Spain, as the multitude of persons who had received royal *mercedes* during his *privanza* could testify (fols. 7–19). Lerma was also a Christian minister who had defended the Christian purity of the Spanish monarchy, a reference to Lerma's role in the expulsion of the Moriscos and his patronage of religious orders (fols. 19–21). But Lerma should be especially remembered because for most of his life "he had on his shoulders an entire world (*tuvo sobre sus hombros un mundo entero*), serving as a new Atlas the most powerful king on earth." "I know," Fray Fernando ended his sermon,

that you were not a king, but you equaled the greatest monarchs in the world. I also know that everyone says that you obtained Philip III's *privanza* using common human means, but I must defend you by saying that your ascent was founded on your virtues, your religiosity, and your love for God. These are the qualities that made you dominant over Fortune during so many years. And even if the entire world celebrated your downfall, they were wrong because nothing can cast you down from the throne of your magnificence (fol. 36).

[60] Fray Fernando de Araque, *Sermón en las honras que el convento de San Vicente Ferrer de la ciudad de Plasencia hizo al Ilustrísimo y Excelentísimo Señor Cardenal Duque de Lerma* (Salamanca, 1625). Further references in the text.

Epilogue: The end of the *privado*

During the reign of Philip IV the Duke of Lerma remained a subject of discussion at court where contradictory images of the former *valido* proliferated. Certain courtiers and royal servants disagreed with the charges the new regime brought against Lerma and believed that, although the crisis of the monarchy could only be understood as the result of actions taken during the reign of Philip III, the accusations against Lerma had been intentionally exaggerated to allow Olivares to seize power. Juan de Vitrián, a harsh critic of the reign of Philip III and of the king himself, claimed that nothing was worse than for a king to select a sole favorite, as Philip III had done, but that if he had to, it was better to choose someone like Lerma, "one of the best *privados* in the world being moderate and equal (*mediano, moderado e igual*) in his public actions .... in his ambitions for the state, and in his greed for wealth."[1]

During Olivares's *privanza* Lerma's government and particularly his international policies were also cited as alternatives to the new favorite's policies. Although it is not known whether any of Lerma's followers actively tried to promote his ideas and policies, there is evidence that by the 1630s he was being depicted as a good and peaceable favorite because he had attempted to accommodate the concerns of the many members of the court and to preserve peace as the best way to conserve Spain's power and reputation. Vitrián, for example, after almost twenty years of war under the leadership of Philip IV and Olivares, attacked the prevailing view that all favorites who promoted "peaceful" policies were attempting to control the king, a belief, Vitrián commented, that drove many to criticize the Twelve Years Truce with Holland signed in 1609. Against this interpretation Vitrián claimed that the best ministers, the ones who truly are able to help kings conserve their crowns, "are the peaceful ones and not those who always promote conflicts," and although excesses are never good, it is better to be too peaceful than too bellicose.[2]

Lerma's personality and policies were often juxtaposed to those of Olivares, who was depicted by his enemies as an overeager and absolutist favorite who listened to no one and who pressed for an aggressive international policy that in the end brought defeat and decline. One of the best examples of such a contrasting portrayal appears in a pair of books by Matías de Novoa. De Novoa's flattering

---

[1] Vitrián, *Las memorias de Felipe de Comines*, vol. II, p. 208. [2] *Ibid.*, vol. II, pp. 66, 442.

Historia de Felipe III depicts both Lerma and Philip III in very positive terms, whereas his *Historia de Felipe IV, rey de España* portrays Olivares as a tyrant and ultimately responsible for the ruin of Spain.[3] It is difficult to know, however, whether Novoa's and others' positive views of Lerma at this time resulted from factional struggles at court or reflected popular opinion. There has never been a study of the activities of Lerma's followers during the reign of Philip IV, or studies comparing the criticism leveled against Lerma and Olivares. The evidence collected by several scholars does suggest that Lerma was the subject of a much smaller number of satires, even during the period from 1618 to 1621, than was Olivares during his *privanza*, especially after his fall in 1643.[4] Despite these favorable evaluations, by the 1640s Lerma began to be perceived as a minor character, frequently relegated to the margins of Spanish history, described most often as a favorite preoccupied with riches and social status, an insecure minister unable or unwilling to promote programs aimed at imposing royal power.

Lerma himself had been banished, his policies had been supplanted, and his reputation had been diminished. But certain aspects of his *privanza* cannot be discounted. Despite claims of a radical rupture between Lerma's practices and those of the Count-Duke of Olivares, Lerma's discourses of legimation and many of his administrative methods as well remained central to political and institutional life during the reign of Philip IV. Lerma's *privanza* had indeed created new political contexts, which had to be accommodated by those who aspired to the king's favor. The history of the *valimiento* of Olivares also demonstrates that, despite criticism of Lerma and Philip III, by the late 1610s monarchs and their supporters had become convinced that a favorite/prime minister was necessary to the expansion of royal power.

It is important to differentiate between Olivares's public statements and his actual practice. Publicly, he insisted that he was not the king's favorite but his minister (ironically, a distinction Lerma also maintained). But neither he nor his supporters put forward any new theories to legitate and institutionalize his power. They merely attempted to discredit former favorites without questioning the institution of the *privanza*, a strategy Virgilio Malvezzi, Olivares's propagandist, clearly articulated when he wrote that "the *privanza* is like the monarchy; if it is in good hands, it is very good; if it is in bad hands it is terrible."[5]

Indeed, from the very inception of Philip IV's reign it was evident that continuity would dominate the political discourse on favorites. On 4 May 1621, a few days after

---

[3] On Novoa's ideas, see the introduction of Cánovas del Castillo to his edition of Novoa's works. Novoa, for example, held Olivares responsible for the rebellions of Portugal and Catalonia in 1640; see Elliott, *The Count-Duke*, p. 658.

[4] See Egido, *Sátiras políticas*, pp. 83–104 (Lerma and Philip III), and pp. 105–79 (Olivares and Philip IV); and García de Enterría, *Sociedad y poesía de cordel*, pp. 310–11 (Lerma), and pp. 313–14 (Olivares).

[5] Virgilio Malvezzi, *Historia del marqués Virgilio Malvezzi* [1640], in Juan Yáñez, *Memorias para la historia de don Felipe III, rey de España* (Madrid, 1773), p. 23.

Epilogue

Philip III's death, and in the presence of Philip IV and Olivares, Fray Gerónimo de Florencia, preaching at a funeral mass for the late king, advised the new rulers that to protect the well-being of the community the king needed at his side a high-ranking servant, whom Florencia called "the father of the king . . ., a *privado* and a confidant who should be in charge of all public affairs."[6] His views and, more importantly, Fray Juan de Maldonado's theories, were reproduced in dozens of mirrors-for-favorites, a genre that reached its apex during Olivares's *privanza*. Mártir Rizo, an expert on royal favorites, defined the favorite as the king's "good friend and minister" and contended that the ideal government was a personal monarchy as long as the monarch had at his side a just favorite who acted as the king's *alter ego*.[7] Virgilio Malvezzi went even further in a treatise on royal favorites inspired by Olivares's *valimiento* in which he presented them as perfect and unselfish creatures in the service of crown and country.[8] The positive discourse on favorites in seventeenth-century Spain was so strongly rooted in the political culture that, even after Olivares's fall in 1643, some writers who had supported him continued to defend royal favorites and their role in the ruling of the monarchy. This was the case, for example, with Fray José Laínez, who in his *El Josué esclarecido*, a book dedicated to Philip IV, still sympathetically described the favorite as "the king's prime minister . . . a character defined in the Holy Scripture as the king's friend . . . and who is the king's right hand, or better a king without crown."[9]

Lerma's legacy included not only a theoretical legitimization of the royal favorite but also an administrative system that remained central to the implementation of royal power during the first half of the seventeenth century. Like Lerma, Olivares became the most important man in the everyday ruling of the monarchy; he promoted the creation of special councils and *juntas* to implement royal orders and accumulated numerous offices, for himself and for his relatives, allies, and creatures. Using his capacity for patronage, the new favorite constructed a complex system of patron–client networks which extended to all corners of the Spanish monarchy and operated to concentrate all power at the center. This informal chain of command made it possible for the king and his favorite to circumvent any political obstacles posed by royal institutions and the various kingdoms.[10]

---

[6] Gerónimo de Florencia, *Sermón que predicó a la majestad católica del rey Don Felipe Quarto* (Madrid, 1621), fols. 26v–27v.

[7] Juan Pablo Mártir Rizo, *Norte de príncipes (1626) y Vida de Rómulo*, ed. José Antonio Maravall (Madrid, 1988), p. 64; see also his *Historia de la vida de Lucio Anneo Séneca, español* [1626], ed. B. de la Vega (Madrid, 1944), pp. 72–3, and his *Historia de la muy noble y leal ciudad de Cuenca* [1629], facsimile edn. (Barcelona, 1979), fol. 60.

[8] Virgilio Malvezzi, *Il ritratto del privato cristiano* [1635], ed. Maria Luisa Doglio (Palermo, 1993), p. 35; Malvezzi's book was translated into Spanish in 1635 and into English in 1647.

[9] Fray José Laínez, *El Josué esclarecido. Caudillo, vencedor de reyes y gentes* (Madrid, 1653), p. 506; see also his *El privado cristiano deducido de las vidas de Joseph y Daniel* (Madrid, 1641). On theories on favorites during Olivares's *privanza* see Tomás y Valiente, *Los validos*, chaps. 2.2, and 3.2; on continuity between Lerma and Olivares see Antonio Feros, "Images of Evil, Images of Kings."

[10] On the continuity of forms of ruling promoted by Lerma and Olivares see Feros, "Lerma y Olivares."

Another justification for the royal *validos*, also indicative of the seventeenth-century perception of them as necessary instruments, was their function as the monarch's protective shield. The need to protect the monarch from criticism in order to guarantee political stability was emphasized by, for example, Fray Juan de Santa María in 1615. "It is time," he wrote, "to finish with this ancient and bad custom of imputing to the king all those resolutions undesirable to the people."[11] Santa María believed that such a role belong to the king's counselors rather than to the king's favorite; however, in the political conditions generated after 1550 (a period when the royal councils began to be viewed as an institutional limitation upon the king's capacity for independent action) it was the royal *privado* who acted as a shield by taking into his hands many of the most potentially damaging political tasks, such as the distribution of royal patronage, the promotion of royal officials, and the day-to-day administration of the monarchy, thus enabling the king, at least in theory, to preserve his aloofness from political controversy and protect his reputation.

Lerma's success in this capacity was, however, rather limited. If, as Philip III's favorite and chief minister, he did not entirely destroy his own reputation, his actions as the king's *valido* appear to have destroyed Philip III's reputation forever. Perhaps the fault lies less with Philip or with Lerma, for that matter, than with the insoluble dilemma posed by two theories of the time. It had been impossible to reconcile the theoretical justification of a favorite as *de facto* prime minister with the existing theory of the king's unique majesty and his duty to rule alone.

Depictions of Philip III as a weak king, a *rex inutilis* in the language of the period, began to circulate immediately after his death in March 1621. Many satires with explicit characterizations appeared. One was especially cruel:

Here lies the best of the good monarchs, but so wretched that although many cried for his death, only a few missed him. He gave himself to the desires of others, he surrendered himself to the villainous power of others ... [everyone seemed to have reached the same conclusion]: if the king does not die, the kingdom will die (*si el rey no muere, el reyno muere*).[12]

Similar images of Philip III were also promoted officially. Fray Francisco de Barreda, for example, insisted on such a presentation in a sermon he preached in Toledo during a funeral mass in commemoration of the late king. Philip III, Barreda told his audience, was indeed a man of many virtues, some of them detrimental to his reputation as a ruler. The king's humble spirit, despite his obvious intelligence, had moved him "to judge himself inferior to all. Ultimately, this was the reason why he had delegated the government of the monarchy to others."[13]

---

[11] Santa María, *República y policía christiana*, p. 100.
[12] A copy of this satire was sent by Alonso de Aguado to Jeroni Pujades in a letter dated May 1621; see Pujades, *Dietari*, vol. III, p. 305.
[13] Fray Francisco de Barreda, *Sermón a la muerte de Philipo III* (Toledo, 1621), fols. 29r–v.

Visions of Philip III as a *rex inutilis* influenced the descriptions of his reign for decades after his death. During the late 1620s and early 1630s at least three biographies of Philip III were published: Baltasar Porreño's *Dichos y hechos del señor rey don Phelipe III el Bueno* (1626); Ana de Castro Egas's *Eternidad del rey don Felipe Tercero, nuestro señor el piadoso* (1629); and Gil González Dávila's *Historia de la vida y hechos del ínclito monarca, amado y santo don Felipe Tercero* (1632). In all three Philip III is construed as a virtuous individual, extremely religious, almost a saint, and a good husband and father. But very little is said about him as a ruler, except that he expelled the Moriscos and was extremely liberal. In contrast, all three biographers present Lerma as the person who played the most active role in the decision-making process. Castro Egas went even further noting that Philip III was a worthy ruler not because of his royal virtues but because of his decision to appoint Lerma as his *alter ego*.[14]

To accept the estimation of Philip III as a weak king unduly dependent upon his favorite may be to accept the over-simplifications of the contemporary political debate. Other monarchs, before and after Philip III, had favorites, but Spaniards did not consider them weak monarchs. To understand why Philip III was so labeled, historians must consider political developments other than the existence of a favorite and the discourse to justify his role in the monarchy.

In *The Prince*, Machiavelli wrote

we are successful when our ways are suited to the times and circumstances and unsuccessful when they are not. For one sees that, in the things that lead to the end which everyone aims at, that is, glory and riches, men proceed in different ways ... and each of these different ways of acting can be effective [if] their ways of acting conform with the conditions in which they operate.[15]

When Philip III became king, his behavior, especially his decision to have a sole favorite, suited the political circumstances of the time, and answered to many contemporary expectations.[16] Although Philip III and Lerma knew that they had to consolidate royal power by developing mechanisms, behaviors, and discourses that enhanced the king's power,[17] they failed to grasp the necessity of also having a monarch who showed initiative and independence as Philip II had done. By delegating the visible, public role of ruling the monarchy to Lerma, a natural consequence of having a favorite, according to some of his contemporaries, Philip III came to be perceived as a monarch who renounced his duties as a ruler. Philip III's words on his deathbed – "If Heaven gives me life, I will rule in a completely different manner" – indicate that he understood his own mistake.[18] The dominant political culture of the time demanded that the monarch enhance royal power by

---

[14] Ana de Castro Egas, *Eternidad del rey don Felipe Tercero, nuestro señor el piadoso. Discurso de su vida y santas costumbres* (Madrid, 1629), fols. 3v–5v.   [15] Machiavelli, *The Prince*, pp. 85–6.
[16] See above, chaps. 2 and 3.   [17] See above, chap. 4.
[18] See above, chap. 12.

appearing as the leading player at court, the active force that moved the monarchy, the true lord of his realm and subjects.

The idea that the consolidation of royal power required an active and publicly visible ruler became central to political discourse especially after the 1610s. In this period, as John H. Elliott has noted, a new generation of courtiers, men like Olivares and his supporters, showed itself more aggressive and more interested in the possibilities of power than in its limitations.[19] They believed that a king should be modeled after Philip II or even after Henry IV of France. Political writers began to value what they called the "royal virtues" over the "personal virtues" of the ruler. "Politics," here understood as the imposition of reason of state on behalf of the king's interests, was gaining precedence over "ethics," the moral character of the king and, thus, over his obligations to the commonwealth.

This political change can be best understood by contrasting different views on royal virtues, like those expressed, for example, by Erasmus in his influential *The Education of a Christian Prince* (1516), and by royal supporters in seventeenth-century Spain. "If you can be a prince and a good man at the same time, you will be performing a magnificent service," Erasmus wrote. Certainly, he continued, "It is quite possible to find a good man who would not make a good prince, yet one cannot be a good prince without at the same time being a good man."[20] By the late sixteenth century, and certainly in the early seventeenth century, attitudes had changed considerably, at least with respect to absolute monarchical power. A tyrant who disregarded the personal virtues necessary to a good monarch was, no doubt, still viewed as a bad ruler, but by the reign of Philip III concerns about tyrants were being displaced by concerns about "weak" kings. Bodin had already called attention to this problem in the late sixteenth century by stating, to use the words of L. Alston, that "a weak, overly generous king who runs his realm by allowing governance to pass into the hands of unworthy favorites, [sets up], in fact, a thousand tyrannies instead of one." An authoritarian monarch, at least to certain courtiers, appeared more desirable than an "excessively weak, pusillanimous, incompetent" one, who could be "a greater disaster to the kingdom than one who appears to be a tyrant."[21]

Juan de Vitrián expressed similar views in the mid-seventeenth century. To preserve his authority – or, as Vitrián asserted, to conserve "the despotic government of the monarchy" – the monarch had to present himself as the real and sole king, and as a flawless "divinity." But being a good king was not necessarily equivalent to being a good person. "A common man is called good if he does good things and lets others mistreat him. But a king is bad if he lets others mistreat him because he is a public person and when he is mistreated the whole kingdom suffers."[22] As the head of the body politic, the "king must be superior to the rest . . .

[19] Elliott, "Yet another crisis?" pp. 309–10.   [20] Erasmus, *The Education of a Christian Prince*, p. 51.
[21] L. Alston in Sir Thomas Smith, *De Republica Anglorum*, ed. L. Alston (Cambridge, 1906), p. 3.
[22] Vitrián, *Las memorias de Felipe de Comines*, vol. I, p. 224. Further references in the text.

[always remembering] that in ruling a monarchy royal virtues are far more important than personal ones" (vol. I, p. 310). Many rulers exemplified this ideal, but
three excelled: Philip II, Henry IV of France, and Tiberius, who was "a great
statesman despite the fact that he was a bad person" (vol. II, p. 71). Unlike Lerma,
Olivares seemed to understand very well that as the king's prime minister it was his
duty to press Philip IV to become a public and active monarch to ensure that his
image would outshine that of his father despite the fact that both monarchs relied
on favorites/prime ministers during their reigns. Olivares promoted Philip II as the
model of kingship which Philip IV should follow to restore the public preeminence
of the king to its former glory.[23]

But although Olivares was able to avoid some of Lerma's most blatant flaws, in
the end he could not prevent the public from perceiving him as the real ruler and
Philip IV as a "king in name alone." The presence of a favorite/prime minister had
begun to be viewed as an impediment to strengthening royal power. Few expressed
this view better than Diego de Saavedra y Fajardo, a writer and diplomat who had
collaborated with Olivares during his *privanza*. In his influential *Idea de un príncipe
político-cristiano representada en cien empresas*, published in 1640, Saavedra noted
that in the last decades rulers throughout Europe had favorites/prime ministers
because all of them believed this was best for the government of their monarchies
and the protection of their interests. Saavedra y Fajardo even recognized that
favorites had often shown good intentions, had attempted to reinforce the power of
the king, and had promoted the well-being of the community. Their genuine efforts
and desires were, however, futile because every initiative developed under the
guidance of a *privado* was immediately perceived as the manifestation of self-
interest and as proof of a desire to usurp, not to reinforce, the king's power and
sovereignty.[24] In other words, Saavedra and many of his contemporaries (even
those who promoted the king's absolute power) thought that, given the discourse
on the role and power of the king, the existence of a favorite/chief minister (no
matter what theories were used to legitimate his public role) would inevitably raise
questions about the nature of the political system and, more important, the
personal and political capacities of the monarch.

After Olivares's fall in 1643, Philip IV apparently realized how necessary it was
that he be perceived as a monarch in control of his own destiny. Thus began a new
phase of development for the early modern state in Spain. Although thankful to
Olivares for support and assistance, Philip IV now knew that a public favorite was a
political liability. Perhaps the writer who best summarized contemporary sentiments on this topic was Fray Marcos Salmerón in a book, *El príncipe escondido.
Meditaciones de la vida de Cristo desde los doce hasta los treinta años*, published in

---

[23] Elliott, *The Count-Duke*, chap. 5; and "Power and Propaganda in the Reign of Philip IV," in his *Spain and its World*.

[24] Diego de Saavedra y Fajardo, *Idea de un príncipe político-cristiano*, empresa 50, pp. 362–3.

1648.[25] Salmerón's main concern was to delineate the causes of the Spanish monarchy's decline, but unlike the *"políticos,"* who, according to Salmerón, believed that the cause of decline could be attributed to "natural forces and the movements of the stars" (pp. 185–6), he ascribed the downturn suffered by the crown to the tyrannical government promoted by favorites such as Lerma and Olivares, with their defense of "reason of state" theories. Salmerón went even further; he claimed that the principal cause of the decline in the authority of the Spanish monarchy was the simple existence of a favorite-prime minister. "These individuals," he wrote, "as a result of their tyranny and inferior dispositions are the ones who provoke the monarchy's complete perdition and ruin, as we can see in ancient history but also in our recent experiences" (p. 188).

Philip IV expressed his own views in a letter to Sor María de Agreda, one of his spiritual counselors, in January 1647. Reminding her that even the wise and prudent Philip II had selected a group of servants to help him rule the monarchy, Philip IV assured her that "this kind of government has taken place in all monarchies, ancient and modern, because in all monarchs have had a principal minister or a close servant," who helped their masters rule the kingdom because it could not be done without assistance. Philip also acknowledged that after Olivares's fall he continued to have a favorite: "It is true that I gave my confidence and approval to one of my servants [Don Luis de Haro] who grew up with me." But he immediately qualified this admission by claiming that, "I always *refused to give him [Haro] the character and name of minister* to avoid past troubles" and especially to avoid being perceived not as the king but as the shadow of a king.[26] Philip IV's decision indicated the end of the *privado* as *de facto* prime minister. This change also affected other European monarchies, as Jean Berenguer has indicated in his seminal article "Le Problème du ministériat au xviie siècle."[27] In Spain, as in France, the end of the prime minister in the middle of the seventeenth century did not mean the restoration of "traditional" forms of government but renewed attempts to consolidate an absolute monarchy. Demonstrating the strength of the monarchical system and its capacity to refashion itself and adapt to changing conditions, Spanish rulers and their supporters continued to defend the idea of personal monarchy, presenting the king as sole possessor of sovereignty. But, in contrast to the time of Lerma's and Olivares's *privanzas*, expansion of royal power during the eighteenth century took place through the promotion of institutional, not personal, methods of government (*juntas, intendentes,* and *secretarios de estado y despacho*).[28] The views of the Spanish monarchs, who from the early eighteenth

---

[25] Further references in the text.
[26] Philip IV to Sor María de Agreda, Jan. 1647; cf. Tomás y Valiente, *Los validos*, pp. 172–3. Emphasis added.
[27] Jean Berenguer, "Le Problème du ministériat au xviie siècle," *Annales*, 29 (1974).
[28] On these developments see Escudero, *Los secretarios*, vol. I, pp. 281–316; and Fernández Albaladejo, *Fragmentos*, pp. 353–454.

century were members of the House of Bourbon, could be summarized in the words of the French Bourbon king Louis XIV to his heir. Disturbed by the opposition to Richelieu and Mazarin, and the experience of the Fronde, Louis XIV became acutely aware of the dangers of having a favorite/chief minister:

As to the persons who were to support me in my work, I resolved above all not to have a prime minister, and if you and my successors take my advice, my son, the name will forever be abolished in France, there being nothing more shameful than to see on the one hand all the functions and on the other the mere title of king.[29]

This was the advice that Spanish rulers, his own descendants, followed until well beyond the end of the *ancien régime*.

[29] Louis XIV, *Mémoires*, p. 31; see also pp. 238–40. For similar views in Spain see the commentary by Juan de Espínola Baeza on his Spanish translation of Richelieu's political testament: *Testamento político del Cardenal Duque de Richelieu, Primer Ministro de Francia en el Reinado de Louis XIII* (Madrid, 1696), esp. pp. 214, 224, 240, 268. On theories on royal favorites after Olivares's fall see Tomás y Valiente, *Los validos*, chaps. 1.1, 2.1, and 3.

Bibliography

MANUSCRIPT SOURCES

Archivo de los Duques de Lerma, Toledo: *legs.* 1, 11, 40, 52
Archivo General de Indias, Seville
  Audiencia de Lima: *leg.* 6.
  Indiferente General: *legs.* 614, 746, 748, 827, 855.
Archivo General del Palacio Real, Madrid
  Expedientes Personales: *cajas* 28/42; 35/23; 50/24; 135/50; 214/15; 233/21; 450/24;
    521/26; 533/14; 548/4; 588/15; 661/15; 913/45; 1048/26; 1064/2.
  Sección Histórica: *cajas* 103, 113, 191; *leg.* 3.
Archivo General de Simancas, Valladolid
  Cámara de Castilla
    Diversos de Castilla: *legs.* 34–6.
    Libros de Cédulas, bks. 160–95.
    Memoriales y Expedientes: *legs.* 120–451, 796–98, 802–17, 821, 824, 825, 834, 839, 844,
      849, 853, 858, 863, 868, 873, 878, 882, 890, 900, 910, 920, 930, 940, 950, 960, 970, 980,
      990, 1000, 1010, 1020, 1030, 1040, 1050, 1060, 1070, 1080, 1090, 1100, 1110.
    Visitas: *legs.* 2792, 2793, 2794, 2796.
  Consejo y Juntas de Hacienda: *legs.* 376–77, 409, 80.
  Dirección General del Tesoro: *leg.* 335.
  Estado:
    Corona de Castilla: *legs.* 152–5, 182–266.
    España: *legs.* 1492–5, 2636–45.
    Indiferente de España y Norte: *leg.* 4126
    Negociación de Alemania: *leg.* 711.
    Negociación de Flandes: *legs.* 634, 2023–6.
    Negociación de Portugal: *legs.* 434–8.
    Gracia y Justicia: *legs.* 621, 890, 897.
    Secretarías Provinciales: *leg.* 13
    Patronato Real: *cajas* 71, 85, 87–90.
Archivo Histórico Nacional, Madrid
  Consejos Suprimidos: *legs.* 4410–22, 7124, 13192, 13193, 37616, 51708. lib. 724.
  Estado: *leg.* 6408. bks. 81, 162, 613, 737–8, 801, 807, 823–4, 832, 859, 863–4, 870, 921.
  Ordenes Militares, Expedientes de Caballeros.
Archivo de Protocolos de Madrid: Protocolo 1848.
Biblioteca Francisco de Zabálburu, Madrid: *carps.* 132, 133, 134.

Bibliography

Biblioteca Nacional de Madrid: Mss 294, 722, 852, 960, 981, 983, 1007, 1174, 1492, 1739, 1858, 1923, 2229, 2237, 2239, 2346–9, 2352, 2355, 2394, 2445, 2751, 3011, 3031, 3207, 3277, 3826, 4072, 5570, 5585, 5785, 6020, 6590, 6713, 6778, 6896, 7377, 7423, 8180, 8512, 8526, 8740, 8741, 8888, 9078, 9087, 9198, 9405, 10334, 10662, 10758, 11000, 11032, 11044, 11070, 11077, 11087, 11260/44, 11264/22, 11317/22, 11569, 11773, 12179, 1260/6, 12914, 13239, 17772, 17858, 17881, 17887, 17995, 18190, 18191, 18275, 18430/1–4, 18419, 18422, 18434, 18657/16, 18665/28, 18716/l–18, 18718/55, 18721/ 46, 18724/6–36, 18725, 18728/4l, 18731/26 and 36, 19344, 20260/30.
Biblioteca del Palacio Real, Madrid: Mss 1829, II-767, II-1557, II-1688, II-1763, II-1896, II-2153, II-2227, II-2422–3, II-2546, III-3428, III-6467.
British Library
Additional, Mss 10238: "De los moriscos de España por el padre Ignacio de las Casas (1605–7)."
Additional, Mss 28378: "Correspondence of the Marquis de Poza with Don Christoval de Mora and others between the 15th of December, 1595, and the 20th of January, 1613."
Additional, Mss 28379: "Letters and minutes of Christoval de Mora, 1594–1598."
Additional, Mss 28422–5: Correspondence of Don Juan de Borja with the Duke of Lerma.
Additional, Mss 28426: Letters to don Juan de Borja, conde de Ficalho, viceroy of Portugal.
Egerton, Mss 311: "Libro de las peregrinaciones que el Católico rey don Phelipe Segundo, de gloriosa memoria, mandó hacer al padre Diego de Salazar Marañón de la Compañía de Jesús por la salud, vida y feliz sucesión de su querido y amado hijo y rey nro. sr. don Phelipe III."
Egerton, Mss 2055: "Official reports on commercial affairs, 1602–1693."
Sloane, Mss 3610: "Tratados varios tocantes a cosas de España."
Instituto Valencia Don Juan, Madrid: envíos 29, 43, 44, 45.
Real Academia de la Historia, Madrid
Mss. 9/3507.
Colección Luis de Salazar y Castro: N-71.
Colección Pellicer: vol. 23.

PRINTED WORKS

Acevedo, Fernando de. *Copia de una carta de Fernando de Acevedo a la ciudad de Córdoba en razón de la concesión del servicio de millones* (Madrid, 1619).
Adams, Simon. "Favourites and Factions at the Elizabethan Court," in Ronald G. Asch and Adolf M. Birke, eds., *Princes, Patronage and the Nobility* (Oxford, 1991).
Alamos de Barrientos, Baltasar. *Norte de príncipes* [*c.* 1600], ed. Martín de Riquer (Madrid, 1969).
Aforismos al Tácito español [1614], ed. José A. Fernández-Santamaría, 2 vols. (Madrid, 1987).
Discurso político al rey Felipe III al comienzo de su reinado [1598], ed. Modesto Santos (Madrid, 1990).
Suma de preceptos justos, necesarios y provechosos en consejo de Estado al rey Felipe III siendo príncipe [*c.* 1599], ed. Modesto Santos (Madrid, 1991).

Printed works

Alberi, Eugenio. *Le Relazioni degli Ambasciatori Veneti al Senato durante il Secolo Decimosesto*, Ser. I, vol. V (Florence, 1861).

Alburquerque, Martín de. *Jean Bodin na península ibérica* (Paris, 1978).

Alcocer y Martínez, Mariano, ed. *Consultas del Consejo de Estado*, 2 vols. (Valladolid, 1930–2).

Allen, Paul. "The Strategy of Peace: Spanish Foreign Policy and the 'Pax Hispanica,' 1598–1609," Ph.D. diss., Yale University, 1995.

Almansa y Mendoza, Andrés de. *Cartas de Andrés de Almansa y Mendoza* [1620s] (Madrid, 1886).

Anderson, Perry. *Lineages of the Absolutist State* (London, 1974).

Angulo Iñiguez, Diego and Pérez Sánchez, Alfonso E. *Historia de la pintura española* (Madrid, 1969).

Aquinas, Thomas. *Commentary on the Nicomachean Ethics of Aristotle*, ed. C. I. Litzinger, 2 vols. (Chicago, 1964).

Araque, Fray Fernando de. *Sermón en las honras que el convento de San Vicente Ferrer de la ciudad de Plasencia hizo al Ilustrísimo y Excelentísimo Señor Cardenal Duque de Lerma* (Salamanca, 1625).

Argensola, Bartolomé Leonardo. "De cómo se remediarán los vicios de la corte y que no acuda a ella tanta gente (1611)," *RABM*, 8 (1978).

Arias Montano, Benito (attrib. to). *Aforismos sacados de la historia de Publio Cornelio Tácito por el doctor Arias Montano, para la conservación y aumento de las monarquías* (Barcelona, 1609).

Aristotle. *Los ocho libros de república del filósofo Aristóteles, con unos breves y provechosos comentarios para todo género de gentes y particularmente para los que tienen cargo de público gobierno*, trans. Pedro Simón Abril (Zaragoza, 1584).

La ética de Aristóteles, trans. Pedro Simón Abril [1580] (Madrid, 1918).

La política, trans. Pedro Simón Abril [1579] (Madrid, 1919).

The Politics, ed. S. Everson (Cambridge, 1988).

Armstrong, C. A. F. "The Golden Age of Burgundy," in A. G. Dickens, ed., *The Courts of Europe. Politics, Patronage and Royalty* (New York, 1977).

Arrieta Alberdi, Jon. *El Consejo Supremo de la Corona de Aragón (1494–1707)* (Zaragoza, 1994).

Artola, Miguel. *La hacienda del antiguo régimen* (Madrid, 1982).

Asch, Ronald G. *The Thirty Years War. The Holy Roman Empire and Europe, 1618–48* (New York, 1997).

Avilés Fernández, Miguel. "La censura inquisitorial de 'Los seis libros de la República,' de Jean Bodin," *Hispania Sacra*, 37 (1985).

Aymard, Maurice. "Friends and Neighbors," in *A History of Private Life. III: Passions of the Renaissance*, ed. Roger Chartier; trans. Arthur Goldhammer (Cambridge, Mass., 1989).

Azcona, Tarsicio. *Isabel la Católica* (Madrid, 1964).

Aznar Cardona, Pedro. *Expulsión justificada de los moriscos españoles* (Huesca, 1612).

Bacon, Francis. *Francis Bacon: A Critical Edition of the Major Works*, ed. Brian Vickers (Oxford, 1996).

Baillie, Hugh Murray. "Etiquette and the Planning of State Apartments in Baroque Palaces," *Archaeologia*, 101 (1967).

Bibliography

Baker, Keith Michael. *Inventing the French Revolution* (Cambridge, 1990).

Baldi, Camillo. *Politiche considerationi sopra una lettera de Anton Perez al Duca di Lerma del modo de acquistar la gratia del suo signore, e acquistata conservare* (Bologna, 1623).

Baldini, A. Enzo, ed. *Botero e la "ragion di stato"* (Florence, 1992).

Barbiche, Bernard. "L'Exploitation politique d'un complot: Henri IV, le Saint-Siège et la conspiration de Biron (1602)," in Yves-Marie Bercé and Elena Fasano Guarini, eds., *Complots et conjurations dans l'Europe moderne* (Rome, 1996).

Barozzi, Niccolò and Guglielmo Berchet, eds. *Relazioni degli Stati Europei. Lette al Senato dagli Ambasciatori Veneti nel secolo Decimosettimo*, Serie 1: *Spagna*, vol. 1, (Venice, 1856).

Barreda, Fray Francisco de. *Sermón a la muerte de Philipo III* (Toledo, 1621).

Barros, Alonso de. *Filosofía cortesana moralizada* [1587], ed. Trevor J. Dadson (Madrid, 1987).

Barthes, Roland. *On Racine*, English trans. Richard Howard (Berkeley, 1992).

Beceiro Pita, Isabel. "Educación y cultura de la nobleza (siglos XIII–XV)," *Anuario de Estudios Medievales*, 21 (1991).

Beik, William. *Absolutism and Society in Seventeenth-Century France. State Power and Provincial Aristocracy in Languedoc* (Cambridge, 1985).

Benigno, Francesco. *La sombra del Rey*, trans. Esther Benítez (Madrid, 1994).

Benítez Sánchez-Blanco, Rafael, and Eugenio Ciscar Pallarés, "La iglesia ante la conversión y expulsión de los moriscos," in Antonio Mestre Sanchís, ed., *Historia de la iglesia en España. IV: La iglesia en la España de los siglos XVII y XVIII* (Madrid, 1979).

Berenguer, Jean. "Le problème du ministériat au XVIIe siècle," *Annales*, 29 (1974).

Bergin, Joseph. *Cardinal Richelieu. Power and the Pursuit of Wealth* (New Haven and London, 1985).

Bermúdez de Pedraza, Francisco. *Por los secretarios de Vuesa Majestad* (n.p., n.d.).

Panegírico legal: preeminencias de los secretarios del rey, deducidas de ambos derechos (Granada, 1635).

Hospital real de corte (Granada, 1644).

El secretario del rey [1620], facsimile edn. (Madrid, 1973).

Birch, Thomas, ed. *Memoirs of the Reign of Queen Elizabeth*, 2 vols. (New York, 1970).

Bireley, Robert. *The Counter-Reformation Prince* (Chapel Hill, N.C., 1990).

Bitton, Davis, and Ward A. Mortensen. "War or Peace: A French Pamphlet Polemic, 1604–1606," in Malcolm R. Thorp and Arthur J. Slavin, eds., *Politics, Religion and Diplomacy in Early Modern Europe. Essays in Honor of De Lamar Jensen* (Kirksville, Mo., 1994).

Bloch, Marc B. *The Historian's Craft*, English trans. Peter Putnam (New York, 1954).

Bodin, Jean. *Los seis libros de la república*, trans. Gaspar de Añastro Isunza [1590], ed. José Luis Bermejo Cabrero, 2 vols. (Madrid, 1992).

Bombín Pérez, Antonio. *La cuestión de Monferrato (1613–1618)* (Vitoria, 1975).

Bonney, Richard. "Absolutism: What's in a name," *French History*, 1 (1987).

Boronat y Barrachina, Pascual. *Los moriscos españoles y su expulsión. Estudio histórico-crítico*, 2 vols. (Valencia, 1901).

Borrelli, Gianfranco. *Ragion di stato e leviatano. Conservazione e scambio alle origini della modernità politica* (Bologna, 1993).

Botero, Giovanni. *Los diez libros de la razón de estado* [1593], trans. Antonio de Herrera y Tordesillas (Madrid, 1613).

Printed works

Practical Politics, ed. George Albert Moore (Washington, D.C., 1949).

The Reason of State, ed. P. J. Waley and D. P. Waley (London, 1956).

Bouza Alvarez, Fernando Jesús. "Portugal en la monarquía hispana (1580–1640): Felipe II, las cortes de Tomar y la génesis del Portugal católico," Ph.D. diss., Universidad Complutense de Madrid, 1987.

Del escribano a la biblioteca. La civilización escrita europea en la alta edad moderna (siglos XV–XVII) (Madrid, 1992).

"Corte es decepción. Don Juan de Silva, conde de Portalegre," in José Martínez Millán, ed., *La corte de Felipe II* (Madrid, 1994).

"La majestad de Felipe II. Construcción del mito real," in José Martínez Millán, ed., *La corte de Felipe II* (Madrid, 1994).

"La nobleza portuguesa y la corte madrileña hacia 1630–1640. Nobles y lucha política en el Portugal de Olivares," *Mélanges de la Casa Velázquez*, 35 (1999).

Imagen y propaganda. Capítulos de historia cultural del reinado de Felipe II, (Madrid, 1998).

Boyden, James Mark. *The Courtier and the King. Ruy Gómez de Silva, Philip II, and the Court of Spain* (Berkeley and Los Angeles, 1995).

Brancalasso, Juan Antonio. *Los diez mandamientos de la corte* (Naples, 1609).

Laberinto de Corte (Naples, 1609).

Braudel, Fernand. "Conflits et refus de civilisation: espagnols et morisques au XVI siècle," *Annales*, 14 (1947).

Brightwell, Peter. "The Spanish System and the Twelve Years' Truce," *English Historical Review*, 89 (1974).

"The Spanish Origins of the Thirty Years' War," *European Studies Review*, 9 (1979).

"Spain and Bohemia: The Decision to Intervene, 1619," *European Studies Review*, 12 (1982).

Brown, Jonathan. "Enemies of Flattery: Velázquez' Portraits of Philip IV," *Journal of Interdisplinary History*, 17 (1986).

Brown Jonathan, and John H. Elliott. *A Palace for a King* (New Haven, 1980).

Brumont, Francis. "Le Pouvoir municipal en Vieille-Castile au Siècle d'Or," *Bulletin Hispanique*, 87 (1985).

Buisseret, David. *Henry IV* (London, 1984).

Bunes Ibarra, Miguel Angel de. *Los moriscos en el pensamiento histórico. Historiografía de un grupo marginado* (Madrid, 1983).

La imagen de los musulmanes y del norte de Africa en la España de los siglos XVI y XVII (Madrid, 1989).

Bunes Ibarra, Miguel Angel, and Mercedes García-Arenal. *Los españoles y el norte de Africa, siglos XV–XVII* (Madrid, 1992).

Burke, Peter. *The Fabrication of Louis XIV* (New Haven, 1992).

Bustamante García, Agustín. *La arquitectura clasicista del foco vallisoletano (1561–1640)* (Valladolid, 1983).

Cabrera, Fray Alonso de. *Sermones del maestro Fray Alonso de Cabrera*, ed. Manuel Mir (Madrid, 1906).

Cabrera de Córdoba, Luis. *Relaciones de las cosas sucedidas en la corte de España, desde 1599 hasta 1614 [c. 1614]* (Madrid, 1857).

Historia de Felipe II, rey de España [c. 1609], 4 vols. (Madrid, 1877).

De historia, para entenderla y escribirla [1611], ed. S. Montero Díaz (Madrid, 1948).

Bibliography

Calabria, Antonio. *The Cost of Empire. The Finances of the Kingdom of Naples in the Time of Spanish Rule* (Cambridge, 1991).

Calendar of State Papers and Manuscripts Relating to English Affairs Existing in the Archives and Collections of Venice, and in other Libraries of Northern Italy, ed. Rawdon Brown, vols. VII–XVII (London, 1885–1911).

Cámara Muñoz, Alicia. "El poder de la imagen y la imagen del poder. La fiesta en el Madrid del Renacimiento," in *Madrid en el Renacimiento* (Madrid, 1986).

Cameron, Keith. *Henri III. A Maligned or Malignant King? Aspects of the Satirical Iconography of Henri de Valois* (Exeter, 1978).

Camos, Marco Antonio. *Microcosmia y gobierno universal del hombre cristiano* (Barcelona, 1592).

Campanella, Tommaso. *La monarquía hispánica*, ed. Primitivo Mariño (Madrid, 1982).

Cano de Gardoquí, José Luis. *La cuestión de Saluzzo en las comunicaciones del imperio español (1588–1601)* (Valladolid, 1962).

Caparrós Esperante, Luis. *Entre validos y letrados. La obra dramática de Damián Salucio del Poyo* (Valladolid, 1987).

Carducho, Vicente. *Diálogos de la pintura* [*c.* 1636], ed. Francisco Calvo Serraller (Madrid, 1979).

Carlos Morales, Carlos Javier de. *El Consejo de Hacienda de Castilla, 1523–1602* (Avila, 1996).

Carnero, Antonio. *Historia de las guerras civiles que ha habido en los estados de Flandes desde el año 1559 hasta el de 1609 y las causas de la rebelión en los dichos estados* (Brussels, 1625).

Caro Baroja, Julio. *Los moriscos del reino de Granada (Ensayo de historia social)* (Madrid, 1957).

Cartas y avisos dirigidos a don Juan de Zúñiga, virrey de Nápoles en 1581 (Madrid, 1887).

Carter, Charles Howard. *The Secret Diplomacy of the Habsburgs, 1598–1625* (New York, 1964).

Carvajal y Mendoza, Luisa de. *Epistolario y poesías*, ed. Camilo María Abad (Madrid, 1965).

Casey, James. *The Kingdom of Valencia in the Seventeenth Century* (Cambridge, 1979).

Castiglione, Baldassare. *Il Libro del Cortegiano* [1528], ed. Amadeo Quondam (Milan, 1981).

El cortesano, trans. Juan Boscán [1534], facsimile edn., 2 vols. (Madrid, 1985).

Castro Egas, Ana de. *Eternidad del rey don Felipe Tercero, nuestro señor el piadoso. Discurso de su vida y santas costumbres* (Madrid, 1629).

Cauvin, Mary Austin. "The *Comedia de Privanza* in the Seventeenth Century," Ph.D. diss., University of Pennsylvania, 1957.

Cervantes Saavedra, Miguel de. *Obras completas*, ed. Angel Valbuena y Prat (Madrid, 1943).

Teatro completo, ed. Florencio Sevilla Arroyo and Antonio Rey Hazas (Barcelona, 1987).

Cervera Vera, Luis. *El conjunto palacial de la villa de Lerma* (Valencia, 1967).

Chartier, Roger. *On the Edge of the Cliff. History, Language, and Practices*, trans. Lydia G. Cochrane (Baltimore, 1997).

Checa Cremades, Fernando. *Pintura y escultura del Renacimiento en España, 1450–1600* (Madrid, 1983).

"Felipe II en el Escorial: la representación del poder real," in *El Escorial: arte, poder y cultura en la corte de Felipe II* (Madrid, 1989).

Checa Cremades, Fernando, and José Miguel Morán, *El coleccionismo en España* (Madrid, 1985).

Printed works

Chittolini, Giorgio. "The 'Private,' the 'Public,' the State," in Julius Kirshner, ed., *The Origins of the State in Italy, 1300–1600* (Chicago, 1996).

Ciasca, Raffaelle, ed. *Istruzioni e relazioni degli ambasciatori genovesi*, vol. I: *Spagna, 1494–1617*; vol. II: *Spagna, 1619–1635* (Rome, 1955).

Cicero. *Libro de Marco Tulio Cicerón en que trata de los oficios, de la amicicia, de la senectud, añadiéndole agora nuevamente las paradoxas y el sueño de Scipión*, trans. Francisco Tamara and Juan Jarava (Salamanca, 1582).

On Duties, ed. M. T. Griffin and E. M. Atkins (Cambridge, 1991).

Cioranescu, Alexandre. *Le Masque et le visage. Du baroque espagnol au classicisme français* (Geneva, 1983).

Clavero, Bartolomé. *Tantas personas como estados* (Madrid, 1986).

Antidora. Antropología católica de la economía moderna (Milan, 1991).

Razón de estado, razón de individuo, razón de historia (Madrid, 1991).

Contarini, Simeone. "Relación que hizo a la República de Venecia Simón Contarini al fin del año 1605," in Luis Cabrera de Córdoba, *Relaciones de las cosas sucedidas en la corte de España, desde 1599 hasta 1614* [c. 1614] (Madrid, 1857).

Cortes de los Antiguos Reinos de Castilla y León. 5 vols. (Madrid, 1857).

Costa, Giovanni da. *Ragionamiento sopra la triegua de Paesi Bassi* (Genoa, 1610).

Covarrubias Orozco, Sebastián de. *Tesoro de la lengua castellana o española* [1611], facsimile edn. (Madrid, 1984).

Cuartas Rivero, Margarita. "El control de los funcionarios públicos a finales del siglo XVI," *Hacienda Pública Española*, 87 (1984).

Cueto, Ronald. *Quimeras y sueños: los profetas y la monarquía católica de Felipe IV* (Valladolid, 1994).

Danvila y Burguero, Alfonso. *Don Cristóbal de Moura, primer marqués de Castel Rodrigo (1538–1613)* (Madrid, 1900).

Danvila y Collado, Manuel. *El poder civil en España*, 6 vols. (Madrid, 1885–6).

"Nuevos datos para escribir la historia de las Cortes de Castilla en el reinado de Felipe III," *BRAH*, 8 (1886).

Diario de un estudiante de Salamanca. La crónica inédita de Girolamo da Sommaia (1603–1607), ed. George Haley (Salamanca, 1971).

Diccionario de Autoridades [1726], 3 vols., facsimile edn. (Madrid, 1969).

Dios, Salustiano de. *El Consejo Real de Castilla (1385–1522)* (Madrid, 1982).

Gracia, merced y patronazgo real. La Cámara de Castilla entre 1474–1530 (Madrid, 1993).

Documentos relativos al archiduque Alberto de Austria, Codoin, 42–3 (Madrid, 1863).

Domínguez Ortiz, Antonio. *La sociedad española en el siglo XVI*, 2 vols. (Madrid, 1963).

Crisis y decadencia de la España de los Austrias (Madrid, 1969).

Las clases privilegiadas en el antiguo régimen (Madrid, 1973).

Domínguez Ortiz, Antonio, and Bernard Vincent. *Historia de los moriscos* (Madrid, 1978).

Ebreo, Leone. *Dialoghi di Amore*, trans. Garcilaso de la Vega, el Inca, 1590, facsimile edn. (Seville, 1989).

Egido, Teófanes. *Sátiras políticas de la España moderna* (Madrid, 1973).

Eguiluz, Federico. *Robert Persons, "el architraidor"* (Madrid, 1990).

Eiras Roel, Antonio. "Desvío y 'mudanza' de Francia en 1616," *Hispania*, 100 (1965).

"Política francesa de Felipe III: las tensiones con Enrique IV," *Hispania*, 118 (1971).

Bibliography

Elias, Norbert. *The Court Society*, trans. Edmund Jephcott (New York, 1983).

The Civilizing Process: The History of Manners and State Formation and Civilization, trans. Edmund Jephcott (Oxford, 1994).

Elliott, John. H. *Imperial Spain* (London, 1963).

The Revolt of the Catalans (Cambridge, 1963).

Richelieu and Olivares (Cambridge, 1984).

"Yet another crisis?" in Peter Clark, ed., *The European crisis of the 1590s* (London, 1985).

The Count-Duke of Olivares. The Statesman in an Age of Decline (New Haven, 1986).

Spain and its World, 1500–1700 (New Haven, 1989).

"A Europe of Composite Monarchies," *Past and Present*, 137 (1992).

Elliott, John H. and Laurence B. Brockliss, eds., *The World of the Favourite* (New Haven and London, 1999).

Elliott, John H., and J. F. de la Peña, eds. *Memoriales y cartas del conde duque de Olivares*, 2 vols. (Madrid, 1978–81).

Entrambasaguas, Joaquín de. *Una familia de ingenios: Los Ramírez de Prado* (Madrid, 1943).

Erasmus, Desiderius. *The Education of a Christian Prince*, ed. Lester K. Born (New York, 1965).

Collected Works, ed. A. H. T. Levi, vol. XXVII (Toronto, 1974).

The Correspondence of Erasmus, ed. A. H. T. Levi (Toronto, 1974).

Escagedo y Salmón, Mateo, ed. "Los Acebedos," *Boletín de la Biblioteca Menéndez y Pelayo*, 5–9 (1923–7).

Escobar, Jesús Roberto. "The Plaza Mayor of Madrid: Architecture, Urbanism and the Imperial Capital, 1560–1640," Ph.D. diss. Princeton University, 1996.

Escudero, José Antonio. *Los secretarios de estado y del despacho*, 4 vols. (Madrid, 1976).

"Los poderes de Lerma," *Homenaje al profesor García-Gallo*, 2 vols. (Madrid, 1996), vol. II, pp. 47–103.

Espejo, Cristóbal. *El Consejo de hacienda bajo la Presidencia del Marqués de Poza* (Madrid, 1924).

"Enumeración y atribuciones de algunas juntas de la administración española desde el siglo XVI hasta el año 1800," *Revista de la Biblioteca, Archivo y Museo del Ayuntamiento de Madrid*, 8 (1931).

Euben, J. P. "Corruption," in Terence Ball, James Farr, and Russell L. Hanson, eds., *Political Innovation and Conceptual Change* (Cambridge, 1989).

Felipe II. "Instrucción del señor Don Felipe II a don Diego de Covarrubias, obispo de Segovia, presidente de Castilla" [1588], *Seminario Erudito de Valladares*, 30 (1790).

Felipe III. *Cartas de Felipe III a su hija Ana, Reina de Francia (1616–1618)*, ed. Ricardo Martorell Téllez-Girón (Madrid, 1920).

Fernández Albaladejo, Pablo. *Fragmentos de Monarquía* (Madrid, 1992).

Fernández Alvarez, Manuel. "Las instrucciones políticas de los Austrias Mayores: Problemas e interpretaciones," *Gesammelte Aufsätze zur Kulturgeschichte Spaniens*, 23 (1967).

Fernández Alvarez, Manuel, ed. *Corpus Documental de Carlos V*, 4 vols. (Salamanca, 1973–9).

Fernández de Caso, Francisco. *Discurso en que se refieren las solemnidades y fiestas con que el excelentísimo señor duque celebró en su villa de Lerma la dedicación de la Iglesia Colegial y traslaciones de los conventos que ha edificado allí* (n.p., 1617).

Printed works

Oración gratulatoria al capelo del ilustrísimo y excelentísimo señor cardenal duque (n.p., 1618).

Fernández Conti, Santiago. "La nobleza cortesana: don Diego de Cabrera y Bobadilla, tercer conde de Chinchón," in José Martínez Millán, ed., *La Corte de Felipe II* (Madrid, 1994).

Fernández Martín, Luis. "La marquesa del Valle. Una vida dramática en la corte de los Austrias," *Hispania*, 39 (1979).

Fernández de Medrano, Juan. *República mixta* (Madrid, 1602).

Fernández de Navarrete, Pedro. *Conservación de monarquías y discursos políticos* [1626], ed. Michael D. Gordon (Madrid, 1982).

Fernández de Oviedo, Gonzalo. *Libro de la cámara real del príncipe don Juan y oficios de su casa y servicio ordinario* [1530?], ed. J. M. Escudero (Madrid, 1870).

Batallas y quinquagenas, ed. Juan Pérez de Tudela (Madrid, 1983).

Fernández-Santamaría, José A. *Reason of State and Statecraft in Spanish Political Thought (1595–1640)* (Lanham, Md., 1983).

Feros, Antonio. "Lerma y Olivares: la práctica del valimiento en la primera mitad del seiscientos," in John H. Elliott and Angel García Sanz, eds., *La España del Conde-Duque de Olivares* (Valladolid, 1990).

"Vicedioses pero humanos: el drama del rey," *Cuadernos de Historia Moderna*, 14 (1993).

"Twin Souls: Monarchs and Favourites in Early Seventeenth-century Spain," in Richard Kagan and Geoffrey Parker, eds., *Spain, Europe and the Atlantic World: Essays in Honour of John H. Elliott* (Cambridge, 1995).

"El viejo Felipe y los nuevos favoritos: formas de gobierno en la década de 1590," *Studia Histórica*, 17 (1997).

"Images of Evil, Images of Kings: the Contrasting Faces of the Royal Favourite in Early Modern Political Literature, *c.* 1570–*c.* 1650", in John H. Elliott and Laurence W. Brockliss, eds., *The World of the Favourite* (New Haven and London, 1999).

Ferraro, Domenico. *Tradizione e ragione in Juan de Mariana* (Milan, 1989).

Ferrer Valls, Teresa. *La práctica escénica cortesana: de la época del emperador a la de Felipe III* (London, 1991).

Florencia, Gerónimo de. *Sermón que predicó a la Majestad del rey don Felipe III en las honras que su Majd. hizo a la serenísima reina doña Margarita su mujer, en San Gerónimo el Real de Madrid a 18 de noviembre de 1611* (Madrid, 1612).

Sermón que predicó a la majestad católica del rey Don Felipe Quarto (Madrid, 1621).

Florit, José M. "Inventario de los cuadros y otros objetos de arte de la quinta real llamada 'La Ribera' en Valladolid," *Boletín de la Sociedad Española de Excursiones*, 14 (1906).

Fonseca, Cristóbal de. *Discursos para todos los evangelios de Cuaresma* (Madrid, 1614).

Fonseca, Damián de. *Justa expulsión de los moriscos de España* (Rome, 1612).

Relación de lo que pasó en la expulsión de los moriscos del reino de Valencia (Rome, 1612).

Fortea Pérez, José Ignacio. *Monarquía y cortes en la corona de Castilla. Las ciudades ante la política fiscal de Felipe II* (Salamanca, 1990).

"El servicio de millones y la reestructuración del espacio fiscal en la Corona de Castilla (1601–1621)," in José Ignacio Fortea Pérez and Carmen Cremades Griñán, eds., *Política y hacienda en el Antiguo Régimen* (Murcia, 1993).

Foucault, Michel. *Power/Knowledge: Selected Interviews and Other Writings 1972–1977* (London, 1980).

Bibliography

Furió Ceriol, Fadrique. *El concejo y consejeros del príncipe* [1559], ed. Diego Sevilla (Valencia, 1952).

Gachard, M. *Collection des voyages des souverains des Pays-Bas*, 3 vols. (Brussels, 1874).

Galasso, Giuseppe. *Alla periferia dell'impero. Il regno di Napoli nel periodo spagnolo (secoli XVI–XVII)* (Turin, 1994).

Galino Carrillo, María Angeles. *Los tratados sobre educación de príncipes, siglos XVI y XVII* (Madrid, 1948).

Gállego, Julián. *Visión y símbolos en la pintura española del siglo de oro* (Madrid, 1984).

García, Carlos. *La oposición y conjunción de los dos grandes luminares de la tierra, o la antipatía de franceses y españoles* [1617], ed. Michel Bareau (Alberta, 1979).

García Arenal, Mercedes. *Los moriscos* (Madrid, 1975).

Inquisición y moriscos: los procesos del tribunal de Cuenca (Madrid, 1978).

García Cárcel, Ricardo. "The Course of the Moriscos up to Their Expulsion," in Angel Alcalá, ed., *The Spanish Inquisition and the Inquisitorial Mind* (Highland Lakes, N.J., 1987).

García-Cuenca Ariati, Tomás. "El Consejo de Hacienda (1476–1803)," in Miguel Artola, ed., *La economía española al final del Antiguo Régimen* (Madrid, 1982).

García de Enterría, María Cruz. *Sociedad y poesía de cordel en el barroco* (Madrid, 1973).

García García, Bernardo José. *La pax hispánica. Política exterior del duque de Lerma* (Leuven, 1996).

García Rámila, Ismael. *El gran burgalés don Diego Gómez de Sandoval, primer conde de Castro (1385–1455)* (Burgos, 1953).

Garrido Aranda, Antonio. *Moriscos e indios: precedentes hispánicos de la evangelización en México* (Mexico City, 1985).

Gascón de Torquemada, Gerónimo. *Gaceta y nuevas de la corte de España desde el año 1600 en adelante*, ed. Alfonso de Ceballos-Escalera y Gila (Madrid, 1991).

Gauna, Felipe de. *Relación de las fiestas celebradas en Valencia con motivo del casamiento de Felipe III*, ed. Salvador Carretes Zacarés, 2 vols. (Valencia, 1926).

Gea Ortigas, María Isabel. *El Madrid desaparecido* (Madrid, 1992).

Geertz, Clifford. *Negara. The Theatre State in Nineteenth-Century Bali* (Princeton, 1980).

Gelabert, Juan E. "Sobre la fundación del Consejo de Hacienda," in José Ignacio Fortea Pérez and Carmen María Cremades Griñán, eds., *Política y hacienda en el Antiguo Régimen* (Murcia, 1993).

La bolsa del rey. Rey, reino y fisco en Castilla (Barcelona, 1997).

Giesey, Ralph. "The President of Parlement at the Royal Funeral," *The Sixteenth Century Journal*, 6 (1976).

Gil, David Bernabé. "La fiscalidad en los territorios peninsulares de la corona de Aragón durante la época de los Austrias," in José Ignacio Fortea Pérez and Carmen María Cremades Griñán, eds., *Política y hacienda en el Antiguo Régimen* (Murcia, 1993).

Gil Pujol, Xavier. "De las alteraciones a la estabilidad," Ph.D. diss., University of Barcelona, 1990.

Gilbert, Felix. *Machiavelli and Guicciardini* (Princeton, 1965).

Goldberg, Edward L. "Artistic Relations between the Medici and the Spanish Courts, 1587–1621: Part I," *The Burlington Magazine*, 138 (1996).

Printed works

Gombrich, E. H. *The Image and the Eye. Further Studies in the Psychology of Pictorial Representation* (Oxford, 1982).

Symbolic Images. Studies in the Art in the Renaissance (Chicago, 1985).

"Getting the Picture," *New York Review of Books*, 40/5 (1993).

Gómez de Sandoval Manrique de Padilla, Francisco. *Memorial dirigido por don Francisco Gómez de Sandoval Manrique de Padilla, duque de Lerma, al rey Felipe IV contra una demanda del fiscal don Juan de Chumacero de Sotomayor, sobre las donaciones y mercedes que le hizo Felipe III al abuelo del litigante* (n.p., n.d.).

González de Amezúa y Mayo, Agustín. "Cómo se hacía un libro en nuestro siglo de oro," in González de Amezúa y Mayo, *Opúsculos histórico-literarios*, vol. 1 (Madrid, 1951).

González de Cellorigo, Martín. *Memorial de la política necesaria y útil restauración a la república de España* [1600], ed. José L. Pérez de Ayala (Valladolid, 1991).

González Dávila, Gil. *Teatro de las grandezas de la villa de Madrid, corte de los reyes católicos de España* (Madrid, 1623).

Historia de la vida y hechos del ínclito monarca, amado y santo don Felipe Tercero [1632] (Madrid, 1771).

González Palencia, Angel, *Gonzalo Pérez, secretario de Felipe II*, 2 vols. (Madrid, 1946).

González Palencia, Angel, ed. *La Junta de reformación* (Valladolid, 1932).

ed. *Noticias de Madrid, 1621–1627* (Madrid, 1942).

Gracián Dantisco, Lucas. *Galateo español* [1585], ed. Ciriaco Pérez Bustamante (Madrid, 1943).

Gracián de la Madre de Dios, Jerónimo. *Diez lamentaciones del miserable estado de los ateístas de nuestro tiempo* [1611], in *Beatus vir, carne de hoguera*, ed. Emilia Navarro de Kelley (Madrid, 1977).

Greenblatt, Stephen. *Shakespearean Negotiations* (Berkeley, 1988).

Greengrass, Mark. *France in the Age of Henry IV. The Struggle for Stability* (London, 1984).

Guadalajara y Xavier, Marco de. *Memorable expulsión y justísimo destierro de los moriscos de España* (Pamplona, 1613).

Guevara, Antonio de. *Aviso de privados o despertador de cortesanos* [1539], ed. A. Alvarez de la Villa (Paris, 1914).

Menosprecio de corte y alabanza de aldea [1539], ed. Asunción Rallo Gruss (Madrid, 1984).

Gurmendi, Francisco de. *Doctrina física y moral de príncipes* (Madrid, 1615).

Guzmán, Diego de. *Vida y muerte de doña Margarita de Austria, reina de España* (Madrid, 1617).

Halperín Donghi, Tulio. *Un conflicto nacional: moriscos y cristianos viejos en Valencia* (Valencia, 1980).

Headley, J. M. "Campanella, America, and World Evangelization," in Karen Ordahl Kupperman, ed., *America in European Consciousness, 1493–1750* (Chapel Hill, 1995).

Tommaso Campanella and the Transformation of the World (Princeton, 1997).

Hermosilla, Diego. *Diálogo de los pajes* [c. 1543] (Madrid, 1989).

Herrera, Pedro de. *Traslación del Santísimo Sacramento a la iglesia colegial de San Pedro de la villa de Lerma* (Madrid, 1618).

Herrera y Tordesillas, Antonio de. *Elogio a don Juan de Zúñiga Bazán y Abellaneda, primer duque de Peñaranda* (Madrid, 1608).

Bibliography

Herrero García, Miguel. "La monarquía teorética de Lope de Vega," *Fenix*, 3 (1935).

Ideas de los españoles del siglo XVII (Madrid, 1966)

Hespanha, Antonio M. *História das instituições* (Coimbra, 1982).

La gracia del derecho. Economía de la cultura en la edad moderna (Madrid, 1993).

Hess, A. C. "The Moriscos. An Ottoman Fifth Column in Sixteenth-century Spain," *American Historical Review*, 74 (1968).

Hinojosa y Navajeros, Ricardo. *Despachos de la diplomacia pontificia en España* (Madrid, 1896).

Holles, John. *Letter book of John Holles*, in *Historical Manuscripts Commission: Manuscripts of the Duke of Portland*, vol. IX, (London, 1923).

Howell, James. *Epistolae Ho-Elianae. The Familiar Letters of James Howell*, ed. Joseph Jacobs, 2 vols. (London, 1892).

Huarte de San Juan, Juan. *Examen de ingenios para las ciencias* [1575], ed. Esteban Torre (Madrid, 1977).

Huemer, Frances. *Corpus Rubenianum Ludwig Burchard. Part XIX: Portraits* (London, 1977).

Hurstfield, Joel. *Freedom, Corruption and Government in Elizabethan England* (Cambridge, 1973).

Hurtado de Mendoza, Antonio. *Discursos de Antonio de Mendoza*, ed. Marqués de Alcedo (Madrid, 1911).

Iñiguez de Lequerica, Juan, ed. *Sermones funerales en las honras del rey nuestro señor don Felipe II, con el que se predicó en las de la serenísima infanta doña Catalina duquesa de Saboya* (Madrid, 1599).

Iñurritegui Rodríguez, José María. *La gracia y la república. El lenguaje político de la teología católica y el "Príncipe Cristiano" de Pedro de Rybadeneyra* (Madrid, 1998).

Israel, Jonathan I. *The Dutch Republic and the Hispanic World, 1606–1661* (Oxford, 1982).

The Dutch Republic. Its Rise, Greatness and Fall, 1477–1806 (Oxford, 1995).

Jackson, Richard A. "The Sleeping King," *Bibliothèque d'Humanisme et Renaissance*, 31 (1969).

Jago, Charles. "Aristocracy, War and Finance in Castile, 1621–1665," Ph.D. diss., Cambridge University, 1969.

"The Influence of Debt on the Relations between Crown and Aristocracy in Seventeenth-Century Castile," *Economic History Review*, 26 (1973).

"Habsburg Absolutism and the Cortes of Castile," *American Historical Review*, 86 (1981).

"Fiscalidad y cambio constitucional en Castilla, 1601–1621," in José Ignacio Fortea Pérez and Carmen María Cremades Griñán, eds., *Política y hacienda en el Antiguo Régimen* (Murcia, 1993).

"Taxation and Political Culture in Castile, 1590–1640," in Richard Kagan and Geoffrey Parker, eds., *Spain, Europe and the Atlantic World. Essays in Honour of John H. Elliott* (Cambridge, 1995).

Jarava, Juan de. *Problemas o preguntas problemáticas* (Alcalá de Henares, 1546).

Juderías, Julián. "Los favoritos de Felipe III: don Pedro de Franqueza, conde de Villalonga y secretario de estado," *RABM*, 13 (1909).

Kagan, Richard L. *Lucrecia's Dreams. Politics and Prophecy in Sixteenth-Century Spain* (Berkeley, 1990).

Printed works

Kamen, Henry. *Philip of Spain* (New Haven, 1997).

Kantorowicz, Ernst H. *The King's Two Bodies* (Princeton, 1957).

Keniston, Hayward. *Francisco de los Cobos, Secretary of the Emperor Charles V* (Pittsburgh, Pa., 1960).

Kennedy, Ruth Lee. "The Madrid of 1617–25. Certain Aspects of Social, Moral, and Educational Reform," in *Estudios Hispánicos en Homenaje a Archer M. Huntington* (Wellesley, Mass., 1952).

Kertzer, David I. *Ritual, Politics and Power* (New Haven, 1984).

Kettering, Sharon. *Patrons, Brokers, and Clients in Seventeenth-Century France* (New York, 1986).

Kirk, Douglas. "Instrumental Music in Lerma, c. 1608," *Early Music*, 23 (1995).

Kirsch, Arthur. "Shakespeare's Tragedies," in John F. Andrews, ed., *William Shakespeare. His World, His Work, His Influence*, vol. II (New York, 1985).

Kivelson, Valerie A. "The Devil Stole His Mind: The Tsar and the 1648 Moscow Uprising," *American Historical Review*, 98 (1993).

Koenigsberger, H. G. *The Practice of Empire* (Ithaca, 1969).

Estates and Revolutions. Essays in Early Modern European History (New York, 1971).

"The Statecraft of Philip II," *European Studies Review*, 1 (1971).

Kooi, Christine. "Popish Impudence: The Perseverance of the Roman Catholic Faithful in Calvinist Holland, 1572–1620," *Sixteenth Century Journal*, 26 (1995).

Kossmann, E. H. "The Singularity of Absolutism," in R. Hatton, ed., *Louis XV and Absolutism* (London, 1976).

Kusche, Maria. *Juan Pantoja de la Cruz* (Madrid, 1964).

Ladero Quesada, Miguel Angel. *La hacienda real de Castilla en el siglo XV* (Seville, 1973).

Los Reyes Católicos: La corona y la unidad de España (Valencia, 1989).

Lagomarsino, David. "Court Factions and the Formulation of Spanish Policy towards the Netherlands (1559–1567)," Ph.D. diss., Cambridge University, 1973.

Laínez, Fray José. *El privado cristiano deducido de las vidas de Joseph y Daniel* (Madrid, 1641). *El Daniel cortesano* (Madrid, 1644).

El Josué esclarecido. Caudillo, vencedor de reyes y gentes (Madrid, 1653).

Lerma, Duque de. *Descripción e inventario de las rentas, bienes y hacienda del cardenal duque de Lerma* (Valladolid, 1622).

Lhermite, Jehan. *Le Passetemps*, ed. Ch. Ruelens, 2 vols. (Antwerp, 1890–6).

Liedtke, Walter A. *The Royal Horse and Rider. Painting, Sculpture and Horsemanship, 1500–1800* (New York, 1989).

Liñán y Verdugo, Antonio. *Guía y avisos de forasteros que vienen a la corte* [1620], ed. Edisons Simons (Madrid, 1980).

Lipsius, Justus. *Epistolario de Justo Lipsio y los españoles (1577–1606)*, ed. Alejandro Ramírez (Madrid, 1966).

Los seis libros de la política, o doctrina civil, que sirven para el gobierno del reino o principado, trans. Bernardino de Mendoza [1604], ed. Javier Peña Echevarría and Modesto Santos López (Madrid, 1997).

Loomie, Albert J. *Spain and the Early Stuarts, 1585–1655* (Aldershot, 1996).

López Bravo, Mateo. *Del rey y de la razón de gobernar* [1616], ed. Henry Méchoulan (Madrid, 1977).

Bibliography

López de Hoyos, Juan. *Real aparato y suntuoso recibimiento con que Madrid recibió a la serenísima reina doña Ana de Austria* [1572], facsimile edn. (Madrid, 1976).

López Madera, Gregorio. *Excelencias de la monarquía y reino de España* (Madrid, 1597).

López Torrijos, Rosa. *La mitología en la pintura española del siglo de oro* (Madrid, 1985).

López de Villalobos, Francisco. *Algunas obras*, 2 vols. (Madrid, 1886).

López de Zárate, Francisco. *Varias poesías* (Madrid, 1619).

Louis XIV. *Mémoires for the Instruction of the Dauphin*, ed. Paul Sonnino (New York, 1970).

Lovett, A. W. *Philip II and Mateo Vázquez de Leça: the Government of Spain (1572–1592)* (Geneva, 1977).

Early Habsburg Spain, 1517–1598 (Oxford, 1986).

Luhmann, Niklas. *Love as Passion*, trans. Jeremy Gaines and Doris L. Jones (Cambridge, Mass., 1986).

Luxán Meléndez, Santiago de. "El control de la hacienda portuguesa: la Junta de Hacienda de Portugal, 1602–1608," in José Ignacio Fortea Pérez and Carmen María Cremades Griñán, eds., *Política y hacienda en el Antiguo Régimen* (Murcia, 1993).

Lynch, John. *The Hispanic World in Crisis and Change, 1598–1700* (Oxford, 1992).

MacCurdy, Raymond. *The Tragic Fall: Don Alvaro de Luna and Other Favorites in Spanish Golden Age Drama* (Chapel Hill, N.C., 1978).

Machiavelli, Niccolò. *The Prince*, ed. Quentin Skinner and Russell Price (Cambridge, 1988).

Madariaga, Juan de. *Del senado y de su príncipe* (Valencia, 1617).

Maltby, William. *Alba: A Biography of Fernández Alvarez de Toledo* (Berkeley, 1983).

Malvezzi, Virgilio. *David perseguido* (Madrid, 1635).

Retrato del privado cristiano político deducido de las acciones del conde duque (Bologna, 1635).

Historia del marqués Virgilio Malvezzi [1640], in Juan Yáñez, *Memorias para la historia de don Felipe III, rey de España* (Madrid, 1773).

Historia de los primeros años del reinado de Felipe IV, ed. D. L. Shaw (Madrid, 1968).

Il ritratto del privato cristiano [1635], ed. Maria Luisa Doglio (Palermo, 1993).

Mantuano, Pedro. *Casamientos de España y Francia* (Madrid, 1618).

Marañón, Gregorio. *Antonio Pérez (el hombre, el drama, la época)*, 2 vols. (Madrid, 1951).

Maravall, José Antonio. *Teoría española del estado en el siglo XVII* (Madrid, 1944).

Las Comunidades de Castilla (Madrid, 1963).

March, José M. *Niñez y juventud de Felipe II*, 2 vols. (Madrid, 1941–2).

Mariana, Juan de. *Obras del Padre Juan de Mariana*, ed. F. Pi y Margall, 2 vols. (Madrid, 1950).

De rege et regis institutione (La dignidad real y la educación del príncipe) [1599], ed. Luis Sánchez Agesta (Madrid, 1981).

Marin, Louis. *Portrait of the King*, trans. Martha M. Houle (Minneapolis, Minn., 1988).

Marineo Sículo, Lucio. *Las cosas memorables de España* (n.p., 1530).

Márquez, Juan. *El gobernador christiano deducido de las vidas de Moisés y Josué, príncipes del pueblo de Dios* (Salamanca, 1612).

"Opúsculo del maestro Fray Juan Márquez: si los predicadores evangélicos pueden reprehender públicamente a los Reyes y Prelados Eclesiásticos," *La Ciudad de Dios*, 46 (1898).

Márquez Torres, Francisco. *Discursos consolatorios al excmo. sr. don Cristóbal de Sandoval y Rojas, duque de Uceda, en la temprana muerte del señor don Bernardo de Sandoval y Rojas, primer marqués de Belmonte, su caro hijo* (Madrid, 1616).

Martí y Monsó, José. *Estudios histórico-artísticos relativos principalmente a Valladolid* (Valladolid, 1898).

"Los Calderones y el monasterio de Nuestra Señora de Portaceli," *Boletín de la Sociedad Castellana de Excursiones*, 83–5 (1908–10).

Martínez Hernández, Santiago. "La nobleza cortesana en el reinado de Felipe II. Don Gómez Dávila y Toledo, segundo marqués de Velada, una carrera política labrada al amparo de la corona," *Torre de los Lujanes*, 33 (1997).

Martínez Millán, José M. "Un curioso manuscrito: el libro de gobierno del cardenal Diego de Espinosa (1512?–1572)," *Hispania*, 53 (1993).

Mártir Rizo, Juan Pablo. *Historia de la vida de Lucio Anneo Séneca, español* [1626], ed. B. de la Vega (Madrid, 1944).

La Poética de Aristóteles traducida del latín [1623], ed. Margerete Newels (Cologne, 1965).

Historia de la muy noble y leal ciudad de Cuenca [1629], facsimile edn. (Barcelona, 1979).

Norte de príncipes (1626) y Vida de Rómulo, ed. José Antonio Maravall (Madrid, 1988).

Martire d'Angheria, Pietro. *Epistolario de Pedro Mártir de Anglería*, ed. J. López Toro, 4 vols. (Madrid, 1953–7).

Marvick, Elizabeth W. "Favorites in Early Modern Europe: a Recurring Psychopolitical Role," *Journal of Psychohistory*, 10 (1983).

Matute Peñafiel, Diego. *Prosapia de Cristo* (Baeza, 1614).

Mauss, Marcel. *The Gift. The Form and Reason for Exchange in Archaic Societies*, trans. W. D. Halls (New York, 1990).

Mayerne, Louis de. *The General Histoire of Spaine* [1583], trans. Edward Grimston (London, 1612).

Medrano, Francisco de. *Poesía*, ed. Dámaso Alonso (Madrid, 1988).

Memorial de los artículos que están vistos por los señores del consejo en el pleito entre el señor fiscal y el reino, con el señor cardenal duque de Lerma y sus sucesores (n.p., 1653).

Memorial del pleito de tenuta que es entre don Gregorio de Sandoval Silva y Mendoza, conde de Saldaña por la tenuta y posesión de los bienes de los estados y mayorazgos de Lerma, Cea y Ampudia (n.p., n.d.).

Mendes da Luz, Francisco Paulo. *O Conselho da India* (Lisbon, 1952).

Mercader, Gaspar de. *El prado de Valencia* [1600], ed. H. Merimée (Toulouse, 1907).

Merriman, Roger B. *The Rise of the Spanish Empire*, vol. IV (New York, 1962).

Mira de Amescua, Antonio. *La segunda de don Alvaro (Adversa Fortuna de don Alvaro)*, ed. N. E. Sánchez-Arce (Mexico City, 1960).

Comedia famosa de Ruy López de Avalos (Primera parte de don Alvaro de Luna), ed. N. E. Sánchez-Arce (Mexico City, 1965).

Mitchell, Banner. *The Majesty of the State. Triumphal Progresses of Foreign Sovereigns in Renaissance Italy (1494–1600)* (Florence, 1986).

Moffitt, John F. "Rubens's *Duke of Lerma, Equestrian* amongst 'Imperial Horsemen,'" *Artibus et Historiae*, 15 (1994).

Moncada, Sancho de. *Restauración política de España* [1618], ed. Jean Vilar (Madrid, 1974).

Montalto Cessi, Donatella. "L'immagine dell'imperio e della Spagna nella circolazione delle idee politiche in Spagna dal XVI al XVII secolo," in Massimi Ganci and Ruggiero Romano, eds., *Gobernare il mondo. L'imperio spagnolo dal XV al XIX secolo* (Palermo, 1995).

Monter, William. *Frontiers of Heresy. The Spanish Inquisition from the Basque Lands to Sicily* (Cambridge, 1990).

Morán, José Miguel. "Felipe III y las Artes," *Anales de Historia del Arte*, 1 (1989).

Morel-Fatio, Alfred. *L'Espagne au XVIe. et au XVIIe. siècle* (Paris, 1878).

Moreno Villa, J., and F. J. Sánchez Cantón. "Noventa y siete retratos de la familia de Felipe III por Bartolomé González," *Archivo Español de Arte y Arqueología*, 38 (1937).

Morford, Mark. *Stoics and Neostoics. Rubens and the Circle of Lipsius* (Princeton, 1991).

Morreale, Margherita. *Castiglione y Boscán: el ideal cortesano en el renacimiento* (Madrid, 1959).

Mousnier, Roland. *The Assassination of Henry IV*, trans. Joan Spencer (New York, 1973).

Mousset, Albert. *Felipe II* (Madrid, 1917).

Moxó, Salvador de. *De la nobleza vieja a la nobleza nueva. La transformación nobiliaria castellana en la baja Edad Media* (Madrid, 1969).

Muir, Edward. *Ritual in Early Modern Europe* (Cambridge, 1997).

Muñoz Jiménez, José Miguel. "Fray Alberto de la Madre de Dios y la arquitectura cortesana: urbanismo en la villa de Lerma," *Goya*, 211–12 (1989).

Muto, Giovanni. *Le finanze publiche napolitane tra riforme e ristaurazione* (Naples, 1980).

Nader, Helen. "Habsburg Ceremony in Spain: The Reality of the Myth," *Historical Reflections/Réflexions Historiques*, 15 (1988).

Narbona, Eugenio de. *Doctrina política civil* (Madrid, 1621).

Navarro Latorre, J. *Aproximación a Fray Luis de Aliaga, confesor de Felipe III* (Zaragoza, 1981).

Neale, J. E. *Essays in Elizabethan History* (London, 1958).

Newcome, Mary. "Genoese Drawings for the Queen's Gallery in El Pardo," *Antichità Viva*, 29 (1990).

Novoa, Matías de. *Historia de Felipe III, rey de España* [*c.* 1640s], *Codoin*, 60–1 (Madrid, 1875).

Historia de Felipe IV, rey de España [*c.* 1640s], *Codoin*, 69, 77, 80, 86 (Madrid, 1876–6).

Nueva recopilación de las leyes del reino, 5 vols. (Madrid, 1982).

Núñez de Salcedo, Pedro. "Relación verdadera de todos los títulos que hay en España" [1597], *BRAH*, 73 (1918).

Ochoa, Eugenio, ed. *Epistolario español*, 2 vols. (Madrid, 1952).

Oestreich, Gerhard. *Neostoicism and the Early Modern State*, trans. David McLintock; ed., Brigitta Oestreich and H. G. Koenigsberger (Cambridge, 1982).

Ordenanzas del Consejo de Hacienda de 1554, 1579, 1593, 1602 y 1621. (n.p., n.d.).

Orgel, Stephen. *The Illusion of Power* (Berkeley, 1975).

Orso, Steven N. *Philip IV and the Decoration of the Alcázar de Madrid* (Princeton, 1986).

Ossorio y Gallardo, Angel. *Los hombres de toga en el proceso de Don Rodrigo Calderón* (Madrid, 1918).

Osten Sachen, Cornelia von der. *San Lorenzo el Real de El Escorial* (Bilbao, 1984).

Pagden, Anthony. *Lords of all the World. Ideologies of Empire in Spain, Britain and France c. 1500–c. 1800* (New Haven, 1995).

Printed works

Paravicini, Werner. "The Court of the Dukes of Burgundy. A Model for Europe?" in R. G. Asch and A. M. Birke, eds, *Princes, Patronage and the Nobility. The Court at the Beginning of the Modern Age*, c. *1450–1650* (Oxford, 1991).

Parker, Geoffrey. *The Army of Flanders and the Spanish Road, 1567–1659* (Cambridge, 1972).

Philip II (Boston, 1978).

The Thirty Years' War (London, 1984).

"David or Goliath? Philip II and his World in the 1580s," in Richard Kagan and Geoffrey Parker, eds., *Spain, Europe and the Atlantic World. Essays in Honour of John H. Elliott* (Cambridge, 1995).

The Grand Strategy of Philip II (New Haven, 1998).

Parrott, David. "The Mantuan Succession, 1627–31: A Sovereignty Dispute in Early Modern Europe," *English Historical Review*, 112 (1997).

Patrizi, Francesco. *Del reino y de la institución del que ha de reinar* [1470s], trans. Enrique Garcés (Madrid, 1591).

Paz y Meliá, Antonio, ed. "Correspondencia del conde de Lemos con don Francisco de Castro, su hermano, y con el príncipe de Esquilache (1613–1620)," *Bulletin Hispanique*, 5 (1903).

ed. *Documentos del archivo y biblioteca del excmo. sr. duque de Medinaceli* (n.p., n.d.).

Pellicer de Tovar, José. *Lecciones solemnes a las obras de don Luis de Góngora y Argote* [1630], facsimile edn. (New York, 1971).

Pelorson, Jean-Marc. "La Politisation de la satire sous Philippe III et Philippe IV," in *La Contestation de la société dans la littérature espagnole du siècle d'or* (Toulouse, 1981).

Perdices, Luis. *La economía política de la decadencia de Castilla en el siglo XVII* (Madrid, 1996).

Pérez, Antonio. *Relaciones y cartas*, ed. Alfredo Alvar Ezquerra, 2 vols. (Madrid, 1986).

Pérez Bustamante, Ciriaco. "Los cardenalatos del duque de Lerma y del cardenal infante don Fernando," *Boletín de la Biblioteca Menéndez y Pelayo*, 7 (1934).

La España de Felipe III (Madrid, 1983).

Pérez de Herrera, Cristóbal. "Carta apologética al doctor Luis del Valle defendiendo su buena intención al publicar su obra sobre los males y remedios del Reino," *Codoin*, 18 (Madrid, 1874).

Pérez Martín, María Jesús. *Margarita de Austria, reina de España* (Madrid, 1961).

Pérez Mínguez, Fidel. *Don Juan de Idiáquez. Embajador y consejero de Felipe II* (San Sebastian, 1935).

Pérez Moreda, Vicente. *La crisis de mortalidad en la España interior, siglos XVI–XIX* (Madrid, 1980).

Peters, Edward. *The Shadow King. Rex Inutilis in the Medieval Law and Literature, 751–1327* (New Haven, 1970).

Phelan, John Leddy. *The Millennial Kingdom of the Franciscans in the New World* (Berkeley, 1970).

Pineda, Fray Juan de. *Los treinta libros de la monarquía eclesiástica, o Historia universal del mundo*, 5 vols. (Barcelona, 1594).

Pinheiro da Veiga, Tomé. *Fastiginia o fastos geniales* [1605], ed. Narciso Alonso Cortés (Valladolid, 1916).

Pinto Crespo, Virgilio. *Inquisición y control ideológico en la España del siglo XVI* (Madrid, 1983).

Bibliography

Pizzolato, Luigi. *La idea de la amistad*, trans. José Ramón Monreal (Barcelona, 1996).

Pliny the Elder. *Historia natural de los animales*, trans. Jerónimo de Huerta (Madrid, 1603).

Pocock, J. G. A. *The Machiavellian Moment* (Princeton, 1975).

"The Concept of a Language and the *métier d'historien*: Some Considerations in Practice," in Anthony Pagden, ed., *The Languages of Political Theory in Early-Modern Europe* (Cambridge, 1987).

"Texts as Events: Reflections on the History of Political Thought," in Kevin Sharpe and Steven N. Zwicker, eds., *Politics of Discourse. The Literature and History of Seventeenth-Century England* (London, 1987).

"Machiavelli and the Rethinking of History," *Rivista di Storia delle Idee Politiche e Sociali*, 27 (1994).

Porreño, Baltasar. *Dichos y hechos del señor rey don Phelipe III el Bueno* [1626], in Juan Yáñez, *Memorias para la historia de don Felipe III, rey de España* (Madrid, 1773).

Dichos y hechos del señor rey don Phelipe Segundo el Prudente [1624] (Madrid, 1949).

Pujades, Jeroni. *Dietari de Jeroni Pujades*, ed. Josep Maria Casas Homs, 4 vols. (Barcelona, 1975–6).

Pulido Bueno, Ildefonso. *La real hacienda de Felipe III* (Huelva, 1996).

Quevedo y Villegas, Francisco de. *Epistolario completo de don Francisco de Quevedo*, ed. Luis Astrana Marín (Madrid, 1946).

Obras completas, ed. Felicidad Buendía, 2 vols. (Madrid, 1960).

Política de Dios y gobierno de Cristo, ed. James O. Crosby (Madrid, 1966).

Ramírez de Prado, Lorenzo. *Consejo y consejeros de príncipes* [1617], ed. Juan Beneyto (Madrid, 1958).

Ranke, Leopold von. *La monarquía española de los siglos XVI y XVII* (Mexico City, 1946).

Ranum, Orest. *Richelieu and the Councillors of Louis XIII* (Oxford, 1963).

"Courtesy, Absolutism, and the Rise of the French State, 1630– 1660," *Journal of Modern History*, 52 (1980).

Reglá, Joan. *Estudios sobre los moriscos* (Barcelona, 1974).

Riba García, Carlos, ed. *Correspondencia privada de Felipe II con su secretario Mateo Vázquez, 1567–1591* (Madrid, 1959).

Ribadeneira, Pedro de. *Patris Petri de Ribadeneira confessiones, epistolae aliaque scripta inedita* [*Monumenta Historica Societatis Iesu*, 60] (Madrid, 1923).

Obras escogidas del Padre Pedro de Ribadeneira, ed. Vicente de la Fuente (Madrid, 1952).

Ribeiro, Michaele. *De ludis lermensibus epistola* (Madrid, 1617).

Ricard, Robert. *The Spiritual Conquest of Mexico* (Berkeley, 1966).

Richelieu, Armand du Plessis, Cardinal Duc de. *Testamento político del Cardenal Duque de Richelieu, Primer Ministro de Francia en el Reinado de Louis XIII*, Spanish trans. Juan de Espínola Baeza (Madrid, 1696).

Rivera Blanco, José J. *El palacio real de Valladolid* (Valladolid, 1981).

Roa Dávila, Fray Juan. *De regnorum iustitia* [1591], ed. Luciano Pereña (Madrid, 1970).

Rodríguez-Salgado, M. J. "The Court of Philip II of Spain," in Ronald G. Asch and Adolf M. Birke, eds., *Princes, Patronage, and the Nobility. The Court at the Beginning of the Modern Age, c. 1450–1650*, (Oxford, 1991).

Rodríguez Villa, Antonio. *Ambrosio Spinola, primer marqués de los Balbases* (Madrid, 1904).

Etiquetas de la casa de Austria (Madrid, 1913).

Printed works

Rodríguez Villa, Antonio, ed. "El emperador Carlos V y su corte (1522–1539): Cartas de D. Martín de Salinas," *Boletín de la Academia de la Historia*, 93 (1903).

Correspondencia de la infanta archiduquesa, doña Isabel Clara Eugenia de Austria, con el duque de Lerma y otros personajes (Madrid, 1906).

Rojas Villandrando, Agustín. *El buen república* (Salamanca, 1611).

Rooney, Peter Thomas. "Habsburg Fiscal Policies in Portugal, 1580–1640," *Journal of European Economic History*, 23/3 (1994).

Roses, Christian Hansen. *Ensayo sobre el pensamiento político del padre Juan de Mariana* (Santiago de Chile, 1959).

Round, Nicholas. *The Greatest Man Uncrowned. A Study of the Fall of Don Alvaro de Luna* (London, 1986).

Ruano, Eloy Benito. "Recepción madrileña de la reina Margarita de Austria," *Anales del Instituto Madrileño*, 1 (1966).

Rubens, Peter Paul. *Letters of Peter Paul Rubens*, ed. Ruth Saunders Magurn (Cambridge, Mass., 1971).

Rubio, José María. *Los ideales hispanos en la tregua de 1609 y en el momento actual* (Valladolid, 1937).

Ruiz Montiano, Gaspar. *Espejo de bienhechores y agradecidos: que contiene los siete libros de beneficios de Lucio Aneo Séneca* (Barcelona, 1606).

Saavedra y Fajardo, Diego de. *Idea de un príncipe político-cristiano representada en cien empresas* [1642], facsimile edn. (Murcia, 1985).

Sainz Rodríguez, Pedro. *Evolución de las ideas sobre la decadencia española* (Madrid, 1962).

Salazar, Juan de. *Política española* [1619], ed. Miguel Herrero García (Madrid, 1945).

Salinas, Conde de. "Dictamen del conde de Salinas en que se examinan las prerogativas de la corona y de las cortes de Portugal" [1612], ed. Erasmo Buceta, in *Anuario de Historia del Derecho Español*, 9 (1932).

Salmerón, Fray Marcos. *El príncipe escondido. Meditaciones de la vida de Cristo desde los doce hasta los treinta años* (Madrid, 1648).

Sánchez, Magdalena. "Confession and Complicity: Margarita de Austria, Richard Haller, S.J., and the Court of Philip III," *Cuadernos de Historia Moderna*, 14 (1993).

The Empress, the Queen, and the Nun: Women and Power at the Court of Philip III of Spain (Baltimore, 1998).

Sánchez Alvarez, Mercedes, ed. *El manuscrito misceláneo 774 de la Biblioteca Nacional de París. (Leyendas, itinerarios de viajes, profecías sobre la destrucción de España y otros relatos moriscos)* (Madrid, 1982).

Sandoval, Prudencio de. *Chrónica del ínclito emperador de España, don Alonso VII* (Madrid, 1600).

Historia de la vida y hechos del emperador Carlos V [1604–6], ed. Carlos Seco Serrano, 3 vols. (Madrid, 1955).

Santa María, Juan de. *República y policía christiana* [1615] (Naples, 1624).

Sarmiento de Acuña, Diego. "Cartas escogidas de las escritas a don Diego Sarmiento de Acuña, conde de Gondomar, o reunidas por éste," *RABM*, 5–6 (1901–2).

Correspondencia oficial de don Diego Sarmiento de Acuña, conde de Gondomar, ed. Antonio Ballesteros y Beretta (*Documentos inéditos para la historia de España*, vols. I–IV (Madrid, 1936–45)).

Schoenfeldt, Michael C. *Prayer and Power. George Herbert and Renaissance Courtship* (Chicago, 1991).

Schroth, Sarah. "The Duke of Lerma and the Art at the Court of Philip III," Paper presented at the meeting of the Society for Spanish and Portuguese Historical Studies, St. Louis, 1987.

"The Private Collection of the Duke of Lerma," Ph.D. diss., New York University, 1990.

Seneca. *Los dos libros de la clemencia*, trans. Alonso de Revenga (Madrid, 1626).

Epistolae Morales, ed. Richard M. Gummere, 3 vols. (London, 1925).

Sepúlveda, Jerónimo de. *Historia de varios sucesos y de las cosas notables que han acaecido en España y otras naciones desde el año de 1584 hasta el de 1603*, ed. Julián Zarco Cuevas (Madrid, 1924).

Serrano i Sanz, Manuel. *Apuntes para una historia de escritoras españolas*, 3 vols. (Madrid, 1975).

Sharpe, Kevin. *Sir Robert Cotton, 1586–1631. History and Politics in Early Modern England* (Oxford, 1979).

Shergold, N. D. *A History of the Spanish Stage* (Oxford, 1967).

Sieber, Claudia. "Madrid: A City for a King," paper presented at the meeting of the Society for Spanish and Portuguese Historical Studies, St. Louis, 1987.

Siete partidas del rey Don Alfonso el Sabio, Las. 3 vols. (Madrid, 1989).

Silva, Juan de. *Instrucción de don Juan de Silva, conde de Portalegre, cuando envió a don Diego su hijo a la corte* (n.p., n.d.).

Cartas de don Juan de Silva, conde de Portalegre, a los reyes Felipe II y Felipe III, y a diferentes ministros, sobre materias diplomáticas, desde 1579 hasta 1601, Codoin, 43 (Madrid, 1863).

Simón Díaz, José. *Relaciones de actos públicos celebrados en Madrid (1541–1650)* (Madrid, 1982).

Simón Tarrés, Antonio. "Política exterior," in Antonio Domínguez Ortiz, ed., *Historia de España*, vol. VI (Barcelona, 1988).

Skinner, Quentin. "The Principles and Practice of Opposition: The Case of Bolingbroke versus Walpole," in Neil McKendrick, ed., *Historical Perspectives. Studies in English Thought and Society in Honour of J. H. Plumb* (London, 1974).

The Foundations of Modern Political Thought, 2 vols. (Cambridge, 1978).

Machiavelli (New York, 1981).

Smith, Hilary Dansey. *Preaching in the Spanish Golden Age. A Study of Some Preachers of the Reign of Philip III* (Oxford, 1978).

Smith, Sir Thomas. *De Republica Anglorum*, ed. L. Alston (Cambridge, 1906).

Smuts, R. Malcolm. "Public Ceremony and Royal Charisma: the English Royal Entry in London, 1485–1642," in A. L. Beier, David Cannadine, and James M. Rosenheim, eds., *The First Modern Society. Essays in English History in Honour of Lawrence Stone* (Cambridge, 1989).

Starkey, David. "Representation through Intimacy," in Ioan Lewis, ed., *Symbols and Sentiments*, Ioan Lewis (London, 1977).

The Reign of Henry VIII. Personalities and Politics (London, 1985).

Stradling, Robert A. *Philip IV and the Government of Spain, 1621–1665* (Cambridge, 1988).

Strong, Roy. *Art and Power* (Berkeley, 1984).

Printed works

Suárez, Francisco. *De legibus* [1612], ed. Luciano Pereña, 6 vols. (Madrid, 1971–7).

Suárez Fernández, Luis. *Nobleza y monarquía* (Valladolid, 1975).

Suárez Fernández, Luis, ed. *Documentos acerca de la expulsión de los judíos* (Valladolid, 1964).

Suárez de Figueroa, Cristóbal. *Hechos de don García Hurtado de Figueroa* (Madrid, 1613).

Tacitus. *Complete Works*, ed. Moses Hadas (New York, 1942).

Tanner, Marie. *The Last Descendant of Aeneas. The Hapsburgs and the Mythic Image of the Emperor* (New Haven, 1993).

Tapié, Victor Lucien. *France in the Age of Louis XIII and Richelieu* (Cambridge, 1984).

Tate, R. B., ed. *Directorio de príncipes* [1493] (Exeter, 1977).

Thompson, I. A. A. *War and Government in Habsburg Spain, 1560–1620* (London, 1976).

Crown and Cortes. Government, Institutions and Representation in Early-Modern Castile (Aldershot, 1993).

"Castile: Polity, Fiscality, and Fiscal Crisis", and "Castile: Absolutism, Constitutionalism, and Liberty," in Philip T. Hoffman and Kathryn Norberg, eds., *Fiscal Crises, Liberty, and Representative Government, 1450–1789* (Stanford, 1994).

Thompson I. A. A. and Bartolomé Yun Casalilla, eds. *The Castilian Crisis of the Seventeenth Century: New Perspectives on the Economic and Social History of Seventeenth-Century Spain* (Cambridge, 1994).

Tirso de Molina. *El vergonzoso en palacio*, ed. Everett Hesse (Madrid, 1983).

Tomás y Valiente, Francisco. "El gobierno de la monarquía y la administración de los reinos en la España del siglo XVII," in *Historia de España Ramón Menéndez Pidal*, vol. XXV (Madrid, 1982).

Los validos en la monarquía española del siglo XVII (Madrid, 1982).

Torras Ribé, Josep M. *Poders i relacions clientelars a la Catalunya dels Austria* (Barcelona, 1998).

Torres, Juan de. *Filosofía moral de príncipes* (Madrid, 1596).

Tovar Martín, Virginia. "La entrada triunfal en Madrid de doña Margarita de Austria (24 de octubre de 1599)," *Archivo Español de Arte*, 61 (1988).

Trevor-Roper, Hugh. "The General Crisis of the Seventeenth Century," in Trevor Aston, ed., *Crisis in Europe, 1560–1660* (London, 1965).

Tuck, Richard. *Philosophy and Government, 1572–1651* (Cambridge, 1993).

Tueller, James Blaine. "Good and Faithful Christians: Moriscos and Catholicism in Early Modern Spain," Ph.D. diss., Columbia University, 1997.

Ulloa, Modesto. *La hacienda real de Castilla en el reinado de Felipe II* (Rome, 1963).

Ungerer, Gustav. *La defensa de Antonio Pérez contra los cargos que se le imputaron en el proceso de visita (1584)* (Zaragoza, 1984).

Urrea, Jesús. "La Plaza de San Pablo como escenario de la corte," in *Actas del I Congreso de Historia de Valladolid* (Valladolid, 1999).

Válgoma y Díaz-Varela, Dalmiro de la. *Norma y ceremonia de las reinas de la Casa de Austria* (Madrid, 1958).

Varela, Javier. *La muerte del rey. El ceremonial funerario de la monarquía española (1500–1850)* (Madrid, 1990).

Varela, Julia. *Modos de educación en la España de la contrarreforma* (Madrid, 1984).

Vargas Hidalgo, R. "Documentos inéditos sobre la muerte de Felipe II y la literatura fúnebre de los siglos XVI y XVII," *BRAH*, 192 (1995).

Vega Carpio, Lope Félix de. *Epistolario de Lope de Vega Carpio*, ed. Agustín González de Amezúa, 4 vols. (Madrid, 1941–3).

El peregrino en su patria [1604], ed. Juan Bautista Avalle-Arce (Madrid, 1973).

Fábula de Perseo o la Bella Andrómeda, ed. Michael D. McGaha (Kassel, 1985).

Obras escogidas de Lope de Vega, ed. Federico Carlos Sainz de Robles, 3 vols., 2nd edn. (Madrid, 1987).

Vera y Figueroa, Juan Antonio de. "Fragmentos históricos de la vida de don Gaspar de Guzmán," *Seminario Erudito de Valladares*, 2 (1787).

(under name of Vera y Zúñiga) *El Embajador* [1620], facsimile edn. (Madrid, 1947).

Verdú, Blas. *Engaños y desengaños del tiempo, con un discurso de la expulsión de los moriscos de España* (Barcelona, 1612).

Vicens Vives, Jaume. "Estructura administrativa estatal en los siglos XVI y XVII," in Vicens Vives, *Coyuntura económica y reformismo burgués* (Barcelona, 1969).

Vilar, Jean. *Literatura y sociedad* (Madrid, 1973).

Villamediana, Conde de. *Poesía impresa completa*, ed. José Francisco Ruiz Casanova (Madrid, 1990).

Villari, Rosario. *The Revolt of Naples*, trans. James Newell (Cambridge, Mass., 1993).

Vitrián, Juan de. *Las memorias de Felipe de Comines con escolios propios*, 2 vols. (Antwerp, 1643).

Vives, Juan Luis. *Obras completas*, ed. Lorenzo Riber, 2 vols. (Madrid, 1948).

Waquet, Jean-Claude. *Corruption. Ethics and Power in Florence, 1600–1770*, trans. Linda McCall (University Park, Pa, 1992).

Wethey, H. E. *The Paintings of Titian. II: The Portraits* (London, 1971).

Whigham, Frank. *Ambition and Privilege. The Social Tropes of Elizabethan Courtesy Theory* (Berkeley, 1984).

Williams, Patrick. "Philip III and the Restoration of Spanish Government, 1598–1603," *English Historical Review*, 88 (1973).

"Lerma, Old Castile and the Travels of Philip III of Spain," *History*, 73 (1988).

Williams, Penry. *The Tudor Regime* (Oxford, 1979).

Winwood, Ralph. *Memorials of Affairs of State in the Reigns of Queen Elizabeth and James I*, 3 vols. (London, 1725).

Wormald, Jenny. "James VI and I: Two Kings or One?" *History*, 68 (1986).

Yáñez, Juan. *Memorias para la historia de don Felipe III, rey de España* (Madrid, 1773).

Yelgo de Vázquez, Miguel. *Estilo de servir a príncipes, con ejemplos morales para servir a Dios* (Madrid, 1614).

Yndurain, Francisco. *Los moriscos y el teatro en Aragón* (Zaragoza, 1986).

Yun Casalilla, Bartolomé. *Sobre la transición al capitalismo en Castilla* (Salamanca, 1987).

Zapata, Luis de. *Miscelánea* [1590s], *Memorial Histórico Español*, 11 (Madrid, 1859).

Index

Index

Carvajal and Mendoza, Luisa de, nun, 49–50
Casa, Giovanni della, writer, 40
Castel Rodrigo, Cristóbal de Moura, Marquis of
favorite and principal adviser to Philip II, 17, 28, 31–2, 41, 43–6, 114, 133, 144
sumiller de corps to Prince Philip, 17, 22
and Lerma, 60
and Portugal, 217
Castiglione, Baldassare, writer and humanist, 36, 73
Castile, 148, 190
economic situation, 214, 216
Castro, Ana de, writer, 266
Castro, Cristóbal de, writer, 111–12
Castro, Rodrigo de, Archbishop of Seville, Lerma's uncle, 39
Castro y Sandoval, Fernando de, Lerma's nephew, 95
Catalonia, 51, 129, 159, 183, 217
Cerda, Catalina de la, *see* Lerma, Duchess of
Cervantes Saavedra, Miguel de, writer and playwright, 126–7, 165
Charles V, Holy Roman Emperor, and King of Spain, 15, 37, 73, 74, 82–3, 145, 149
Charles Emmanuel I, Duke of Savoy, 145, 163, 204, 205, 213–14, 249
and Mantuan War, 231–4
Chinchón, Diego Fernández de Córdoba, Count of, counselor of state, principal adviser to Philip II, 22, 32, 60
Cicero, 23, 121
Ciriza, Juan de, secretary of state, 256
Cobos, Francisco de Los, private secretary to Emperor Charles, 74
comuneros, revolt of the, Castile (1520–1), 37, 102
Contarini, Simeone, Venetian ambassador, 115
Córdoba, Fray Gaspar de, confessor of Philip III, 67, 128, 157
Cornwallis, Sir Charles, English ambassador, 164
Corral y Arellano, Diego de, counselor of Castile, 251
corruption during Lerma's government, 140
Cortes
Aragon, 143
Castile, 84, 112, 144, 153–6
Costa, Giovanni da, writer, 196
Councils, 12, 24–6, 84, 87
Aragon, 129, 228
Cámara de Castilla, 56, 132
Cámara de Indias, 132
Castile, 16, 27, 45, 59, 131, 132, 134, 186, 221, 223, 228

and royal patronage, 192
and factional conflict, 219, 221, 228–9
and the crisis of the monarchy, 250–2
Finance, 28, 129, 132, 133, 134
reorganization of, 156–7
and *juntas* of finance, 158, 172, 189–90
accused of mishandling royal finances, 169
and political corruption, 178–9
and the crisis of Castile, 214–17, 223
Indies, 132, 133–4, 220
Inquisition, 59
Italy, 239, 246
Military Orders, 131
Portugal, 60, 113, 127, 133, 161, 217, 218, 230
State, 28, 36, 48, 49, 50, 60, 61, 87, 132, 145, 256
reorganization of, 53, 111
and the government of the monarchy, 113–14, 127
and the financial duties of the kingdomn, 154, 218
and the crisis of Castile, 250
and royal patronage, 191
and the expulsion of the *Moriscos*, 201, 203
and the conflict in the Netherlands, 193, 194, 195, 197
and the war against Savoy, 232–4
and the rebellion of Bohemia, 243–5
and Philip III's international policies, 252
War, 52, 132
court
factional struggles, 15–16, 218, 230–1, 235–6, 239, 247–9
royal household, 16, 92–3
palace offices, 16–17, 92–3
move from Madrid to Valladolid, 86–8
currency
vellón: minting under Philip III, 153

Dávila, Roa, writer, 21
Diego de Austria, son of Philip II, 15, 16
donativo, 153
Dutch Republic, *see* United Provinces

Eboli, Ruy Gómez de Silva, Prince of, favorite of Philip II, 16, 27, 38, 111
education, of monarchs in early modern Spain, 11 *ff.*
Elizabeth, Queen of England, 80–1, 163, 201
England, 55, 144, 145, 149–50, 152, 163–4, 177, 193, 196, 197, 200, 205, 225, 232, 240, 241, 252

Index

CAMBRIDGE STUDIES IN EARLY MODERN HISTORY

Henry IV and the Towns: The Pursuit of Legitimacy in French Urban Society, 1589–1610
S. ANNETTE FINLEY-CROSWHITE
The Limits of Royal Authority: Resistance and Obedience in Seventeenth-Century Castile
RUTH MACKAY
Defiled Trades and Social Outcasts: Honor and Ritual Pollution in Early Modern Germany
KATHY STUART
The Other Prussia: Royal Prussia, Poland and Liberty, 1569–1772
KARIN FRIEDRICH
Kingship and Favoritism in the Spain of Philip III, 1598–1621
ANTONIO FEROS

Titles available in paperback marked with an asterisk*

The following titles are now out of print:

French Finances, 1770–1795: From Business to Bureaucracy
J. F. BOSHER
Chronicle into History: An Essay in the Interpretation of History in Florentine Fourteenth-Century Chronicles
LOUIS GREEN
France and the Estates General of 1614
J. MICHAEL HAYDEN
Reform and Revolution in Mainz, 1743–1803
T. C. W. BLANNING
Altopascio: A Study in Tuscan Society 1587–1784
FRANK MCARDLE
Gunpowder and Galleys: Changing Technology and Mediterranean Warfare at Sea in the Sixteenth Century
JOHN FRANCIS GUILMARTIN JR
The State, War and Peace: Spanish Political Thought in the Renaissance 1516–1559
J. A. FERNÁNDEZ-SANTAMARIA
Calvinist Preaching and Iconoclasm in the Netherlands, 1544–1569
PHYLLIS MACK CREW
The Kingdom of Valencia in the Seventeenth Century
JAMES CASEY
Filippo Strozzi and the Medici: Favor and Finance in Sixteenth-Century Florence and Rome
MELISSA MERIAM BULLARD
Rouen during the Wars of Religion
PHILIP BENEDICT
The Emperor and His Chancellor: A Study of the Imperial Chancellery Under Gattinara
JOHN M. HEADLEY
The Military Organisation of a Renaissance State: Venice c. 1400–1617
M. E. MALLETT AND J. R. HALE
Neostoicism and the Early Modern State
GERHARD OESTREICH